100 BEST ROMANTIC RESORTS OF THE WORLD

**Perfect Places in All Price Ranges
for Honeymooners and Others in Love**

Third Edition

by

Katharine D. Dyson

The
Globe
Pequot
Press

GUILFORD, CONNECTICUT

Photo credits: pp. 2, 50: courtesy Little Palm Island; p.5: courtesy Curtain Bluff; pp. 6, 296: courtesy Turtle Island; pp. 18, 31, 106, 146, 154: by J. Dyson; p. 39: courtesy Tashiro Marketing & Advertising, Inc.; p. 47: copyright © Walt Disney World; p. 69: courtesy Sheila Donnelly & Associates; p. 82: courtesy The White Barn Inn; p. 85: courtesy The Wauwinet; p. 98: courtesy Karen Weiner Escalera Associates; p. 103: courtesy Woodstock Inn; p.117 courtesy La Pinsonniere; p. 133: courtesy M. Silver Associates; p. 151: courtesy Little Dix Bay, Rosewood Resort; p. 167: courtesy Sans Souci Lido; p. 170: Half Moon Golf, Tennis, and Beach Club; p. 214: photo by J.B. Weir; p. 223: courtesy La Casa que Canta; p. 226: courtesy Las Hadas; p.238: courtesy ITT Sheraton Corporation; p. 241: courtesy The Feathers Hotel; p. 257: photo by J. Jerrik; p. 271: courtesy Hotel Danieli; p. 273: Foto Vasconi; p. 283: copyright © Nick Passmore 1992, all rights reserved; p. 287: courtesy Bedarra Bay Resort; p. 293: courtesy Silky Oaks Lodge; p. 303: courtesy Hotel Bora Bora; all others by Kathie D. Dyson.

Cover design by Lana Mullen

Interior design by Nancy Freeborn/Freeborn Design

Cover photos: background: Eric Kamp/Index Stock; inset: Wallace Garrison/Index Stock

Library of Congress Cataloging-in-Publication Data
Dyson, Katharine D.
    The 100 best romantic resorts of the world : perfect places in all price ranges for honeymooners and others in love / by Katharine D. Dyson. — 3rd ed.
        p. cm. — (100 best resorts series)
    First ed. published under title: The 100 best honeymoon resorts of the world. 1996.
    ISBN 0-7627-0624-4
    1. Hotels—Guidebooks. 2. Resorts—Guidebooks. 3. Couples—Travel—Guidebooks.
    4. Honeymoons. I. Title: Hundred best romantic resorts of the world. II. Dyson, Katharine D. 100 best honeymoon resorts of the world. III. Title. IV. Series.

TX907 .D97 2000
647.94'025—dc21

                                        00-020942

Manufactured in the United States of America
Third Edition/Second Printing

To my husband, John, for his never-ending
support and patience.

Author's Thanks

B ecause the quality of a resort can change dramatically in a short time, I have ensured that each place comes with a first-person, recent recommendation, preferably (and in most cases) mine. However, because of the time constraints involved in researching and writing such a book, it would have been physically impossible for me to personally revisit each of the one hundred resorts within the allotted time frame and still get the material to the publisher on deadline. Thus I am indebted to many fellow travel writers and others who have generously helped me put together an accurate, up-to-date account of these one hundred most romantic resorts around the globe.

My deepest appreciation to the following people who helped me update this third edition: Lynn and Scott Prowitt-Smith, who shared their impressions of their honeymoon resort, Maroma, Mexico, with me; Risa Weinreb, for her contributions in Hawaii, Tahiti, and Morocco; Christopher Pinckney, for Hyatt Regency Aruba and Sandals St. Lucia, where, he and his wife, Cathy, report, their honeymoon was a perfect "ten"; Georgina Kassalty, for Hyatt Regency Grand Cayman and Melhana Plantation; and Merrie Murray, for Four Seasons Maui. Thanks also to Frank "Poncho" Shiell, for all his help in Ixtapa/Zihuatanejo; Leslie Lefkowitz, The Ritz-Carlton; Richard Kahn, of Kahn Travel Communications; Abbe McCracken, M. Silver Associates; Meryl Pearlstein, of Karen Weiner Escalera Associates; Marcella Martinez, of Marcella Martinez Associates; Karen Preston, of Leading Hotels of the World; Mary Homi, of Mary Homi International Public Relations; Theresa Scanlon and Clif Cooke, of *Jax Fax Travel Marketing Magazine;* Geri Bain, of *Modern Bride;* and Lea Lane, Sara Southworth, and Roberta Graff. Also thanks to world travelers Jeanne and Jack Klinge.

Contents

Introduction 1

The United States and Canada 11
    Arizona 12
    California 17
    Colorado 38
    Connecticut 41
    Florida 43
    Georgia 55
    Hawaii 57
    Maine 76
    Massachusetts 84
    New Mexico 91
    New York 93
    Vermont 97
    West Virginia 105

    Canada 109
        Alberta 109
        Quebec 117

The Caribbean and Bermuda 121
    Anguilla 122
    Antigua 125
    Aruba 128
    Bahamas 131
    Barbados 137
    Bermuda 139
    British Virgin Islands 145
        Virgin Gorda 145
        Peter Island 153
    Cayman Islands 157
        Grand Cayman 157
    Dominican Republic 160
    Grenada 162

Jamaica 165

Nevis 180

Puerto Rico 185

St. Kitts 190

St. Lucia 192

St. Martin 205

U.S. Virgin Islands 208

    St. John 208

Latin America and Mexico 212

Costa Rica 213

Mexico 216

Europe 236

Austria 237

England 239

France 254

Germany 261

Greece 263

    Lemnos 263

Italy 266

Portugal 276

    Madeira 279

Scotland 282

Asia and the Pacific 286

Australia 287

Fiji 295

French Polynesia 299

Indonesia 305

Thailand 313

Africa 316

Morocco 317

South Africa 319

Indexes 323

Introduction

E ach of the "100 Best Romantic Resorts of the World" has unique, special qualities—some may even be a bit quirky. In my travels and research, I came across some marvelous places that perhaps didn't quite fit the definition of a full-service resort. Nonetheless, because they are especially romantic and may be just what you're looking for, I've included them in the book.

All of the 100 Best have the following characteristics in common:

1. Romantic setting
2. Best in category/region for overall quality
3. Primarily caters to vacationers seeking recreation, entertainment, and escape from the "real world"
4. Easy to reach
5. Safe location
6. Excellent, friendly service
7. One or more restaurants on or within walking distance of the property
8. Spiffy clean and superbly maintained
9. Appeals to couples in love
10. Offers good value

Romantic setting. This is highly subjective. What will it be? A cabin in the woods, a castle on a hilltop, an over-the-water bungalow, a thatched beachfront cottage? I invite you to browse through these profiles and decide for yourself.

Best in category. It might have made my job easier had I simply selected the most expensive and exclusive places in each region. Expense doesn't necessarily add up to value, though, and since many honeymooners are just starting out, I've included a number of reasonably priced resorts as well as the pricier hotels to give you a range of choices—all which represent the best in their price category for ambience and quality.

Recreation, entertainment, and escape. These resorts are more than just a place to spend the night. Most have pools and/or beaches for swimming, tennis courts, and fitness facilities. Recreation covers a wide spectrum—it might be skiing, hiking, horseback riding, sailboarding, or croquet—and entertainment could be anything from soft piano music to disco. The bottom line is that these resorts cater to travelers who are on vacation, rather than on a business trip. The 100 Best exist for fun and romance.

Little Palm Island, Florida

Easy to reach. The majority of the resorts in this book are within reasonable traveling distance of North America. This is particularly important for honeymooners. After all the excitement of the wedding festivities, you could very well be exhausted. It would help if your trip to your destination is a quick and easy one. I have, however, included some properties in exotic faraway places for those who feel adventurous and have the time.

Safe location. You want to feel safe and secure. Going to an iffy area with a history of turbulence is not a good idea if you want to relax and simply enjoy each other. The 100 Best are located in what are considered (at press time) safe, stable areas, but remember that no matter where you go, you should always take necessary precautions, such as putting your money in traveler's checks, stowing cash in two or three different places, and bringing along an ATM card, often the best way to get additional cash abroad. Carry all the "must have" items with you on the plane (don't check them with your luggage) and put your valuable items in the hotel safe. Better yet, leave expensive jewelry at home, and you won't have to worry about it.

Excellent, friendly service. When you order room service at 3:00 a.m., you'd like to get your order before the sun rises. When your waiter greets you at the table, it would be nice to see a smile. All these things help make your resort experience a fine one.

Choice of restaurants. It's good to have two or more places to eat, ranging from gourmet/formal to casual. A range of prices, ambience, and kinds of cuisine is also important. The most important element, however, is good food, whether the resort has one restaurant or several, or is located in an area where there are several good restaurants.

Clean and superbly maintained. There's nothing like a leaky faucet dripping in the middle of the night or a dust ball behind a chair to turn the romance level down a notch or two. The 100 Best get high ratings in the cleanliness and maintenance departments.

Appeals to couples in love. Now here's where it gets tricky. I discovered some great resorts that met all my other criteria except this one. Perhaps the kids took over the pool most of the day. Or the resort was just too exclusive, geared to the hopelessly well off and out of reach to all but 2 percent of our readers (who probably already know where they are jetting off to and don't need anyone to tell them where to go). Resorts like these didn't make it.

Good value. Very important. I tried to eliminate any place that was unreasonable or doing the "big rip-off." If prices are steep to begin with and you know it, you can budget for it. If rates at first sound reasonable and then the cash register starts ringing up every time you go waterskiing, play an hour of tennis, or walk into the nightclub, your good deal starts to drift into the sunset. Whenever possible, I have listed romance packages and other plans that give you the biggest bang for your buck. And remember: Even if a package is not listed in the book, ask the resort if it offers any special plans, such as ones for tennis, scuba diving, or golf. Many do; they just may not promote them.

One of the best bets for some budget-minded travelers is the all-inclusive resort, where one price pays for everything, including drinks, meals, and sports activities. No surprises here at checkout time.

Helpful Tips for Using This Book

Each resort profile in this guide begins with a complete description of the resort, including its special features, ambience, decor, cuisine, and activities offered. Following the description is a section of at-a-glance information about the resort—types of accommodations, rates, sports and facilities available, and so on. Most of this information is self-explanatory, but the following clarification of a few items should help you utilize this book to the fullest as you plan your romantic holiday.

Rates: Each resort has its own unique way of putting together its rate schedule. Although I have tried to give you the rates in as consistent a manner as possible, you will see several variations on such details as seasons—some offer seasonal rates, some do not. In some cases package rates are quoted. I have given you my best shot in describing these rates so that you can understand what is and is not offered.

Following are terms used throughout the book in reference to rates.

Rack Rates: Published rates—usually the top retail price without any discounts

MAP: Modified American Plan; includes accommodations, breakfast, and dinner

AP: American Plan; includes accommodations, breakfast, lunch, and dinner

EP: European Plan; includes no meals

Package Rates: Promotional packages geared in some cases to specific-interest groups such as honeymooners. Most include a number of extra features, such as champagne and room upgrade.

All-Inclusive: Usually this means that the rate includes accommodations, all meals, sports, and other activities. A truly all-inclusive rate will include all beverages, including name-brand liquors; some even include the wedding ceremony. Occasionally resorts advertise an all-inclusive rate but still require you to pay for your beverages. Read the fine print and make sure you know what you're buying.

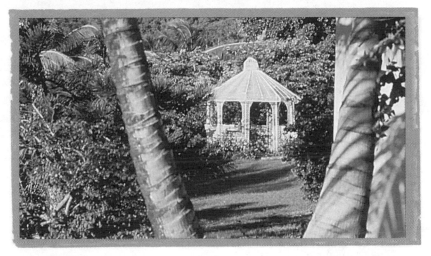

Curtain Bluff, Antigua

Room Upgrade: This means getting a better room than you paid for. It is dependent on whether one is available and is usually not guaranteed.

Seasonal Rates: Prices are geared to the time of year and can vary widely from hotel to hotel. The high season is the most expensive and is the time when the resort is the busiest. In the Caribbean this means the colder months; in Europe it's usually spring, summer, and fall; in New England it is often fall foliage season; and in Bermuda, it's summer. Christmastime is also considered high season by many places. Low-season rates are the least expensive and are available when the resort is not in such great demand. Some resorts do not use season designations but instead give you a schedule of periods during the year with corresponding rates. Some offer just one year-round rate. ("Shoulder" season rates are those between high and low.)

Deposit: Deposit and refund policies vary greatly with each hotel. Some require only a guarantee with a credit card. Typically you get your money back if you cancel within a particular period. Check with the hotel and be sure you understand their policy

Exchange Rates: You'll find that some of the rates in this book are in U.S. dollars, others in local currency. Often when a hotel has a U.S. representative, you'll find rates quoted in U.S. dollars. Some hotels, however, quote only in their local money. To convert to U.S. dollars, look up the exchange rate in the daily paper (usually in the business section).

Arrival/Departure: Transfers mentioned under this item refer to the resort's arrangements for getting you from and to the airport—by bus, boat, van, private car, or otherwise.

Weddings: If you want to get married at your honeymoon destination, make sure you inquire well ahead of time as to residency requirements, documents required, and so on. Your travel agent, resort, and/or country tourism office representative in the United States can help you with this.

A Note About Electricity: Dual-voltage appliances such as hair dryers often have a special switch that allows you to convert to either 110 or 220 volts. You will also, however, need a special plug for your appliances when traveling to many places out of the country. Hardware stores generally sell these plugs in sets.

Tips for Those Planning a Honeymoon

Attention to the following details can make the difference between having an OK honeymoon and a great one.

1. Book a late flight the morning after the wedding, when possible.

2. Know what your budget is and work within these limits. If money is tight, look into an all-inclusive resort, where you know ahead of time what you'll spend. Many resorts sound reasonably priced until you add up all the extra charges. Checkout time can be a mind-blower.

3. Book the best room you can afford. Complaints from returning honeymooners tend to focus on the quality of their accommodations.

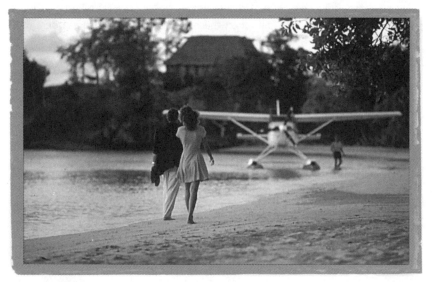

Turtle Island, Fiji

4. Ask about bed size. In some parts of the world, double beds may be smaller than what you'd expect. In Europe you'll find a lot of twin-bedded rooms, so if you're Europe-bound, you might want to ask for a "matrimonial bed."

5. Both the bride and the groom should take part in deciding where to go and how much to spend.

6. Unless you want to keep your honeymoon a secret, let the hotel know ahead of time that you are newly married (your travel agent can do this for you). Honeymooners often enjoy special perks, such as champagne and breakfast in bed.

7. It is often helpful to be in the travel agent's office while your room is being booked so that you can answer any special questions the hotel might have.

8. If being directly on the beach overlooking the water is very important to you, make sure the hotel and the room you book are just that. Sometimes properties advertised as "beachfront hotels" are in reality not right on the beach, but close by. Rooms may also have a view of the garden instead of the water.

9. Ask about the best way to get from the airport to your resort. Are you being met? Do you need to look for someone in particular? How much is a taxi or van service?

10. If you are renting a car, find out ahead of time about insurance requirements. Check with your credit card company to see if you are covered by collision damage waiver.

11. Check what travel documentation you will need and get everything in order. Carry two forms of photo identification in two separate places. If you lose one you'll still be able to get on the plane with the other. Remember, a valid photo ID is required to board. No ID, no flight.

12. On international travel it is good to fax hotels a few days before your arrival date to reconfirm your arrangements. This is particularly important when the booking was made well in advance. This is one vacation you want to make sure runs like clockwork. Your travel agent should do this for you, but be sure to request that it be done.

13. I highly recommend purchasing trip cancellation insurance. If you have to cancel for any reason (heaven forbid), you'll get your deposit back. Ask your travel agent about this.

14. If you are traveling to a place such as Africa or the South Pacific, check with your doctor or local health authority to find out if you need any special inoculations or medicines to take either prior to or during your trip. In some areas you must show proof that you are up to date on certain disease-preventing immunizations (e.g., yellow fever and malaria) in order to enter the country.

15. If you are not leaving for your vacation destination until a day or two after your wedding, you may want to stay at a relaxing, romantic inn on your first night. Most couples find they are quite exhausted after the festivities and need some time to unwind.

16. Book your airline seats at the same time you make plane reservations. This is also the time to order special meals if you have any dietary restrictions.

Honeymoon Countdown

Don't wait until the last minute to plan your honeymoon. Good groundwork can really pay off when it comes to lining up the perfect romantic holiday. Here are some guidelines.

- Five months before your wedding: Select a travel agent, read up on destinations, and nail down your budget. Be sure to include spending money in your calculations.

- Four months: Decide where you're going and book your reservations with your travel agent.

- Three months: Get your travel documents together. Allow up to six weeks to process the paperwork for a new passport. Applications are available at the main branch of your local post office and at U.S. government passport agencies.

- Two months: Get your confirmation numbers for hotel, airlines, rental cars, and so forth

- One month to one week: Purchase film for your camera. Check to make sure your camera batteries are working. Get out the converter plugs for your hair dryer, and so on, or purchase them from a hardware store. Confirm your reservations and get your traveler's checks.

This book offers a wide range of resorts to choose from. You and your partner should look through it individually and select a few establishments that appeal to each of your tastes. Then compare notes and narrow down the list to the ones that sound wonderful to both of you. The next step is to contact your travel agent for brochures and more information.

Tips for Packing

1. The layered look is in. Temperatures in many areas can soar one day, plunge the next.

2. Limit your color choices to basics. Gray, white, black, and beige work. Add color with silk scarves, belts, and jewelry.

3. Take costume jewelry. Take nothing you couldn't bear losing unless you wear it all the time.

4. Bring no more than three pairs of shoes unless you want to squeeze in a pair of sandals.

5. Pack mix-and-match outfits—shirts, slacks, etc.—that can be worn two or more times in different combinations.

6. Wear your bulkiest (and most comfortable) things on the plane.

7. Think silk, tercel, and anything else that is thin and will not wrinkle easily.

8. Pack or wear a basic all-purpose jacket. Black works great.

9. Don't carry large bottles of anything. Use small bottles, containers, and plastic bags. Film cartridge canisters are handy for things like pills and pins.

10. Put together a mini-medicine kit (just in case), and carry it in a small sandwich size baggie.

11. Before you pack, lay everything you want to take out on your bed. Put aside all those things that you absolutely can't live without. Pack them. Put everything else back in the closet.

12. Take a midsize wheely bag and a small carry-on. Bring nothing you cannot easily move yourself and preferably carry on the plane. Movability is flexibility. And remember that cars in Europe are smaller than most of those in the United States.

My hope is that your holiday will be far more romantic than you ever dreamed; that you'll have the opportunity to get off the beaten track and create memories that will last a lifetime as you discover what is unique and special about a place, its people, and its traditions.

If you have any suggestions for how this guide could be improved, please feel free to e-mail your comments to editorial@globe-pequot.com, or send them to The Globe Pequot Press, Reader Response, P.O. Box 480, Guilford, Connecticut 06437.

The prices and rates listed in this guidebook were confirmed at press time. We recommend, however, that you call establishments to obtain current information before traveling.

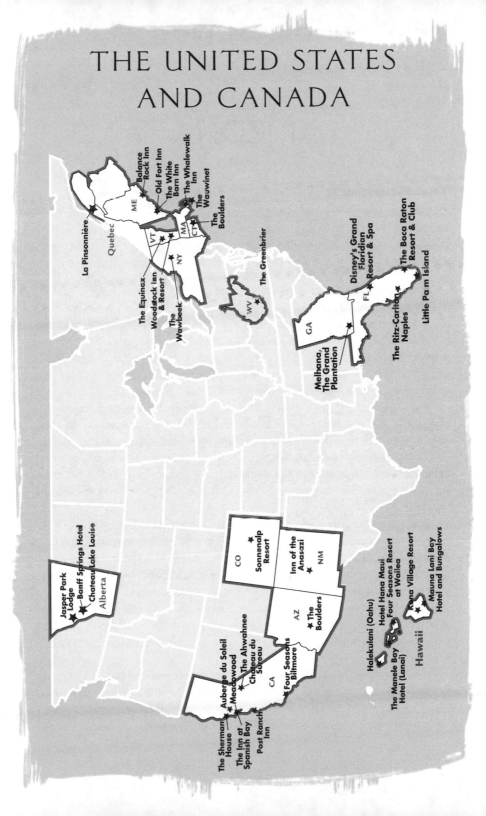

THE UNITED STATES
AND CANADA

ARIZONA

≋

The Boulders

Location: Nestled in the high Sonoran Desert northeast of Phoenix and Scottsdale, Arizona, on 1,300 acres.

Romantic Features: Vast beauty of the desert setting; fireplaces in your private casita; hikes on the magnificent grounds; balloon rides over the desert.

A s you approach the resort, you see just ahead some huge, reddish boulders. At first you don't see the resort itself—it blends so well into its environment. Individual casitas are molded into the terrain; colors blend perfectly. Here and there you catch a view of the golf courses with their green tees and greens looking very much like neat toupees sitting on the red-tan desert ground. This is The Boulders, one of the country's most romantic resorts and absolute heaven for those who also want to play golf.

You know you are in the desert. The air is hot yet dry. The days are sunny and warm, the nights cool. The sky goes on forever. Giant fingers of the saguaros, several times as tall as you are and much older, stick up out of the desert scrub, silhouetted against the brilliant sunset skies and morning sunrises—just as in the postcards, but better because you are here. In the evening you will probably hear the cries of a coyote, maybe even see one on your stroll to dinner.

Granite boulders, their edges rounded and smoothed by millions of years of wear, sit one atop another in a bit of a hodgepodge, just as they have lain for centuries, like silent sentries watching over the desert. Tucked in the crevices and cracks and rooted in the land are the flowers and plants of this rich desert environment, home to more than 2,500 species of plant life and more than 600 species of birds. From its conception those who carved The Boulders into the desert did so with great ecological sensitivity. The architect camped on the grounds for fifteen months studying the light and the land before he created the master plan.

The 160 casitas, made of earth-tone adobe, were hand-molded and rubbed to follow the contours of the rocks, and, like the ancient boulders themselves, hard edges were softened and rounded. Plants that had to be uprooted to make room for construction were replanted. A desert garden, with each species

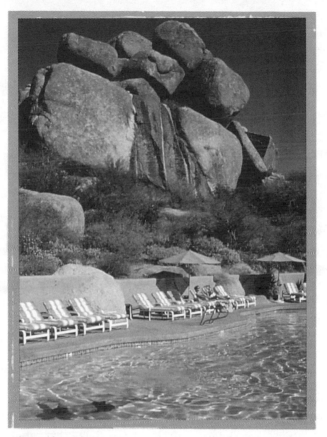

The Boulders, Arizona

labeled, was planted along the winding walkway leading from the reception area to the golf clubhouse.

Each individual casita has a sitting area and fireplace, a balcony or patio, a minibar, a large tiled bath with a vanity, and comfortable leather chairs, ottomans, and sofas upholstered in flame stitch and earthy fabrics reflecting the rich colors and patterns of the desert. Stone floors, hand-hewn beamed ceilings, area rugs, baskets, clay pots, and regional art objects and paintings add to the Southwestern ambience. Lights are perfectly placed for reading or for romance. And many of the Indian weavings and paintings hanging on the walls are for sale—just ask.

Life at The Boulders revolves around the main lodge and the two superb golf courses. The pool area is also popular. The wall around the pool is interrupted here and there by boulders that were never moved but were instead incorporated into the design. A trail nearby leads up a steep, rocky hill; at the top you get sweeping views of the beautiful Sonoran Desert with its armies of erect saguaro cactus and low-growing bushes and flowers.

Inside the lodge you'll find no sharp corners or edges; everything is rounded just like the exteriors. In the main lounge a lofty ceiling has been installed using the latilla and viga method of construction: Spokes of wood radiate from a center "pole" much like a giant umbrella. Adobe walls are brightened by original artwork, such as an 1890s chief's blanket and antique tapestries.

Every evening as the sun goes down and things get cooler, the giant fireplace inside the lodge and the one just outside the entrance are lit, sending the sweet spicy odor of shaggy juniper into the air. The aroma lingers the next day, buoyed by additional fires in the restaurants and casitas.

The five restaurants at The Boulders place a strong emphasis on healthful eating. You can enjoy food such as mesquite-grilled meats and fish, roast range chicken, anchiote-basted veal chop with sun-dried tomato orzo, grilled salmon and quesadilla with Anaheim chiles. In keeping with its commitment to fresh food, the resort has introduced a new foraging program. Its foraging chef seeks out local farmers who produce organically grown fruits and vegetables, finds sources for fresh meat and special seafood items like "diver scallops," and harvests such things as cactus fruits right from the desert.

You really don't have to leave the grounds to find both a variety of restaurants and a change in moods. Through its large windows the Latilla restaurant affords marvelous views of the Sonoran landscape and a softy lit waterfall. The Palo Verde restaurant, with its colorful exhibition kitchen, features Southwestern cuisine and regional specialities served indoors or on the terrace.

The informal Boulders Club, located in the golf course clubhouse, is another popular choice for lunch and dinner. You can eat in the main dining room or on the deck overlooking the fairways and mountain foothills. Also try the Discovery Lounge in the main lodge for live entertainment during the evening and for cocktails.

In El Pedregal marketplace, you'll find The Bakery Cafe, which serves homemade pastries and sandwiches. The Cantina del Pedregal, also in the marketplace, focuses on Mexican cooking.

At The Boulders you also have another choice: You can stay "home" and enjoy a private breakfast or dinner on your balcony or patio or get cozy in front of your fireplace while the wood fire blazes away.

The Boulders' two excellent golf courses have been carefully integrated into the landscape. One ancient cactus sits smack in the center of a rather formidable sandtrap: The saguaro was there when the golf course was built, so the trap was simply constructed around it. These are true desert courses: No plants are growing here that are not indigenous to the area, and local grasses are used that require much less water than the type normally associated with golf courses. Named by *Golf Magazine* as a Gold Medal Golf Resort 1999–2000, The Boulders treats its players to stunning vistas from elevated tees—on one hole you actually tee off from the top of a boulder.

In addition to the two golf courses, The Boulders Club, a private country club reserved exclusively for resort guests and club members, includes a Tennis Center with eight Plexi-cushioned courts, a pro shop, and another pool. Clinics and private lessons are offered daily.

A 1,600-square-foot fitness center plays homage to the philosophy "A Natural Approach to Fitness." Programs include aerobics, hiking, biking, and flexibility exercises. The Sonoran Spa features a number of special treatments, such as the hot rock massage, reflexology, Swedish and sports massages, the setting sun aloe wrap, and other unique body treatments utilizing the natural healing properties of desert herbs—not a bad way to wind up the day.

For the ultimate romantic indulgence, try the spa's couple's massage. Two therapists come to your casita with massage tables, and after the massages the lights are turned low, the music is turned on, and a warm bath with aromatic oils is drawn. A candle is lit to complete the mood for romance as the therapists quietly leave.

Those who love the outdoors will find much to do here. You can explore the area on horseback or hike on the Apache Trail, which passes by lakes, volcanic rock formations, and awesome buttes. You can take a sunset jeep tour or a moonlight horseback ride. Or tackle the desert trails on foot or bike; ask for a special hike and gourmet picnic lunch designed just for the two of you. There is also rock climbing and night-vision hikes using infrared goggles. You can spend hours in the colorful market area, El Pedregal, which contains more than forty boutiques, restaurants, and art galleries, plus an amphitheater where many kinds of performances are scheduled.

Just as any great resort cannot stand on its physical beauty and facilities alone, The Boulders goes to the top of the class for its personal people skills. You are greeted warmly on your arrival, and if you come back for more visits (and you will), you are remembered and catered to. And who wouldn't want to return? This is one super place.

Author's Note: The Sonoran Desert is in full spring bloom February through May.

Address/Phone: P.O. Box 2090, 34631 North Tom Darlington Drive, Carefree, AZ 85377; (480) 488–9009; fax: (480) 488–4118

E-mail: ssmith@grandbay.com

Web Site: www.grandbay.com

U.S. Reservations: (800) 553–1717

Owner/Manager: William J. Nassikas, president, Mark Vinciguerra, vice-president and general manager

Arrival/Departure: Pickup at either the Scottsdale or the Phoenix Airport can be arranged; with prior permission private planes can land at the Carefree Airport. A helicopter landing pad is also located on-site.

Distance from Scottsdale Airport: 13 miles, 30 minutes; 33 miles from Phoenix Sky Harbor Airport

Distance from Phoenix: 16 miles

Accommodations: 160 adobe-style guest casitas; 45 one-, two-, and three-bedroom Pueblo Villas

Best Room/Suite: If you like water views, try one of the casitas near the end, overlooking the pond

Amenities: Air-conditioning, ceiling fans, wood-burning fireplaces, minibars, large dressing area, TV, toiletries, padded hangers, umbrella, room service, telephone, robes

Electricity: 110 volts

Sports and Facilities: Two championship 18-hole golf courses; Tennis Park, featuring 8 Plexi-cushioned courts and pro shop; Fitness Center with Aerobic Studio, weight room, heated outdoor lap pool, hiking program; desert jeep tours, hot air ballooning, horseback riding; spa

Dress Code: Casual smart

Weddings: Can be arranged

Rates/Packages: $175–$545 per room for casitas; $325–$720 for a one-bedroom/den pueblo villa. Sonoran Romance, $1,550–$2,858, including 4 nights' casita accommodations, breakfasts, dinners, gift, and hot-air balloon ride or en-suite couple's massage.

Payment/Credit Cards: Most major

Deposit: Two-night deposit or half the package rate to be applied to first and last night's stay. Cancel 3 weeks in advance of arrival date for full refund.

Government Taxes: 10.67 percent tax on accommodations; 7.4 percent tax on food and beverage charges

Service Charges: $18 per night in lieu of cash gratuities for all resort personnel, excluding food and beverage

CALIFORNIA

≋

The Ahwahnee

Location: Inside Yosemite National Park

Romantic Features: Spectacular vistas of forests, waterfalls and mountains; miles of trails to explore on foot and horseback; private cottages in the woods

Sounds of birds, the rustle of grasses and trees, glimpses of a coyote, badger, or even a bear along with awesome views of rock cliffs, redwoods, rivers, and lakes await those who visit The Ahwahnee and Yosemite National Park The main attraction here is nature, which provides the perfect getaway destination for those who love the outdoors.

The Ahwahnee is nestled in the heart of Yosemite Valley, an ideal location as just getting in and out of the center of the park can take an hour or more. Yosemite is huge. There are rustic cottages nearby, operated by the Yosemite Concession Service Corporation, as is The Ahwahnee. But if you are looking for any kind of luxury and a candlelit dinner at the end of a day of exploring the more than 350 miles of marked trails, climbing a mountain, or taking a horseback ride through the hills, then The Ahwahnee is the place to be.

When Lady Astor, England's first female member of Parliament, came to Yosemite in the early 1920s she thumbed her nose at her unheated room and bathroom, which was down the hall. She checked out and returned to the gentler comforts of the city. This prompted Stephen T. Mather, director of the National Park Service, to order that a new luxury hotel be built to attract more people to his beloved park.

Since the seven-story granite-and-timber structure and cottages were built The Ahwahnee has welcomed such important guests as Queen Elizabeth II, President John F. Kennedy, Judy Garland, Winston Churchill, and Ronald Reagan.

From the beginning the theme of the furnishings and decor was derived from Native American culture. The public rooms are massive with soaring ceilings that replicate the park's towering pines and giant sequoias. Large windows as well as the long outdoor terrace are oriented toward Glacier Point and Sentinel Dome. Pull out your binoculars and look carefully; you may be able to spot someone climbing the sheer rock faces.

Although it was used as a Navy hospital for three years during World War II, it has primarily served as a gracious place to stay in the woods. Over the years it has been refurbished and redecorated, but some things have stayed the same. The original big oak tables, wrought-iron chandeliers in the Great Lounge, the

The Ahwahnee, California

beautiful Native American carpets hanging on the walls, and the intricate rubber mosaic tiles in the entrance lobby are still here.

Accommodations are located in the main lodge and in the cottages which are strung along paths leading from the hotel. Beautifully decorated in Native American prints and rusts, browns, black, greens, and blues, the rooms have all necessary amenities, including cable television and minifridges.

For privacy the cottages are great and come with stone patios furnished with a wrought-iron table and chairs. You won't see much beyond the trees that surround the cottages, and the decor is a bit more rustic; still you have basically the same amenities as the rooms in the main lodge along with a small dressing room, separate vanity area, and a sitting area. Most cottages are furnished with king-size beds with wood headboards edged by a twig border. A few cottages are furnished with double beds.

Inside the lodge, the Great Lounge is huge. I paced it off at 100 feet long, but no one was quite sure just what the room dimensions are—the fireplace is large enough to roast a cow. The dining room is equally impressive, especially at night when the chandeliers and candles set a romantic mood. For casual dining and drinks you can order such items as turkey quesadillas, salads, and sandwiches in the bar.

You will probably run out of time before you run out of things to do in Yosemite. In addition to the obvious—hiking, biking, riding, climbing—have the hotel pack a lunch basket or stop at the convenience store for some wine, bread, and cheese. Then drive up to Tuolumne Meadows, stopping at Tenaya Lake for a picnic by the shore. The lake is surrounded by tall pines and the north side is blessed by a lovely sand beach. The lake is sparkling clean and swimmable if you like your water briskly cool.

Keep in mind that the drive up to Tuolumne is about 50 miles and takes about one and one-half hours. You can visit the giant sequoias on the way or head to Mariposa for a guided tour of the massive trees with trunks so large that you could drive a truck through the middle.

For an overview of the valley, sign on for a two-hour valley floor tour, a 26-mile journey in an open-air tram. (If you are driving a convertible, you can use a map and do it yourself.) If you like to paint, join one of the art classes that are offered every day.

If you want a break head to The Ahwahnee pool for a soothing swim and soak up the dramatic views from your lounge chair.

Address/Phone: Yosemite National Park, Yosemite, CA 95389; (209) 372–1407; fax (209) 372–1463

Web Site: www.yosemitepark.com

U.S. Reservations: (559) 252–4848; fax (559) 456–0542

Owner/Manager: Val Hardcastle, general manager

Arrival/Departure: Car rentals available at San Francisco and Oakland Airports

Distance from San Francisco Airport: 214 miles (4 to 5 hours); Fresno Airport, 105 miles (2½ hours)

Distance from Yosemite: Right in the park

Accommodations: 127 rooms and cottages

Best Room/Suite: Mary Tresidder Room (605), a minisuite with balcony and huge bath; The Duke's Suite (602), a spacious suite with a king bed, library, fireplace; cottages for those who want rustic privacy

Amenities: Hair dryer, minirefrigerator, TV, coffeemaker (cottages), toiletries, robes, ice service, concierge service, valet parking, turndown service, complimentary morning coffee, *USA Today* delivered to your door

Electricity: 110 volts

Sports and Facilities: Pool, walking, hiking, fishing, horseback riding, mountain climbing, Alpine and cross-country skiing, ice skating, art classes, river rafting, golf at Wawona outside the valley

Dress Code: Jackets required in main dining room, dinner only

Weddings: Can be arranged

Rates/Packages: $265.20 per couple per night for rooms; $611.99–$857.72 for suites. Romance Package (January 30–March 5) $849 for 3 nights including accommodations, in-room candlelight dinner, one breakfast in bed,

picnic lunch, champagne, rose, and gifts (available Sunday through Thursday).
Payment/Credit Cards: Most major
Deposit: By credit card
Government Taxes: 10 percent
Service Charges: Not included

≋≋≋

Auberge du Soleil

Location: Thirty-three–acre olive grove in the Rutherford foothills.
Romantic Features: Knockout views of Napa Valley's most illustrious vineyards (each room has a private deck and fireplace); half-mile nature trail studded with more than sixty sculptures.

L ocation, location, location is yours to savor at this luxury resort in the heart of Napa Valley wine country. Snuggled in an olive grove in the eastern foothills, Auberge du Soleil overlooks a tapestry of vineyards, stone wineries, and the rugged ridge of the Mayacamas Mountains. A Relais & Chateaux property, it's the perfect hideaway for couples wanting to sample the best of the wine country lifestyle—tasting rooms and fine restaurants, smart boutiques and antiques stores, hot air ballooning and bicycling.

Auberge cossets guests in tranquil beauty from the moment they enter the lobby with its oversize floral display placed on a massive wood and stone table. The grounds are spectacular, with gardens and courtyards cached in nooks and crannies accented by pergolas, fountains, and gigantic pots overflowing with ivy geraniums.

A four-acre olive grove provides a unique venue for appreciating alfresco works in the inn's sculpture garden. The collection of sixty works by well-known local and national artists are fun and unique. A shapely pair of stone legs sprawl under a tree; cheerful metal flowers "grow" in the gardens; a dancer turns on her toe in the wind; giant nails are hammered in the ground; colorful rings frolic on the hillside.

Accommodations are tucked into two-story cottages staggered up the hillside. Stuccoed in warm earth tones, each cottage has a patio or terrace. Inside, the decor is class, not flash, embellished with cool Mexican tile floors and rawhide chairs. Color schemes percolate in vibrant hues of hot pink and yellow. Two new cottages are a whopping 1,800 square feet and come with nonstop views and every imaginable amenity.

Everything encourages you to relax, from the two chaise lounges poised on the terrace with the comfortable padded cushions, chairs for two, and sofas with huge overstuffed pillows. Music is piped from a CD/stereo player, logs are

Auberge du Soleil, California

laid in your fireplace, and candles and amber bath salts wait by the side of the tub (some units have Jacuzzis for two.) The king-size bed is primped with a medley of colorful pillows; live orchids and flowers are everywhere, arranged in vases, floating languidly in glass bowls, and spilling over earthenware urns. Original art work including large canvasses and three-dimensional pieces reflect the sunny warmth of the Napa Valley.

If perfection lies in details, Auberge has it all figured out. Light switches are marked for location, including one to spotlight the art . . . even the extra roll of toilet paper comes "gift wrapped" with a bow. Both drawer and closet spaces are ample, and the wet bar includes a refrigerator stocked with regional wines and cheeses.

In fine weather (almost a certainty here in Northern California), you'll enjoy basking by the lovely swimming pool, heated to a comfy 85 degrees year-round. Broad wooden decks provide plenty of space for sunning, while a flotilla of market umbrellas seem to mirror the contours of distant mountain peaks. Tennis players can hone their strokes on three hard courts. Although the workout room equipped with exercise bike, stair machine, and free weights is small, it features incredible valley views.

You will certainly want to explore several of Napa's more than 220 vineyards. Ask Auberge to prepare a picnic basket for your day in the valley, and pick up a special wine along the way.

For wining and dining there's the Auberge du Soleil Restaurant, with meals served either indoors in a country-French dining room or outdoors on a trellis-covered wooden deck with awesome views of the valley. No need to worry about a chilly evening while savoring the sunset—overhead heaters keep you cozy. Service is friendly, not intrusive. Advice on wine and cuisine choices is delivered by the maître d' and highly knowledgeable waiters.

Inviting menu choices include roasted poussin de Lyon in a chanterille ragout (one of executive chef Andrew Sutton's favorites), golden trout with scallops and butter leeks, ravioli filled with escargot in a sorrel creme, salad with beet risotto, salmon tenderloins with roasted asparagus, and lavender honey glacé with a lavender tuile. You can start off with the Seven Sparkling Sins, which includes Russian osetra caviar, sautéed foie gras, truffled quail eggs, and other tantalizing tastes. All of course paired with one or more wines from Auberge's extensive wine list.

Time your reservation so that you catch the last glow of the sun going down, flaming behind the mountains. By dessert, the stars will be twinkling out *good night.*

Address/Phone: P.O. Drawer B, 180 Rutherford Hill Road, Rutherford, CA 94573; (707) 963–1211; fax (707) 963–8764

E-mail: info@aubergedusoleil.com

Web Site: www.aubergedusoleil.com

U.S. Reservations: (800) 348–5406; Relais & Chateaux, (800) RELAIS 8

Owner/Manager: Philippa Perry, general manager

Arrival/Departure: Car rentals available at airports; limousine service available from San Francisco at $175 each way.

Distance from San Francisco Airport: 65 miles north (1½ hours)

Distance from Rutherford: 5 minutes

Accommodations: 50 rooms one-, two-, and three-room suites, each with valley views and fireplaces

Best Room/Suite: The Upper Suites are the most spectacular, with a huge patio and large living room

Amenities: Air-conditioning, fireplace, refrigerator stocked with wine and cheese, TV, VCR, coffeemaker, toiletries, basket of snacks, skylights in bath, double sinks, some rooms with Jacuzzis, hair dryer, valet, 24-hour room service, down comforter, bathrobes, slippers, twice-daily maid service, full-service beauty salon, voice mail

Electricity: 110 volts

Sports and Facilities: Swimming pool and large sundeck; whirlpool, massage, and steam rooms; small workout room; three tennis courts (instruction available). Golf, horseback riding, bicycling, hot air ballooning, and jogging nearby.

Dress Code: Casually smart

Weddings: Can be arranged

Rates/Packages: $400–$600 per couple per night for rooms; $800–$950 for suites; $2,500 for private cottages.

Payment/Credit Cards: Most major

Deposit: Prepayment is required at time of booking to secure your reservation. Your reservation will be confirmed in writing upon receipt of full payment. Reservations must be canceled 14 days prior to scheduled arrival date to receive a refund.

Government Taxes: 10.5 percent

Service Charges: Not included

≈≈≈

Chateau du Sureau

Location: Poised in the foothills of the Sierras on nine wooded acres south of Yosemite National Park.

Romantic Features: Balconies and fireplaces, canopy beds, intimate dining in The Estate by the Elderberries.

This red-roofed palace with its stone tower, balustrades, gardens, and wrought-iron balconies beckons to all the Romeos and Juliets in the world. There may be plenty to explore in nearby Yosemite, but Chateau du Sureau, a member of the Relais & Chateau group, seduces you to linger. Discover unusual treasures—one-of-a-kind pieces of furniture, accessories, and art work, all carefully collected by Erna Kubin-Clanin, Chateau du Sureau's owner, whose inspiration and superb taste is revealed throughout the property, which consists of the Elderberry Restaurant, the Chateau, and the exquisite new two-bedroom Villa Sureau.

Hand-painted ceilings and alcoves, a 1780s tapestry, Oriental carpets, period prints, urns, china, beamed ceilings, tall arched windows, period light fixtures, a 1,000-year-old floor obtained from a chateau in Paris, gardens, and the herringbone pattern brick fireplace in the Grand Salon.

Growing up in Vienna, Austria, castles and romance were woven into Erna's dreams from an early age. In 1962 Erna came to New York, found her way to Yosemite, and was responsible for turning the rather lackluster Redwood Inn into one of the finest restaurants around.

When it came time for her to renew the lease, the government clamped down on the use of parkland, sending Erna hunting for a new challenge. She found it: nine wooded hillside acres full of pines, black oak, manzanita, and elderberry bushes reminding her of her native land. First she built her restaurant, Elderberry House, named for the elderberries she found on the property.

Chateau du Sureau, California

Over the door she placed a sign quoting Oscar Wilde I HAVE THE SIMPLEST OF TASTES: I WANT ONLY THE BEST. That's what she demanded and that's what her customers got. The restaurant's reputation for superb cuisine and meticulous service brought diners from San Francisco and beyond, people like Robert DeNiro and Kevin Bacon. One day Craig Claibourne stopped in. His glowing article in the *New York Times* that followed brought "foodies" from everywhere to Erna's restaurant. Reservations were hard to get. Erna's success with the restaurant served as a springboard for the fulfillment of Erna's second dream: to build a place where people could stay overnight in complete comfort.

With her new husband, Rene, Erna built the ten-room Chateau du Sureau and, most recently, the two-bedroom Villa Sureau. She has used her creative talents and boundless energy to fill the rooms with authentic antiques and other unique pieces gathered from around the world.

Each room is different and named after Provençal herbs and flowers: elderberry, thyme, rosehip, sweet geranium, mint, lavender, chamomile, rosemary, and saffron. The Saffron Room is decorated in bold golds and yellows and boasts a handsome 1834 Napoleonic ebony armoire and bed inlaid with ivory; the Lavender Room features delicate lavender-and-white fabrics and wall coverings and the Elderberry Room has a canopy bed with blue-and-white flowered drapes. Baths are trimmed in hand-painted French tile and beds are dressed with down duvets and Italian linens. There are massive four-poster beds, sleigh beds, canopies with flowing side draperies, fireplaces, and oversize tubs. Fresh flowers are everywhere.

An ornate gazebo overlooks a pond, a nice place to sip a cup of tea or a cocktail; nearby, a giant chess game is tucked into its own garden setting.

Four full-time gardeners keep flowers and shrubs looking their best and supply fresh blooms for arrangements and herbs and vegetables for the kitchen. Staff is always on hand to see that your every wish is granted. Chambermaids dressed in crisp black uniforms with ruffled white aprons deliver room service orders, make the beds, resupply fluffy fresh towels, and keep everything spotless.

Chef James Overbaugh presides over the award-winning kitchen creating a California-French cuisine with fresh fruits, vegetables, and meats. A six-course prix-fixe dinner in the red-toned candlelit dining room costs $68; lunch is about $14.50 to $18.50. The menu changes each night and might include grilled foie gras with apples, braised turnips and elderberry grappa emulsion, vegetable couscous, brochette of rib eye and shiitake mushrooms with boudin noir mashed potatoes and celery root and black trumpet sauce—topped off by semolina flummery, a white and dark chocolate pâté plum sorbet. The wine list offer more than 700 choices; be sure to stop at the wine cellar bar for a drink.

The newest addition to Erna's kingdom Villa Sureau, goes over the top in elegance and amenities and is furnished with turn-of-the century pieces from France. Original art, stained-glass windows, massive carved wood doors, fireplaces, highly polished marble-topped tables, full-length gold-gilt mirrors, Oriental carpets, crystal chandeliers, a king-size bed swathed from floor to ceiling with filmy turquoise-and-gold organdy, hand-painted trompe l'oeil detailing, a grand piano, library of leather-bound books, and an opulent black-marble bath with columns—Nero would love it. There is a private gate, a garden with a fountain, and another beautiful bedroom. And let's not forget the butler.

At Chateau du Sureau, fairy tales do come true.

Address/Phone: 48688 Victoria Lane, Oakhurst, CA 93644; (559) 683–6800; fax (559) 683–0800

E-mail: chateau@sierratel.com

Web Site: www.chateausureau.com

U.S. Reservations: (559) 683–6800; Relais & Chateaux, (800) RELAIS 8

Owner/Manager: Erna Kubin-Clanin; Lucy Royse, director

Arrival/Departure: Car rentals available at San Francisco and Oakland Airports

Distance from San Francisco Airport: 210 miles (3 hours); Fresno Airport, 35 miles (45 minutes)

Distance from Yosemite: 17 miles

Accommodations: 10 rooms and suites plus the 2-bedroom Villa Sureau

Best Room/Suite: It's a tough call. The Lavender Room's balcony overlooks the pool; the Rosehip Room features Empress-period furniture and a tub-for-two with a view out a large window; Mint has a wonderful wide canopy; Elderberry, a corner room, is decorated in blue and yellow and has a high vaulted ceiling. If you really want to splurge, take the Villa Sureau. All rooms are no-smoking.

Amenities: Hair dryer, CD/VCR stereo system, toiletries, robes, TVs on request

Electricity: 110 volts

Sports and Facilities: Pool, chess, walking, hiking; Yosemite about 17 miles away

Dress Code: Jackets requested in main dining room

Weddings: Can be arranged for guests staying in the Chateau. In addition to the gazebo and gardens, there is a mini-chapel in the Chateau with just three pews.

Rates/Packages: $325–$525 per room per couple, including full European breakfast and complimentary bar in the Grand Salon; $2,500 for Villa Sureau with a private butler

Payment/Credit Cards: Most major

Deposit: 50 percent at time of booking; cancel 7 days prior to arrival for refund less 10 percent service fee.

Government Taxes: 9 percent

Service Charges: 12 percent

≋≋≋

Four Seasons Biltmore

Location: Across the street from Butterfly Beach, in the exclusive Montecito enclave.

Romantic Features: Beachfront setting, Roaring Twenties panache (the hotel opened in 1927), glamorous public areas.

The Four Seasons Biltmore reigns as the red-tile–roofed queen of Santa Barbara. You can't beat the vintage 1920s style or the California dream setting, with the deep-blue Pacific glimmering just across the way.

The resort glows with the burnished patina of a classic. It opened in 1927 as part of the original Biltmore chain; the property became a Four Seasons resort in 1987. Over the years the clientele has included everyone from Douglas Fairbanks to Michael Douglas and President Ronald Reagan. (The Reagan ranch is located in the nearby Santa Ynez foothills.)

Set on nineteen acres, the Spanish-Mediterranean resort is composed of a main building plus separate wings and cottages. Public areas resemble the castle of a Spanish grandee, with high, coffered ceilings; thick, red-tile floors; and hand-painted tiles adorning the corridors and stairways. Red-tile or flagstone walkways ramble past bright green lawns and impeccable flower borders.

Giant blue gum trees, broad Monterey cypress, and spreading camphor trees shade the grounds.

Accommodations all differ in layout and view; there are also separate cottages poised along the back ridge of the property in a lush garden setting. Furnishings reflect classic good taste and have recently been updated using rich colors and fabrics. You can slide open the white plantation shutters for an airy country cottage feel. Extremely well laid out, the white-marble bathrooms are replete with such nice touches as Chinese ceramic containers to hold cotton balls. Some rooms have fireplaces, balconies, or private patios.

The new executive chef, Martin Frost, who had garnered top notices while at the Four Seasons Nevis in the Caribbean, now presides over the Biltmore's superb three restaurants. Dining in The Patio is like eating in a country garden—there's even a glass roof with retractable panels to open or close to fit the weather's moods. The nightly buffet earns raves, and Sunday brunch is a Santa Barbara tradition, with huge platters of fresh seafood, a stir-fry table, omelet and Belgian waffle stations, and lots more.

Afternoon tea is served in the Sala Lounge, an elegant drawing room beautified with a high, open-beamed ceiling and a fireplace. La Marina is known for romantic dining, with flowers, candlelight, and arched windows framing the seaward view. In addition to a la carte selections, Chef Frost presents a four-course tasting menu, where choices might include squab with scallion polenta and mission figs, followed by roast tenderloin of veal. Heading to a polo match or into Santa Barbara wine country? The hotel can customize a picnic basket for you.

Guests enjoy preferred tee-time privileges at Sandpiper Golf Course, one of the top-rated public golf layouts in the country, and the newly opened Rancho San Marcos. For tennis players there are three lighted courts. On the property you'll also find an eighteen-hole putting green, croquet, and shuffleboard; the concierge can make arrangements for sportfishing, horseback riding, and sailing.

The recently refurbished workout room comes with an ocean view—along with treadmill, bikes, free weights, and stair machines—and lolling by the Olympic-size swimming pool on the edge of the Pacific makes life luxuriously wonderful. But the biggest treats of all may just be the guest privileges at the Art Deco–era Coral Casino, a private club that has been the center of Santa Barbara social life for over half a century.

Address/Phone: 1260 Channel Drive, Santa Barbara, CA 93108; (805) 969–2261; fax (805) 565–8323

U.S. Reservations: (800) 332–3442

Owner/Manager: Managed by the Four Seasons Hotels & Resort

Arrival/Departure: Transfers can be arranged; car rentals available at airport

Distance from Santa Barbara Airport: 12 miles

Distance from downtown Santa Barbara: 2 miles (5 minutes)

Accommodations: 217 rooms and suites, many with balconies or private patios and fireplaces

Best Room/Suite: Cottage suites; Odell Cottage suite is top of the heap

Amenities: Ceiling fan, hair dryer, 3 phones, VCR, TV, in-room safe, air-conditioning, minibar, bathrobes, AM/FM clock radio, toiletries; in-room spa treatments available, 24-hour room service, twice-daily maid service, shoe shine

Electricity: 110 volts

Sports and Facilities: 3 tennis courts, 2 swimming pools, bicycles; golf and whale-watching expeditions nearby (February to mid-April)

Dress Code: Casually elegant

Weddings: Can be arranged

Rates/Packages: $270–$450 per couple per night for a room; $800 for a suite. Romance package (3 days, 2 nights) $800–$950 per couple; includes welcome bottle of champagne, dinner for two at La Marina restaurant.

Payment/Credit Cards: Most major

Deposit: Deposits are required within 14 days of making reservation. Cancellations are accepted with a full refund up to 72 hours prior to the expected arrival date.

Government Taxes: 10 percent

Service Charges: Not included

≋

The Inn at Spanish Bay

Location: In the Del Monte Forest on the south coast of the Monterey Peninsula.

Romantic Features: Fireplaces; views of the sun setting over the sea.

You pass through the staffed gate of Pebble Beach's highly privileged enclave that juts into the Pacific, drive along the narrow winding roads, and turn into the landscaped entrance of The Inn at Spanish Bay, one of the famed Pebble Beach Resorts. It has all the things you require in a top-rate hotel: beautiful flowers and grounds, bellmen, multiple restaurants, elevators, a pool, a golf course, a tennis complex, a health club, walkways along the beach, and miles of sea to ponder.

Golfing couples will be in heaven. Laid along the sea and winding among the snaggly shrubs, trees, and grass is the often windy Links at Spanish Bay. The area's newest golf course, designed by Robert Trent Jones, Jr., Tom Watson, and Frank "Sandy" Tatum, is reminiscent of Scotland's wild and gritty dune classics. Pebble Beach, a course on every golfer's wish list, is just down the way. As a guest at Spanish Bay, you have a good shot of getting tee times at Pebble Beach Resorts' other two courses on the Peninsula.

Tennis players will appreciate the eight-court complex, and fitness buffs will be more than happy with the full-service health club.

At Spanish Bay red-tile–roofed groups of interconnected low-rise buildings huddle close to the shoreline, inviting walks along the sea to catch the early morning mists or the glowing sunsets. The 17-mile drive is a popular route for bikers; Carmel-By-The-Sea, Clint Eastwood's trendy domain, is just fifteen minutes away.

This low-key resort is high on service and luxury. Airy rooms decorated in soft tones of creams and sand echo the grassy dunes just outside. Comfortable chairs flank the corner fireplace—just flick a switch and the fire comes to life. A bar is stocked with every imaginable snack and beverage; the spacious Italian-marble baths are roomy enough for two. Rooms are so comfortable, they're hard to leave. They come with overstuffed pillows, sofas, and chairs; downy comforters; and large balconies.

When it comes time to eat, you have several choices. Roys is always popular; The Bay Club, decorated in warm colors and wood paneling, serves great Northern Italian cuisine; the Clubhouse Bar and Grill is perfect for lunch or dinner after golf, and for a change of pace, there are the facilities and restaurants of the Lodge at Pebble Beach.

Be sure to catch the plaintive sounds of the lone bagpiper as he walks the course at sunset. It's just one of the traditions at Spanish Bay you'll long remember.

Address/Phone: 2700 17-Mile Drive, Pebble Beach, CA 93953; (831) 647–7500; fax (831) 644–7955

U.S. Reservations: (800) 654–9300

Owner/Manager: Gary Davis, general manager

Arrival/Departure: Car rentals available at San Francisco International, Monterey, San Jose, and Oakland Airports.

Distance from San Francisco Airport: 130 miles (2–3 hours); Monterey Airport, 7 miles (15 minutes)

Distance from Carmel-By-The-Sea: 3 miles

Accommodations: 270 rooms and suites

Best Room/Suite: Ocean-view suites

Amenities: Hair dryers, clock radios, phones, TVs, irons, toiletries, wall safe, double vanities, minibar

Electricity: 110 volts

Sports and Facilities: Golf, 8 Plexi-paved tennis courts (2 lighted), health club, pool, sauna, steam room, walking, hiking, biking, horseback riding

Dress Code: Resort casual

Weddings: Can be arranged

Rates/Packages: $330–$450 per couple, per night for rooms; $650–$2,075 for suites; golf $165–$225 per person

Payment/Credit Cards: Most major

Deposit: By credit card

Government Taxes: 10.5 percent

Service Charges: $17 per room per day

≈≈≈

Meadowood Napa Valley

Location: In the heart of the Napa Valley wine region, just outside the charming town of St. Helena.

Romantic Features: Wood-burning fireplaces; private cottages hidden up a long, winding lane; great spa facilities (a well-kept secret).

You'll be treated like Napa Valley landed gentry while staying at this luxury resort located in the area's most prestigious country club. Meadowood Napa Valley is a picture-perfect property tucked into a 250-acre vale off the Silverado Trail. A member of the Relais & Chateaux group, this elegant hideaway is surrounded by vineyards and trees.

You'll feel as though you've stepped back in time when you enter the turn-of-the-century farmhouse-style lobby, with its huge fireplace, bowls of apples ready for the taking, and glass-fronted cabinets filled with books and knick-knacks. It almost feels as though you're in New England. Meadowood's casual, clubby atmosphere reflects hominess and coziness, not glitz; it's conducive to doing nothing—yet it offers all the facilities of a full-service luxury resort.

Over the years the property served as a Christmas tree farm and rice paddy, before being groomed into one of the area's preeminent country clubs in the 1960s. The resort itself opened in 1984, and today guests rub shoulders with the "who's who" of Napa Valley, especially during the many top social events that are held here, including the annual Napa Valley Wine Auction in June.

Guests dwell in gray clapboard cottages, which look part Martha's Vineyard, part California wine country, with gables, white trim, cathedral ceilings, and stone fireplaces. There is more than a little romance in these gracious abodes nestled into the woods of tall California oaks and conifers. What a place to go and hide out—with the scent of pine permeating the airy rooms, a fine Chardonnay resting in an ice bucket next to two flutes, plush down comforters, and piles of fat pillows stacked on the king-size bed; and in the cooler months,

Meadowood Napa Valley, California

a cozy fire crackling in your fireplace. With room service available, who needs to go anywhere?

One of the best features of the cottages are the wraparound porches, each with an oh-so-private sitting area furnished with chairs and tables. In your room you'll find rattan furniture, a writing desk and minibar, and tasteful decor. Bathrooms are spacious and come with all the modern comforts. Some cottages have kitchenettes.

Meadowood offers a tantalizing array of choices for the sports-minded. In addition to miles of hiking and walking trails, where it would not be unusual for a deer or two to cross your path, you can swim in two pools and play croquet on the primped and clipped croquet lawns, which are trimmed as meticulously as a golf green and have wickets just the thickness of a nickel wider than the ball.

You can shake out your golf game on the resort's nifty and narrow nine-hole course, play tennis, explore the area by bike, or be pampered with a variety of soothing treatments at the health spa. The aerobics room provides a setting for classes ranging from a thirty-minute abs-intensive workout to yoga, and the air-conditioned exercise room features Cybex equipment, bikes, stair machines, and more. The masseur will even do treatments in your room—one of life's great happinesses.

Want to check out Napa Valley and the grapes? You can get an overview of more than one hundred vineyards from a lofty perch in a hot air balloon, or you can hop in a car and explore the area. Pick up a loaf of sourdough bread (a specialty in the region), a bottle of wine, and some good cheese and have a picnic on the way. Meadowood can help you with directions and suggestions for visiting not only the vineyards but also the scores of art galleries and boutiques in the vicinity.

The Restaurant at Meadowood offers the most extensive wine list in the valley, with more than 600 selections. Practically every vineyard in the valley is represented, and bottles are all fairly priced. Overlooking gnarled oaks and the golf course, the dining room makes an especially pretty picture at night, with floral displays, table lamps, and spotlighted watercolors. The menu tempts you with country-style rack of lamb with rice, beans, fennel, tomatoes, wilted arugula, olives, and garlic sauce or chilled Dungeness crab with three caviars, mango, and avocado, and lemon-cilantro vinaigrette. Desserts are hard to resist, but the flourless chocolate cake is rich enough to satisfy the most audacious of chocoholics. All this, of course, is accompanied by a fine wine—would you expect anything less here!

Breakfast, lunch, and dinner are served in the casual Meadowood Grill, and snacks and a limited lunch menu are available during the summer months at the Poolside Terrace. The food and other services are delivered by a caring, attentive staff in a friendly, unobtrusive manner.

Meadowood is a peaceful and unspoiled sanctuary in the midst of one of the nation's most interesting areas. Little more than an hour's drive from San Francisco, it is an exceptional retreat that has great charm and style. With its woodsy privacy it can help you put the outside world on hold.

Address/Phone: 900 Meadowood Lane, St. Helena, CA 94574; (707) 963–3646; fax (707) 963–3532

U.S. Reservations: (800) 458–8080; Relais & Chateaux, (800) RELAIS 8

Owner/Manager: Seamus McManus, managing director; H. William Harlan, managing partner

Arrival/Departure: Limousine service available from airport

Distance from San Francisco Airport: 70 miles; Santa Rosa Airport, 20 miles; Oakland Airport, 60 miles

Distance from downtown San Francisco: 70 miles

Accommodations: 85 rooms are scattered throughout the property. All rooms have a private entrance and porch; some are located in the woods overlooking the pool, others by the tennis courts and golf course fairways, and 13 are located in the Croquet Lodge. All have king-size beds; most have fireplaces.

Best Room/Suite: The Hillside Terrace cottages, set deep in the woods, with huge porches, stone hearths, and plenty of privacy

Amenities: Air-conditioning, TV, minibar, toaster, coffeemaker, hair dryer, terry robes, toiletries, duvets, fireplaces in most rooms; fresh fruit basket, newspaper, room service

Electricity: 110 volts

Sports and Facilities: 7 championship tennis courts, 2 regulation croquet lawns, 2 pools (1 is a heated, 25-yard pool and is open year-round), 9-hole golf course, bicycling, hiking trails; full-service health spa with sauna, Jacuzzi, classes, quality equipment, and massage treatments

Dress Code: Informal; casually elegant attire requested for dinner at The Restaurant; white clothing and flat-soled shoes are required on the croquet lawns.

Weddings: May be arranged by calling (707) 963–3646; e-mail: catering@ meadowood.com

Rates/Packages: $395–$2,915 per couple per night

Payment/Credit Cards: Most major

Deposit: Guarantee with 2-night deposit (use a credit card); cancel 14 days prior to arrival for refund

Government Taxes: 10.5 percent

Service Charges: Not included

≋≋

Post Ranch Inn

Location: On ninety-eight acres amid the seaside cliffs of Big Sur.

Romantic Features: Endless views of the Pacific from the villas' ridge-top perches; a large, night-lighted outdoor hot tub on the edge of a cliff; guided nature hikes; on-staff tarot reader and astrologer; stargazing through a 10-inch Meade electronic tracking telescope.

They sometimes have problems with deer grazing on the roofs. That challenge reflects the uniqueness of Post Ranch Inn, a magnificent resort located in one of the most majestic spots on earth—Big Sur. Opened in 1992, Post Ranch was the first new hotel in nearly twenty years to debut along this untamed, almost mythological coastline, which over the decades has attracted avant-garde writers and actors such as Henry Miller, Jack Kerouac, and Orson Welles. Big Sur was one of America's last frontiers, a place where roads did not arrive until the 1930s, electricity until the 1950s.

To win the approval of development-abhorring locals and legislators, the resort had to meet stringent environmental standards. In part, the property was planned by Bill Post III, whose great-grandfather had homesteaded the land (he paid $4.00 an acre for 160 acres) some 130 years previously. The resultant enclave manages to feel both rustic and futuristic—*Star Wars* meets the Old West.

Planked with redwood, the accommodations seem more like private houses than hotel rooms. Although rooms vary in layout and view, all offer the same amenities and square footage and make extensive use of gold-gray rajah slate, quarried by hand in India, for the floors. Railings and doors in Cor-Ten steel weather to the same brown-red tone of the neighboring oaks and madrone trees. Furnishings are comfortable, with features such as curvilinear sofas or window seats. Color schemes of blue, green, and earth tones soothe the spirit. Bathrooms are embellished with slate and granite; many have tubs next to windows positioned so that no one can see you but you can enjoy a 100-mile view. Bath towels are thick, the down comforters plump.

Tree Houses live up to their name, built on stilts so as not to disturb the adjoining redwoods. Walls are angled to maximize views and privacy. Personal favorites are the Ocean Houses, which hunker into the ridgeline—the terrain rising from the back to form the sod-covered roofs, the aforementioned salad bar for perambulating deer. Out front, views of the Pacific surge to the horizon. The fireplace is arranged so that you can view it from both the living room and the bathroom.

Because Michael Freed and Myles Williams, Post Ranch's creators, wanted to spotlight the splendor of nature rather than the playthings of man, distractions are kept to a minimum. Rooms have no TVs (though they do come with pretty nifty stereo/CD systems), and there are no tennis courts or golf courses. What you have are miles of big-country hiking trails through redwood forests into the valleys snaking hillward behind Highway 1. Some guided hikes are offered, including nature treks and off-property hikes; herb garden talks are also available. The lap pool awaits, a warm 80 degrees year-round. A fitness room offers a step machine, free weights, and exercise machines; yoga classes are held poolside in the morning. Dramatic seascapes can be enjoyed at Pfeiffer and Andrew Molera Beaches, both less than 5 miles to the north.

Rates include an elaborate continental breakfast, served in your room or in the restaurant. Choices generally include fresh fruits, home-baked breads, granola, and quiche. Floor-to-ceiling glass windows (each of which took nine people to carry into position during construction) of the Sierra Mar restaurant afford cliff-hanging views of the water. So as not to compete with the vistas, decor is simple, with slate floors and a big fireplace.

Superintended by executive chef Craig von Forester, the Californian menu dallies with flavors from around the world. Entrees might feature a grilled venison chop with fermented black beans or John Dory (a fish that is like sole) with lemongrass, papaya, chili, and roasted peanuts. Prices run $58 per person for the four-course, prix-fixe dinner. The wine list is phenomenal, encompassing 2,000 different wines.

Not much is known about the Ohlone Indians, the original inhabitants of the Northern California coast. From their celebrations only a line from a song remains, "dancing on the brink of the world." From your cliffside perch at Post Ranch Inn, you'll probably experience a similar feeling of joy.

Address/Phone: P.O. Box 219, Highway 1, Big Sur, CA 93920; (831) 667–2200; fax (831) 667–2824

U.S. Reservations: (800) 527–2200

Owner/Manager: Michael Freed and Myles Williams, general partners; Larry Callahan, general manager

Arrival/Departure: Easily accessible by car

Distance from Monterey Airport: 35 miles south; 90 miles south of San Jose Airport; 150 miles south of San Francisco International Airport

Distance from Carmel: Approximately 30 miles south; 150 miles south of San Francisco

Accommodations: 30 villas, each with ocean or mountain views, in four styles: 5 Ocean Houses recessed into ridge with sod roofs, 7 Tree Houses on stilts, 10 Coast Houses, 2 Mountain Houses, and 6 guest accommodations in three-level Butterfly House

Best Room/Suite: Top-of-the-line Ocean Houses hang on the brink of the cliff and feature private, slate-floored terraces. These often book up way in advance.

Amenities: Wood-burning fireplace, bathtub/Jacuzzi, satellite stereo/CD music system, in-room massage table, coffeemaker, minibar, toiletries, terry cloth robes, hair dryer

Electricity: 110 volts

Sports and Facilities: A "basking pool" (a giant hot tub); fitness center and spa; hiking and walking trails

Dress Code: Casually smart

Weddings: Can be arranged

Rates/Packages: $395–$695 per couple per night

Payment/Credit Cards: Most major

Deposit: Reservations require guarantee or deposit in advance. Cancellations must be made 7 days in advance.

Government Taxes: 10 to 15 percent

Service Charges: Not included

≋

The Sherman House

Location: In the Pacific Heights neighborhood of San Francisco

Romantic Features: Fireplaces; elegant rooms with down duvets and feather mattresses; candlelit dining; intimate walled gardens

You couldn't ask for a better address: right in the heart of San Francisco's trendiest neighborhood within walking distance of Union Street, Fisherman's Wharf, and dozens of boutique shops and cafes. Certainly music patron and piano importer Leander Sherman thought so when he built his grand home here in 1876. Over the years he entertained the cream of the music and art world, including Lillian Russell, Ignace Paderewski, Enrico Caruso, Victor Herbert, and other famous highbrows.

The Sherman House, a white, impeccably groomed villa constructed in the French-Italianate-Victorian style, is distinguished by its decorative exterior, mansard roof, balustraded balconies, and wide staircase leading up to the original entrance. The villa is surrounded by a profusion of flowers and tiered garden rooms reminiscent of England's Hidcote.

Inside it gets even better. Meticulously restored by the owners and furnished by well-known interior designer William Gaylord, who looked to France's Second Empire for his inspiration, each room is decorated to the nines. Each is quite different.

Gaylord combed antiques shops and markets around the world to find authentic period pieces to bring back to the Sherman House. There is an antique

The Sherman House, California

Flemish tapestry, an ornate fantasy of a birdcage modeled after a French chateau and inhabited by some cheery chirpy finches, a hand-painted frieze, plumply upholstered sofas and chairs, heavy brocade and silk draperies, enormous Oriental carpets, and other eclectic treasures gleaned from antiques dealers and auction houses.

A wide double stairway leads from the soaring ballroom-size three-story music and recital room up to the library and gallery. All the public rooms are very grand, showcasing glittering crystal chandeliers, bronze urns, original oil paintings, china figurines, sterling silver candelabras, parquet floors, high ceilings, marble-topped tables, and a grand piano. In the restoration, the original 1870s patterns for the plaster work were used for the ornamentation on walls, ceilings and columns.

Guest rooms and suites are located in the main house and the carriage house set in the gardens. Some rooms feature cozy cushioned window seats tucked into bay windows; all but one have queen-size beds and working wood-burning fireplaces—there's even a second fireplace in the bathroom of Suite 202. There are private terraces with views of the bay, rooms with high beamed ceilings, and a suite with a private garden patio.

Black-granite baths, faux-cherry moldings and paneling, plump pillows, fabulous embossed and damask linens, and four-poster beds completely surrounded by bed draperies are just a few of the elaborate features. Although most rooms are furnished in Second Empire, Gaylord used the classic nineteenth-century Beidermeier in one room; ornate Jacobean in another.

The Sherman House has a pond, a gazebo, a guest-only dining room—perfect for a quiet dinner—and a sunny breakfast room with a black-and-white tile floor and lots of leaded windows. Nestled into corners of the gardens with the lightly splashing fountain nearby are small wrought-iron tables and chairs, inviting you to enjoy breakfast or lunch amidst the flowers.

Address/Phone: 2160 Green Street, San Francisco, California 94123; (800) 424 5777; (415) 563–3600; fax (415) 563–1882

U.S. Reservations: (800) 424–5777; Relais & Chateau, (800) RELAIS 8

Owner/Manager: Christine Berlin, general manager

Arrival/Departure: Car rentals available at San Francisco and Oakland Airports

Distance from San Franisco International Airport: 15 miles (½ hour)

Distance from San Francisco: In the heart of city

Accommodations: 14 rooms and suites in main house and carriage house

Best Room/Suite: Carriage House Suite 503, where you wake up to a view of the Golden Gate Bridge. The suite has a canopy bed, sunken living room, and large brick-patio balcony. Very private.

Amenities: Air-conditioning, hair dryers, clock radios, phones, TVs, toiletries, VCR, CD stereo player/cassette deck, wall safe, robes, umbrella

Electricity: 110 volts

Sports and Facilities: All attractions of San Francisco just outside the door

Dress Code: Jacket requested at dinner

Weddings: Can be arranged

Rates/Packages: $360–$850 per couple per night, including breakfast, valet parking, and evening wine and hors d'oeuvres

Payment/Credit Cards: Most major

Deposit: By credit card

Government Taxes: 14 percent

Service Charges: Included

COLORADO

≈≈≈

Sonnenalp Resort

Location: Three separate houses set in the center of Vail near the covered bridge; within walking distance of just about everything.

Romantic Features: Sitting by a blazing fire in your suite while the snow falls softly just outside; sleeping under fluffy down duvets; moonlight sleigh ride; European ambience.

You don't have to go all the way to Austria to find the archetypal European ski and mountain resort. Just grab your skis and head to Vail, where the Fässler family has created a resort that fairly sings with charms of the Old World. The Sonnenalp is actually three separate inns within easy walking distance of one another. Each has its own restaurants and personality, yet the facilities of all are open to Sonnenalp's guests.

The Austria Haus Club & Hotel, located next to Vail's covered bridge, is the smallest and coziest. It has a bar, a Jacuzzi, a sauna, on-site ski storage, and an intimate lobby with a large fireplace. Many of the thirty-seven rooms, with their antique brick and barn-board walls and washed pine furniture, overlook picturesque Gore Creek.

The Sonnenalp Resort of Vail, winner of *Snow Country Magazine's* National Design Award for ski area lodges and hotels, consists of the elegant Ludwig's Restaurant, the more casual Bully Ranch Restaurant, and the King's Club Lounge, with its piano bar and library.

Sonnenalp Resort, Colorado

The light, airy, 5,000-square-foot spa features a 1,200-square-foot indoor/outdoor pool, indoor and outdoor Jacuzzis, a sauna, steam rooms, and an exercise room with the latest in exercise and weight-lifting equipment. You can also pamper yourself with various massages, seaweed wraps, and other soothing treatments. The spa has lots of windows affording great views of the beautiful mountain world just outside.

The largest and most luxurious of the three inns, Sonnenalp Resort of Vail has eighty-eight suites decorated with handcrafted woodwork, original artwork of Native American scenes, gas fireplaces, cozy sitting areas, European fixtures, and warm, natural wood furniture. Bathrooms have heated marble floors, double sinks, and large tubs just right for soaking out kinks acquired on the ski slopes.

With its white exterior trimmed with wooden balconies and stone arches and a roofline that swoops over towers and gables, Sonnenalp Resort of Vail is reminiscent of a lovely palace chalet. Covered with snow, it's a picture postcard. Send this one to your friends, and they won't believe it's not somewhere in the Alps.

At the Swiss Hotel & Spa, just half a block away from Sonnenalp Resort of Vail, you'll find a European treatment spa offering aromatherapy and massage and body treatments as well as facials, manicures, and other pampering services. The spa also has an indoor Jacuzzi, an outdoor heated pool, a cold plunge pool, a fitness room, Finnish saunas, Turkish steam rooms, and a juice bar as well as a full bar serving beverages and light meals.

The fifty-seven rooms and two suites at the Swiss Hotel & Spa feature pine armoires and beds, Alpine decor, and views of the creek or the village. Be sure to try the fondue and raclette, specialties at the Swiss Chalet Restaurant.

The Cosmetique Boutique and the Sonnenalp Shop, located in the Swiss Hotel & Spa, feature a tempting array of items, including jewelry, accessories, perfumes, and unique gifts.

During the summer months Sonnenalp is a wonderful base for those who love hiking, biking, swimming, horseback riding, tennis, and exploring this lovely mountain area. The Sonnenalp Golf Club features an eighteen-hole, links-style course.

If you've got Europe on your mind but want to leave your passports at home, Sonnenalp is highly recommended.

Address/Phone: 20 Vail Road, Vail, CO 81657; (970) 476–5656; fax (970) 476–1639

E-mail: sonnenalp@vail.net

Web Site: www.sonnenalp.com

U.S. Reservations: (800) 654–8312; fax (970) 476–8066

Owner/Manager: Johannes Fässler, owner/general manager

Arrival/Departure: Colorado Mountain Express shuttle service available at $48 per person, one-way

Distance from Denver International Airport: 2 hours; Eagle County Airport is only 35 miles to the west

Distance from Denver: 100 miles west

Accommodations: Sonnenalp Resort of Vail, 2 rooms, 88 suites; Swiss Hotel & Spa, 57 rooms, 2 suites; Austria Haus Club & Hotel, 433 rooms and 4 suites.

Best Room/Suite: Suites in Sonnenalp Resort of Vail; spacious Bald Mountain Suite overlooks creek and comes with a separate bedroom; large living room with fireplace and minibar; and a great bathroom with separate shower, double sinks, and soaking tub. Lodgepole Suite also roomy and luxurious, with fireplace, soaking tub, separate sitting area, minibar, and view of Vail Village or Gore Creek. Creekside Room in Austria Haus Club & Hotel has view of mountain and creek and is cozy and less expensive.

Amenities: Hair dryer, bathrobes, iron and ironing board, toiletries, telephone, TV, VCR, down duvet, minibar, air-conditioning (Sonnenalp Resort of Vail only). Suites have fireplaces, minibar, double vanity, soaking tub, balcony, separate living room, and loft.

Electricity: 110 volts

Sports and Facilities: Vail Ski area has 4,000 skiable acres serviced by 25 lifts; in addition to Alpine and cross-country skiing, you can go snowboarding, snowshoeing, bobsledding, paragliding, dogsledding, snowmobiling, and ice skating; 18-hole golf course with pro shop, pool, and clubhouse; outdoor Jacuzzi, indoor and outdoor heated pools; 2 European spas; 4 tennis courts

Dress Code: Casual; jacket and tie requested for Ludwig's restaurant only

Weddings: Can be arranged

Rates/Packages: Romance in the Rockies, $149–$219 per person, double occupancy, including suite accommodations, flowers, champagne, chocolate-covered strawberries, breakfast, and dinner (rates higher in winter season)

Payment/Credit Cards: Most major

Deposit: 1 night's lodging due within 10 days of booking; full payment due 30 days (60 during holiday period) prior to arrival. Cancellations made 30 days (60 for holiday period) or more prior to arrival, forfeit $50 per room. Cancellations made less than 30 days, forfeit all monies held on account.

Government Taxes: 8 percent

Service Charges: Not included

CONNECTICUT

The Boulders

Location: Overlooking Lake Waramaug in Connecticut's Litchfield Hills.
Romantic Features: Rustic beauty by the lake; four-poster beds; dining on the terrace.

New Preston, Connecticut, is barely an eye blink when you drive through it on Route 202. But hang a left onto Route 45 and you'll immediately see a tight enclave of little shops and cafes. Farther down the road you'll come to Lake Waramaug and The Boulders, my choice for your overnight stay if you're looking for an intimate lakeside inn. It may be rustic in appearance with its brown shingle and stone exterior and knotty-pine lounge, but it is pure country luxury in its accommodations, food, service, and charm. There's a lot to do here if you love nature, hiking, and water sports. Winter enthusiasts will also appreciate its location: close to New England's major ski areas.

The Boulders is a classy inn, with seventeen rooms and suites and a restaurant, carefully tended by the innkeepers and owners, Dutch-born Kees Adema and his wife, Ulla, who came here from Germany. Dating from 1895, when massive rocks carried down nearby Pinnacle Mountain were incorporated into the thick-walled structure of this bold shingled mansion, The Boulders appeals to an upscale clientele. But according to Ulla, "It by no means should be considered fancy. Our guests who come back year after year are like friends coming home for a holiday."

There are four rooms and two suites in the main house; four double cottage rooms and three rooms in the carriage house. The guest cottages are more private and feature fireplaces, refrigerators, sitting areas, and decks overlooking the lake, but the decor is less imaginative than that in the main house, whose rooms are individually decorated and furnished with authentic antiques and cheerful printed fabrics and may feature window seats, king-size beds, bay windows, and canopy beds as well as sitting areas. Take a close look at the beautiful lamps located throughout the inn. The hand-cut lampshades were created by Ulla—an art she still practices when she finds the time. Not an easy thing when you're looking after guests.

The lounge, spacious and comfortable, is an inviting place to sit and sip a cup of tea, read a book, or simply enjoy the views of the lake through the large windows. Here in this eclectically furnished room, you can help yourself to an apple from a bowl set on a marble-topped table or borrow a book from the shelves near the fireplace. In summertime you can head to the boat house and take out the canoes and paddleboats or borrow one of the bikes and ride around the lake or into town. A vineyard is just down the road.

The Boulders has garnered a well-deserved reputation for its restaurant operations. Breakfast and dinner are served in the dining room overlooking the lake or on the terrace in warmer months. Both fish- and meat-based dishes are included on the limited but tempting menu. You might find pan-seared red snapper with shaved-fennel salad, black bean cake, and saffron mussel broth or veal osso buco with orecchiette pasta. Herbs and vegetables from The Boulders' own gardens, as well as produce, game, and cheese from local farmers, are used whenever possible. Try the superb foie gras, and select a vintage wine from the impressive and extensive wine list.

Address/Phone: East Shore Road (Route 45) New Preston, CT 06777; (800) 55 BOULDERS; (860) 868–0541; fax (860) 868–1925

E-mail: boulders@bouldersinn.com

Web Site: www.bouldersinn.com

U.S. Reservations: (800) 552–6853

Owner/Manager: Kees and Ulla Adema

Arrival/Departure: Arrangements can be made for pickup at Bradley Airport, Hartford, or at Albany Airport, New York. Most guests arrive by car.

Distance from Bradley Airport (Hartford): 45 miles (approximately 1 hour)

Distance from Hartford: 45 miles

Accommodations: 17 rooms and suites located in the main inn, a carriage house, and cottages

Best Room/Suite: I love the traditional rooms with the large four-poster beds in the main house. However, if you want more privacy, ask for the guest houses, which come with their own fireplaces, whirlpool tubs, and decks.

Amenities: Hair dryer, telephone, radio, coffeemaker; air-conditioning; some have ceiling fans, wood-burning fireplaces, refrigerators, whirlpool tubs, TV, toiletries, padded hangers

Electricity: 110 volts

Sports and Facilities: Hiking trail, private beach, boats, biking, ice skating, fishing; golf and horseback riding nearby

Dress Code: Casual smart

Weddings: Can be arranged

Rates/Packages: Double room rates with breakfast and dinner, $295–$345; room with breakfast, $225–$275. Deduct $50 weekdays November 1–May 1; add $50 for Friday and Saturday June–October.

Payment/Credit Cards: Most major

Deposit: Guarantee with credit card; one night's lodging or one-half of total stay required; cancel 14 days or more prior to arrival date for full refund less a processing fee

Government Taxes: 6 percent

Service Charges: 15 percent

FLORIDA

The Boca Raton Resort & Club

Location: On a 356-acre estate on Florida's Gold Coast, in Palm Beach County.
Romantic Features: Private beach; Sunday brunch in the Cloister; the view at sunset from the Tower.

D reamers, risk-takers, moguls, and millionaires all contributed to the mystique of Florida's Boca Raton Resort & Club, beginning with Ponce de León, who sailed along these shores looking for the "Fountain of Youth" in 1513. He was followed by Spanish conquistadors and pirates.

In the early 1920s the famed architect Addison Mizner bought 17,500 acres here to create a great resort, and proceeded to do so in grand style. In 1926 the Cloister Inn was the most expensive one-hundred-room hotel ever built up to that time. Today it is the fantasy centerpiece for the Boca Raton Resort & Club, still a superb resort. In 1993 it underwent a $70 million renovation program, further enhancing its guest rooms and public areas, and since 1990 about $10 million has been spent annually on property upgrades and maintenance. The physical beauty of the setting and buildings, combined with the sports facilities and top-notch staff, adds up to one great honeymoon resort.

This imposing complex on Florida's Gold Coast offers something for every taste. The most dramatic and romantic section is the original six-story Cloister, redolent of Florida in the 1920s, displaying Moorish, Mediterranean, and even Gothic touches. Modeled after a Spanish castle, the Cloister is a harmonious blend of Venice and Palm Beach, with a dash of ancient Greece and Rome thrown in for extra flavor. Flower-filled tropical courtyards, hidden gardens, barrel-tile roofs, and dusky archways all contribute to the mystique of this creamy pink palace. The fountain in the center of the courtyard is a sculpture of an alluring nude woman said to be modeled after a mistress of the architect.

The Cloister lobby is filled with columns, mosaics, and beamed ceilings of ornate pecky cypress. Furnishings feature Mizner's rare antiques from old churches and universities in Spain and Central America. At the far end a little museum highlights the resort's history.

Other sections of the sprawling resort, which hugs the Atlantic, the inland waterways, and rolling golf links, are connected by free water taxi and shuttle service. They include the twenty-seven–story Tower, Boca Beach Club, Palm Court Club, and Golf Villas, all with lovely accommodations and all with a different focus.

There are Mediterranean-style or modern terraces over the water or twinkling high-rise views, Jacuzzis or kitchens, balconies or patios. The Boca Beach Club, which is casual and quiet, is steps from the water. Golf Villa Apartments, located on the fairways, are spacious, private, and secluded. Tower rooms have panoramic windows with sweeping views of the coast—very sophisticated. And the quiet, Mediterranean-type Cloister boasts the Palm Court Club, a floor with a private concierge and special amenities. Depending on your interests and whether you prefer the dreamily historic, the pounding surf, or the convenience of rolling out of bed and onto the greens, the choice is yours. You could even spend some nights in more than one section, as the resort aims to please in any way possible.

Everything here is pristine and delightful and reflects the good life. Walkways are lush with flowers, the sand is sparkling, the shops are brimming with stylish goods, the well-prepared food is presented with snap. Even the tropical birds in the Cloister have spotless cages and gourmet fruit.

A perfect day in Boca might start with breakfast in the grand old Palm Court, a water-taxi ride over to the ½ mile of private beach, and a leisurely lunch at the open-air poolside bar. In the afternoon you might bike or play croquet, swing a racquet, or play eighteen holes. Or maybe board a private charter for some deep-sea fishing off Boca's famous reefs—now free of pirates.

Most of the sports activities require a fee, so budget accordingly. For example, bike rentals are $7.00 per hour for a half-day, $20.00 a full day. Sailboarding is $25.00 per hour and snorkeling is $9.00 per hour. Greens fees are $120.00 (eighteen holes) and $90.00 (nine holes); cart rentals are $25.00. If you are into a particular sport in a big way, you should ask about the special packages, such as golf or tennis plans, which might be your best deals. Boca's Resort Course is currently undergoing an extensive redesign and reconfiguration of each hole. Expect more water, elevation changes, and an island green.

The dine-around plan is a good way to enjoy any of the resort's several indoor and outdoor restaurants. Dinner might be Florida stone crabs at Nick's Fishmarket at the Beach Club or fresh pasta at The Italian Restaurant on the twenty-seventh floor of the Tower, with far-reaching views from Palm Beach to Miami Beach. You might want to end the evening at Malone's Magic Bar, one of the resort's several nightclubs and lounges with live entertainment.

And then, of course, there's always a walk under the streaming bougainvillea and magic moon. Perhaps the Fountain of Youth *was* discovered around here, after all.

Address/Phone: 501 East Camino Real, P.O. Box 5025, Boca Raton, FL 33431-0825; (561) 447–3000; fax (561) 447–3183

U.S. Reservations: (888) 498–BOCA

Owner/Manager: Michael F. Glennie, president; David Feder, vice president and general manager

Arrival/Departure: Taxis available at airports

Distance from Ft. Lauderdale Airport: 24 miles; Palm Beach Airport, 28 miles; Miami International Airport, 45 miles

Distance from Palm Beach: 22 miles

Accommodations: 963 rooms and suites in four areas: the Cloister, the Tower, the Golf Villa Apartments, and Boca Beach Club

Best Room/Suite: Boca Beach Club rooms with ocean views

Amenities: Air-conditioning, hair dryer, ceiling fans, minibar, safe, TV, telephone, bathrobes, toiletries, marble baths, magnifying makeup mirror; room service

Electricity: 110 volts

Sports and Facilities: 30 clay tennis courts, 4 racquetball courts, 2 fitness centers, two 18-hole golf courses, driving range, putting green, private beach, 5 pools, 25-slip marina, most water sports, private beach club, deep-sea fishing, sailing, scuba diving, snorkeling, sailboarding, Waverunners, bicycling

Dress Code: Casually elegant

Weddings: Can be arranged

Rates/Packages: $140–$325 per couple per night (summer); $190–$440

(spring and fall); $240–$580 (winter). Romance Packages available from $574 per couple for 2 nights.

Payment/Credit Cards: Most major

Deposit: 1 night's deposit for rooms, $250 for packages; cancel 24 hours to 21 days prior to arrival date for refund, depending on time of year

Government Taxes: Not included

Service Charges: $9.00 per room per day

≋

Disney's Grand Floridian Resort & Spa

Location: On forty acres in the heart of Walt Disney World Resort on the west side of Seven Seas Lagoon, between the Magic Kingdom and the Polynesian Resort.

Romantic Features: The whole of Walt Disney World at your doorstep; opulent Victorian-style accommodations; luxurious spa.

If you thought Walt Disney World was just for kids, think again. This area, with all its various attractions, is one of the top honeymoon destinations in the world. And within this complex of fun and games, the Grand Floridian Resort & Spa is just about the most romantic of the places you can stay. Special honeymoon suites overlook the palm-shaded pool and lazy lagoon of this Victorian-style hotel that rests like an oasis right in the heart of all the action just beyond its entrance.

Designed in the grand manner of the Victorian era and reminiscent of the setting for *The Great Gatsby,* the Grand Floridian, with its sprawling white facade accented by gabled roofs, intricate latticework, and ornate balustrades, is set amid gardens and lawns planted with canary palms, magnolias, hibiscus, and other lush tropical flora. This grand hotel boasts wide verandas with wicker rockers, more than 120 miles of decorative scrollwork, white towers, and a red-shingle roof.

A curious touch in the lofty, five-story atrium lobby is an open-cage elevator that whisks guests up and down. Look up and admire the lobby's ceiling, with its three illuminated stained-glass domes, ornate chandeliers, and metal scrolls.

Rooms, which are located in a 225,000-square-foot main building and in five lodge buildings, carry out the early 1920s mood, though the colors used are softer and lighter. Applied with flair are printed wall coverings coordinated with fabrics, light woods, marble-topped sinks (but with old fashioned–looking fittings), and Victorian woodwork. Most rooms have two queen-size beds; some have kings. Suites include a parlor plus one or more bedrooms.

Grand Floridian Resort & Spa, Florida

The mood may hark back to the turn of the century and the days of John D. Rockefeller and Thomas Edison, but the amenities are pure twentieth-century modern, with monorail service and air-conditioning—the monorail stops right beside the Grand Lobby. The resort has five restaurants, four lounges, two snack bars, five shops, a pool, a 9,000-square-foot spa and health club, a marina, and children's facilities.

The opportunities for fun and romance are seemingly unlimited. At the spa you can unwind with a soothing massage, a native Floridian floral bath, or a hydrating paraffin body wrap. Or rent a boat from the marina and explore the lagoon. At Epcot you can visit the cultures and entertainment worlds of many countries as well as thrill at the sharks and tropical fish at The Living Seas. You can ride the spine-tingling Thunder Mountain at the Magic Kingdom; whiz down the 120-foot-high Summit Plummet from the top of Mt. Gushmore at the sixty-six-acre Blizzard Beach water park; thrill to an alien encounter in Tomorrowland; and dodge (imaginary) flying objects at the 3-D exhibit, "Honey, I Shrunk the Audience." Later, back in the resort, you can dine by candlelight in the privacy of your room and enjoy a moonlit walk on the white sand beach.

You can go nightclub hopping at Pleasure Island (yes, that man's eyes in the portrait at the Adventurers Club really do follow you), where you will most likely laugh at the comedians at the Comedy Warehouse, and dance up a storm at the Mannequins Dance Palace. See how films are made and special effects created at Disney's MGM Studios and shop at the many, many stores.

Restaurants at the Grand Floridian range from the formal fare served in Victoria & Albert's to the hamburgers and hot dogs of Gasparilla Grill and Games. At V&A's the menu changes daily, and what you get depends on what is available in the local market that day. Selections include fresh seafood and meat. A nice touch is the red rose you are given when you arrive.

For a market-fresh blend of Florida and Mediterranean cooking, try Citricos, and for Southern specialties head for the Grand Floridian Cafe. The 1900 Park Fare serves a Disney-character breakfast and dinner buffet; Narcoosee's features a variety of seafood. All serve baked goods prepared in the hotel bakery.

At the close of the evening, the night sky lights up at Epcot with a spectacular display of fireworks during IllumiNations 2000, a laser and water spectacular—it's guaranteed you'll see stars!

Address/Phone: P.O. Box 10,000, Lake Buena Vista, FL 32830-1000; (407) 824–3000; fax (407) 824–2968

U.S. Reservations: (407) W–DISNEY

Owner/Manager: Georgina Sussan, general manager

Arrival/Departure: Transfers included in the Grand Honeymoon package

Distance from Orlando International Airport: 26 miles

Distance from Orlando: 25 miles southwest

Accommodations: 901 rooms and suites, including Standard, Concierge, and Lodge

Best Room/Suite: Honeymoon rooms have all the amenities included in the Concierge rooms, with a few differences. Some are octagonal; some have balconies; some Jacuzzis. Lodge suites, located in a separate building, enjoy such special amenities as afternoon tea, complimentary continental breakfast, and hors d'oeuvres and wine. For high rollers try the Roosevelt Suite, which has 3 rooms, 5 private balconies, 2 bedrooms with king-size canopy beds, and oversize bathrooms, including a Jacuzzi in the master bath. The living room has a complete entertainment center, with a stereo system, CD player, VCR, and 52-inch wide-screen TV.

Amenities: Air-conditioning, ceiling fans, hair dryer, telephones, minibar, in-room safe, bathrobes, turndown service, room service, iron and ironing board (on request), and toiletries. Concierge rooms and suites also include special shampoos and lotions, slippers, VCR, continental breakfast, tea, hors d'oeuvres, and late-night dessert and cordials. Down pillows, refrigerator, and microwave can be requested.

Electricity: 110 volts

Sports and Facilities: A 275,000-gallon swimming pool, beach, marina, water sports, health club, exercise room, saunas, massage room; also in the Disney complex are 5 championship golf courses, tennis courts, jogging paths, horseback riding, ponds and pools for swimming and boating.

Dress Code: Casual; dressier if you want to dine at Victoria & Albert's

Weddings: Disney plays fairy godmother to more than 1,000 couples who come to tie the knot here. The glass-enclosed Fairy Tale Wedding Pavilion, set on an island in the Seven Seas Lagoon, offers a magical site for the ceremony. You can also arrange with Disney's wedding department for a wedding and Cinderella reception at the Grand Floridian or a Sunset Beach wedding. Call (407) 828–3400 for wedding details.

Rates/Packages: The 3-night Grand Honeymoon package, priced from $2,670 per couple, includes accommodations, unlimited admission to Disney World attractions; unlimited use of bicycles; canoes; sail-, pedal-, and rowboats; use of Disney's transportation facilities; breakfast, lunch, and dinner daily at a variety of locations; personalized prearrival itinerary planning; roundtrip airport transfers; one selection from Disney's Flex Features, such as photo session or keepsake collector's box; light snacks and refreshments; fireworks cruise; 50-minute spa treatment; admission to Cirque du Soleil; private golf and tennis lessons, and use of health club.

Payment/Credit Cards: Most major

Deposit: 2-night deposit at time of booking to cover first and last nights' accommodations; refundable if canceled up to 15 days prior to arrival

Government Taxes: 11 percent sales tax on rooms; 6 percent on food

Service Charges: Some gratuities are included in honeymoon packages

≋

Little Palm Island

Location: Off the tip of Little Torch Key, 120 miles southwest of Miami and 28 miles east of Key West.

Romantic Features: Your own thatched cottage—it's like being in the South Pacific, only you don't have to knock yourself out getting there.

I t used to be a rustic fishing retreat for America's presidents and high-profile stars. It still attracts people like Mario Andretti, Robert Wagner, Jill St. John, and Ivana Trump, but Little Palm Island is no longer rustic. The South Seas–style thatched bungalows, which stand on stilts amid the more than 250 coconut palm trees, tropical foliage, and gardens of this idyllic island Shangri-la, just 3 miles offshore in the Lower Florida Keys, come with air-conditioning, whirlpool baths, king-size beds, and fully stocked minibars. Little Palm Island, which opened as a public resort in 1988, succeeds in combining the best of both worlds.

Once your boat pulls into the pier—and that's the only way you get here—you leave behind things like TVs, cars, alarm clocks, and telephones. There's one public phone located in a former outhouse (used by Truman, they say), but

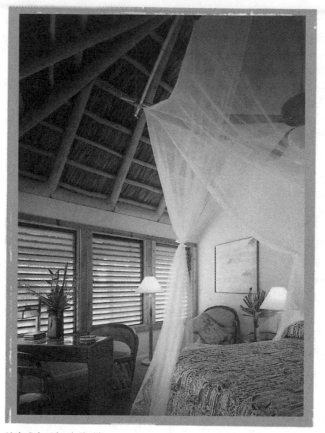

Little Palm Island, Florida

that's it. So look around, stroll along the gravel paths that link the cottages to the pool area and beach, find a hammock, settle in, and relax. Since young children are not allowed here, you'll have the pool and the beach all to yourself.

You share the island, maintained as a nature preserve, with a variety of species of birds and animals, including herons, parrots, manatees, Key deer, and loggerhead turtles, which lay their eggs each year on the beach. A recently completed $2 million landscape program includes a Zen garden.

The sugar-white sand beach runs in a thin strip around the five-acre island and broadens out at one end, where you'll find a vast tidal flat, home to a fascinating number of birds and other creatures, which are best seen in the early morning or evening. During the day, from your lounge on the beach you need only plant your pink flag in the sand to summon a member of the ever-watchful staff, who will be quick to take your drink or snack order.

Sunsets are special here. Look carefully and you can see the green flash just as the sun drops below the horizon. Walk completely around the island in the early evening and watch the colors brighten and mellow.

Your suite has a soaring pitched ceiling of thatch and bamboo, a ceiling fan, a king-size bed draped with a filmy white net canopy, a really comfortable Guatemalan lounger, a sitting area, wraparound sundecks, a dressing area, and a bathroom decorated with Mexican tile.

Although each bathroom comes with a whirlpool tub, the most popular way to freshen up is to use your outdoor shower, which is enclosed by bamboo walls and is totally private. On Little Palm's list of ways to conserve natural resources is the suggestion to "shower with a friend."

Louvered wood walls (with screens) open to let the sea breezes in—you rarely need to turn on your air-conditioning; some never do. Your sitting area has natural wicker and rattan chairs and sofas with cushions in brightly hued tropical fabric. Linens are changed daily by the staff unless requested by guests not to do so.

Of course you'll have to make major decisions, like whether to go snorkeling or try out one of the canoes, whether to loll at the lagoonlike pool or head to the spa for a massage. Since the water off the beach is usually too shallow to swim in, you'll need the pool for your lap work. Nearby are superb dive sites for scuba enthusiasts. Just 3 miles away, Looe Key, a long reef protected by the National Park Service, stretches for miles and is home to myriad multicolored fish and other sea creatures.

There is a small library with a good selection of books to borrow, and nearby are hammocks strung in the trees. You also have a hammock on your deck—at Little Palm, hammocks are in. And if you really can't stand all this serenity and good living, you can sneak down to the Quarter Deck, which is located on the dock, and rent a TV/VCR.

You can dine indoors in the main restaurant, located in the new poolside Great House, or outside on the terrace. You can also dine at the casual, literally on-the-beach restaurant, where your dining chairs and table sit on wood "island" platforms set right on the sand. And the food prepared by executive chef Adam Votaw is as good as it looks—using mostly fresh local ingredients.

Especially tasty are the fresh dolphin, grouper, tuna, grilled salmon, rack of lamb, and homemade soups and pastas. Fresh herbs and seasonings are just right, sauces splendid, desserts impossible to resist. On Thursdays you really get a chance to test your eating capacity with the seven-course Gourmet Night, and on Sundays it's brunch time. Everything's accompanied by a bottle of red or white from Little Palm's impressive wine cellar.

Physically, Little Palm Island is fifteen minutes from shore; psychologically, it's another world, where cares wash away and romance blooms.

Address/Phone: 28500 Overseas Highway, Little Torch Key, FL 33042, (305) 872–2524; fax (305) 872–4843

E-mail: getlost@littlepalmisland.com

Web Site: www.littlepalmisland.com

U.S. Reservations: (800) 3–GET LOST; Relais & Chateaux, (800) RELAIS 8

Owner/Manager: Paul Royall, general manager

Arrival/Departure: Transfer and van service to the Little Torch Key Shore Station (mile marker 28.5) is available from both Key West and Marathon Airports. Little Palm's shuttle service will meet you and take you to their shore station, where you will board a boat for the 3-mile, 15-minute ride to the island. Limousine service can also be arranged from Miami International for the 2½-hour drive through the Florida Keys to the station. Little Palm Air provides seaplane service to the island from Ft. Lauderdale, Miami, Marathon, and Key West for an additional fee. Advance notice is required for all of these services.

Distance from Miami International Airport: 120 miles; Key West International Airport, 28 miles

Distance from Key West: 28 miles

Accommodations: 30 one-bedroom suites are located in 15 thatched-cottage bungalows; 2 suites in Eagle's Nest houseboat

Best Room/Suite: Although all rooms have a view of the sea, those directly facing the open ocean are tops.

Amenities: Air-conditioning, minibar, wet bar, coffee bar, whirlpool bath, outdoor shower, ceiling fans, bathrobes. (TVs, telephones, and alarm clocks are "banned" from the island. There is one public phone, located in the former outhouse, and it takes credit cards only.)

Electricity: 110 volts

Sports and Facilities: Pool, beach, full-service spa, exercise room; sailing, kayaking, canoeing, fishing, snorkeling; pontoon boats, and Sun-Kat motorized lounge chairs can be rented; deep-sea fishing, scuba diving, guided nature tours can be arranged

Dress Code: Casual elegance

Weddings: Can be arranged

Rates/Packages: $700–$1,700 per suite per night; dinner plans available at additional cost

Payment/Credit Cards: Most major

Deposit: First and last nights' lodging at time of booking, refundable if canceled no later than 30 days prior to arrival date; $50 service charge applies. Deposit will be forfeited if canceled 30 days or less prior to arrival date.

Government Taxes: 11.5 percent

Service Charges: 10 percent

≋≋≋

The Ritz-Carlton, Naples

Location: In Naples, on the west coast of Florida.
Romantic Features: Luxurious rooms with views of the sea; Old World elegance.

The internationally acclaimed Ritz-Carlton name conjures up all sorts of romantic notions: elegantly appointed rooms, marble baths with oversize tubs and Jacuzzis, king-size beds that seem even larger, thick terry bathrobes, exquisite cuisine, and, of course, twenty-four–hour room service—all you have to do is place a quick call and your order will be fulfilled at a moment's notice.

The Ritz-Carlton, Naples, does not disappoint. Built in 1983 on twenty acres of waterfront property on the famed Gold Coast in Naples, the hotel evokes Old World Mediterranean grandeur with its classic arches, stone fountains, and manicured gardens with unexpected vistas at every turn.

A huge veranda dotted with Southern-style rocking chairs overlooks the gardens and swimming pool. Tall Palladian windows frame views of the Gulf of Mexico and flower-bedecked courtyards. Garden benches are strategically placed near fountains amid flowers. If one distinction of a grand hotel is a palatial lobby, then the creators of the Ritz-Carlton score a ten. It's a beauty. And set off against a quiet color scheme of rose and green are some 250 magnificent pieces of antique furniture and art.

For afternoon relaxation you can head to the lobby lounge, which hosts a tea every afternoon, complete with Devonshire cream and scones, or if something more potent tempts you, you can order cocktails while seated in cozy armchairs and sofas.

Rooms and suites are beautifully furnished with armoires, a writing desk, club chairs, and fine art. All rooms have a separate dressing area with vanity and a marble bath with an oversize tub. There are twenty-eight suites, including twenty-two gulf-view one-bedroom suites, four two-bedroom suites with extended parlor, and two Presidential Suites.

For those who like their creature comforts orchestrated to the highest possible level, there is The Club, a lofty place in more ways than one: It's located on the top floors and is accessible only by private elevator (you get a special key). Here you enjoy the services of a private concierge devoted exclusively to your needs. Continuous food and beverage services, complimentary cocktails, newspapers, magazines, ice service, and more goodies are all provided in the lounge's warm, living room atmosphere.

When it comes to accolades for cuisine, the Ritz-Carlton, Naples, is no slouch either. Its restaurants (five in all) have garnered more awards than any other hotel in the state of Florida and are right up there with the best in the world. And at the Ritz there is sure to be a dining facility that fits your mood, whether it be formal or very casual.

The newly remodeled main dining room is devoted to classic cuisine in the Grand Hotel tradition—elegant, sophisticated, and very romantic. Silks, chandeliers, French doors, oil paintings, piano music, and all that good stuff set the mood. On the more casual side, the Beach Pavilion, an open-air cottage-style restaurant located directly on the gulf beach, is open for breakfast and lunch. Nightly entertainment is on tap at The Club, featuring a potpourri of music from the 1960s through the 1990s.

Three miles of pure white sand beach on the warm, calm Gulf offer up a variety of water activities, including sailing and catamaran cruising, and there is a super pool for the serious lapper. Tennis enthusiasts have a choice of hard or clay surfaces on six lighted courts, and a pro shop, a beverage bar, and professional instruction are available. Golfers can head out to Tiburón, a Greg Norman–designed twenty-seven–hole golf course located 3 miles east of the Ritz-Carlton, Naples. The Ritz golf coordinator will set it all up for you.

The romantic pièce de résistance is the hotel's fleet of personal limousines, which are available for transportation to and from the airport and for shopping sprees.

Address/Phone: 280 Vanderbilt Beach Road, Naples, FL 33963; (941) 598–3300; fax (941) 598–6690

Web Site: www.ritzcarlton.com

U.S. Reservations: (800) 241–3333

Owner/Manager: William A. Hall, general manager

Arrival/Departure: Taxis available at Ft. Myers Airport; transfers can be arranged

Distance from Southwest Florida International Airport (Ft. Myers Airport): 25 miles (35 minutes)

Distance from Naples: 10 miles from center of town

Accommodations: 463 rooms and suites with views of the Gulf of Mexico

Best Room/Suite: Ocean-view Club rooms

Amenities: Hair dryer, air-conditioning, toiletries, bathrobes, telephone, some with fax and computer hookups; separate dressing area with vanity; minibar, remote-controlled TV, personal wall safe; twice-daily maid service, 24-hour room service, afternoon ice delivery

Electricity: 110 volts

Sports and Facilities: Heated pool, fitness center, 6 tennis courts, water sports, billiard room, bicycles, golf nearby

Dress Code: Two of the restaurants require gentlemen to wear jackets and ties; others are casual.

Weddings: Can be arranged. The hotel has a full-time wedding coordinator.

Rates/Packages: From $395 per couple per night for a room; from $725 for a suite; Presidential Suites (good if you're an oil sheik), $3,500

Payment/Credit Cards: Most major

Deposit: First and last nights' room rate and tax; cancel 7 days prior to arrival date for refund

Government Taxes: 8 percent sales tax

Service Charges: Not included

GEORGIA

Melhana, The Grand Plantation

Location: The Red Hills of Georgia, 4 miles south of Thomasville.

Romantic Features: Shaded walks under moss-draped canopies of oak; tea by the koi pond; a stroll by the creamy moon flowers as they open in the dusky evening on the back veranda; carriage rides through the grounds.

Had Melhana been on the market when Scarlett and Rhett were looking for a home, they would most certainly have considered this plantation to be their mimosa. In fact Melhana, the Grand Plantation, was the site for the original screening of *Gone with the Wind,* held in The Showboat, the owner's private on-site theater designed to resemble a river vessel. Melhana is one of seventy-one historic plantations in the south Georgia/north Florida area.

This blush-colored antebellum plantation, which along with thirty other buildings spreads over forty acres of gardens and tree-fringed lawns, was until the late 1980s a grand private estate. Over the years well-known guests including Jackie Kennedy, Joan Crawford, and Julie Moran were invited to soak up the tranquility of this gracious Southern estate, where the scent of magnolias drifts through the air and moss hangs heavy on the spreading branches of old oaks.

Melhana dates back to the nineteenth century when it was built and once occupied more than 7,500 acres. In the late 1800s the main house and gardens were expanded, followed by the construction of stables, a carriage house, milking and dairy barns, groom's cottage, greenhouse, other cottages, and formal gardens. The original antebellum house, today known as the Pink House, contains several rooms, a formal dining room, and other public areas.

Great care was taken in the renovations and restoration of the property, which took place in 1995/1996. Original brass door fittings, light fixtures, even the robe hooks in the Pool House and original, hand-painted trash and laundry receptacles that still show the original artists signature, have been preserved.

Guest accommodations are located in the Pink House as well as in cottages and buildings on the property. Each of the rooms and suites is unique, but most feature original heart-pine floors, custom-made king-size beds know as "Beds of Roses," imported linens, and feather pillows. Some rooms have Jacuzzi tubs; most have fireplaces. For those desiring total privacy, there is the Hibernia Cottage, with its own formal garden and a marvelously lavish bath.

The Squirrel's Cottage offers three additional rooms, which surround a common living area and kitchen. The Village at Melhana and the Dairy Barn/Foshalee Building offer all the amenities of the main house as well as a village atmosphere. Live shows and other seasonal events are often held here.

For fun and after hours there is swimming in the lovely pool flanked by terraces, gardens, and a stunning pool house built in the early 30s. From the pool house, a series of French doors open onto a brick-and-marble walled courtyard. You can also play tennis on the clay courts, luxuriate in the spa, ride through the grounds and local area by horse-drawn carriage, go horseback riding, play croquet, and explore nearby Thomasville.

All meals are served in the gracious formal dining room in the Pink House or on the verandah, which is furnished with comfortable wicker chairs. Or for a lovely decadent welcome to a new day, have a gourmet breakfast delivered on silver service. Afternoon tea also is served daily in the Hanna Gathering Room; complimentary cocktails are offered in the evening.

At Georgia's only historic plantation receiving overnight visitors, you are able to experience the forgotten luxuries of a grand experience in an unrushed and world-class atmosphere while enjoying all the amenities of a modern day resort.

Address/Phone: 301 Showboat Lane, Thomasville, GA 31792; (888) 920–3030 or (912) 226–2290; fax (912) 226–4585

Web Site: www.Melhana.com.

U.S. Reservations: (888) 920–3030

Owner/Manager: Mr. and Mrs. Charlie E. Lewis, owners

Arrival/Departure: Complimentary shuttle service from Tallahassee Regional Airport

Distance from Tallahassee Airport: 35 miles (45 minutes)

Distance from Thomasville: 4 miles; Jacksonville, Florida,156 miles; Atlanta, Georgia, 230 miles

Accommodations: 30 rooms in main house and cottages, some with fireplaces and Jacuzzis

Best Room/Suite: Hibernia Cottage with its private gardens and a hammock for two. The Melrose or Winnstead Suites in the Pink House are also good choices.

Amenities: Air-conditioning, hair dryers, bathrobes, toiletries; nightly turn-down service features homemade treats; 24-hour room service; lending library

Electricity: 110 volts

Sports and Facilities: Pool, tennis (outdoor on clay courts), fitness spa, croquet, moonlit horse-drawn carriage rides, guided tours of Melhana's formal gardens. Equestrian packages (featuring Western and English riding lessons) and quail shooting packages (in season) are also available. Golf, biking, sailing, deep-sea fishing excursions; antiques and collectibles shopping; historic home and site tours; Gulf Coast beaches; skeet shooting sessions and walking bird hunts can be arranged nearby.

Dress Code: Casual smart; jackets required for gentlemen for dinner in The Dining Room.

Weddings: A range of elegant indoor and outdoor venues is available for weddings and receptions. The Sunken White Garden (seats 180) overflows with flowers; the Koi Pond is surrounded by magnificent oaks; and the Pool House is popular. A special butterfly release is used instead of rice or grain to send the bride and groom on their way.

Rates/Packages: The Inn at Melhana (Pink House) $250–$450; Hibernia Cottage $450; the Village at Melhana $285–$650; the Squirrel's Cottage $300–$400. All rates are per night, double occupancy, and include continental breakfast. The Swept Away package (4 days/3 nights), starting at $1,200 per couple, includes suite accommodations, champagne and imported chocolates upon arrival, wine hour each evening, full plantation breakfast each morning, candlelight dinner one evening, fresh flowers, and massage.

Payment/Credit Cards: Most major

Deposit: One night's room rate or 50 percent of the entire stay's rate due at the time of the reservation. To ensure a refund of your deposit, allow 4 days' notice for 1 night, 10 days' for 2–6 nights, 15 days' for 7 days or more.

Government Taxes: 5 percent

Service Charges: Not Included

HAWAII

Four Seasons Resort Maui at Wailea

Location: On fifteen waterfront acres between the slopes of the Haleakala Crater and the Pacific shore in Wailea, along Maui's southwestern coast.

Romantic Features: Total pampering in magnificent garden setting; breathtaking views of the rugged volcanic coast and moonlit surf; huge marble bath with separate soaking tub; the ultimate romantic dinner for two on a grassy knoll, high above the sea; limo picnic lunch with champagne; outdoor massages along the ocean; Bougainvillea Trail.

Everything about the Four Seasons Resort Maui at Wailea since the resort opened in 1990 is as it should be—geared for the pleasure of its guests. Most would agree that chilled towels, ice water, and Evian mist brought to your poolside cabana throughout the day are not necessities. But boy are they appreciated! The Four Seasons' propensity for pampering and attention to detail have helped it earn the distinction of ranking consistently among the top hotels in the world.

The young, energetic staff look more like winners from central casting for a new California surfing movie than their real-life roles as dispensers of goodwill, frosty drinks, and fluffy towels. Four Seasons in Maui has managed to put together a great package, combining exquisite facilities with superb personnel.

A study of elegance and style, the property has the look and feel of a plantation home settled in perfect harmony with its seaside surroundings. The lofty, open design integrates the vibrant blues of the Pacific with pastel-colored walls, floor-to-ceiling wooden shutters, ceiling fans, and plump-cushioned rattan couches. Gentle trade winds keep a profusion of white orchids in constant motion. Scattered throughout the lobby and other (un)common areas are pieces of art and period furniture.

Measuring a generous 600 square feet, the guest rooms are both elegant and comfortable and are decorated in a decidedly tropical mode. The in-room safe is simple to use; the light in the closet, a welcome touch; and sitting on your bedside table is a reading light.

Catering to the diversity of its many guests, the Four Seasons maintains the delicate balance between too much activity and not enough, and successfully separates activities geared for children and adults. With two pools, water sports galore, a health club, a jogging trail, aerobics, and more, there is no lack of things to do. Sea kayaks and water scooters are available nearby.

A special surprise (priced at $215) awaits the unsuspecting: A trail of flower petals is laid from your bedroom door to a drawn bubble bath. Candles, CD music, roses, and champagne set the mood. At the heart of the resort, royal palms define the borders of a large swimming pool, which boasts an adjacent computer-controlled fountain; it's programmed to react to the whims of the trade winds so its spray keeps within defined boundaries. Two Jacuzzis spill into the pool; one is for adults only. Hundreds of flowers follow a sweeping stairway from the upper lobby to the pool area and beyond. Beneath the stairway two tropical birds greet visitors as they pass. A manicured lawn between the pool and Wailea Beach provides an additional lounging area, and even the sand is water-cooled, making it easygoing on bare feet when the sun is hot.

Nearby a waterfall cools guests as they swim in the smaller, second pool, effectively hidden by tropical plants. The resort also has two tennis courts; cold, wet towels are provided.

Dining options abound and range from casual to elegant haute cuisine. Seasons, the resort's award-winning signature restaurant, is a treat for even the most assiduous gourmet. The offerings are varied and exceptional: island seafood with upcountry Maui greens; tropical fruit charlotte and papaya coulis, for example. All are presented with pride in a pleasing, open setting with wonderful ocean views.

Soft breezes and a breathtaking view also factor in at the Pacific Grill, where guests can enjoy a sumptuous buffet breakfast, lunch, and/or dinner. For more casual dining there is Ferraro's at Seaside for informal fare served during the day. At night try Seaside for authentic Italian cuisine. Watch the sunset while enjoying seductive Italian music.

A car isn't necessary, as other dining options, shops, and golf are just a short walk away along Wailea's 2-mile ocean pathway. A complimentary shuttle is also available within the Wailea Resort. However, if you want to go off on your own and go exploring, you will probably want to rent a car for a couple of days. There is a lot to see and do on Maui. You can get up early in the morning, be driven up to the top of the volcano, and then ride back down the mountain on a bike, and you can visit some of the small nearby villages and browse in the shops. Or you can stay just where you are on your lounge and wait for someone to come by and refresh you with a light mist of cool water.

Address/Phone: 3900 Wailea Alanui, Wailea, Maui, HI 96753; (800) 334–6284 or (808) 874–8000; fax (808) 874–2222

U.S. Reservations: (800) 332–3442 or (800) 334–6284

Owner/Manager: Shimizu Corporation, owner; Thomas Steinhauer, general manager

Arrival/Departure: Airport limousine transfers; Avis rental cars; motorcoach minibus and van service can be arranged

Distance from Kahului Airport: 17 miles

Distance from Kihei: 4 miles

Accommodations: 380 spacious rooms and suites, all with one or more lanais (porches); 85 percent have ocean views

Best Room/Suite: Ocean-view or executive suite

Amenities: Air-conditioning, ceiling fans, hair dryer, bathrobes, room safe, double vanity as well as separate vanity, built-in refrigerator bar, separate soaking tub, TV, cosmetic mirror, toiletries, spacious lighted closet; complimentary morning coffee, beans and grinder; twice-daily maid service, valet parking

Electricity: 110 volts

Sports and Facilities: 2 pools, 2 Jacuzzis, beach, use of 3 golf courses at Wailea Golf Club, tennis at the 14-court Wailea Tennis Center (including 3 grass courts), complimentary use of 2 on-site tennis courts lighted for night play, health club with exercise machines and steam room; running paths, snorkeling, scuba diving, sailing instruction, aerobics, aqua exercise, power walking

Dress Code: Casual elegance

Weddings: The resort offers a number of wedding packages ranging from $2,500 for the Ku'uipo Wedding, with ceremony, leis, solo musician, and a bottle of champagne, to the Lokelani Wedding, priced at $10,000, a more elaborate affair. Popular sites for the ceremony include the Seasons Garden, the Luau Grounds, the Sculpture Gardens, and a grassy knoll above the ocean.

Rates/Packages: $305 per couple per night for a room with a garden view; $575–$875 for an executive suite; $670–$1,270 for a room or suite on the Club floor; $700–$2,800 for a one-bedroom suite. Romance for All Seasons package, priced at $4,900 per couple, gives you limo transfers from airport, champagne, bathrobes, dinner for two, a dozen roses, limo picnic with champagne, and either 3 nights in a one-bedroom oceanfront suite and a Cadillac DeVille or convertible rental, or you can choose 7 nights in an ocean-view room and the use of a convertible. The 3-night Romantic Interlude package, with convertible rental car, champagne, and dinner for two, is $1,625–$1,915 per couple.

Payment/Credit Cards: Most major

Deposit: 1-night deposit plus tax; refund if canceled 7 days prior to arrival

Government Taxes: 11.41 percent

Service Charges: Not included

≈≈≈

Halekulani

Location: On five oceanfront acres on Waikiki Beach, Oahu.

Romantic Features: At twilight sounds of Hawaiian music floating up to your balcony overlooking the sea; candlelit dinner on your own private lanai.

R ecently I visited Oahu. My home for a few days was Room 1463, one of 456 white-on-white rooms in the quietly posh Halekulani—tucked into the middle of Waikiki Beach between the high-rise Outrigger Reef and the 1852-room Sheraton Waikiki—not at first glance a great location for vacationers seeking privacy and quiet refinement. Indeed, some might wonder if the Halekulani hadn't stopped to rest at Waikiki on its way to Maui but decided to stay. A good idea, I discovered, as I soon got caught up in the excitement and fun of the country's eleventh largest city. There was so much to do and see in and around Honolulu, and at the end of the day nothing was better than returning to the Halekulani, an elegant oasis within steps of all the hustle and bustle.

Originally a private oceanfront estate, the Halekulani has been welcoming guests since 1917. Over the years ownership has changed and buildings have been built and demolished and built again. What remains of the original hotel is a 1930s building (now called the "main building") that has been incorporated into the overall design, consisting of five interconnected structures. Throughout the resort you'll find lots of marble, Italian terrazzo, and fine woods in creating this Hawaiian oasis.

From your languorous lanai you'll see the exquisite oval pool and, beyond that, the beach and sea. Halekulani, which means "house befitting heaven," has everything you'll require to make it your own personal paradise.

Wraparound lanais with nonstop views of the sunsets, the sea, and Diamond Head are only the beginning. Decorated in soft whites and neutrals enlivened by the color of orchids and flowers so perfect you'll wonder if they're real, rooms are furnished with rattan and upholstered furniture, glass-top tables, king-size beds, louvered-window walls, and plush carpets. Everything is quietly elegant. You'll not find any Hawaiian clichés lurking in the decorating schemes of these rooms.

Baths have marble vanities, ceramic tiles with outrigger motifs, and mirrored doors opening into a closet. Open the louvered doors on the other (bedroom) side of the closet and you can watch the surfers ride the waves while you relax in your tub. You'll also have a desk, plenty of drawers, extra shelves in the closet, padded hangers, an in-room safe, a minibar, and a TV that slides into a wall cabinet. The Halekulani gets my vote for the best-designed room I've ever seen: not necessarily the largest or the poshest, but a space perfectly crafted for its size in visual beauty and ease of use. Even the toiletries, which are in small, sleek containers, fit into your hand or cosmetic bag just right.

Your room comes with all the amenities you'd expect, such as hair dryers and state-of-the-art phones, but there is more. A phone in the enclosed toilet area, spa-type bottled water, and lovely little pillow gifts each night—ranging from shells to orchids, all attached to a soft sweet message—pamper guests. Even your laundry rates special treatment: It comes back carefully wrapped in tissue in a wicker basket. And they really go over the top with honeymooners and deliver champagne to help celebrate the happy occasion.

Your opportunities for dining are no less impressive. Orchids, an oceanside indoor/outdoor restaurant open for all meals, specializes in international seafood cuisine along with Hawaiian items created by chef Jean-Pierre Maharibateha. Living up to its name, this three-tiered restaurant has live orchids placed throughout it.

House Without a Key, another indoor/outdoor restaurant, serves breakfast, lunch, and sunset cocktails with Hawaiian entertainment and dancing under the stars each night. Arrive in time to watch the sun go down — it's one of the best seats in town for this nightly spectacle.

French-style meals are served at La Mer, an elegant indoor restaurant in the main building, with great ocean views and high accolades from those who rate. You'll find several Hawaiian-produced products on the menu, such as yellow-fin tuna, Kula tomatoes, and Big Island lobster. Plates appear at your elbow like a series of gifts. Even the names of your dishes, like fine wines, need to be rolled across the tongue: Tartares of Hamachi, Ahi, and Salmon with Three Caviars and Three Coulis, and Baked Moano Fillets with Opakapaka Mousse and Lobster Medallions.

Tea is served every afternoon in the living room in the main building, and cocktails hold center stage in Lewers Lounge each evening.

I took a tour of "the back of the house," those places tourists don't normally see. Very impressive. I saw the yogurt and ice-cream machines at work, chocolates being dipped, and exotic flowers being artfully arranged. In the bakery the wonderful aromas of freshly baked rolls and breads and the miniature muffins reminded me it was getting time for yet another meal.

Halekulani offers a full range of water sports as well as a fitness room and sight-seeing programs. And I loved the pool. A simple, elegant large oval, it has no diving boards, slides or waterfalls—just a huge orchid "painted" in mosaic glass tiles on the bottom. It really takes your breath away and only gets more beautiful as night falls.

Even when the hotel is full, there is never a need for you to do the early-morning scramble to stake out your territory on a favorite chaise with your towel. There are more than enough chairs, tables, and lounges.

You may never want to leave the grounds, but if you do there's a whole other world out there filled with fun and excitement. If you want action like an outrigger canoe ride, party time every Sunday at Duke's just down the beach, or shopping at the countless upscale stores, you'll find that almost everything is within a five- to ten-minute walk. Discos, nightclubs, streetcars—all close by. Catch the latest exhibit at the Contemporary Museum; picnic in the park and lie back on a blanket while the Hawaiian Royal Band plays the "Kamehameha Waltz." Try some rainbow-flavored shaved ice from the Waiola Store; shop for wild-looking veggies in Chinatown; pick up a yummy *malasala* (fluffy Portuguese doughnut) at Leonard's Bakery; and eat some great Thai food at Singha. Cap off the evening in the Hard Rock Cafe.

If you really feel adventurous, hop on a bus and go to Hanauma Bay for some snorkeling, hike up to the top of Diamond Head for a fabulous view of Honolulu, or explore Waimea Falls Park on the North Shore, where you can sit on a rock overlooking the beach and watch the sailboarders.

At sunset on Halekulani's terrace of the House Without a Key, sip a cool

Chardonnay or Mai Tai as Kanoe Miller, elegantly dressed in a long brown velvet skirt and white Victorian-style blouse, dances gracefully under an aged Kiawe tree to lilting Hawaiian music played by the trio just behind her. With a backdrop of palms and the sea and the sun sinking slowly, turning the sky a rich pink, you'll find it hard to believe you are but a few yards from Waikiki Beach. Here, it would seem, you can have it all.

Staying at Halekulani may not be at the low end of the budget scale, but for your vacation of a lifetime, it's worth going the extra mile.

Address/Phone: 2199 Kalia Road, Honolulu, HI 96815-1988; (808) 923–2311; fax (808) 926–8004

Web Site: www.halekulani.com

U.S. Reservations: (800) 367–2343

Owner/Manager: Patricia Tam, general manager

Arrival/Departure: Taxis available at airport; one-way is approximately $25; limousine service is $80; city bus $1.00; airport express bus $7.00; complimentary limousine service is provided for those staying in the Presidential and Royal Suites

Distance from Honolulu Airport: 11 miles (25 minutes)

Distance from Honolulu: You're in the center of the Waikiki action; downtown Honolulu is 4 miles (15 minutes) away

Accommodations: 456 rooms and suites, located in five low-density buildings ranging in height from 2 to 17 stories; 95 percent have ocean views. Most rooms are alike; you pay for the view.

Best Room/Suite: Diamond Head ocean-front suites are also roomy and overlook the famous Diamond Head; corner ocean-view suites, with 1,620 square feet, have a separate bedroom, bathroom, powder room, living room, wet bar and dining area. Club ocean-view suites are 720 square feet and come with two lanais, bedroom/sitting area, bathroom, wet bar, and cozy bay window

Amenities: Air-conditioning, hair dryer, remote color cable TV, minirefrigerator with overhead cabinet and bar accessories, 3 telephones, adjustable reading lamps, TV audio in bathroom, in-room safe, separate glassed-in shower with thermostatic control, makeup mirror, bathrobes, wooden coat and satin dress hangers, private-label toiletries; 24-hour room service, twice-daily turndown service; complimentary admission to myriad art and cultural venues in Oahu.

Electricity: 110 volts

Sports and Facilities: Large 46-by-82-foot pool; beach center where you can arrange outrigger canoes, surfing, snorkeling, deep-sea fishing, sailboarding, and golf and tennis lessons; fitness room with scheduled workouts and classes as well as massages

Dress Code: Tropical elegance

Weddings: The Halekulani does a lot of weddings, each one personalized. The resort has its own floral shop, and bridal-gown rental shops are within walking distance. Usually a marriage license and a minister can be arranged through the concierge desk; gazebo on the grounds is a popular wedding site.

Rates/Packages: Rates per couple $310–$520 per night; from $700 for suites; 8-day/7-night honeymoon packages from $3,059; 4-day/3-night packages from $1,489

Payment/Credit Cards: Most major

Deposit: Guarantee with credit card. Cancel 72 hours (Hawaiian time) prior to arrival date and credit card will not be charged.

Government Taxes: 4.16 percent state tax; 7.25 percent occupancy tax (total 11.41 percent)

Service Charges: Not included

≋

Hotel Hana Maui

Location: Eastern end of the island, in Maui's back pocket.

Romantic Features: Quiet, secluded area recalls Old Hawaii; private Jacuzzis on bungalow decks overlooking Pacific.

Geography has played a key role in making Hotel Hana Maui one of the most romantic resorts in Hawaii. Located on the eastern end of Maui, which was formed when the volcano Haleakala erupted, Hana is isolated from the more developed touristy areas by deep valleys and ravines dividing this part of the island from areas around Kahana and Kaanapali, which lie in the shadow of another volcano. In order to reach Hana, you embark on a breathtaking journey along the Hana Highway, called one of the most beautiful roads in the world.

Around many of the 617 bends of the road, which twists and wiggles along the rugged coastline, waterfalls bubble and gush, falling into deep pools of clear mountain water—bring your bathing suit and take a dip in these clean, cool mountain "Jacuzzis." Jungle vegetation, lush and dense, cloaks the hills in a rich, dark green blanket damp with moisture and glistening in the sun, which filters through during the fickle mood shifts in the weather. If you're driving a convertible, you'll find you may be raising and lowering your roof several times during the 50 or so miles of your ride, which takes about three hours. The sea is seldom out of view, and the scenery is spectacular. Watch out for parked vehicles—photo opportunities are enticing, and cars stop frequently along the route.

Finally, after crossing about fifty-four bridges along the Hana Highway (from Kahului), you come to the small town of Hana. There's not much here except

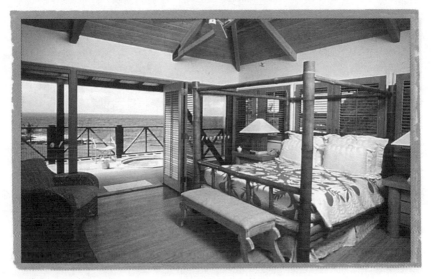

Hotel Hana Maui, Hawaii

for a couple of small stores, a bank, a post office, a gas station, and a restaurant. And Hotel Hana Maui. Sitting prettily on the very end of the island, below the rainy slopes of Haleakala, this hideaway resort is located on sixty-six acres of rolling, landscaped grounds.

This land was once devoted to the production of sugarcane and later to raising cattle. In the early fifties Hotel Hana Ranch was created by Paul Fagan, the owner of the 14,000-acre Puu O Hoku cattle ranch, specifically to accommodate Fagan's wealthy friends. There are still several thousand head of cattle on the property, but the hub of activity for most who find their way here is the hotel itself. It's not very flashy, nor does it have a long, sandy beach. It doesn't even have much of a golf course—just a three-hole pitch-and-putt layout.

But once you check in and stroll around the gardens and lawns, richly planted with heliconias, exotic palms, and a wide variety of flowering shrubs, and walk to the top of the hill overlooking the coast, where waves crash against jagged black rocks, the spell of Hana will soon captivate. Whether you stay in one of the garden cottages or in the traditionally styled Sea Ranch cottages, you'll appreciate the appointments and details that make this place so special. Live orchids growing out of ceramic containers and baskets, original Hawaiian arts and crafts, four-poster bamboo beds, quilt bedspreads, rattan furniture, and beautiful tiled baths designed so that you don't need a curtain or door lend an air of low-key elegance.

Bleached hardwood floors, stone countertops, and carpets of split bamboo, along with muted natural colors of whites, tans, and soft browns, appeal to those who love things that are natural, not overdone. Soaps come in the shapes of shells, bathrobes are yakuta-style, towels are thick and thirsty.

Your view from your trellised patio or deck could be a fragrant garden or the sea. The one-story cottage suites are quite different from the Sea Ranch accommodations. Cottage suites are nestled into the gardens, and the views from the patios are of flowers and palms and towering trees. You'll find it hard to resist scooping up the petals from the plumeria trees, which drop their fragrant blossoms along the walkways.

The Sea Ranch cottages have spacious decks, and some come with private Jacuzzis that overlook the sea. Louvered-window walls allow the sea breezes to cool the rooms, which are comfortable, quiet, and very private.

Hana has a number of recreational facilities on the grounds or nearby. A 1932 Packard sedan takes you on a five-minute ride to a silver-black sand volcanic beach right down the road, a beach James Michener called the most perfect crescent beach in the Pacific. The beach is public but never crowded, and the hotel has its own changing and refreshment house, where you can get fresh towels and lunch. You can also ask the hotel to pack a picnic lunch for you.

Early risers may want to join the morning walk. You can also go horseback riding along the sea or follow the trails up the lower slopes of Haleakala, where you can see exotic birds and plants in the rainforest. An excursion to Ulaino brings you to lovely waterfalls and a stream you can swim in as well as an idyllic pond called the Blue Pond. Very private and romantic.

You can also go bicycle riding; play tennis, croquet, and sand volleyball; or practice your golf on the three-hole pitch and putt, where tees are marked by coconuts. Take a nature hike into the forest, or head to the Wellness Center, located near the pool at the top of a grassy hill above the sea, where you'll find the latest in fitness equipment. Aquacise classes are offered daily; massages are also available.

The dining room, with its beautiful garden view and dramatic 35-foot open-beamed ceiling, is located in the main building. It overlooks the gardens and features a range of Hawaiian specialties along with Polynesian, American, and Oriental cuisine. The chef uses lots of local produce, such as herbs, vegetables, taro, coconut, mango, and bananas. The Paniolo Bar, on the covered lanai overlooking the bay, is the place to go for those who want to relax after dinner. The more casual Hana Ranch Restaurant is open daily for breakfast and lunch and on Friday and Saturday for dinner. Wednesday is pizza night, always popular with guests and local residents.

The marvelous Hana Coast Gallery and the library are also located in the main building. The gallery features the finest in genuine Hawaiian art and master crafts, including paintings, pottery, sculpture, wooden bowls, and rare antique floral prints.

You'll find the staff extremely friendly and helpful. Most live in the village and walk to work. Some have been employed at the hotel since its opening in 1946!

At Hotel Hana Maui you won't find a TV or even a clock in your room. You won't be able to track down a disco or a Jet Ski. What you will find here is a quiet beauty and people who genuinely care about pleasing you.

The Hotel Hana Maui casts its spell with exquisite subtlety. Serene and lovely, it's a resort romantics must discover at some point in their lifetimes. A honeymoon is a good place to start.

Address/Phone: P.O. Box 9, Hana, Maui, HI 96713-9989; (808) 248–8211; fax (808) 248–7202

U.S. Reservations: (800) 321–4262

Owner/Manager: Larry Mayo, acting general manager

Arrival/Departure: By car from Kahului Airport: A 55-mile drive along the scenic (and winding) Hana Highway. If you're going to rent a car, make arrangements before you leave, and rent the car in Kahului. You'll pay more if you rent in Hana, and only Dollar has an office there. By air: A 15-minute flight to Hana from Kahului Airport by Air Molokai or Aloha Island Air. You can also fly from Honolulu to Hana via Aloha Island Air (90 minutes) or take a private charter or private helicopter. The hotel's open jitney picks up guests at all flights coming into Hana Airport and transports them to the property, a 10-minute ride.

Distance from Kahului Airport: 55 miles

Distance from Hana: Located in town; 50 miles from Kahului

Accommodations: 93 rooms and suites, including garden lanais and Sea Ranch cottages on the ground sloping to the seacoast on the Pacific side

Best Room/Suite: Ranch cottages with private Jacuzzis

Amenities: Coffee bar with coffeemaker, grinder, and selection of Kona coffee beans; hair dryer, toiletries; ceiling fans and refrigerator with ice maker

Electricity: 110 volts

Sports and Facilities: Beach, tennis court, pool, 3-hole pitch-and-putt course; hiking, horseback riding, snorkeling, croquet, volleyball

Dress Code: Casual by day; dressier during evening

Weddings: The wide veranda of the Plantation House and the beautiful lawn and gardens are popular sites

Rates/Packages: $395–$795 per couple, per day, including tennis, bicycles, snorkeling, and beach equipment; $95 per person, per day for breakfast, lunch, and dinner; $75 for breakfast and dinner. Honeymooners get 15 percent off rack rates as well as dinner one evening, champagne, and a massage for two.

Payment/Credit Cards: Most major

Deposit: 1 night, guaranteed with credit card

Government Taxes: 10.17 percent
Service Charges: 15 percent

≋

Kona Village Resort

Location: On eighty-two acres amid palms, gardens, and historic fishponds along a natural black-and-white beach on Kahuwai Bay.
Romantic Features: Luxury hales (cottages), each designed in a different Polynesian style, such as Tahitian, Fijian, and Samoan; privacy protected when you place coconut at door; private massage for two in garden setting; private Jacuzzis.

N ative grass shacks were never like the luxurious hales that loll along the crystal-blue bay at Kona Village Resort, a hideaway strung around peaceful lagoons and blessed by a natural black-and-white speckled beach. The setting is something of a miracle—a small oasis of coco palms and beach that was left untouched by a fiery lava flow in 1801. Today Kona Village remains a lush, eighty-two-acre paradise of emerald lawns and mirror-still ponds. It's a quiet retreat for simple pleasures: watching a coconut drift in with the tide or stopping to watch the nightly "water ballet" by the resident manta rays, which softly swirl near shore.

Located at the site of an ancient Hawaiian fishing community, the resort resembles an old Hawaiian village. Its paths are edged by fragrant pikake and plumeria blossoms, and bungalows are thatched with coconut fronds and planted on stilts beside the ocean and lagoons or on lava fields. The resort is, in fact, the largest group of thatched buildings in the state of Hawaii. Local materials, such as coral, stone, and koa and ohia woods, are used extensively.

Inside, however, twentieth-century accoutrements include king-size beds in most accommodations, a refrigerator stocked with juices and soft drinks, modern bathrooms, and dressing rooms. The designs of the hales reflect nine different Polynesian cultures. The Hawaiian accommodations, for example, have steeply pitched thatched roofs, while the Maori feature boldly patterned fronts and carved figures on the rooflines. Interiors are paneled with wood, and ceilings are lined with lauhala matting. Furnishings might include rattan chairs and tropical-print spreads. The hales are also notable for what they don't have—in-room telephones, radios, or television. Instead of air-conditioners, ceiling fans enhance nature's cooling trade winds. A coconut placed in front of your hale's door alerts the staff to leave you alone.

Every mealtime is special, from the macadamia-nut pancakes with coconut syrup at breakfast to duck breast with taro leaves and mango coulis at dinner.

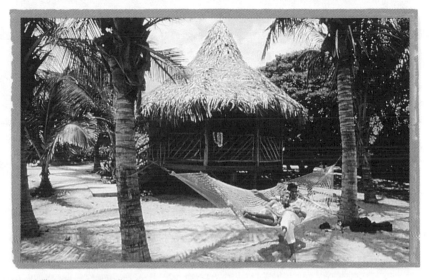

Kona Village Resort, Hawaii

Friday and Monday nights the resort hosts a traditional luau, one of the most authentic in the islands—many Big Island residents drop by to enjoy the feast. Kailua pig is roasted in the imu (underground oven), accompanied by other delicacies, such as lau lau (pork and fish in taro leaves) and lomi salmon.

Afterward a Polynesian revue showcases Pacific Island dances, including the Samoan fire dance and hip-quivering Tahitian tamure. Another favorite is the paniolo steak cookout, with ukulele music to accompany the kiawe-grilled steaks.

A bevy of water sports activities are available for guests, including outrigger canoeing and glass-bottom boat excursions. In addition to the crescent shaped swimming beach, the property offers two freshwater pools and a whirlpool. The resort has three lighted outdoor Plexi-paved tennis courts; you can take advantage of the complimentary adult clinic or sign on for the round-robin series for practice and fun.

At the new Oceanside Massage Hale, a variety of massages from lomi lomi to Thai and cranial-sacral therapy soothe weary travelers.

The grounds also include many Hawaiian archaeological sites, including fishponds, house sites, and shelter caves. You can learn more about Hawaiian culture on several different excursions, including historical walks, tide-pool explorations, and petroglyph tours highlighting the powerful depictions of turtles, fish, dogs, and humans.

About half of the guests at Kona Village have stayed at the resort previously. You'll probably want to add your names to the roster of returnees soon.

Address/Phone: P.O. Box 1299, Kailua-Kona, HI 96745; (808) 325–5555; fax (808) 325–5124

E-mail: kvr@aloha.net

Web Site: www.konavillage.com

Owner/Manager: Fred Duerr, general manager

U.S. Reservations: (800) 367–5290 or (800) 423–5450 (in Hawaii)

Arrival/Departure: Transfers included in honeymoon package

Distance from Keahole-Kona Airport: 6 miles

Distance from Kailua-Kona: 15 miles

Accommodations: 125 thatched hales (cottages) in nine architectural styles

Best Room/Suite: The luxurious Lava Tahitians are set out on the lava rock along the ocean, away from other hales. The Sand Marquesans are also very luxurious and are located on the water, with lots of greenery to provide privacy.

Amenities: Ceiling fans, hair dryer, toiletries, king-size bed, dressing room, refrigerator stocked with juices and soft drinks, coffeemaker

Electricity: 110 volts

Sports and Facilities: Sunfish sailboats, outrigger canoes, snorkeling, new Oceanside spa, and 3 lighted tennis courts all available on premises; nearby activities include five 18-hole championship golf courses, horseback riding, deep-sea fishing

Dress Code: Tropically casual

Weddings: The resort's wedding coordinator sees to everything from ministers to marriage licenses. Wedding packages are available.

Rates/Packages: $450–$795 per couple per night, including breakfast, lunch, and dinner daily. Prices also cover most resort activities, including tennis, kayaking, Sunfish sailing, historical and petroglyph tours, airport transfers in the Big Island, and more. The Honeymoon Hideaway package costs $1,275–$2,325 per couple for three nights; $3,025–$5,393 for seven nights. It includes all meals, accommodations, and a line-art reproduction of your honeymoon hale. Couples can also choose one optional activity: a snorkel/sail, body massage, tennis lesson, or one-tank scuba dive (certification required).

Payment/Credit Cards: Most major

Deposit: 2 nights' deposit; guarantee with credit card

Government Taxes: 11.42 percent

Service Charges: Not included

≋

The Manele Bay Hotel

Location: Southeastern coast of Lanai.

Romantic Features: White sand Hulopoe Beach; serene courtyard gardens; two hotels for the price of one—stay at Mahele Bay and enjoy facilities at the upcountry Lodge at Koele.

A dozen years ago the island of Lanai was about a twenty-five–minute flight from—and about fifty years behind—Honolulu. With 98 percent of the land owned by Dole Food, Lanai was called the Pineapple Island, a laid-back world with one funky hotel and a one-room airport.

All that changed in the early 1990s with the debut of two elegant new sister resorts, among the most luxurious in Hawaii. In the short time they have been open, the hotels have wowed rich and famous guests such as Kevin Costner and Billy Crystal and hosted major sporting events such as the Merrill Lynch Senior Shoot-Out on the PGA tour.

Playful spinner dolphins often visit Hulopoe Bay, Lanai's best beach and the setting for the Manele Bay Hotel, which opened in May 1991. Architecturally, the resort combines both Hawaiian and Mediterranean detailing, with arcaded loggias and sloping roofs. White walls and a sea-green tile roof harmonize with plush lawns and ochre pathways. To maintain an intimate feeling, individual wings surround garden courtyards, each with a different theme, such as Hawaiian, Japanese, or bromeliad.

In the lobby, murals by John Wullbrandt depict the legend of Kaululaau, said to have chased evil spirits from the island. Honoring Lanai's pineapple-plantation heritage, bronze chandeliers incorporate leaves and fruit in their design; vintage Hawaiian prints line the corridors.

As you stroll through the lush grounds, you'll encounter staff members diligently pursuing perfection—perhaps a wizened gardener raking imaginary leaves from an immaculate lawn, or a housekeeper polishing a bronze urn until it's mirror bright.

Rooms are very large and decorated in chinoiserie chic, with bamboo-framed chairs, porcelains poised on the armoire, and a four-poster bed. Spacious bathrooms sparkle with marble floors and counters and a separate glass stall shower. In addition to the usual shampoos and soaps, the lavish toiletries basket also includes hairspray, a miniloofah, and prethreaded needles. The lanai (terrace) is designed to be enjoyed and is furnished with a plump-cushioned chaise lounge and two comfy armchairs. About half of the rooms have ocean views.

A diamond-bright crescent, Hulopoe is one of the loveliest beaches in the islands. When conditions are calm, there's good snorkeling along the rocks at the left (as you face the ocean). Among the hotel's facilities the only downside is the health club, which is tiny and stuffed in a side corridor (the entry looks like a broom closet).

Through the hotel, guests can arrange various excursions, including a snorkel cruise aboard the Trilogy trimaran. They can also sign on for an ocean rafting trip along Lanai's coast, which is lined by 1,000-foot cliffs and secret coves.

For dining-with-a-view, you can't top the outside terrace of the Ihilani, with sound effects courtesy of the rustling palm fronds and wash of surf. The menu centers on Hawaiian regional cuisine. Accented by crystal chandeliers and murals, the Ihilani formal dining room re-creates the splendor of the Hawaiian monarchy and serves a French Mediterranean cuisine. Save room for one of the chocolate desserts, made with Hawaiian-grown cocoa beans.

The Lodge at Koele, Manele Bay's sister property, is also extremely Hawaiian—but in a way mainlanders rarely imagine Hawaii to be. The upland setting—a cool 1,700-foot elevation where hills often wear clouds like misty halos—resembles a scene more from *The Sound of Music* than *South Pacific*. Styled after a turn-of-the-century plantation estate, the resort features high beamed ceilings, twin 30-foot stone fireplaces in the Great Hall, and spacious verandas arranged with phalanxes of wicker armchairs.

Although Koele feels as though it has purred along in Grand Hotel perfection for at least a century or two, it only opened in April 1990. Connoisseurs can happily browse among rarities, ranging from a Burmese elephant howdah in the foyer to the eighth-century Persian painting in the music room. At the same time, the ambience is friendly, thanks to interior designer Joszi Meskan's sprightly touches, such as monkeys cavorting among the 8-foot-tall chandeliers.

Coddling remains the byword here, from the butter-soft suede armchairs in the library to the real down pillows on your bed. Rooms encourage relaxing, with a lavishly cushioned window seat, two wicker armchairs, and a four-poster bed crowned with pineapples. Bathrooms feature exotic blue-marble countertops paired with Italian tile floors and hand-painted cups from Portugal. Look carefully at the walls—they're painstakingly handpainted, not papered.

Lanai is golfers' heaven, with two spectacular eighteen-hole layouts. Designed by Jack Nicklaus, the championship Challenge at Manele opened in December 1993 to immediate acclaim. Every hole on the course offers an unobstructed ocean vista. Upland, the Experience at Koele, designed by Greg Norman and Ted Robinson, boasts panoramic views and several dramatic elevation drops from tees to greens.

It all adds up to the perfect choice for couples who love outdoor adventures by day and sumptuous accommodations at night.

Address/Phone: P.O. Box 310, Lanai City, HI 96763; (808) 565–7700; fax (808) 565–2483

U.S. Reservations: (800) 321–4666

Owner/Manager: Michael Slosser, general manager

Arrival/Departure: Complimentary airport and island shuttle transportation included

Distance from Lanai Airport: 9 miles (15 minutes)

Distance from Koele: 7 miles (12 minutes)

Accommodations: 250 rooms and suites

Best Room/Suite: If you want to splurge, ask for one of the suites that includes butler service (e.g., the midpriced Mauka Mini Suite); deluxe ocean-front rooms are also very romantic.

Amenities: Air-conditioning, ceiling fans, hair dryer, minibar, toiletries, TV, radio, clock; coffee/tea service, 24-hour room service. Some suites have butler service.

Electricity: 110 volts

Sports and Facilities: 36 holes of championship golf, 6 tennis courts, 1 swimming pool, snorkeling, free introductory scuba-diving course. The hotel can arrange scuba diving and snorkel sails.

Dress Code: Casually elegant

Weddings: Can be arranged

Rates/Packages: $325–$625 per couple per night for a room; $675–$2,500 for a suite

Payment/Credit Cards: Most major

Deposit: 2-night deposit required within 14 days of the reservation request. Deposits will be refunded in full when cancellations are received at least 14 days prior to arrival.

Government Taxes: 10.17 percent

Service Charges: Not included

≋

Mauna Lani Bay Hotel and Bungalows

Location: On twenty-nine oceanfront acres at Kalahuipua'a, on the Big Island's Kohala Coast.

Romantic Features: Two white sand beaches; fifteen acres of ancient, spring-fed Hawaiian fishponds plus pools teeming with tropical fish; fine restaurants.

Its name means "mountain reaching heaven," a perfect visual for honeymooners, who will feel as though they've come close to finding paradise at the Mauna Lani Bay Resort. Located on the sunny, dry (only 7 inches of rain annually) Kohala Coast, this six-story hotel presents a bold, contemporary design. Shaped like an arrowhead thrust seaward toward Makaiwa Bay, Mauna Lani Bay is a true-blue haven fringed by pearl-white beaches. The lobby reflects a spare elegance, with koi ponds and banks of orchids, torch ginger, and birds of paradise flanking the atrium. Jet-weary travelers are immediately soothed by the whoosh of waterfalls, view of the sapphire-blue Pacific, and friendly ministrations of the concierge, who checks you in.

The resort is built around fifteen acres of ancient fishponds, once *kapu* (forbidden) to all but Hawaiian royalty. They're stocked with mullet, awa, and lemon butterflies, whose brilliant colors swirl like an aquatic kaleidoscope. Paths encourage peaceful wanderings.

Decorated in serene tones of white and sand, each of the accommodations measures more than 550 square feet and has a private lanai. Ceiling fans, polished teak furnishings, and live orchids complement the tropical oasis decor. Top-of-the-line accommodations are the five bungalows—private houses, really, encompassing more than 4,000 square feet. Each has a private swimming pool and whirlpool spa and is served by a butler who can handle everything from unpacking your bags to grilling mahi-mahi on the barbecue. Steven Spielberg and Roseanne are among the celebrities who have roosted amid the sumptuous decor, accented by koa wood, marble, and crystal.

The signature restaurant is the celebrated Canoe House, which has won accolades in magazines such as *Bon Appétit*. Poised on the brink of the ocean, it offers diners ringside views of the polychromatic Kohala Coast sunsets. The Pacific Rim menu highlights choices such as wok-fried *lilikoi* (passion fruit), shrimp, and lemongrass-crusted ono (a fish). The Honu Bar is open for late-night music and dancing. In all, Mauna Lani has five restaurants.

Carved from a sixteenth-century lava flow, the two championship golf courses (home to the annual Senior Skins golf tournament) present dramatic juxtapositions between stark black lava rock, smooth emerald turf, and an ever-changing sea. Meanwhile *Tennis Magazine* has included the ten Plexi-pave tennis courts on its list of top fifty U.S. resort facilities. The roster of activities also includes aerobics classes, hula and lei-making lessons, beach picnics, and more. At the Mauna Lani Health Spa, options range from low-impact aerobics classes at water's edge to lomi lomi, a Hawaiian-style massage.

For relaxing and sunning Mauna Lani's two beaches are regarded as some of the finest on the Big Island. Try to snare one of the private cabanas, and lie back on the two-person lounge chairs shaded by a cabriolet roof. One of Hawaii's best scuba-diving locales, the waters off the Kohala Coast are stippled with lava tubes, archways, caves, canyons, and coral heads. Favorite sites include

Turtles Reef, a cleaning station for Hawaiian green sea turtles. Dive packages are available.

According to Hawaiians, Mauna Lani Bay is set on sacred ground. Perhaps that explains the tremendous feeling of mana (spiritual power) that the resort exerts over all those who visit. •

Address/Phone: 68–1400 Mauna Lani Drive, Kohala Coast, HI 96743; (808) 885–6622, fax (808) 885–1484

E-mail: maunalani@maunalani.com

Web Site: www.maunalani.com

U.S. Reservations: (800) 327–8585; (800) 367–2323; (808) 885–6622; (800) 992–7987 (in Hawaii)

Owner/Manager: Bill Sayce, general manager

Arrival/Departure: Taxis available at airport; transfers can be arranged

Distance from Keahole-Kona Airport: 25 miles north

Distance from Kona: 34 miles north

Accommodations: 345 rooms; 5 bungalows with private swimming pools and 24-hour butler service; 23 ocean villas. Over 92 percent of the accommodations have ocean views.

Best Room/Suite: Bungalows with pools; ocean villas

Amenities: Oversize TV (with cable) and on-command movies, honor bar, electronic safe, refrigerator, makeup mirror, toiletries, hair dryer, robes; concierge service

Electricity: 110 volts

Sports and Facilities: 36 holes of golf, 10 tennis courts, heated swimming pool, health club; sailing, snorkeling, sailboarding, boogie boarding, and surfing. Scuba diving and deep-sea fishing can be arranged.

Dress Code: Casually elegant

Weddings: The director of Weddings and Romance can arrange all the details, from formal weddings to nuptials in a helicopter. A favorite site is a little island in one of the fishponds.

Rates/Packages: $350–$620 per couple per night for a room; $970 for a suite; $525 for a one-bedroom villa; $4,550 per night for a bungalow. Romantic Interludes (3 nights): $1,665 per couple for oceanfront accommodations. Additional nights, $450. Includes a bottle of champagne and chocolate-dipped strawberries, lei greeting, rose petal turndown, candlelight dinner, daily breakfast in bed, picnic basket, and gifts. Couples can also custom-design their own romance package, with options ranging from limousine service to a private dinner accompanied by a violin serenade.

Payment/Credit Cards: Most major

Deposit: 2-night deposit required to guarantee reservation

Government Taxes: 11.16 percent
Service Charges: None

MAINE
≈≈≈

Balance Rock Inn

Location: On Frenchman Bay just 2 blocks from Main Street
Romantic Features: Wood-burning fireplaces; private suites with Jacuzzis and saunas; sunrise over the water; dreamy vistas from your private balcony; close proximity of forests and mountains of Acadia National Park.

The foggy mist was just burning off as we took a brisk morning walk looping from the entrance of Balance Rock to Main Street down to the sea and along the shore path that passes splendid seaside mansions, most of them private. Back at the inn we headed to the columned veranda overlooking the pool and Frenchman Bay beyond. Sipping a cup of freshly brewed coffee, we settled back into the thick cushions of a large wicker chair and considered our options for the day before going to the dining room for a breakfast of fresh fruit, Belgian waffles, and homemade breads.

Bar Harbor, Maine, with its fresh brisk air, spectacular seashore and mountains—wait until you see Acadia National Park—has to be one of the best places on earth to unwind and fall in love with your mate all over again.

In the mid to late 1800s, the Astors, Fords, Rockefellers, Carnegies, and Vanderbilts came to Bar Harbor and Mount Desert Island to built opulent summer homes overlooking the sea. They called them "cottages," but these sprawling mansions—averaging more than ten bedrooms with their columned verandas, rolling lawns, and gardens—could hardly be called your normal two-bath/three-bedroom getaway haven. In those days, this was the place to come to take in the fresh brisk sea air, throw lavish parties and unwind from the stress of banking, land deals, and corporate mergers.

A devastating fire in 1947 wiped out more than seventy of these mansions; World War II and the Great Depression finally ended the years of extravagance. Still, the scenic beauty of Bar Harbor along with the 41,000 acres of Acadia National Park encompassing glacier-carved mountains and lakes, granite outcroppings, and forests, was too good. Bar Harbor was rebuilt and today, although located more than halfway up Maine's rocky coastline—not exactly in most people's back yard—Bar Harbor continues to draw those who love the sea, the outdoors, and a laid-back life style.

Balance Rock Inn, Maine

Certainly Michael Miles and his wife, Nancy Cloud, thought so when they came from Boston to vacation in 1978. In fact they liked it so much that Michael, an advertising executive, and Nancy, a psychiatric social worker, decided to chuck the Massachusetts scene and settle into a whole new life as innkeepers of Ledgelawn Inn and later Balance Rock Inn, the former oceanfront retreat of Alexander Maitlin, who made his fortune developing railroads in Key West, Florida.

Balance Rock Inn, a sprawling gray-shingled mansion with white trim and black shutters named for the ice-age boulder that sits on the property, enjoys a marvelous location on a secluded cul-de-sac just 2 blocks from Main Street's shops and restaurants.

The grandeur of the former private summer residence has been restored. Coffered ceilings, intricate moldings, fluted pilasters, and arches are artfully painted in mauves, creams, and grays. Floral and paisley wallpaper complement the period-reproduction furniture, such as Queen Ann sofas, wing chairs, and a player piano. Flowers are everywhere.

French doors lead onto the veranda and windows are flanked by flowing mauve silk moire drapes. Fireplaces in the living room and dining room cheer up a crisp, cool day. Early risers can pour a cup of tea or coffee in the lounge.

Each of the seventeen guest rooms and suites have private baths. Some have whirlpool tubs; some have fireplaces, saunas, decks overlooking the sea, and Select Comfort airbeds that allow you to adjust the firmness on each side.

Although Balance Rock does not have a restaurant, it is still more of an inn than a B&B. There are bellmen to help with the luggage and for those who request it, there is turndown service. In addition to a full breakfast, tea is served in the afternoon and cigars and cocktails are offered at the veranda bar in the evening. "We'll serve drinks as long as people want to stay up," says Michael, who loves good wines and stocks an impressive wine cellar. If you prefer privacy, you can take a bottle of wine or champagne to your room.

Besides lounging at the pool or in the Jacuzzi, sipping tea on the veranda, or watching the boats go by on the bay, there is plenty to do in the area. You can take a harbor cruise, go whale watching, hike and bike in Acadia National Park, browse the many interesting shops, and try restaurants like the fun and funky Freddie's Route 66 and Galyn's, an affordable great little place with a creative menu; the crabcakes are delicious and, of course, you can't go wrong ordering whole Maine lobster.

This is a place where the salty air, cries of seagulls, and the distant sound of a fog horn set the mood. Even when the pavement is hot enough to fry eggs in New York, here the air cools and refreshes.

Address/Phone: 21 Albert Meadow, Bar Harbor, ME 04609; (800) 753–0494; (207) 288–2610; fax (207) 288–534

E-mail: barhbrinns@aol.com

Web Site: www.barharborvacations.com

U.S. Reservations: (800) 753–0494 or Destinnations New England (800) 333–4667; fax (508) 790–0565; E-mail: destinn@capecod.net

Owner/Manager: Michael Miles and Nancy Cloud

Arrival/Departure: Rental cars available at Portland (3½ hours driving time) and Bangor Airports (1¼ hours driving time) or Logan International Airport (Boston, 5½ hours driving time).

Distance from Bar Harbor Airport: 13 miles; Bangor Airport, 45 miles

Distance from downtown Bar Harbor: 2 blocks from center of town

Accommodations: 14 rooms and 3 suites. Most have king-size beds, marble baths, private balconies or patios, and water views.

Best Room/Suite: Room 306 has a huge deck, whirlpool bath, water views from your bed, and is very private; Room 205 has a king-size bed, separate living room with fireplace, whirlpool bath, and sauna.

Amenities: Air-conditioning, TV, hair dryer, terry robes, toiletries, 300-count linens, phones, VCRs; fireplaces in some rooms; many with whirlpool tubs or saunas and luxury "Select Comfort" beds

Electricity: 110 volts

Sports and Facilities: Heated pool; small gym; walking, hiking, biking

Dress Code: Informal

Weddings: Can be arranged

Rates/Packages: $175–$525, including breakfast; packages available, including Honeymoon Special: Add $75 to rate for champagne, fresh flowers and fruit, chocolates, special gift, and trolley ride through Bar Harbor.

Payment/Credit Cards: Most major

Deposit: 2 nights or fewer, payment in full required; 3 nights, 2-night deposit; 4 nights or more, 50 percent deposit; cancel 10 days prior to arrival for refund less $30 booking fee

Government Taxes: 7 percent

Service Charges: None

Closed: End of October to end of April

≈≈≈

Old Fort Inn

Location: A block from the ocean in Kennebunkport.

Romantic Features: Canopy beds and fireplaces; tucked-away seclusion; walks along the coast.

I t's just a short trek along a wooded trail to an unobstructed view of President George Bush's summer "White House" (although in this case, it's gray). You probably won't be invited to stay there on your vacation, so the next best thing is to check into the Old Fort Inn.

Innkeepers and owners, David and Sheila Aldrich, came here from California twenty years ago, just at the time, David says, "The B&B business was coming into its own. We hadn't really planned on moving to Maine, but we heard the place was for sale and decided to check it out." David, then a marketing manager for a major oil company, and his wife, Sheila, who at that time was a flight attendant, liked what they saw, bought the inn, and changed their lifestyle. Since that time they have been constantly working and upgrading the place.

"If we ever have the desire to stop working on it, it will be time to move on," says David, who explains that they do go back to California during the winter when the inn is closed.

Rustic yet with all the comforts of a first-rate country lodge, the Old Fort Inn is tucked into the woods off a side road yet is only a ten-minute walk into the center of town and the rugged Atlantic shore. The inn comprises a huge barn built around 1880, which houses a reception area, a Great Room with massive hand-hewn beams and brick fireplace, and an antiques shop crammed with vintage toys, furniture, artifacts, memorabilia, and other items. In the Great Room, a life-sized soft sculpture of an old-time piano player sits poised over the keys of a real life piano; French doors lead out to the pool and garden patio.

Sixteen recently renovated rooms and suites are located in the Carriage House. Each room has been uniquely furnished with a mix of antiques and period reproductions. Some have four-poster beds with crocheted canopies, fireplaces, and hand-stenciled borders. Appointments are eclectic and include items like mahogany armoires, lots of pillows, lace swags, leather-bound books, and framed vintage photos of someone's ancestors. One of the suites holds an antique chamber pot stocked with current magazines, Spode dishes displayed under a glass table top, and an oak hutch set with pewter plates. All rooms feature well-coordinated fabrics and wall coverings in soft shades of blues, greens, mauves, and mustards.

You may need to do a treasure hunt to find the television, which may be hidden in a piece of furniture that looked like a bureau. But you won't have any trouble finding the lights. The Carriage House may be more than one hundred years old, but the amenities are ultramodern. There are wonderful reading lights by the bed with easy-to-reach switches. Baths have state-of-the-art vanities and fixtures as well as heated tile floors.

Appreciated extras include fresh toffees on the coffee table, just-baked cookies delivered when you arrive, creamy white blankets encased in two sheets, and soft down or nonallergenic pillows.

David, an accomplished cook, prepares a lavish breakfast buffet, perhaps featuring malt waffles or crepes but always including fresh fruit and juices, yogurts, and cereals. You serve yourself using a large flat basket as a tray. Eat in the Great Room, carry your breakfast out to the pool or patio, or take it to your room for a private feast.

Nearby the Old Fort Inn are wonderful boutiques, art galleries, and restaurants to discover. Stroll by the historic homes built by wealthy sea captains and bike along the coast.

Address/Phone: Old Fort Avenue, P.O. Box M30, Kennebunkport, ME 04046; (207) 967–5353; fax (207) 967–4547

E-mail: oldfort@cybertours.com

Web Site: www.oldfortinn.com

U.S. Reservations: Destinnations New England (800) 333–4667; fax (508) 790–0565; E-mail destinn@capecod.net

Owner/Manager: David and Sheila Aldrich

Arrival/Departure: Portland (45 minutes driving time); Logan International Airport (Boston, 1½ hours driving time)

Distance from Portland: 35 miles; Boston, 80 miles

Distance from downtown Kennebunkport: 10-minute walk

Accommodations: 16 rooms and suites.

Best Room/Suite: Number 212 is a large corner minisuite with a queen canopy bed, fireplace, and views of the woods.

Amenities: Air-conditioning, TV, hair dryer, terry robes, Neutrogena toiletries, phones, iron, VCR, minibar with microwave oven, refrigerator, dishes, cutlery, and cupboards; heated tile floors in baths. Some rooms have fireplace and many have whirlpool tubs.

Electricity: 110 volts

Sports and Facilities: Freshwater pool, garden; tennis; walking, hiking, biking

Dress Code: Informal

Weddings: Can be arranged

Rates/Packages: $145–$310, including breakfast

Payment/Credit Cards: Most major

Deposit: 1 night's deposit for up to 3 nights stay; 2 nights' deposit 4 or more nights; cancel 15 days prior to arrival for refund

Government Taxes: 7 percent

Service Charges: None

Closed: After first weekend in December until May 1

≈≈≈

The White Barn Inn

Location: In historic Kennebunkport.

Romantic Features: Elegant candlelight dining in a rustic barn; wood-burning fireplaces; whirlpool baths for two; poolside cottage.

The White Barn Inn, a cozy enclave consisting of cottages, an 1850s homestead and two 170-year-old barns, has been carefully crafted by owner Laurence Bongiorno, to meet the expectations of guests who come to Kennebunkport looking for privacy, luxury and over-the-top dining. They are not disappointed.

Bongiorno has raised the bar when it comes to setting standards for country inns. Handpainted furniture, CD stereo systems, steam showers, fireplaces, a heated infinity granite-and-stone pool, and an award-winning restaurant where the cuisine and service live up to the highly romantic ambience, all score points in the above and beyond column.

There are contrasts here and they all seem to work. Rustic beams and formally attired waiters; primitive farm implements and white linen table cloths; elaborate international cuisine and simply grilled local fish; 40 foot ceilings and intimate cottages; primitive antiques and contemporary art.

In the main house, once the Boothbay boarding house, there are twelve rooms featuring whimsically painted beds and original art. The four garden rooms have queen-size sleigh beds, fireplaces, and whirlpool baths. The seven

The White Barn Inn, Maine

junior suites are furnished with four-poster king beds and come with sitting areas, fireplaces, and spacious marble baths with whirlpool baths.

May's Cottage, one of the most romantic places to stay, is located by the pool and has a king-size bed, double-sided fireplace, living room, whirlpool bath, and steam shower. The new loft suite features a private deck, cathedral ceilings, and a private entrance as well as a king-size bed, oversized marble bath, steam shower, and whirlpool bath.

All rooms are decorated with a mix of traditional furnishings and contemporary accents with coordinated fabrics and wallcoverings that are stylish and handsome, not cutesy Americana. Furniture is mostly nineteenth-century polished traditional pieces such as carved mahogany four-poster beds and Chippendale chairs. Mantels frame wood-burning fireplaces.

Bedspreads are creamy white matelasse; towels are thick and luxurious. On your bedside table, you'll find a bottle of water and you may decide to delve into one of the current novels left for you to read.

Breakfast—including fresh-squeezed juices, eggs, cheeses, cereals, and breads —is served in the main house dining room each morning; tea is served in the parlor in the afternoon during the cooler months around a roaring fire. Port is offered as a fitting nightcap, perhaps after a brisk walk around town.

The White Barn Inn restaurant is adjacent to the cottages. As you walk into the lofty candlelit room, you'll see at once the huge window wall framing a changing tableau each season: in the spring, brilliant displays of flowers and greenery; at Christmas, close to twenty trees all silvery with balls, bows, and white lights dusted with snow. A pianist plays soft dinner music and service is attentive, not intrusive. If ever you were looking for a place to pop the question, this is it.

Table-to-floor white linen cloths topped by fanciful silver sculptures (of New England wildlife creatures such as lobsters and pheasants crafted by French artist Gerard Bouvier from silver spoons, forks, knives, and other flatware) along with elegant brocade upholstered chairs are juxtaposed against the rustic barn-siding backdrop of highly varnished wide board floors, soaring ceilings, and displays of oldtime farm equipment and antique signs. A bar with a highly polished brass top is tucked into a corner.

And if the setting isn't enough to ooh and ahh you, the highly acclaimed and artfully presented cuisine prepared by executive chef, Jonathan Cartwright, will tip the scales (and probably yours). Paying homage to Maine produce and seafood, Chef Cartwright combines regional fish, seafood, game, and poultry with unusual ingredients such as truffles, wild mushrooms, and quail eggs. The prix-fixe menu at $67 changes weekly and features items such as steamed lobster on fettucine with a cognac butter sauce, chargrilled native salmon, roasted lamb rack, and Grand Marnier custard. Meals start with an amusé bouche from the chef, perhaps a bit of chicken liver mousse with truffles.

Small dinner parties of twelve or less can enjoy private dining in the Wine Room, which is decorated with a mural of Tuscany by local artist Judith Harden and an Italian chiaro marble floor. More than 7,000 bottles of fine wine are stored here.

During the summer, a light bistro menu is offered poolside from 12:30 to 2:00 P.M. consisting of baguette sandwiches, salads, and brick oven pizza. And of course frosty drinks.

The White Barn Inn celebrates all seasons. In the summer lawns, flowers, and shrubs invite you to linger; in the winter the courtyard is alive with tiny white lights that glow against the snow and purple light of night creating a beautiful fairyland. Spring is light and lacy with new flowering shrubs and trees; fall is bold and colorful.

There's not much nightlife in Kennebunkport, but then who needs it.

Address/Phone: P.O. Box 560C, Beach Street, Kennebunkport, ME 04046; (207) 967–2321; fax (207) 967–1100

E-mail: innkeeper@whitebarninn.com

Web Site: www.whitebarninn.com

U.S. Reservations: Contact the hotel directly.

Owner/Manager: Laurence Bongiorno, proprietor; William Mozingo, innkeeper

Arrival/Departure: Rental cars available at Portland (35 minutes driving time) or Logan International Airports (Boston, 1½ hours driving time).

Distance from Portland Airport: 25 miles

Distance from Logan International Airport: 80 miles

Distance from downtown Kennebunkport: In town

Accommodations: 25 rooms and suites

Best Room/Suite: May's Cottage, with a double-sided fireplace, living room, whirlpool bath, and steam shower. Loft Suite features a private deck, cathedral ceilings, private entrance, king-size bed, oversized marble bath, steam shower, and whirlpool bath.

Amenities: Air-conditioning, TV, hair dryer, terry robes, CD stereo systems, toiletries, phones, complimentary tea and port, turn-down service. Some have fireplaces, whirlpool tubs, steam showers, and decks.

Electricity: 110 volts

Sports and Facilities: Heated pool, canoeing, tennis, biking, horseback riding, whale watching, and picnics can be arranged

Dress Code: Informal

Weddings: Can be arranged

Rates/Packages: $190–$450, including breakfast; packages available

Payment/Credit Cards: Most major

Deposit: Required (depends on length of stay); cancel 30 days prior to arrival during summer (high season) for full refund; 14 days in low season.

Government Taxes: 7 percent

Service Charges: None

MASSACHUSETTS
≈≈≈

The Wauwinet

Location: On the northeastern end of the island of Nantucket.

Romantic Features: Walks on windswept beaches; bike rides; picnics in a secluded cove.

The weathered clapboard houses and tucked-away gardens brimming over with hollyhocks, black-eyed Susans, and cascades of roses tumbling over white picket fences are all part of Nantucket's inescapable charm. At the heart of it all is one of the oldest inns on the island, The Wauwinet.

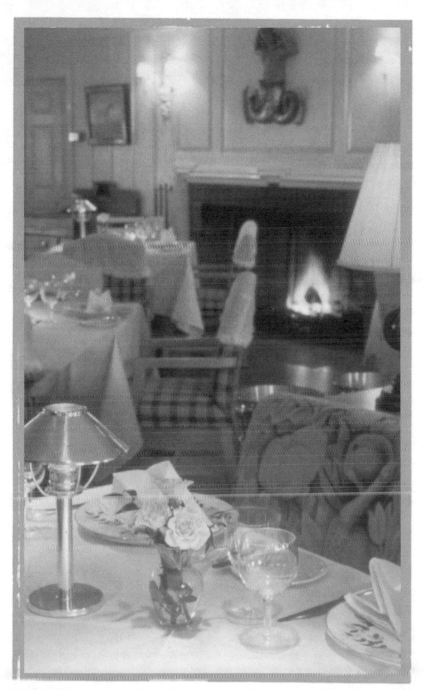

The Wauwinet, Massachusetts

Located just about as far away as you can get from the noise and complexities of everyday life, The Wauwinet stands firmly planted on its grassy carpet, a bastion of peace and tranquility.

Its traditions reach back to the mid-1800s, when the inn was a restaurant, known as Wauwinet House, that served shore dinners to guests arriving by boat. In 1876 it became an inn and soon emerged as not only a Nantucket social center but a hot spot for Northeasterners to head for their vacation. It went through a period of decline until 1986, when Bostonians Stephen and Jill Karp purchased the property, restoring it to the tune of $3 million. A more recent facelift has resulted in new wall treatments, upholstery, furniture, and artwork.

Flanked by Nantucket Bay on one side and the Atlantic Ocean on the other, The Wauwinet is New England at its best. Its gables, porches, and lawns invite guests to sit back in the comfortable wicker chaises and white lawn chairs to gaze out at magnificent, endless ocean views, gentle dunes, and wispy gardens of wildflowers and roses all around. Sandy paths cut through the low-lying shrubs lead to the sea and to private, buff-colored beaches.

Rooms are individually decorated, many with an eclectic mix of English-style period pieces, country antiques, and casual wicker. Chintz and stenciling add to the warmth of the decor; headboards are iron or upholstered. Around the rooms you'll find special touches such as baskets, hatboxes, books, and woodcarvings.

You have all the amenities you could wish for to ensure that you will be sublimely comfortable—extra things like Egyptian cotton bathrobes; armoires with soft, scented hangers; eyelet-trimmed linens; bottled water beside your bed; and fresh flowers. Windows are large, letting in lots of fresh air and light; ceilings are high.

Topper's, one of the best-known and most respected restaurants on Nantucket, is located right at The Wauwinet. Topper's award-winning cuisine and wines continually garner rave reviews. You can dine alfresco on the umbrella-shaded Bayview Terrace or eat inside in two indoor dining rooms. The executive chef, Chris Freeman, uses local produce, such as bushberries and cranberries, as well as fresh fish and seafood to prepare his American cuisine with a light touch. Service is polished and gracious; wines, superb and recently the restaurant received the Grand Award, the highest honor given by *Wine Spectator.*

The inn's jitney is available to take you into Nantucket town, always an interesting excursion. (You can also bicycle in.) Once the largest whaling center in the world, Nantucket has a fascinating museum that details the history of the whaling industry. The town's streets are lined by more than 800 homes built between 1740 and 1840, many owned by whaling captains. You can spend hours browsing through the countless small shops, cozy restaurants, and art galleries. And take time to check out the harbor, where there are many lovely yachts riding at anchor or tied to the wharfs.

For a more intimate outing, ask the staff to prepare a gourmet basket lunch and take the *Topper, Too* launch to a secluded beach for a lazy afternoon of sunning and swimming.

Activities and sports at The Wauwinet are centered on Nantucket's natural assets. You can swim; go out in the inn's many boats and sailing craft; hike, bike, and jog through the trails that wind through the area; or play tennis or croquet. Golf can be arranged nearby.

During the crisper months, which some feel are the very best, after a walk through the dunes you can head to the cozy library, sit before the fire, and sip sherry or port.

Once you've stayed there, when you define the word *bliss,* you'll naturally think Wauwinet.

Address/Phone: P.O. Box 2580, Wauwinet Road, Nantucket, MA 02584; (508) 228–0145, fax (508) 228–6712

U.S. Reservations: (800) 426–8718

Owner/Manager: Stephen and Jill Karp, owners; Russ and Debbie Cleveland, innkeepers

Arrival/Departure: If you want to get there in a hurry, you can fly from Hyannis via Island Air for about $40 one-way (800–698–1109) or take Nantucket Air (800–635–8787). Cape Air also goes from New Bedford to the island (800–352–0714). Or you can take the ferries from Hyannis operated by either the Steamship Authority (508–540–2022) or Hy-Line Cruises (508–778–2602); the trip ranges from 1 hour and 50 minutes to 2 hours and 10 minutes. Fares are about the same (approximately $22 round-trip) for both lines, but the Hy-Line ships are 20 minutes faster. For about $10 more you can enjoy first-class service on the Hy-Line's run: You sit in a comfortable lounge set up with couches. If you plan on taking your car, make your ferry reservations well ahead of time, especially during the peak summer season. Rental cars are available in town. Complimentary transportation to The Wauwinet from the Steamship Authority dock only (Hy-Line's dock is right down the street).

Distance from Nantucket Airport: 9 miles

Distance from Nantucket town: 9 miles

Accommodations: 30 rooms; 25 located in the inn, 5 in private guest cottages

Best Room/Suite: The inn's rooms have warmth and character; the guest cottages are more private; deluxe rooms have king-size beds

Amenities: Air-conditioning, ceiling fans, hair dryer, TV, VCR, cotton bathrobes, irons and ironing boards, telephone, Crabtree & Evelyn toiletries, scented hangers; evening turndown service, CD player, video library

Electricity: 110 volts

Sports and Facilities: 2 Har-Tru clay tennis courts, jogging, hiking, and walking trails; swimming at 2 private beaches, Sunfish sailing, rowboats; jeep safaris, croquet, bocce, BeetleCat, mountain bikes, fishing, golf; racquetball and squash can be arranged

Dress Code: Smart casual; jackets with or without ties or dress sweaters and slacks are requested for gentlemen dining at Topper's after 6:00 P.M.

Weddings: Can be arranged

Rates/Packages: Rates per couple per night include room, breakfast, cheese, port and wine, tennis, use of bikes, boating, natural history excursions, jitney service into town: $230–$1,170 (spring/fall); $380–$1,400 (summer)

Payment/Credit Cards: Most major

Deposit: Prepayment required. Cancellation penalties apply; must cancel 21 days (or more) prior to arrival date for refund less $35 cancellation fee.

Government Taxes: 9.75 percent room tax

Service Charges: Not included

Closed: Open mid-May to late October

≋

The Whalewalk Inn

Location: In the middle of Cape Cod near Orleans.

Romantic Features: Private cottage tucked into corner of gardens; fire-places; homemade breakfasts; whirlpool tubs.

A saltbox cottage overlooking a meadow of wildflowers; a fireplace fire at the flick of a switch; a one-minute walk to hot coffee and home-made blueberry waffles. Sound good? Then consider The Whalewalk Inn. Nestled in a quiet part of Cape Cod in Eastham, this tranquil oasis sits on three acres of lawn, rolling fields, and gardens dotted with Adirondack chairs.

Converted to a country inn in 1953, an 1830s whaling master's home—a colonial building with lots of paned windows, black shutters, and decorative lattice work along the roof—is the centerpiece of a serene haven that should appeal to anyone who loves the Cape but prefers to do without the fuss at the end of the day.

Decide to come here and you'll have a hard time choosing which room you want. Shall it be the Saltbox Cottage? A suite in the carriage house with its own fireplace and a balcony overlooking the meadows (no need to close the drapes here)? Or do you want one of the highly romantic rooms in the main house or in the converted barn or guest house?

Eastham is not as well known as its busier neighbors, Chatham and Orleans, which makes it all the more appealing to many. Like Eastham, The Whalewalk

The Whalewalk Inn, Massachusetts

Inn is not flashy, formidable, or pretentious. Yet it's just a bike ride away from the Cape's beaches and within a few minutes' drive of such attractions as the Wellfleet Wildlife Sanctuary, the Cape Cod National Seashore, and Heritage Plantation of Sandwich.

The Whalewalk Inn is the kind of place where you can roll out of bed when you feel like it, wander down to the main dining room for breakfast, and stick your head into the kitchen to say Hi to owners Carolyn and Richard Smith, who are preparing your breakfast. Depending on the season, you can have breakfast in the sunny dining room or outdoors on the flagstone garden terrace.

Each morning when Dick ties on his apron and digs into preparing breakfast, you know you're in for some good cooking. Applesauce bread, cranberry or blueberry pancakes, Grand Marnier French toast or apple walnut crepes—he makes them all. He also whips up a mean Granola Breakfast Pizza.

The Smiths, former advertising executives, have put their heart and soul into the place as innkeepers, decorators, cooks, and hosts. They have furnished the inn's common rooms with nineteenth-century antiques from England, France, and Denmark. Sixteen guest rooms and suites have four-poster beds or cottage country beds, comforters, and thick, thirsty towels. Some have fireplaces, wet bars, balconies, and whirlpool baths for two. Unusual accents include artwork by local artists, decorative plates, brass candlesticks, afghans, antique trunks,

and hand-crafted area carpets. All have marvelous bed skirts, lots of plump pillows, and a feeling of airy spaciousness.

Decor is different in each room. One room has a blue-and-white theme;
another is done in green and white and comes with white wicker chairs and set-
tee; and a deluxe room boasts a king-size four-poster pencil bed, and soft rose
drapes and wall coverings.

The Saltbox Cottage is off by itself, tucked into a bower of flowers and
shrubs. It has a queen-size bed, fireplace, sitting area, wet bar, and patio—perfect for honeymooners. The Carriage House contains some of the newer
accommodations. Rooms and suites are extra large and come with fireplaces,
queen beds (some on platforms), private patios or decks, and large tubs and
baths. Wake up to complimentary coffee and tea, which is set up in the hall
each morning.

Whalewalk offers bikes for its cycling guests: A 30-mile bike path is nearby.
You will never run out of things to see and do on the Cape. Besides the obvious—beaches, boating, and whale watching—the Heritage Plantation is well
worth visiting. It contains several extensive exhibits and gardens, including an
art museum, a military museum, a working and very rare 1912 carousel, and a
collection of antique cars. Among the restored automobiles are Gary Cooper's
original 1930 Dusenberg Model J Derham Tourster and the 1909 White Steam
car used by President Howard Taft.

Golfers have ten courses within a twenty-minute drive, and shoppers can go
from town to town to browse through antique stores, art galleries, and boutiques.

On your return from a day exploring or sunning at the beach, you can dig
into some complimentary hors d'oeuvres served either in the living room or, in
warm weather, on the patio. A wet bar and setups are provided. Freshly baked
cookies tempt those with sweet tooths. Try having just one. Impossible!

Address/Phone: 220 Bridge Road, Eastham, Cape Cod, Massachusetts
02542; (508) 255–0617 or (800) 333–4667; fax (508) 240–0017

E-mail: whalewalk@capecod.net

Web Site: www.whalewalkinn.com

U.S. Reservations: Contact the inn or Destinnations New England, (800)
333–INNS

Owner/Manager: Carolyn and Dick Smith

Arrival/Departure: Car rentals available at Boston's Logan International
Airport

Distance from Boston's Logan International Airport: 100 miles (2
hours); Hyannis or Provincetown Airports, 20 minutes

Distance from Eastham center: 10 minutes

Accommodations: 16 rooms and suites in 5 buildings

Best Room/Suite: Saltbox Cottage; deluxe room in main house with two-person soaking tub; queen suite in Carriage House with private deck, fireplace, and whirlpool tub-for-two

Amenities: Air-conditioning, ceiling fans, hair dryers, clock radios, phones, TVs, irons, toiletries. Some have fireplaces, whirlpool baths for two, soaking tubs, refrigerators, stocked pantries, complimentary coffee and tea.

Electricity: 110 volts

Sports and Facilities: Swimming, walking, hiking, biking (bikes on site); golf and horseback riding nearby

Dress Code: Informal

Weddings: Can be arranged

Rates/Packages: $160–$275 per couple per night including breakfast

Payment/Credit Cards: Most major

Deposit: Required (varies according to length of stay and accommodations). Cancel 14 days or more before arrival date for refund, less $25 processing fee.

Government Taxes: 9.7 percent

Service Charges: None

NEW MEXICO

Inn of the Anasazi

Location: In the center of Santa Fe.

Romantic Features: Seductive desert colors; private kiva fireplace; four-poster bed.

I t's only been open since 1991, but its spirit stretches back over 700 years ago to a time when the creative Anasazi Indians lived in cliffs in the southwestern hills. The Indians, who were artistic and in tune with their surroundings, left a heritage of beautiful geometric designs that were found in everyday items such as pottery and weavings.

When the Inn of the Anasazi was built, the creators successfully captured the essence of the culture of this ancient people throughout the inn without imposing any of the clichés often found in such tourism-related endeavors. This place feels as if it has sat here in the heart of historic Santa Fe for many, many years.

Its romantic appeal is in both the low-key, classy way the inn has been designed and the warmth of the people who run it. Each room has its own private kiva fireplace, king-size bed (most rooms) with a fluffy duvet, fine, 100 percent cotton sheets, down pillows, and colors that carry you out to the desert.

Lie back on your bed and look up at the ceiling, which is made of authentic *vigas* and *latillas,* a traditional wooden beam and pole construction. Really interesting and indicative of the kind of thought that went into the inn's design.

The decor is pure Southwestern: massive hand-hewn furniture, Indian blankets, mellow brown leather chairs, stone-top tables; terra-cotta pots filled with cactus, original artwork and crafts by Native American artists, and antique Indian rugs. Baskets woven in Anasazi-style patterns, unpainted sandstone and adobe walls (hand-plastered), wide plank floors, a palette of desert earth tones, and handmade tile baths all add to a mood that is soft and seductive.

The ninety-two-seat restaurant, winner of the AAA (American Automobile Association) Four Diamonds award, serves a lot of fresh, organically grown food purchased from local farmers. The menu, which changes twice a year, is contemporary Southwestern fare and might include grilled corn tortilla soup with ginger pork; Anasazi flatbread with fire-roasted sweet peppers; peanut-and-coconut–grilled prawns with watermelon salsa; and fresh herb-and-lime marinated rack of lamb.

Santa Fe has a lot going for it, and you're just steps away from it all. Right outside Anasazi's bold timbered entrance, you can stroll to the market stands of the Pueblo Indians who sell turquoise and silver jewelry and belts, and you can visit the many art galleries that feature wonderful, handcrafted pots, baskets, and paintings. The inn can arrange for you to visit the ancient Anasazi ruins of Chaco Canyon and see some of the northern pueblos that are in the area. You can also go hiking, whitewater rafting, and fishing. In the winter months you can head to the ski slopes not too far away.

Steeped in the earthy world of the Southwest, the Inn of the Anasazi will enchant those romantics who love the culture and spirit of the West. This place is really well done.

Address/Phone: 113 Washington Avenue, Santa Fe, NM 87501; (505) 988–3030; fax (505) 988–3277

Web Site: www.innoftheanasazi.com

U.S. Reservations: (800) 688–8100

Owner/Manager: Jeff Mahan, general manager

Arrival/Departure: By rail: Amtrak leaves passengers at Lamy, 17 miles from Santa Fe. Shuttle service is available into town by calling (505) 982–8829. By air: Shuttle service, via Shuttlejack, to downtown Santa Fe available at Albuquerque International Airport. Mesa Airlines operates a daily schedule of flights between Albuquerque and Santa Fe Municipal Airport. Transportation can be arranged to hotel. Taxis also available.

Distance from Albuquerque International Airport: 60 miles

Distance from Santa Fe: In the center of town

Accommodations: 59 rooms. Traditional rooms are fairly small; Superior rooms are larger, and Deluxe rooms, the largest, have small sitting areas. 53 rooms have king-size beds; 6 have two twins.

Best Room/Suite: Deluxe or superior rooms

Amenities: Hair dryer, air-conditioning, toiletries with organic bath oils, shampoo and soaps, minibar, bathrobe, TV, VCR, stereo, coffeemaker, safe, two-line phones, 100 percent cotton sheets, duvet, down pillows, stationary bike for use in room on request; room service 6:00 A.M. to 11:00 P.M.

Electricity: 110 volts

Sports and Facilities: Massage therapist; whitewater rafting and horseback riding can be arranged

Dress Code: Southwestern casual

Weddings: Can be arranged

Rates/Packages: $249–$409 per couple per night (March 30–October 31; excludes July and August), $205–$355 (November 1–March 29); $265–$415 (June 29–October 31). Romance packages available. $10 parking fee.

Payment/Credit Cards: Most major

Deposit: 1 night deposit; cancel 72 hours prior to arrival for full refund

Government Taxes: 11.31 percent

Service Charges: Not included

NEW YORK

The Wawbeek on Upper Saranac Lake

Location: Adirondack Great Camp on 1,400 feet of shoreline in Tupper Lake.

Romantic Features: Canoeing on a pine-fringed glassy lake; hikes in the forest; dining on the porches overlooking the water; your own private cabin.

I magine loons gliding on the water, log cabins with private decks, pines so tall they hide in the early morning mist, miles of trails, and balsam-scented fresh air, and you get the picture. God's country. Who wouldn't find romance at the Wawbeek, a turn-of-the-century Adirondack Great Camp. Sprawled on more than forty wooded acres on Upper Saranac Lake, this is the great outdoors at its best—but with such comforts as heated cabins, warm blankets, and a superb restaurant.

The Wawbeek (*Wawbeek* is the Native American word for "big rock") is just one of a handful of Great Camps located in Adirondack State Park, the nation's largest state park. Constructed in the style we now call "Adirondack," these camps were built with dark wood exteriors, often logs, porches with railings made of thick branches, and large central great rooms with stone fireplaces. The dining room was usually located in a separate building with sleeping quarters in one or more other buildings. The camps were used as summer retreats by wealthy families such as the DuPonts, Rockefellers, and Baches, who came to cool off and relax.

Some, such as the Great Camp Sagamore, can be very rustic, with single beds wrapped with Hudson Bay blankets, shared baths, and a waterfront location to die for. Sleeping, eating, and recreational activities are located in buildings throughout the grounds. Meals are served buffet style to guests who eat at large tables communal style, and rates are modest. Once the summer haven for the Vanderbilt family, Sagamore is popular with groups who come to enjoy traditional camp community life.

Then there is The Point, famed former retreat of the Rockefellers and now a member of the Relais & Chateaux group of properties. About the only thing rustic about The Point is the setting: Every luxury imaginable is here, from four-poster canopied beds and antique furniture to wraparound windows. But luxury comes with a price tag: The cost at The Point is more than double that of the Wawbeek.

All these Great Camps are very good at what they do. It just depends on the experience you are looking for and the price you want to pay.

The Wawbeek, my choice for a place that combines a rustic ambience with private cabins and candlelight dining, is managed by co-owners Nancy and Norman Howard, refugees from the corporate world in Connecticut, who preside over this glassy islet-studded lake.

One of Norman's great pleasures is cranking up his party barge to take guests for cruises on the lake. You'll pass a few other Great Camps poking through the woods and, perhaps, an eagle or two soaring overhead.

The Wawbeek has its own fleet of canoes, paddleboats, and Sunfish promising days of water-oriented fun. Land-based amusements include two tennis courts, croquet, and a game house where you can challenge your mate to Ping Pong, pool, darts, or a board game. Some evenings there may even be a campfire with a storyteller or guitar player.

Of the Wawbeek's twenty-one rooms, six are located in Mountain House, a two-story building and one of the original houses built on the property. Some rooms open onto porches where you can look out to the shimmering lake and islands.

There are also several rustic cottages with sitting rooms, efficiency kitchens, pull-out sofas (for emergency snoring relief), and a spacious deck with glimpses of the water.

Other rooms are in the Carriage House, including a spacious corner suite with a private entrance, king-size bed, and deck.

Each cabin comes with a small kitchen; some have sitting rooms, fireplaces, screened porches or decks, and eating areas. Some are tucked into the hillside and are very private. Most have queen- or king-size comfortable beds with good quality linens, blankets, and quilts. All have updated fresh decor in pine green, tan, and brown and are squeaky clean. Books and knitted afghans lend a homey touch.

You'll not find any old tin showers here. Bathrooms are modern, with a tub and shower combo, and for what the Howards say are "all the right reasons," Wawbeek's rooms do not have telephones, TVs, or air-conditioning. However if this creates any sense of panic, these contrivances can be arranged.

Nature trails fan out from the main reception area, leading to the lakefront and dock, to the restaurant, and to a secluded spot at water's edge where you can settle back in one of the Adirondack chairs, read, or simply savor the moment. The Adirondack Park's many hiking trails are right at your doorstep. You might follow the Bloomingdale Bog Trail, only 1.8 miles, or bike along the 7-mile Deer Pond Loop across the way or the 18-mile Paul Smith Loop up the road. Then cool off with a swim. The lake is clean and refreshing.

Nearby there are plenty of places to explore. The Adirondack Museum in Blue Mountain Lake is crammed with a day's worth or more of things to see, such as antique boats, trains, historical exhibits, survival tools, art exhibits, and more. There are miles and miles of canoe routes and mountains to climb like Mt. Baker and Haystack Mountain. Donna and Captain Pohl's spiffy double-decker *WW Durant* offers a variety of cruises on Raquette Lake, including lunch and dinner cruises. The food on board— items such as dilled cheese potato soup and braised duck breast—is remarkably delicious.

Spring, fall, and winter can be lovely here, too. In the fall brilliant red, orange, and yellow leaves drift down, carpeting the trails, and the air is brisk—perfect for long hikes. In the winter pristine snow blankets the ground in great drifts, catching the sunlight and making it sparkle. There are 100 miles of snow-mobiling trails, endless cross-country ski trails, and snowshoeing and Alpine skiing down Big Tupper and Whiteface Mountains. There is ice skating on the lake and dinner and cocktails in the Wawbeek restaurant in front of a blazing fire. Early in February everyone in town turns out for Saranac Lake's Winter Carnival, renowned for its ice castle, and later for the annual Woodchuck Shuffle snow-shoe event.

And Spring. Budding flowers poke up through the melting snow; energy levels turn up a notch or two. Things are waking up. It's a great time for brisk hikes, golf, and other outdoor pursuits—perhaps the Ice Breaker 5-mile canoe race on Saranac River.

All year long in the town of nearby Saranac Lake, there are stores to poke through, concerts, performances at the Pendragon Theatre, and sports events galore from canoe races to ski-jumping contests.

Once back at the Wawbeek, you can look forward to a really fine meal. The Wawbeek restaurant, which sits high on a rocky promontory overlooking the lake, delivers both romantic ambience and exceptional cuisine. Chef Richard Brosseau spins his magic in this woodsy retreat, creating dishes such as Venison Carpaccio, seared Hudson Valley foie gras, farm-raised ostrich loin grilled and served over Yukon Gold mashed potatoes, spiced crusted filet of salmon served with Mediterranean couscous, and a salad of baby lettuces with maple vinaigrette and roasted pecans. Chef Brosseau prides himself on using as many fresh ingredients as he can find, including herbs and berries from the grounds, locally grown vegetables, fresh trout, and regional meats. A farmer in Syracuse grows mesclun, tomatoes, and other vegetables just for him—Richard is known to go to great lengths to get it right.

"When Richard first arrived," says Nancy, "I was giving him a tour of our trails, pointing out the wild flowers along the way as well as a patch of wintergreen. Later in the winter, when he was having trouble finding oil of wintergreen to make his signature homemade ice cream, I reminded him of the wintergreen in the woods. 'Let's go find it,' he said. I cautioned that it was under several feet of snow. 'But it's WINTERgreen,' he replied. Made sense. So off we went trudging through the snow. We dug down at least 3 feet, where we finally found it, green as could be."

It is very quiet here at the Wawbeek—indeed so quiet that the scampering of a squirrel or two across your roof or the hoot of an owl in the night can put you into a momentary state of panic. "Just who is that?" No one. Go back to sleep. Listen to the rustle of the pines. You're in a good place where even the thought of locking your door may seem a bit silly. And when you must finally leave, listen carefully for the sounds of a pileated woodpecker tapping out "good-bye."

Address/Phone: Panther Mountain Road, Tupper Lake, NY 12986; (800) 953–2656; (518) 359–2656; fax (518) 359–2575

E-mail: wawbeek@capital.net

Web Site: www.wawbeek.com

U.S. Reservations: (800) 953–2656

Owner/Manager: Nancy and Norman Howard

Arrival/Departure: Rental cars available at Adirondack Airport just 9 miles from Saranac Lake and Albany Airport.

Distance from Albany Airport: 150 miles (2½ hours)

Distance from Tupper Lake: 10 minutes to village; 15 miles to Saranac Lake

Accommodations: 21 rooms in several buildings, including rustic cottages

Best Room/Suite: Partridgeberry, a secluded cabin with a fireplace, vaulted ceiling, and screened porch; Tamarack, a cottage close to the boat dock with a good view of the water from the corner deck; Mountain House Rooms 5 and 6; Carriage House Number 1

Amenities: Ceiling fans, coffee and tea making facilities, toiletries, grills, kitchens, laundry facilities. Some have fireplaces, fold-out queen-size sofas, daily housekeeping services; Adirondack resourceful hosts!

Electricity: 110 volts

Sports and Facilities: Canoes, paddleboats, Sunfish, sloop; 2 tennis courts; swimming, walking, hiking, biking, skiing, snowshoeing, cross-country skiing, Alpine skiing, ice fishing; golf and horseback riding nearby

Dress Code: Informal

Weddings: Can be arranged

Rates/Packages: $145–$230 per couple, per night (summer); $135–$210 (fall and holidays); $115–$185 (winter/spring), including full breakfast and use of boats, bikes, and snowshoes. Weekly rates start at $595; 3-day rates (winter/spring only) from $85 per night.

Payment/Credit Cards: Most major

Deposit: 50 percent deposit required to hold booking. Balance due on arrival. Cancel 30 days or more before arrival date for refund less 10 percent (60 days if booking more than one sleeping room).

Government Taxes: 7 percent

Service Charges: 10 percent recommended

VERMONT

The Equinox

Location: In the center of Manchester Village, in southern Vermont's Green Mountains.

Romantic Features: Sleigh rides; late evening nightcaps in the cozy Marsh Tavern; en-suite Jacuzzis and fireplaces.

The allure of Vermont's Green Mountains beckons to those who love the outdoors. From your base at The Equinox, a charming country inn resort that holds center stage in the small village of Manchester, you can hike; go horseback riding in the surrounding hills; play golf on a picturesque, par 71, 6,423-yard championship course; swim, fish, and ski. You can even learn off-road driving or falconry.

Close to the ski areas of Bromley and Stratton Mountains, the stately Equinox has a long history of welcoming guests. It started life in the 1700s as the Marsh Tavern (now one of the hotel's restaurants), and by the mid-1800s the hotel had put Manchester Village on the map as one of America's finest year-round destinations. In 1972 the resort was added to the National Register of Historic Places, and in 1991 The Equinox underwent an ambitious renovation program, including the restoration of all public areas and guest rooms as well as the golf course.

Anyone driving through the center of Manchester Village could not possibly miss it. The Equinox, which faces the village green, is simply the most impressive structure in town. It boasts an imposing, white-pillared facade with a long porch set up with green rocking chairs and two wings that create an interior garden courtyard. Just across the street from the front entrance are a number of classy clothing and gift shops—fun to browse through, but bring lots of cash

The Equinox, Vermont

if you intend to buy. Also located here are a number of 200-year-old buildings, including the Congregational church and Bennington County Courthouse.

You'll find the rooms at The Equinox very comfortable. Furnished in a traditional style in muted New England colors, some of these rooms include king-size beds, washed-pine armoires, desks, wing chairs, rich drapes and bedspreads, and marble-tiled baths.

Next door is the newest Equinox addition, the Charles Orvis Inn. Dating back to 1833, this house was originally used to accommodate guests during the winter months, when the main hotel was closed. Today it has been totally rebuilt and houses nine one- and two-bedroom deluxe suites, each with its own working fireplace, living room, dining room, full kitchen, and super appointments. Check in here and you'll have your own private en-suite Jacuzzi and the use of an intimate bar and billiard room.

If you're into golf, perhaps one of the best parts of staying here is that you can easily walk from the hotel to the first tee of one of the loveliest golf courses in New England. The Gleneagles course, originally designed by the legendary Walter Travis, has been improved and updated by the well-known golf course designer Rees Jones. The course's ups and downs will very likely do the same to your score card. It's hilly, challenging, and breathtaking in its beauty. As you hit your ball from the tee on the eighth hole, your ball will soar into the sky against a backdrop of dense green mountains and deep blue skies. Straight ahead is the white spire of a quintessential New England church, nestled at the base of a mountain. On the fifth hole you'll have to wait for those ahead of you to ring a bell before hitting over the blind hill. This is one course you can play again and again without getting bored—there are new challenges around every bend.

The Equinox also has a great fitness spa, located at the back of the hotel's courtyard, as well as three clay tennis courts, a 75-foot heated swimming pool outdoors, and a 47-foot heated indoor pool. You can rent bikes and cycle out to the many trails in the area and play croquet. Hikers have a good selection of wooded mountain trails to explore.

Canoeing trips on the Battenkill River can be arranged, and if you ever wanted to try your hand at fly-fishing or shooting, The Equinox offers lessons on its own Equinox Pond or the Battenkill River. You can also attend the Orvis Fly-Fishing School, the oldest of its kind in the country, and the Orvis Shooting School, located right in Manchester Village.

You can eat breakfast, lunch, and dinner at the Marsh Tavern, a darkish, cozy place that dates back to 1769. You can also enjoy cocktails on the tavern's terrace during July and August. For a more elegant dining experience, head to the grand Colonnade, which features fine continental cuisine and wines and is open for dinner June to October on Wednesday through Sunday evenings and November to May on weekend evenings.

Some nights there is entertainment in the Marsh Tavern, and during the summer months a number of local performing art centers offer an assortment of concerts and theater productions. Come here if you love New England and all it offers. Your accommodations at The Equinox will be supremely comfortable; your choice of activities plentiful if you love exploring the countryside and participating in traditional sports.

Think of any name-brand clothing or sporting goods company and you'll find it in the outlet stores that line the roads leading into town. The stores are housed in attractive New England–style buildings of weathered wood and clapboard, in harmony with the surrounding countryside. If you have some wedding money you want to spend, you can easily fill the backseat of your car with bags full of bargains from Anne Klein, Liz Claiborne, Ralph Lauren, London Fog, Armani, Escada, and Donna Karan, to name a few.

Address/Phone: Historic Route 7A, Manchester Village, VT 05254; (802) 362–4700; fax (802) 362–1595

E-mail: reservations@equinoxresort.com

Web Site: www.equinoxresort.com

U.S. Reservations: (800) 362–4747

Owner/Manager: S. Lee Bowden, president and managing director

Arrival/Departure: Transfers via private car can be arranged at $85 per car, one-way, plus 15 percent gratuity

Distance from Albany Airport: 64 miles (about 1½ hours)

Distance from Manchester Village: In heart of town

Accommodations: 183 rooms and suites, including suites in the Charles Orvis Inn, next door. Most rooms are oversize and offer a choice of garden, village, or mountain views.

Best Room/Suite: Try one of the new one-bedroom suites in the Charles Orvis Inn. Main building suites also good.

Amenities: Toiletries, air-conditioning, telephones, clock radio, ironing facilities, cable TV, in-room movies, bathrobes, fireplaces (some), Jacuzzis (some); concierge services; room service; valet parking

Electricity: 110 volts

Sports: Tennis (3 clay courts), swimming (indoor and outdoor pools), fishing, shooting range, golf, fitness spa with aerobics classes, gym, saunas, croquet; downhill skiing nearby at Bromley and Stratton Mountains; snowmobiling; cross-country skiing on grounds; biking (rentals available at hotel); ice skating (nearby), snowshoeing, nearby hiking trails, horseback riding, canoeing, off-road driving school, falconry school

Dress Code: Casual in Marsh Tavern; jackets required in The Colonnade

Weddings: Can be arranged

Rates/Packages: $169–$589 per couple per night; add $60 per person for breakfast and dinner or $80 for breakfast, lunch, and dinner; Honeymoon Package: $436.25 per person, includes 3 nights in deluxe accommodations (upgrade to suite, if available), flowers, champagne, use of fitness spa and mountain bikes. A Fireside Package, at $492 per person, gives you 2 nights in a one-bedroom town house suite with fireplace, bottle of wine, Equinox tartan throw, breakfast and dinner daily, and use of the fitness spa. Ski and spa packages also available.

Payment/Credit Cards: Most major

Deposit: 1-night deposit required to confirm reservation and will be applied to last night of visit. Refunds will be issued only if cancellation is received 30 days before your scheduled arrival date. Cancellations are subject to a $30 processing fee.

Government Taxes: Vermont rooms and meals tax

Service Charges: $2.50 per room per night housekeeping gratuity

≈≈≈

Woodstock Inn & Resort

Location: Centrally located in Vermont near the New Hampshire border.
Romantic Features: En-suite fireplaces; New England village setting.

If you are dreaming of a honeymoon in New England—with warm fires crackling and snow falling on the mountains, or brilliant fall foliage shading a village green lined by pristine clapboard houses, or perhaps lazy summer days strolling on woodland trails—your fantasies will turn into reality when you arrive in Woodstock, Vermont. At the heart of this beautiful little town of only about 2,500 people lies the stately Woodstock Inn & Resort, a lovely inn built by Laurance S. Rockefeller in 1969 on the site of the original inn and tavern, which dated back to 1793.

It's a resort you can enjoy all by itself. The impressive facilities include a putting green located in the courtyard of the inn; the Woodstock Country Club, with its superb golf course, Woodstock Health & Fitness Center, and Ski Touring Center; the nearby Suicide Six ski area; and many planned activities. But just outside your door is the delightful village of Woodstock, with all its eighteenth- and nineteenth-century homes, interesting shops, covered bridges, and historic places like the Billings Farm & Museum, an active historical museum and working dairy farm depicting what farm life was like in the nineteenth century, and the Marsh-Billings-Rockefeller National Historical Park.

Furnished in Colonial style, with soft reds, greens, and blues, the rooms—fifty recently renovated—are bright and cheery, many opening onto a central courtyard, where the putting green is located. Many have fireplaces—just ask and the staff will lay the logs for you. Beds are covered with handmade quilts and hand-loomed coverlets; bookshelves are filled with hardbacks and paperbacks; and built-in cupboards and bureaus give you plenty of storage space. You also have white louvered blinds that you can close when you wish privacy, as well as modern tile and marble baths.

The lobby area is most inviting, especially on a cold day when the massive, 10-foot fireplace is blazing away. Exceptional original artwork in various styles ranging from primitive to contemporary is located throughout the inn along with antique fixtures, lamps, and furniture.

You can dine in the main dining room at tables elegantly appointed with fine linen and gas lamps or enjoy a more casual meal in the Eagle Cafe. Particularly appealing is Richardson's Tavern, where you can settle into a comfortable sofa in front of the fireplace and sip a cognac before heading to your room. The cozy bar area is a popular gathering place.

Just a five-minute walk down South Street from the inn is the Woodstock Country Club. Here you'll find the 6,001-yard, eighteen-hole, Robert Trent Jones–designed golf course. It's narrow and lined with more than eighty bunkers and has some nasty water hazards guaranteed to give wild hitters more than a few nightmares—the Kedron Brook comes into play on all but six of the eighteen holes. (You might want to leave your driver in the car.) It's also one of the most interesting little courses you'll find in New England.

The 40,000-square-foot recently refurbished Woodstock Health & Fitness Center, located about 1 mile farther south from the Woodstock Country Club, has two indoor tennis courts, two squash courts, two racquetball courts, a 30-by-60-foot lap pool, a whirlpool, a gym, a massage room, and a croquet court. Tennis buffs can enjoy ten outside tennis courts.

In the winter the golf operations turn into the Woodstock Ski Touring Center. Ski trails lace the golf course and beyond, and equipment for sale or rent occupies the space where in the summer you find golf bags, balls, and accessories.

The personal, user-friendly Suicide Six ski area, which opened in 1937, has twenty-two trails in addition to the Face, which is served by two chairlifts and a beginner area with a J-bar. Although the more advanced skiers may prefer to head to nearby Killington, Suicide Six is still a good choice for skiers of all levels who want a pleasant, challenging ski experience. Here you'll find a ski school, ski shop, cafeteria, and lounge-restaurant in the Base Lodge.

Other activities at your fingertips include hiking, biking, horseback riding, fishing, and cultural performances (Dartmouth College's Hopkins Center for the Performing Arts is just a half-hour's drive away). There are also complimentary evening movies at the inn, morning coffee, and afternoon tea and cookies in the Wicker Lounge, a greenhouselike lounge.

Your best bet, if you want to play golf or ski, is to look into a package that

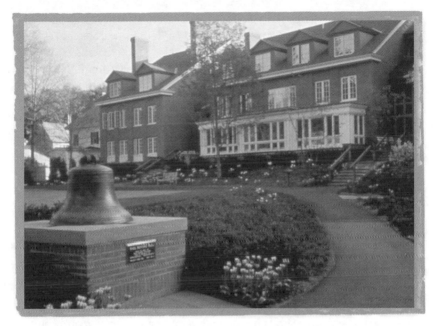

Woodstock Inn & Resort, Vermont

includes these activities. Otherwise you will be charged for the use of many of the sports facilities. For example, greens fees are $44.00 to $75.00 per person; tennis is $11.50 to $14.00 per person, per hour, and inn guests pay $9.75 per person for the use of the racquetball or squash courts. The use of the pool, sauna, steam room, whirlpool, exercise room, and croquet court is complimentary for Woodstock Inn guests.

The Woodstock Inn & Resort is a comfortable, friendly hotel boasting a staff that is eager to see to it you have everything you need. It has just enough spit and polish to make it a top-rated property, yet is not pretentious or stuffy. It's a place you'll want to come back to on your first anniversary.

Address/Phone: Fourteen the Green, Woodstock, VT 05091-1298; (802) 457–1100; fax (802) 457–6699

E-mail: email@woodstockinn.com

Web Site: www.woodstockinn.com (reservations accepted online)

U.S. Reservations: (800) 448–7900

Owner/Manager: Chet Williamson, president and general manager; Tom List, inn manager; Chuck Vanderstreet, Woodstock Health & Fitness Center/Country Club/ski area manager

Arrival/Departure: Daily air service available from New York, Hartford, and Boston to Lebanon, New Hampshire. Taxi and car rentals available at Lebanon Airport.

Distance from Lebanon Airport: 15 miles; 138 miles from Albany; 148 miles from Boston

Distance from Woodstock: In heart of town

Accommodations: 144 rooms and suites, 23 with fireplaces

Best Room/Suite: The fireplace rooms or Suites 304 and 349

Amenities: Toiletries, air-conditioning, telephones, clock radio, ironing facilities, cable TV, VCR, bathrobes; fireplace (some); concierge services; room service; valet parking

Electricity: 110 volts

Sports and Facilities: Putting green, outdoor pool, 12 tennis courts (2 indoor, 6 clay, 4 all-weather); 18-hole golf course, practice green, pro shop, practice range; 2 squash courts, 2 racquetball courts; lap pool; whirlpool; 10-station Nautilus room; aerobics room; steam baths, saunas; croquet court; ski trails, Alpine ski center; horseback riding; biking; hiking; fishing

Dress Code: Casual; jackets customary and encouraged in dining room; blue jeans, T-shirts, and swim shorts not permitted on golf course or tennis courts

Weddings: Can be arranged

Rates/Packages: $165–$340 per couple; add $55 per person per day for MAP (breakfast and dinner); honeymoon package at $1,034 per couple includes 3 nights' accommodations, breakfast and dinner daily, 2 days of complimentary sports in season, champagne, and special gift. Classic Romance: $591 per couple, includes 2 nights' accommodations, breakfast daily, one dinner for two, flowers, champagne, cordial nightcap. Tennis, golf, and ski packages available.

Payment/Credit Cards: Most major

Deposit: Two-night deposit required to confirm reservation and will be applied to first and last nights of visit. Refunds will be issued only if cancellation is received one week before your scheduled arrival date. Cancellations are subject to a $15 processing fee.

Government Taxes: 7 percent Vermont rooms and meals tax

Service Charges: Not included

WEST VIRGINIA

≈≈≈

The Greenbrier

Location: On a 6,500-acre estate in the Allegheny Mountains, in White Sulphur Springs, West Virginia.

Romantic Features: Victorian carriage ride followed by private lunch in gazebo; sleigh rides in the Allegheny foothills; fireplaces.

The Greenbrier, a venerable bastion of Southern gentility and great golf, is a destination in itself—a place to come for golf, tennis, hiking in the great outdoors, and other gracious pleasures, such as afternoon tea, carriage rides, late-night hot chocolate, croquet, and horseback riding. Mineral baths, an array of spa treatments, good food, and dancing in the cocktail lounge are all part of the scene here.

Grooms will have to pack their ties and jackets and brides will get to wear their favorite fancies. At The Greenbrier tradition reigns, and dressy attire is required for dinner at two of the resort's six restaurants. Black tie is also acceptable.

When the rich and famous traveled here in the mid-1800s to revive themselves in the famous mineral waters and socialize with their peers, they told their friends they were going to the "Old White." The guest book of this stately grande dame includes such historical greats as Dolley Madison, Andrew Jackson, Thomas Edison, and John F. Kennedy. At least twenty-three presidents have come here to take in the fresh mountain air and Southern hospitality.

The original 400-foot-long building is gone, but in its place a majestic Georgian-style structure with pillars and rows of windows sits like a great European castle in the midst of a sea of green pine. Most impressive.

This is not exactly a place you'd describe as intimate or cozy. Any resort that claims to sit on 6,500 acres is major stuff. However, accommodations such as the cottages and suites give you all the privacy you want along with a generous dash of luxury.

The public and private rooms are truly grand. The designer Carleton Varney orchestrates all the interior decoration, including the creation of new fabric and wallpaper designs every year. Each of the hotel's 672 rooms and suites has its own unique decor. Yards and yards of brightly flowered fabric, richly swagged and draped around the high windows; bed canopies and pillows; upholstered chairs and chaises; and bedspreads create surprising riots of fresh color against walls and carpets of reds, emerald greens, and yellows. No fainthearted application of color here! Furnishings are a combination of traditional period

The Greenbrier, West Virginia

antiques and antique reproductions, along with gilt-framed mirrors, paintings, and Oriental carpets.

In the lofty lounge, in spite of the dramatic black-and-white marble floor and high columns, chairs and tables have been arranged in intimate, inviting groupings conducive to a quiet chat, a game of backgammon, or afternoon tea, to the accompaniment of chamber music.

If you want to hide away in your own cottage, ask for accommodations in one of the guest houses. The cottages are airy and roomy, and each has its own porch, fireplace, oversize tub, wet bar or kitchen, separate parlor, and dressing room.

With the staff of 1,600 outnumbering the guests, you can be totally decadent and do nothing but allow yourself to be pampered. If your journey here has been a long one, perhaps the first place you should visit is the Spa. In addition to a Greek-inspired, Olympic-size pool ringed with pillars and patterned tile work, you'll find whirlpool baths, saunas, herbal wraps, and massages—over eighteen different treatments.

For the more energetic there are aerobics classes, exercise equipment, and other instruments designed for hard labor. There are guided hiking excursions along the miles of mapped and unmapped trails on The Greenbrier grounds and on nearby Kate's Mountain and plenty of tennis courts, indoors and outdoors, along with three great golf courses. Winding through the rolling countryside at the base of the starkly beautiful Allegheny Mountains, these courses give golfers a visual gift as well as a challenge. Newer golfers may prefer the picturesque, gentle-on-your-score Lakeside course. The more competent links mavens can tee off on the championship Nicklaus layout or the Old White, a traditional favorite.

Golf packages are one of the better deals here, giving you unlimited golf, use of a practice range, a professional clinic, and daily club cleaning and storage as well as breakfast and dinner. It is quite a bargain, as the cost to a nonguest for just playing the course is over $200 with cart.

For a special romantic day, Greenbrier's Romantic Rendezvous takes you on a Victorian carriage ride on the grounds and ends at their gazebo, where a waiter serves you lunch. The cost for this treat is $185 per couple.

When it comes time to eat, you have a lot of choices. The main dining room, the largest of the eateries, is an elegant affair with chandeliers, pillars, and ornate plasterwork. Meals, featuring continental and American cuisine, are served with a flourish. The presentation is a work of art. Be sure to save room for the chocolate truffles.

The Drapers Cafe is fun, colorful, and informal. Here you can get breakfast, lunch, and dessert and good things from the soda fountain. For a cozy, intimate meal, try the Tavern Room, which specializes in American food, seafood, and rotisserie selections. (Although rates include breakfast and dinner, you'll pay a surcharge to eat here.)

If you are coming from the golf course, you can stop at the newly opened Sam Snead's for fine dining in a casual setting. You can also catch the latest sports events on TV along with afternoon food and beverages at Slammin' Sammy's, adjacent to Sam Snead's.

There is also the Old White Club for cocktails and dancing and the Rhododendron Cocktail Lounge. In other words, there are plenty of places to eat, suitable for whatever mood you're in.

Many of the vegetables and fruits come from the local markets, and there are local specialties such as fresh trout. The Tavern serves its own ice cream, made daily. Especially popular at breakfast are the warm, homemade muffins and buckwheat cakes. And if you're into watching what you eat, The Greenbrier has introduced its Greenbrier Light Cuisine, with one-third the calories and low-fat.

You won't have to go very far if you want to shop. There is a major shopping arcade right in the main building, with stores like Orvis and The Sam Snead Memorabilia Shop. There is also another group of craft shops on the grounds, selling some really good handicraft items.

Address/Phone: White Sulphur Springs, WV 24986; (304) 536–1110; fax (304) 536–7834

Web Site: www.greenbrier.com

U.S. Reservations: (800) 624–6070

Owner/Manager: Ted J. Kleisner, president and managing director

Arrival/Departure: Amtrak offers train service to The Greenbrier from New York and Chicago, with intermediate stops in Philadelphia, Wilmington, Baltimore, Washington, D.C., Indianapolis, and Cincinnati

Distance from Greenbrier Valley Airport, in Lewisburg: 12 miles (15 minutes)

Distance from Washington D.C.: 250 miles southwest

Accommodations: 670 rooms, 33 suites, 71 guest houses

Best Room/Suite: Guest houses (Paradise Row or Spring Row) or Garden Suites

Amenities: Air-conditioning, hair dryer, clock radio, minibar, toiletries, bathrobes, wet bars or kitchens in some suites, TV, fireplaces in guest houses; nightly turndown service, 24-hour room service

Electricity: 110 volts

Sports and Facilities: 3 golf courses; 20 tennis courts; indoor and outdoor swimming pools; mountain biking; falconry academy; horseback riding; carriage rides; croquet; shooting preserve; whitewater rafting trips; hiking, jogging, and parcourse fitness trails; fishing; bowling; sleigh rides; Golf Academy, Land Rover Driving School, and cross-country skiing. There is also a 29,000-square-foot spa with all sorts of mineral baths, massage, and exercise facilities.

Dress Code: Casual by day; jacket and tie for dinner, except in golf club restaurant

Weddings: Can be arranged

Rates/Packages: $167–$339 per person (double occupancy), including breakfast and dinner. Honeymoon packages are $546 per couple per night, including breakfast, dinner, champagne, and a photo. However, if you're into golf or tennis, you'd do better to take the golf or tennis packages, which are priced from $300 and $270 per person daily, respectively, and give you breakfast, dinner, unlimited golf or plenty of tennis plus a clinic and some balls.

Payment/Credit Cards: Most major

Deposit: $225–$450, depending on time of reservations. Late arrival or early departure causes forfeiture of deposit unless cancellation or changes are made 7 to 15 days in advance, depending on reservation dates.

Government Taxes: 6 percent

Service Charges: $21 per person per day

Canada

ALBERTA
≈≈≈

Banff Springs Hotel

Location: Nestled in the mountains at the confluence of the Bow and Spray Rivers in the Canadian Rockies.

Romantic Features: Castlelike features; awesome views; fresh mountain air; fireplaces; spa treatments and massages for two.

Modeled after a Scottish baronial castle, the Banff Springs Hotel reigns over the majestic mountains and hills that surround it. This massive stone hotel—with it steeply pitched green roofs and gables topped by finials of gold and its gray granite walls, turretlike wings, and arched passageways—would be right at home perched in the Alps. Built in 1888 by the Canadian Pacific Railroad to provide its passengers with an oasis of opulence, it has enough rooms to accommodate a king, a queen, and their entire court.

Called "Castle in the Rockies," grand features include king-sized fireplaces, massive chandeliers, and print fabrics in deep rich tones. The Banff Springs Hotel invites you to have it both ways: the wilderness experience—trail rides, hiking, and biking—along with luxuries like a full service spa, fireplaces, minibars, and tons of shops. Certainly its appeal has attracted its share of notables over the years, including Clint Eastwood, Wayne Gretzky, Ivana Trump, and Tina Turner.

A truly four seasons resort, in the summer flowers overflow in hanging baskets and thrive happily in the gardens, golfers head to the tees, hikers and bikers hit the trails, and whitewater rafters swoosh down the swollen rivers.

In the winter the fireplaces get cranked up, the ski tows start running, and cross-country skiers head out on the miles of trails. And any time of year it's an easy walk to the center of Banff, where a number of shops and cafes beckon to browsers and buyers.

Rooms and suites located in the main building and in the adjacent Manor House are furnished in mostly Victorian style in deep reds, greens, and browns. Unique heritage accessories such as glass bottles, leather-bound books, and brass candlesticks are placed here and there. Views are of the mountains, the pine forests, and the golf course.

On the picturesque twenty-seven–hole golf course, which winds along the valley at the base of the mountains and along the Bow River, wildlife often call the shots. Elk are at times as plentiful as geese. This is especially true in the fall, rutting season, when the big guys get all charged up and herd together all the females they can bully. Rangers are called almost on a daily basis to shoo the elk to the sidelines. (A word of caution: Heed posted warnings and don't try to approach an elk with a camera or a club. The bulls can get testy.)

If you want to kick back and head into the hills, Holiday on Horseback offers hourly and two- to six-day overnight pack trips from its base near the hotel. About a four- to five-hour ride through some pretty spectacular countryside, you'll reach Sundance Lodge, a two-story log house with a wide veranda. The lodge has several bedrooms. Beds are very comfortable and food is plentiful—perhaps a ham or roast beef with all the trimmings and homemade pie. In the evening guests gather around the campfire to swap tales and roast marshmallows. The lodge is solar heated and remarkably warm and cozy. Farther up the trail is Halfway Lodge, for folks who want something even more rustic and a longer trip.

Banff Springs Hotel also participates in the Heritage Mountaineering and Interpretive Hiking Program, offering hikes led by certified mountain guides and naturalists.

At the end of a day's hiking or riding, or just anytime for that matter, the full service European-style Solace Spa and Fitness Centre, a $12 million dollar 35,000-square-foot facility, pampers you with aromatic wraps, refreshing facials, scrubs, baths, and hour-long massages. There is a sauna, Jacuzzi, inhalation room, and steam room as well as a 105-foot saltwater pool divided into lanes for doing laps. In another area mineral water cascades in silvery sheets into three massage pools heated at different temperatures; from there you can step into a larger therapeutic mineral pool and then relax on the cushioned lounges.

Outside there is another heated pool open year-round and a large Jacuzzi. Solace also boasts a fully equipped cardio- and strength-conditioning fitness center and an aerobics theater where daily classes are scheduled. Views of mountains and dense stands of pine all around complete the blissful picture.

With seventeen restaurants and lounges, including Rob Roy, the hotel's signature restaurant, Grapes, an European bistro and wine bar, and Samurai, where you can make a meal out of their California rolls, the only decision you have to make when it comes time to eat is do you turn right or left out of the elevator.

You can spend a week, a month, or more at the Banff Springs Hotel and never tire of things to do or see.

Address/Phone: P.O. Box 960, Banff, Alberta T0L 0C0; (403) 762–2211; fax (403) 762–5755

Web Site: www.cphotels.ca

U.S. Reservations: (800) 441–1414

Owner/Manager: Canadian Pacific Hotels, owner; Edward T. Kissane, regional vice president and general manager

Arrival/Departure: Shuttle service available from Calgary Airport

Distance from Calgary Airport: 80 miles; (1½ hours)

Distance from Calgary: 80 miles

Accommodations: 770 rooms and suites

Best Room/Suite: Tower rooms feature a spiral staircase leading to a loft, which may have a round bed, a Jacuzzi, and great views of the valley.

Amenities: Coffee/teamaker, minibar, TV, radio, hair dryer, bathrobes, iron/ironing board, toiletries; some have fireplaces, parlors, oversized whirlpools, saunas

Electricity: 110 volts

Sports and Facilities: Solace Spa and Fitness Centre features cascading waterfalls, mineral whirlpools, indoor and outdoor saltwater pools, solaria, steam rooms, saunas, and various treatments; 27 holes of golf, 5 tennis courts, hiking, biking, horseback riding, bowling, rollerblading, whitewater rafting, canoeing, fishing, interpretive walks, rock climbing, mountaineering, skiing, heliskiing, snowboarding, ice skating, dogsledding, tobogganing, horse-drawn sleigh rides, curling, hockey

Dress Code: Resort casual; jacket and tie requested in the Rob Roy Room during summer months

Weddings: Can be arranged

Rates/Packages: Canadian Rockies Experience package includes accommodations, meals, unlimited sports, gratuities, and sight-seeing. Summer package is priced from $538 per room per day; winter from $513. Outdoor activities include golf, canoeing, cycling, fishing, hiking, Heritage Mountaineering and Interpretive Hiking Program, sleigh rides, ski lift tickets

Payment/Credit Cards: Most major

Deposit: By credit card

Government Taxes: 12 percent

Service Charges: Sometimes included

Chateau Lake Louise

Location: In Banff National Park in the Canadian Rockies.
Romantic Features: Awesome views of crystal-clear lake and mountains; horse-drawn sleigh rides; fireplaces; moonlight skating.

B uilt in 1913 this white stucco resort is huge, with sweeping vistas of the snow-topped mountains that cradle a stunning glacier-fed turquoise lake. Even at night the lake glows, a shimmery, glassy surface framed by the jagged steep cliffs, pine-clad hills, and striated rock formations that have shifted over thousands of years to slant toward the water. Dark blue velvet skies ringed by patches of misty clouds sparkle with stars. The resort twinkles with tiny white lights, creating an outdoor wonderland. Then daylight. The lake, not large, is a watercolor of reflections fanning out from the narrower end, where the glacier lies receding in the distance.

From the beginning Chateau Lake Louise was built to appeal to guests with outdoor interests. Its orientation to one of the most beautiful lakes in North America and its setting of manicured lawns and gardens surrounded by densely forested mountains laced with hiking, biking, skiing and horseback riding trails, rock faces to climb, and rivers to conquer hold enough interests and challenges to appeal to sportspersons of all skill levels.

Some come simply to soak up the scenery and enjoy a variety of dining experiences. Famous guests have included Queen Elizabeth II, Mary Astor, John Barrymore, Cary Grant, Prince Rainier of Monaco, and many of today's Hollywood celebrities.

With close to 500 rooms and suites, Chateau Lake Louise could hardly be called your cozy inn in the Rockies. Yet within its walls there are intimate spaces, comfortable sofas, warm-paneled wood lounges, and fireside groupings. Built to celebrate the outdoors, the hotel has immense arched windows that frame the mountain peaks and paths that lead to the water's edge and along it.

Rooms and suites are spacious and oriented toward the lake or the mountains. Some have balconies and oversize whirlpool tubs. High ceilings, rich, thick carpets in greens and reds, hand-painted folk art on each guest room door, chandeliers, brass fixtures and wood paneling are featured in public rooms and guest accommodations. Special touches include such items as books on the shelf, glass bottles, and candlesticks. A shopping arcade sells everything from Canadian sweaters and fleeces to jewelry and Irish goods, including wool capes, sweaters, and crystal.

Restaurants include Walliser Stube, specializing in Swiss Alpine cuisine—the fondue and raclette are excellent. For casual dining there is the Poppy Room, serving breakfast, lunch, and dinner, and the Glacier Saloon, where the Old West comes alive. The Edelweiss Dining Room features world-class cuisine, and in the Victoria Dining Room you can experience grand dining in a European atmosphere punctuated by beautiful chandeliers, linens, and china. Backpackers can stock up at the Chateau Deli on water, sandwiches, soups, and desserts; cocktails are available in the Lobby Bar.

Recalling the time one hundred years ago when Swiss guides arrived in the area, greatly boosting the hiking and mountain climbing activities, Chateau Lake Louise has launched its Heritage Mountaineering and Interpretive Hiking Program. There are hikes for all levels, from those just moderately fit to the highly experienced. Certified mountain guides and naturalists take you on a wonderful journey of from four to ten hours.

"Prepare to leave civilization," cautions Naturalist Guide Bruce Bembridge in a hushed tone. The snow continues to fall through the trees, the ice on the path melts into dark wet patches. Snow clings to spiderweb threads hanging from pine branches like Christmas tree icicles. You continue walking down the hill, finally reaching the wide open grounds that lead to the entrance of the hotel. You have left the tiny blue flowers poking through the snow, the views high up and through the spruce and firs of Lake Louise, the teahouse perched on a mountain peak, the chipmunks gathering and cracking nuts. It's all so breathtakingly beautiful.

Address/Phone: Lake Louise, Alberta T0L 1C0; (403) 522–3511; fax (403) 522–3111

Web Site: www.cphotels.ca

U.S. Reservations: (800) 441–1414

Owner/Manager: Canadian Pacific Hotels, owner; David M. Bayne, general manager

Arrival/Departure: Shuttle service available from Calgary Airport

Distance from Calgary Airport: 120 miles; (2½ hours)

Distance from Banff: 36 miles

Accommodations: 489 rooms, including 81 suites; 26 rooms have whirlpools, and 4 are split-level suites with balconies

Best Room/Suite: Junior Suites on upper floors with sitting areas and lake views; the Belvedere Suites, two-level accommodations with balconies overlooking lakes and mountains; Room 303 with its coffered ceiling, wide balcony, and wood paneling is especially grand; Number 536, decorated in the Victorian style, has an elegant living room, balcony, fireplace flanked by bookcases, and a bathroom and powder room.

Amenities: Minibars, hair dryers, TVs, dressing table, toiletries, coffee/tea facilities, iron/ironing board, robes, fan

Electricity: 110 volts

Sports and Facilities: Recreation center with indoor pool, whirlpool, steamrooms, weights and exercise equipment; walking, hiking, canoeing, tennis, fishing, mountaineering, rock climbing, dogsledding, Alpine and cross-country skiing, ice skating, river rafting, golf, guided snowshoeing expeditions, snow-boarding, heliskiing, horse-drawn sleigh rides, curling, hockey, broom ball; guided trail rides and overnight horseback adventures; arcade and video room; art classes

Dress Code: Resort casual; jacket and tie required for Edelweiss Dining Room

Weddings: Can be arranged

Rates/Packages: Canadian Rockies Experience package includes accommodations, meals, unlimited sports, gratuities, and sight-seeing. Summer package is priced from $539 per room per day; winter, from $492. Outdoor activities include canoeing, cycling, fishing, hiking, Heritage Mountaineering and Interpretive Hiking Program, sleigh rides, ski lift tickets

Payment/Credit Cards: Most major

Deposit: By credit card

Government Taxes: 12 percent

Service Charges: Sometimes included

≋≋≋

Jasper Park Lodge

Location: On 903 acres in Jasper National Park, one of North America's largest wilderness areas.

Romantic Features: Awesome views; fresh mountain air; fireplaces; wildlife all around.

It began as an eight-bungalow wilderness retreat at the turn of the century in the 4,200 acre Jasper National Park, a place where people could escape and reconnect with nature. And they came: the Kennedys, John Travolta, Marilyn Monroe, Bob Newhart, and many others who could afford the best.

Today Jasper Park Lodge has grown: more cottages, more facilities, a wonderful main lodge with enormous lounges, shopping arcade, dining rooms, swimming pool, golf clubhouse, and outdoor Jacuzzi. Still, although it now has close to 450 rooms and seven places to eat and drink, it has emerged with its integrity intact. It continues to appeal to anyone who appreciates cool mountain air, walking along lakeshore paths, going to bed hearing the plaintive calls of elk, skipping stones across a white-blue translucent lake, sitting in front of a crackling fire drinking hot chocolate, and heading out to the golf course, ski trails, or other outdoor pursuits for fresh air and exercise.

Jasper Park Lodge, a comfortable enclave of log cabins and cedar chalets, features spacious, well-appointed rooms with all the amenities you could wish for, including padded hangers, minibars, TVs, down duvets, king-size beds, large picture windows, pine armoires, and colorful burgundy, green, and brown print fabrics. Some rooms open onto decks or patios; some have fireplaces and oversized whirlpool baths. One thing is certain, you may be stomping around the grounds and surrounding mountains in your wool socks and hiking boots, but when it comes time to eat or hit the sack, you'll find nothing rough about your accommodations.

Cottages range in size from three bedrooms, each with private bath, to Milligan Manor, with eight bedrooms, nine baths and a 900-square-foot living and dining room. The Point and Overlook, older cabins loaded with charm, feature several well-appointed bedrooms, lofty living room, kitchen, and dining room (Bill Gates and his family rented one of these on a recent vacation). Since all rooms in these multibedroom cabins are complete in themselves, with en-suite baths and outside entrances, they can be rented singly but are also ideal for a group of couples who desire private bedrooms but the use of a central living, dining, and kitchen area.

Those seeking privacy can book their own one-bedroom cabin that sits on a bluff overlooking the water and comes with a separate living room, fireplace, and a whirlpool tub-for-two. Other options include the Whistler king suites, featuring enormous vaulted-ceiling living rooms with fireplaces and kitchens; French doors open onto decks overlooking the lake.

Golfers will find the Stanley Thompson–designed golf course challenging but very playable. Tees on the course, which meanders along the shores of Lac Beauvert, are oriented to mountain peaks and some holes require driving over water. All but three of the holes are fenced to keep elk off the fairways and greens.

Restaurants range from the elegant Edith Cavell Dining Room, serving gourmet cuisine, to the Tent City Sports Pub, a sports bar offering billiards and shuffleboard and pub-style food. When dining at the Edith Cavell, be sure to try the mushroom chowder; it's the best. Also good is the filet of Alberta beef tenderloin on a Yukon Gold potato cake, the fresh lemon curd flan, and the birch and apple cider–basted British Columbia salmon filet. Fresh herb and vegetables grown in Jasper's greenhouse are used in food preparation; breads and pastries are freshly baked.

All the mountain-oriented sports and activities are available at Jasper, including the Heritage Mountaineering and Interpretive Hiking Program and horseback riding. For a memorable adventure arrange a rafting trip with Mount Robson Whitewater Rafting, about forty-five minutes from the hotel in Valemount, B.C. Operated by the Cinnamon family, this company has more than twenty years' experience in taking venturesome travelers down the spectacular Fraser River, the longest river in British Columbia. At the end of the trip, chow down on some of the best veggie or hamburgers you'll ever taste—the recipe is a secret.

Jasper Park Lodge is a peaceful place. Listen very carefully as you walk along the paths and through the pines. Shhh. You may be able to hear the soft tread of the eclectic group of early adventurers who explored the land and climbed the mountains.

Address/Phone: P.O. Box 40, Jasper, Alberta T0E 1E0; (780) 852–3301; fax (780) 852–5107

Web Site: www.cphotels.ca

U.S. Reservations: (800) 441–1414

Owner/Manager: Canadian Pacific Hotels, owner; Kevin Toth, general manager

Arrival/Departure: Shuttle service available from Calgary Airport

Distance from Calgary Airport: 256 miles (4 hours)

Distance from Edmonton: 225 miles

Accommodations: 446 rooms, suites, cabins and chalets

Best Room/Suite: Number 467 (Athabasca) known as the "Honeymoon Cottage"; Whistler king lakeside suites also good

Amenities: Bathrobes, coffeemaker, minibar, TV, radio, hair dryer, iron/ironing board, umbrellas, scales, toiletries, turndown service; some have fireplaces, oversized whirlpool baths

Electricity: 110 volts

Sports and Facilities: Walking, hiking, fishing, mountaineering, rock climbing, dogsledding; Alpine and cross-country skiing, ice skating, river rafting, biking, helihiking, canoeing, sleigh rides, canyon ice crawling, snowmobile tours; 18-hole golf course, 4 tennis courts (hard surface); game room and fitness center with exercise equipment, steamroom and whirlpool; year-round heated outdoor pool; Miette hot springs; guided snowshoeing expeditions; billiards; guided trail rides and overnight horseback adventures

Dress Code: Resort casual

Weddings: Can be arranged

Rates/Packages: Canadian Rockies Experience package includes accommodations, meals, unlimited sports, gratuities, and sight-seeing. Summer package is priced from $493 per room per day; winter, from $440. Outdoor activities include golf, canoeing, cycling, fishing, hiking, Heritage Mountaineering and Interpretive Hiking Program, sleigh rides, ski lift tickets

Payment/Credit Cards: Most major

Deposit: By credit card

Government Taxes: 12 percent

Service Charges: Sometimes included

QUEBEC

≈≈≈

La Pinsonnière

Location: On the banks of the St. Lawrence River, in the picturesque Charlevoix region north of Quebec City.

Romantic Features: Private fireplaces; terraces above the river; whirlpool baths for two.

T his small inn, which lies between the Laurentian Mountains and the tidal flats of the St. Lawrence River, is a real find for those honeymooning in Canada. La Pinsonnière, which means "house of the finches," sits about 200 feet up a bluff overlooking the river, which at this point is wider than one of the Finger Lakes is long. This sprawling white manor house, with its pointed towers and garden setting ringed by tall trees, would seem equally at home on the Loire River in France's château country.

The personal involvement of owners Jean and Janine Authier, who purchased the mansion several years ago and converted it into an inn, is just one reason this property is so special. The Authiers, along with their daughter, Valérie, La Pinsonnière's manager, are committed to providing their guests with an exceptional place to stay and dine. Their restaurant, with its French-trained

La Pinsonnière, Quebec

chef, has already received a number of awards and has gained a reputation for serving some of the finest cuisine in Canada.

In addition to the hotel business, the Authiers have an avid interest in the arts. Contemporary paintings by Quebec artists, many for sale, hang in the dining room and in other places throughout the inn.

Each of the rooms has a personality all its own; several have been recently redecorated. For example, one has a king-size brass bed, fireplace, private sauna, and large whirlpool tub. Another is a vision of romantic Victoriana, with white wicker and rattan furniture, a white marble bath, lace duvet cover, and puffy white cushions.

Some rooms are decorated in muted traditional colors and feature Queen Anne–style furniture, brass lamps, and wing chairs; others are light and airy, decorated in soft sea colors with rattan and pine furniture and French doors leading to terraces overlooking the river.

Large marble baths with designer soaps, fluffy down duvets, classical music, and chairs you can really sink into and fall asleep in, add up to accommodations that are comfortable but not obtrusive.

La Pinsonnière is located in the Charlevoix region, an area known for its rugged cliffs, rolling hills, coves, and exceptional river views. A late afternoon pleasure for the inn's guests is to sit on the terrace of the hotel's lovely large patio and watch the sun set over the tops of the tall cedar, spruce, and birch trees. You can also follow the path that leads down through a cedar forest to the inn's private, rugged beach, a great place for a picnic. Going down the 226 steps is easy. Going up you'll find rustic benches where you can stop and rest or just sit for a while.

The inn may be small, but it still offers a lot of choices for active couples. There is a tennis court, indoor pool, and massage therapists who can pamper you with a variety of soothing treatments.

In the warmer months, you can hike on the trails in the surrounding hills, take a whale-watching cruise, and play golf at nearby Murray Bay. Cruise up the Saguenay Fjord, the world's southernmost fjord, and marvel at the spectacular scenery of sheer rocky cliffs plunging dramatically down to the river. Or visit the artists' town of Baie Saint Paul, a pleasant drive from the inn, where you can browse through about twenty galleries featuring Charlevoix and Quebec painters. There are also many summer theater productions and concerts held nearby.

If you come in the winter, you can cross-country and downhill ski at Mont Grand Fonds, go snowmobiling, ice skating, and dogsledding and at the end of the day curl up in front of a crackling fire in your room or in the lounge.

Want an adventure? In the warmer months you can climb into a red isothermic suit and head off by boat for the world of the belugas and blue whales that inhabit the Saguenay Marine Arctic Park.

Vistas from La Pinsonnière's restaurant, as well as from most of the rooms, are expansive. Large windows afford marvelous views of the rivers, hills, and trees. Dining by candlelight at a beautifully appointed table is a special pleasure. Cuisine centered on continental fare with an emphasis on French cooking includes dishes such as ravioli croustillants de crabe en velouté de cidre, foie gras de canard poelé aux poires confites, and wild mushrooms served in a delicate sauce. A prix-fixe dinner is $50 for four courses plus tax and service charges. The Authiers' 13,000-bottle wine cellar is impressive, and you are invited to participate in frequent wine tastings.

An exquisite romantic hideaway, the inn is a member of the prestigious Relais & Chateaux group.

Address/Phone: Cap-à-l'Aigle, Charlevoix, Quebec G0T IB0 Canada; (418) 665–4431; fax (418) 665–7156

E-mail: pinsonniere@relaischateaux.fr

Web Site: www.relaischateaux.fr/pinsonniere

U.S. Reservations: (800) 387–4431; Relais & Chateaux, (800) RELAIS–8

Owner/Manager: The Authier family

Arrival/Departure: There is a very small airport, St.-Irenée, about 3 miles from the inn; free pickup can be arranged

Distance from Quebec International Airport: 95 miles

Distance from Quebec City: 90 miles

Accommodations: 26 rooms, including 1 suite

Best Room/Suite: Room 312, which has a rosewood king-size bed, whirlpool bath for two, and sauna with a spectacular view of the St. Lawrence River; Room 211, a creamy white confection with king-size bed, white lace duvet cover, double whirlpool, fireplace, marble bath, and deck

Amenities: Hair dryer, toiletries, fireplace (some rooms), TV, telephones, robes, ceiling fans, air-conditioning, and classical music

Electricity: 110 volts

Sports and Facilities: Indoor pool, hiking, beach, tennis, kayaking, skiing, skating, sauna, whale watching, massage therapy

Dress Code: Smart casual; no jackets required for dinner

Weddings: Can be arranged

Rates/Packages: $110–$450 (Canadian dollars) per couple per night, including breakfast, dinner, and service (low season); $140–$450 (high season—warmer months and holidays)

Payment/Credit Cards: Most major

Deposit: 50 percent of total cost of stay required; balance due on arrival. Refundable if canceled 15 days or more prior to date of arrival.

Government Taxes: 7 percent federal; 7.5 percent provincial

Service Charges: Included

Entry Requirements for U.S. Citizens: Proof of citizenship

Closed: November to mid-December

THE CARIBBEAN
AND BERMUDA

Atlantic Ocean

Bermuda
The Reefs
Cambridge
Beaches

FLORIDA

Grand
Bahama

NASSAU
Andros
Island

Sandals Royal
Bahamian Resort & Spa
Ocean Club
THE
BAHAMAS

Long Island

Acklins
Island

San Salvador

Great Inagua

Mayaguana

Grand Turk

HAITI

DOM. REP.

Casa de Campo

CUBA

Sandals Royal Jamaican
Sandals
Dunn's River
Sandals
Ocho Rios
Grand Lido
Sans Souci

Half Moon
Golf, Tennis,
and Beach Club
Sandals
Montego Bay
Swept Away
Negril
Sandals Negril

JAMAICA

Hyatt Regency
Grand Cayman

Cayman Islands

Peter Island Resort
and Yacht Harbour
Caneel
Bay
ST. JOHN

The Bitter End
Yacht Club
Little Dix Bay
VIRGIN
GORDA
TORTOLA

ANGUILLA
Cap Juluca
ST. MARTIN
La Samanna

ST. KITTS

Misbet Plantation Beach Club
The Golden Lemon Inn & Villas

NEVIS

Four Seasons Resort

Hyatt Regency
Dorado Beach

PUERTO
RICO

Horned Dorset
Primavera Hotel

ANTIGUA
Curtain Bluff

GUADELOUPE

DOMINICA

MARTINIQUE

Sandals St. Lucia
Golf Resort & Spa
Windjammer Landing
La Sport

Anse Chastanet
ST. LUCIA

Cobblers
Cove
BARBADOS

Spice Island
Beach Resort
GRENADA

ARUBA

Hyatt Regency
Aruba Resort & Casino

ANGUILLA

≋≋≋

Cap Juluca

Location: Along Maunday's Bay, on the southern coast of Anguilla, the northernmost island of the Caribbean's Lesser Antilles.

Romantic Features: Sugar-white crescent beach; palatial bathrooms, some with private solarium; intimate "garden rooms" for sunning and relaxing near pool.

C ap Juluca's dazzling white towers, turrets, and arches, set against the dense greens of the foliage and clear turquoise of the Caribbean waters, create a fairy-tale village straight out of the pages of *Arabian Nights*. Nothing but brightly hued blossoms of bougainvillea and waving palm fronds comes between you and your view of the sea from your terrace. Set on 179 acres, all the resort's rooms and villas are just steps away from the white, sugary sand crescent beach; no building is higher than the palm trees.

The exteriors of the buildings, with their parapets and domes, are dramatic enough, but wait until you get inside. Rooms are really large—at least 16 feet by 16 feet—and one-bedroom suites go up to 2,200 square feet. Villas, with up to five bedrooms, have private pools set in an enclosed red-tiled garden courtyard. You can rent bedrooms and suites in the pool villas, or you can rent the entire villa yourself for complete privacy. Bathrooms are outrageously opulent, with tons of marble, double sinks, showers, and bidets. Some have double-size bathtubs with headrests; some open onto a private walled solarium furnished with chaises and a table. Louvered windows let the sea breezes slip through, yet preserve your privacy. You can lie back and catch the sun wearing as little as you want or nothing at all.

Rattan furniture with thick cushions, king-size beds, fine linens, potted palms in clay pots, dark Brazilian walnut doors and trim, white walls, and ceramic tile floors in various muted colors provide a sumptuous setting for romance. Unique accessories, such as wooden bowls and sculpture, leather, and clay, as well as beautiful area rugs, inlaid mirrors, and artwork, many imported from northern Africa, are found in some rooms; others lean toward a more European feeling, with traditional period furnishings and accessories.

There are three tennis courts, and the pro schedules round-robin tournaments every week. There are also a fitness center with state-of-the-art equipment and a croquet court set up British style. Complimentary water sports include waterskiing, sailing, and sailboarding. You can also go scuba diving (this is extra), or if you want to set off on your own "True Love" cruise, you can charter a yacht. You can also get a soothing massage.

No one will intrude on your privacy, even while you're on the beach—unless, of course, you plant a red flag in the sand. This means you would like someone to come over and see what you want, whether it be a clean towel or another Sea Breeze. Intimate "garden rooms," partitioned with hedges, are located around the pool. If you want service, just ring a bell.

Cap Juluca's beaches are long and very walkable. The main beach stretches along Maunday's Bay for about a mile. Go around the eastern end of the headland and there is another 2-mile beach running along Cove Bay. In the center of Maunday's Bay beach is an Olympic-size pool, which is surrounded by white market-style umbrellas and tables along with many lounge chairs—a popular gathering place.

Many guests, especially those who have terraces with great sea views, prefer to have breakfast brought to their room. Fresh fruits and juices, muffins and banana bread, and steaming coffee or tea are beautifully set up on your patio table complete with linen and china. You also get a summary of the latest news from the *New York Times* faxed that morning from the States (just in case you've missed it).

One night you may wish to order a West Indian dinner served on your patio. Linger over a bottle of wine from the resort's extensive wine cellar, and see if you can spot the lights of St. Martin or tiny Saba twinkling across the water.

Cap Juluca has two restaurants: the casually elegant Pimms and the more informal George's. Pimms is tucked into the corner of the protected eastern end of the cove and sits just 6 feet from the water's edge. George's is located midway along Maunday's Bay beach and is open all day for casual dining.

After dinner kick off your shoes and walk hand in hand back to your room along the moonlit beach and be lulled to sleep by the sound of waves rolling up on the shores. Or linger at your table at George's for some dancing under the stars.

When you come to Anguilla, don't expect a roaring nightlife. After all, an island where the 30-mile-an-hour speed limit is reinforced by a series of speed bumps and the airport only allows prop planes to land is not a swinging place. Come here if you like to picnic on an uninhabited island or drift away in a hammock in a garden perfumed with the scents of frangipani, jasmine, and orchids.

Address/Phone: P.O. Box 240, Maunday's Bay, Anguilla, Leeward Islands, British West Indies; (264) 497–6666; fax (264) 497–6617

E-mail: helen@capjuluca.com

Web Site: www.capjuluca.com

U.S. Reservations: (888) 8–Juluca; fax (305) 935–3780

Owner/Manager: Cap Juluca Holdings, Inc., owner; Dion Friedland, chairman of the board; Eustace Guishard, general manager

Arrival/Departure: Anguilla is reached via scheduled air service from San Juan (50 minutes) or St. Martin (5 minutes) or via ferry from Marigot in French St. Martin (25 minutes). Guests are met on arrival.

Distance from Wallblake Airport: 8 miles (15 minutes)

Distance from Marigot, St. Martin: 8 miles (25 minutes by ferry); 5 miles from the valley

Accommodations: 58 luxury rooms and junior suites; 7 suites; 6 pool villas

Best Room/Suite: For privacy try the end units: Pool Villa 19 and a room or suite in Villa Building 12

Amenities: Air-conditioning, ceiling fans, private walled terraces, toiletries, refrigerator, stocked minibar, hair dryer, oversize tub (some), solarium (some), bathrobes; kitchen in villas; twice-daily maid service

Electricity: 110/220 volts

Sports and Facilities: 3 Omni-surface tennis courts (2 lighted), croquet; sailboarding, waterskiing, snorkeling, scuba diving; Hobie-Cats, Sunfishes; Olympic-size pool; 6 villa pools; 3 miles of beach; extra charge for use of 32-foot motor cruiser; massages

Dress Code: Casually elegant and sophisticated; no jacket or tie required

Weddings: Can be arranged

Rates/Packages: $400–$3,740 per couple (spring/fall); $310–$2,160 (summer); $665–$4,895 (winter); $745–$5,385 (holidays); includes continental breakfast on your patio, tennis, watersports, entertainment, use of fitness center, tea. Meal plans available. Romantic Rendezvous (7 nights): $3,955–$5,425, includes accommodations, champagne, continental breakfast, 4 dinners, cruise, snorkeling trip, 1 day car rental, and transfers.

Payment/Credit Cards: Most major

Deposit: 3-night deposit within 14 days. Refunds made only when written notice is received by the hotel no later than 21 days prior to scheduled arrival. Other conditions may apply during peak periods.

Government Taxes: 8 percent (except for package where tax is included)

Service Charges: 10 percent (except for package where service charge is included)

Entry Requirements for U.S. Citizens: Return ticket and proof of citizenship required; passport best

ANTIGUA

≋

Curtain Bluff

Location: Situated on Antigua's south shore, on a private peninsula jutting out into the water between two lovely beaches, one on the Atlantic, the other on the Caribbean.

Romantic Features: Terraces overlooking the sea; dancing under the stars; hammocks for two on your own private patio (executive suites); private dinner in the garden gazebo.

I f there is a pot of gold at the end of one of Antigua's most winding, bumpy roads, it has to be Curtain Bluff. It's worth every torturous mile it takes to get you to this superb little resort, which seduces you from the moment you arrive. Consistently rated as one of the best resorts in the Caribbean for almost forty years, Curtain Bluff rises from a narrow peninsula between two beaches, marking the place where the Caribbean and Atlantic meet, and giving you non-stop ocean views from every room. Bougainvillea, hibiscus, oleander, royal palms, and every other tropical flower you can think of line walkways, hug buildings, and fall in great clouds of blossoms from trellises and walls. And wherever you go, you never lose sight of the sea.

Some of the two-story buildings are spread out along the beach—just take a couple of steps from your patio and you can sink your toes into the sand. The villa suites climb gently up the slope of the peninsula. At the top of the bluff sits the home of the owner, Howard Hulford. It's the crown to Curtain Bluff's string of pink and white buildings and the site of weddings as well as cocktail receptions honoring Curtain Bluff's guests.

There was nothing much on the land when Hulford bought the property, but he brought seeds and cuttings from plants he liked from everywhere, started his own nursery, and soon had the grounds flourishing with palms, flowering shrubs, and other tropical plants. Today Hulford says he enjoys spending at least an hour a day tending to his fledgling seedlings and newly grafted shrubs. This attention to detail by a man who once flew planes for a living is just part of the story and helps explain the beauty and seductive influence Hulford and his beautiful wife, Chelle, have created at Curtain Bluff.

All the rooms and suites are decorated with impeccably good taste by Chelle in soft pastels and natural textures—clay pots, baskets filled with flowers, red tile, and an abundance of plants and real art. Rooms are airy and large with spacious patios, rattan furniture, puffy pillows, and natural fiber rugs on the Italian-tile floors. Large sliding doors, which glide like butter, open onto a spacious, well-furnished seaside patio. Ceiling fans (even in some bathrooms) along with louvered side windows let the sea breezes slip in and keep the rooms fresh and pleasantly cool. There is no air-conditioning, nor is it needed.

White walls and high, vaulted cedar ceilings distinguish the multilevel suites. In addition to the seaside patio, there is another, flower-filled open-air patio on the inland side of your suite, with walls just high enough to give you total privacy while letting the breezes in. A roomy hammock big enough for two is slung across a corner. A dining area, bedroom, bath, and another patio are located on the top level.

All the suite bathrooms are large and luxurious, with lots of tile and marble. They boast twin vanities, endless shelf space, a bidet, a walk-in, no-curtain shower, a large tub, and mirrors ringed with small light bulbs. You also enjoy lots of hot water for those long showers and plenty of electricity.

Each year Curtain Bluff closes down for five months in order to refurbish and refresh. Perhaps this is one reason nothing here ever looks tired or worn.

Dining is on an open terrace, where a band plays every evening. Dance under a spreading tamarind tree and a canopy of stars. Chef Ruedi Portmann, a classic Swiss chef who has been at Curtain Bluff since the mid-'60s and was named Caribbean Chef of the Year in 1991, is adept at preparing delicious American and European cuisine. Ingredients are the freshest you can find in the Caribbean: Fish is delivered every day and is filleted right on the property.

Curtain Bluff has an impressive 25,000-bottle cellar. Dust off a bottle of 1983 Louis Roederer Cristal and toast your bride, or try a bottle of '83 Dom Perignon or an '81 Taittinger Brut Reserve.

On Wednesdays you can warm up to reggae at the beach party, which is held at the bay beach. You can have lunch at the beachfront restaurant, where a lavish buffet tempts you with salads, fish, pasta, and meat dishes.

If you want to eat in the privacy of your room or on your patio, just order room service. It's all included in the price.

Straddling the peninsula, the two beaches offer something for everyone. The waters off the ³/₄-mile beach on the Caribbean side are calm, gentle, and great for swimming. You can sailboard, snorkel, sail, or just laze away the hours on the beach. On the other side the Atlantic stirs up more surf and the winds beckon to sailors and those looking for a little more excitement. A new pool, overlooking the bay beach, has a seating area in the water.

Tennis is big here. With four superbly maintained Laykold courts, lessons, clinics, round-robins, tournaments, or just friendly play keeps the action rolling. There's a good-size stadium for spectators to watch their favorite players as well as a squash court and a croquet field.

The fitness center is well equipped with Trotter treadmills, steppers, and the latest in health and fitness equipment. Aerobics classes are held on an adjacent deck.

There are no TVs in the rooms, but there is Television House, perched high on stilts near the tennis courts and fitness center. Guests gather here to watch events like the Super Bowl and the Kentucky Derby.

The ages and interests of guests range from the older, well-heeled traditionalists to active, younger couples. You'll see a lot of Brits here, especially during January and February. From December 19 to April 14 a jacket is required for gentlemen five nights a week; there's no doubt that the guests here like the idea of "dressing up" for dinner and appreciate the traditions that have evolved over the years since 1961, when Curtain Bluff first opened its doors.

At first glance Curtain Bluff may seem a bit pricey at $4,500 to $6,000 for a week (in the deluxe rooms). But everything is included (except wine by the bottle), even the scuba diving and the deep-sea fishing. Curtain Bluff is for those who love a beautiful, warm place by the sea where they can get away and totally unwind while a superb, dedicated group of people see to it that nothing interferes with this vision of what paradise should be.

Address/Phone: P.O. Box 288, Antigua, West Indies; (268) 462–8400; fax (268) 462–8409

Web Site: www.curtainbluff.com

Owner/Manager: Howard W. Hulford, owner and chairman, board of directors; Robert S. Sherman, managing director; Calvert A. Roberts, general manager

U.S. Reservations: (888) 289–9898 or (212) 289–8888

Arrival/Departure: Taxi to and from airport. Local regulations prevent hotel from sending drivers.

Distance from V. C. Bird International Airport: 15 miles (35 minutes)

Distance from St. John's: 9 miles

Accommodations: 63 rooms and suites, all with terraces and all overlooking the sea: 51 deluxe with king-size bed or 2 double beds; the Terrace Room with four-poster king-size bed (popular with honeymooners); 5 one-bedroom suites, 1 junior suite, and 5 executive/deluxe rooms, all with king-size beds

Best Room/Suite: The Terrace Room, with its huge terrace, and the one-bedroom suites

Amenities: Hair dryer, wall safe, ceiling fans, bathrobes, telephones, fresh flowers daily, real hangers; suites have minibars; full room service at no extra charge

Electricity: 110 volts

Sports and Facilities: 4 tennis courts, squash court, putting green, swimming pool, fitness center; waterskiing, sailboarding, scuba diving, snorkeling, sailing, croquet, deep-sea fishing, swimming, aerobics (land and water)

Dress Code: Curtain Bluff has recently relaxed its rule that formerly required gentlemen to wear tie and jacket every evening for dinner. Ties for men, even in peak season, are now optional at dinner. Jackets are required except on Sunday and Wednesday at peak season.

Weddings: Can be arranged. Good locations are the garden gazebo and the terrace of the owner's house.

Rates/Packages: All-inclusive rates include accommodations, three meals daily, all bar drinks, afternoon tea, hors d'oeuvres, tennis, weekly beach party, entertainment, mail service, and water sports including scuba diving. $725–$995 per couple per night (mid-December to mid-April); $555–$795 per couple per night (mid-October to mid-December and mid-April to mid-May).

Payment/Credit Cards: American Express, personal check, traveler's check

Deposit: 3-night deposit; cancellation 30 days in advance for full refund, except for December 16 to January 1, when cancellation must be received before November 1

Government Taxes: 8.5 percent

Service Charges: 10 percent

Entry Requirements for U.S. Citizens: Passport

Closed: Mid-May to mid-October

ARUBA
≈≈≈

Hyatt Regency Aruba Resort & Casino

Location: On Aruba's historic Palm Beach, known for its white, sandy beaches and turquoise waters, on the southwestern coast of Aruba, 14 miles off the coast of Venezuela.

Romantic Features: Terraces overlooking the Caribbean; walking along the white sand beach under the moonlight.

W hen you get to Aruba, don't bother trying to find a weather report in any local newspaper or on the TV. You won't find one, because the weather never changes. All they need to do is to put up a permanent sign reading, "About eighty-two to eighty-three degrees. Clear blue Caribbean skies with an occasional puffy white cloud shaped like popcorn floating by, winds about 16 miles per hour; and no rain. If anything's gonna change, we'll call you." This is just one reason Aruba is one of the more popular island destinations.

There are a lot of hotels here, most of them lined up along the broad, white Palm Beach, which stretches along the southwestern coast for several miles. An all-around good choice for romantics is the Hyatt Regency Aruba Resort & Casino. It's got a lot going for it.

As you check in and feel Aruba's famous trade winds blowing through the expansive, open-air lobby, you'll feel you've wandered back to a classic time of luxury and elegance. There are magnificent chandeliers, wooden beams, Oriental rugs, and frescoes on the walls and ceilings. A sense of Aruban history pervades this relatively new resort: The architecture of the Hyatt borrows from the 1899 Gold Smelting Works of Balashi and Bushiribana on the North Coast of Aruba. The grounds, more lush than the rest of this desert island, do not disappoint.

Just off the lobby, walkways curve down toward the beach along waterfalls and the hotel's cascading, three-tiered pool—check out the two-story water slide. There's also a 5,000-square-foot pool stocked with tropical fish, and there are large aviaries of exotic birds. Here in this lush landscape, you'll find plenty of secluded areas in which to bask in the sun as well as larger patios if you wish to mingle.

The Hyatt's pools end where Aruba's white, sandy Palm Beach begins. The trade winds keep the temperature at a comfortable level, allowing you to loll in the sun with a tropical drink from one of the Hyatt's outdoor bars or to enjoy the shade at one of the resort's thatch-umbrella tables. If you want to be more active, you can join in a game of beach volleyball or go parasailing, scuba diving, sailboarding—something Aruba is known for—or simply float on a raft in the 80-degree Caribbean Sea.

In addition to offering the usual water sports, the hotel's Red Sail Sports Center also features Balia catamaran cruises, canoe rentals, scuba diving, and sunset cruises.

While the turquoise water welcomes visitors with its gently rolling waves on this side of the island, you should pay a visit to the northeastern coast, where rough waves crash in, carving out craggy cliffs. Here the remains of the island's original inhabitants, such as tools and hieroglyphics left in chalk caves, together with twisting rock formations, lend a historical, desert-island feel to Aruba. The windswept, native divi divi trees lean over in 45-degree angles like giant bonsai trees; iguanas perched on rocks, and cacti complete the picture. Land tours of the island are readily available and can be arranged through the Hyatt.

A sporting way to explore the desert landscape is to play a round of golf on Aruba's newly built Tierra del Sol, a championship golf course designed by Robert Trent Jones, Jr., and managed by Golf Hyatt. Located at the base of the island's California Lighthouse, the course is distinctly Aruban in its landscape. All but three holes offer a panoramic view of the Caribbean as you play this challenging course. Built to complement the terrain, the roughs can be nasty. Errant balls find trouble in the form of cacti, divi divi, and native desert grasses; hit it straight and you'll land in wonderfully lush, watered fairways. The Hyatt offers reserved tee times for guests, and clubs can be rented at a reasonable fee.

Dining at the Hyatt gives you a number of options for a variety of tastes. There's Ole, a Spanish and tapas restaurant; Cafe Piccolo, an Italian cafe specializing in regional cuisine; Ruinas del Mar, featuring continental cuisine; and Palms, a casual restaurant serving Caribbean cuisine. Especially appealing is to dine at one of the cozy tables located out among the fountains and weeping walls of the Spanish-influenced hotel building—perfect for special romantic evenings.

Nightly entertainment is not forgotten. The resort's lively Casino Copacabana beckons to those who want to try their hand at blackjack, roulette, craps, or the slots. Bands play for dancing, and entertainment is regularly featured.

With 360 rooms, this is not your small, intimate hotel. It is, however, a superb choice if you're looking for lovely accommodations in a tropical sun and sand destination. It's one of Hyatt's winners.

Author's note: With a reputation for being squeaky-clean and safe, Aruba is popular among honeymooners. Only those bent on finding an island with a colorful, native culture with lots going on locally (politics, industry, working farms, sugar and banana plantations, etc.) may be disappointed. Aruba's main business is tourism; its hotels and casinos are where you'll find most of the action.

Address/Phone: L. G. Smith Boulevard, Number 85, Palm Beach, Aruba; 2978–61234; fax 2978–61682

U.S. Reservations: (800) 233–1234

Owner/Manager: Barry Kaplan, general manager

Arrival/Departure: Taxis and car rentals available at airport

Distance from Queen Beatrix Airport: 7 miles

Distance from Oranjestad: 2 miles

Accommodations: 360 rooms, including 17 suites, 1 Regency Club floor, and 1 Governor's Suite

Best Room/Suite: Suites overlooking the Caribbean

Amenities: Air-conditioning, ceiling fans, minibar, cable TV, direct-dial phone with voice-activated dialing, in-room safe, coffeemaker, radio, hair dryer, toiletries; room service

Electricity: 110 volts

Sports and Facilities: Sailing, snorkeling, sailboarding, deep-sea fishing, 2 lighted tennis courts, volleyball, golf, beach, pools, health and fitness club

Dress Code: Casual

Weddings: Can be arranged

Rates/Packages: $355–$495 per room (winter); $215–$335 (spring and fall); $199–$320 (summer); "Honeymoon Romance" package (per couple): 4 days, from $1,099; 8 days, from $2,159, including accommodations, champagne, breakfast for two on first morning, sunset cruise, massage for two, jeep rental for 1 day, snorkel/sail with lunch on 53-foot catamaran, gratuities included for food and beverage items, service charges, taxes, and clothing discount at Red Sail Sports. Golf and scuba-diving packages also available.

Payment/Credit Cards: Most major

Deposit: Reservations must be secured with deposit within 14 days of verbal confirmation; refundable if cancellation received in writing no later than October 1 for arrivals during Christmas season, 14 days in advance for all other periods

Government Taxes: 6.5 percent, included in honeymoon plan

Service Charges: Included for items on honeymoon plan

Entry Requirements for U.S. Citizens: Proof of citizenship; passport best

BAHAMAS
≋

Ocean Club

Location: On Paradise Island, off the northern edge of Nassau's New Providence Island.

Romantic Features: Intimate courtyard dining; hammocks for two; fountains and gardens.

From the moment you are greeted with a bubbling glass of fine champagne by warm, hospitable people, you know your honeymoon at this small, intimate resort on Paradise Island will live up to its reputation.

In 1995 the owners, Sun International, reopened the Ocean Club after spending $7.5 million on renovating and restoring this little jewel. Once part of billionaire Huntington Hartford's holdings, the Ocean Club's reputation for providing guests with superb service and luxurious accommodations is further enhanced with the addition of modern conveniences like minibars and central air-conditioning. With the Atlantic waters only about 20 yards from the guest rooms and a balcony or patio that takes full advantage of the marvelous sea views, the Ocean Club appeals to those seeking European ambience in a tropical setting.

Whether you are staying in a premier suite, an attractive tennis villa, or any of the other rooms in between, you are sure to be pampered by the kinds of services and amenities Croesus would have desired. Regal, king-size beds, softly colored pastel linens and fabrics, sink-in-your-toes carpeting, noiseless central air-conditioning, designer ceiling fans, stocked minibars, and 27-inch TVs are just the beginning. Bathrooms have state-of-the-art appointments, with imported marble, tile vanities, bidets, scales, and many other features you'd expect to find in fine European hotels, right down to the customized toiletries and bottled water. And something you probably wouldn't find across the "pond"—irons and ironing boards!

But that's not the total picture. Add twenty-four–hour room service, a maid who cleans your rooms three times a day, complimentary shoe shines, free shuttle transportation on Paradise Island, use of the bicycles, and a wonderful fruit basket in your room and you have a pretty good idea of what's yet to come.

The Ocean Club has a remarkable lineup of sports facilities. For the tennis player there are nine Har-Tru clay courts, lighted for night play and free to guests. There are also a teaching pro and a well-equipped pro shop. For golfers there is an award-winning eighteen-hole course less than a mile away that is always open to Ocean Club guests. Greens fees and a cart are $86.

For pool loungers there is a pool adjacent to both the tennis courts and a delightful open-air restaurant serving lunch and cocktails. The beach is one of the prettiest in the Bahamas. It's set in a protected cove and lined with palms and tropical plants, and the sand is white, soft, and deep. Lunch and drinks are served in a terrace restaurant overlooking the water, where you can watch parasailers flying in the brilliant blue sky and luxury liners anchored offshore.

Hammocks-for-two dot the lush lawn just above the staircase to the beach. And in true Cecil B. DeMille fashion, would you believe, doves glide overhead, cooing their blessings.

Beautiful old trees, tropical flowers, and shrubs provide a rich setting for the terraced Versailles Gardens and plush lawns, which are tiered like a wedding cake up a gentle hillside. At the top is a twelfth-century French cloister, which was imported from Europe and rebuilt stone by stone by Hartford. With its marble columns, arches, and statues, it is a lovely place to relax and enjoy the beauty of the gardens and the sea. (It's also a great place to have a wedding ceremony.)

You couldn't ask for a more seductive place to dine than the Courtyard Terrace restaurant, an intimate, outdoor courtyard where tables are arranged around fountains and gardens. With such a setting you'd almost be willing to accept the most mundane of meals, but it will not be necessary. This restaurant is known for serving some of the finest cuisine in the islands. The a la carte menu features items such as Beluga caviar, homemade soups, lobster medallions with a warm sauce surrounded by local vegetables, chateaubriand for two, and a superb chocolate mousse. Dinner for two costs around $86.

Because Sun International owns about 70 percent of Paradise Island, you can use the facilities of their other property, the mega-size Atlantis, which is located less than a mile down the road. At the Atlantis there are twelve different restaurants and a 30,000-square-foot casino, complete with Las Vegas–style shows. The casino is open twenty-four hours a day for the slot machines and from 10:00 to 4:00 A.M. for the gaming tables. If you crave some action, this is

Ocean Club, Bahamas

the place to come, courtesy of the Ocean Club, which runs a free shuttle every half-hour until midnight. The Ocean Club may be close to the action, but it is worlds away from the glitter and glitz of its sibling down the road.

A $40 million expansion program will add 40 new rooms and suites.

Address/Phone: P.O. Box N4–777, Nassau, the Bahamas; (242) 363–3000; fax (242) 363–3703

Web Site: www.sunint.com

U.S. Reservations: Sun International, (800) 321–3000

Owner/Manager: Sun International Bahamas, Ltd., owner; Russell Miller, general manager

Arrival/Departure: Paradise Island Airlines leaves from Miami, Ft. Lauderdale, and West Palm Beach twice a day and lands five minutes from the Ocean Club. All U.S. major carriers fly into Nassau. Transfers can be arranged.

Distance from Paradise Island Airport: 1 mile (5 minutes); Nassau International Airport, 30 minutes

Distance from Nassau: 3 miles (10 to 15 minutes)

Accommodations: 58 newly refurbished rooms, including 4 suites and 5 two-bedroom villas each with private whirlpool (50 new rooms and suites bring the total count to 108)

Best Room/Suite: Suites overlooking ocean

Amenities: Hair dryer, toiletries, central air-conditioning, ceiling fans, iron and ironing board, 27-inch TVs, bathrobes, scales, in-room safe, bidet, minibar; 24-hour room service, laundry and valet service

Electricity: 110 volts

Sports and Facilities: 9 Har-Tru lighted tennis courts; sailing, swimming, snorkeling, Aquacat sailing, kayaking; golf, cycling, croquet

Dress Code: Daytime casual, jackets required for dinner at Courtyard Terrace

Weddings: Can be arranged

Rates/Packages: $375–$765 per couple per night. Ask about honeymoon packages.

Payment/Credit Cards: Most major

Deposit: 2-night deposit, refundable at no charge if canceled 15 days or more prior to arrival date.

Government Taxes: 10 percent room tax; $15 departure tax at airport

Service Charges: $3.00 housekeeping gratuity per person; $2.00 utility gratuity per person.

Entry Requirements for U.S. Citizens: Proof of citizenship; passport best

Sandals Royal Bahamian Resort & Spa

Location: Cable Beach, Nassau, Bahamas.

Romantic Features: Couples only; all-inclusive plan; nonstop activities and seductive minipools; romantic restaurants; private island.

After extensive remodeling and additions, including expansion of the patio and pool areas, new restaurants, and an elegant new spa, The Sandals Royal Bahamian Resort & Spa on Nassau's Cable Beach seems more romantic than ever.

If all those pillars that seem to float on the water and the huge, rather fearsome statue of Neptune that greets you at the entrance seem a bit excessive, the overall impression is nevertheless one of opulence and grandeur. Hard to argue with that.

The elegance of the pink and white exteriors has been turned up several notches—some might say the former Balmoral Club has been "Sandalized." Huge palladium windows, tons of marble, chandeliers, and frescoed ceilings help send the message: "If you're looking for luxury, come here."

Sandals Royal Bahamian has three large pools and two private minipools. Located in the middle of everything, the heated main pool comes with Jacuzzis, waterfalls, a swim-up bar, and even Neptune himself, spouting a stream of water out of his mouth. For cooling off you can sit under the misting pool.

Although the resort is located on the sea and has a moderate-size beach, the best beach is found on Sandals Cay, a private island reached by water shuttle just ½ mile offshore. Besides the wonderful white sand, there is a pool with a swim-up bar, a Jacuzzi, and the Cafe Goombay. Sandals also offers a full range of water sports, including scuba diving.

Accommodations range from beachfront rooms in The Manor House to villas and suites. Furnishings are traditional and elegant, with hand-carved mahogany four-poster king-size beds, flowing flowered fabrics, and comfortable upholstered chairs. Many rooms have balconies or patios.

There will be no need to go off the property when it comes to dining choices: Sandals Royal Bahamian has eight restaurants, ranging from the dazzling crystal room and French-inspired Baccarat restaurant to the casual Cricketers. If Cricketers looks like an authentic English pub, that's because it is; much of the interior was brought here piece by piece from Great Britain.

For late-nighters there is entertainment and a disco. The brash, neon-lit Carnival Resort and Casino, just down the road, is far enough away not to impinge on the romantic mood, yet close enough for those who want a night out to gamble.

For total pampering you can head to the 6,000-square-foot spa, where you'll find a wide choice of European-style services and treatments. Kur baths, Finnish saunas, reflexology, aromatherapy, deep-cleansing facials, and much more are offered here and are about the only items not included in Sandals's all-inclusive price.

Address/Phone: P.O. Box CB-13005, Cable Beach, Nassau, Bahamas; (242) 327–6400; fax (242) 327–6961

U.S. Reservations: (800) SANDALS

Owner/Manager: Stephen Ziadie, general manager

Arrival/Departure: Sandals guests are met at the airport and escorted to the resort

Distance from Airport: 15 minutes

Distance from Nassau: 5 minutes

Accommodations: 406 rooms, suites, and villas

Best Room/Suite: Grande Luxe Oceanfront rooms in The Manor House

Amenities: Air-conditioning, king-size beds, ceiling fans, hair dryer, generous kits of lotions and shampoo, telephones, clock radios, color TVs, and safes; suites also have fully stocked wet bars, terry robes, and *New York Times* faxes

Electricity: 110 volts

Sports and Facilities: 3 freshwater pools, 2 minipools, 5 whirlpools, 2 tennis courts, fitness center; scuba diving, snorkeling, sailboarding, sailing, paddleboats, canoes, kayaks, golf (nearby), pool/billiard tables, volleyball, shuffleboard, croquet, waterskiing; full-service spa (services and treatments are extra)

Dress Code: Casual

Weddings: On-site wedding coordinators arrange all the details, including taking care of the paperwork, leading the couple through the process of getting the marriage license, flowers, music, and reception. "WeddingMoons"—Sandals's term—can be as intimate as a couple getting married in a horse-drawn carriage or under a gazebo with a best man and attendant "borrowed" from the Sandals staff, or it can be an even more elaborate affair, with a reception for a couple's family and friends.

Rates/Packages: All-inclusive rates for 7 nights start at $2,275 per person

Payment/Credit Cards: Most major

Deposit: Guarantee with credit card

Government Taxes: Included

Service Charges: Included

Entry Requirements for U.S. Citizens: Proof of citizenship; passport best

BARBADOS
≋

Cobblers Cove

Location: On west coast of the island.
Romantic Features: Friendly, laid-back ambience; lovely beach.

Not quite as opulent as some of its more pricey neighbors on Barbados's western coast, Cobblers Cove is a jewel of a place: small and casual, yet lovely enough to be wildly romantic. It's the kind of place couples look for when they want to get away and simply enjoy each other for a serene few days. Cobblers is very British in feeling; not slick, not elaborate, just an easy, laid-back kind of place. It offers water sports as well as tennis, but although you'll find Cobblers to be very friendly, no one tries to organize your time or urge you to play volleyball.

The hotel is located on only three acres, and you don't have to go very far to find anything. Water sports? A quick snack or the resort's famous bar drink, the Cobbler's Cooler? Everything's right there.

Each of the two-story, pink-and-white cottages has four suites with sitting rooms and louvered-window walls that open onto terraces or patios. The cottages and the main reception building and restaurant sit amid tropical gardens near the sea. Each suite, decorated in cheery colors, comes with a kitchenette, bamboo and contemporary white furniture, and good-size closets. Although many of the suites are not right on the water, it's still hard to find a "bad" room here. For the most privacy ask for the rooms to the left of the clubhouse (as you're facing the water). Those on the other side mostly overlook the gardens and lawns, where some people like to sit and sunbathe. The upper suites have peaked ceilings and better views.

If you really want to splurge, book the Camelot Suite, which is aptly named. This bilevel little spot of heaven, appropriately decorated in blues and whites, has a massive white four-poster king-size canopied bed; a spacious sitting room; a huge bathroom with whirlpool tub; twin sinks; white marble floors; dhurrie carpets; and a luxurious, upholstered chaise and chairs. Climb the spiral stairway to your private pool on the furnished deck above, where you'll also find a wet bar and nonstop views.

The 1,780-square-foot Colleton Suite, located in the west turret of the Plantation House, delivers total luxury. It has a huge bathroom with a Jacuzzi and neck massage facility, separate sitting room, and bedroom with canopied Empress-size bed. French doors lead onto an expansive sun terrace, where the views are what dreams are made of.

The resort's kidney-shaped pool is not large, so if you find it a little too pop-ulated for your taste, all you have to do is walk about eight steps to one of the loveliest and quietest beaches in Barbados. For the more active there are com-plimentary tennis, waterskiing, sailboarding, and snorkeling right off the beach. The hotel will also make arrangements for you if you want to go deep-sea fish-ing, play golf, or take an island excursion.

The Terrace Restaurant is right by the sea. Here you can enjoy some of the best cuisine on the island, if not the Caribbean. You'll have meals to write home about—guaranteed. French-trained chefs offer new choices every day. The emphasis is on Caribbean specialties with lots of fresh fish, fruits, and vegetables. You can sit on the open-air terrace right by the water and watch the sunset. Music and other entertainment are provided on various nights during the week.

Address/Phone: Road View, St. Peter, Barbados; (246) 422–2991; fax (246) 422–1460

E-mail: cobblers@caribsurf.com

U.S. Reservations: Relais & Chateaux (800) RELAIS–8 or (212) 856–0115; fax (212) 856–0193; Karen Bull Associates, (800) 890–6060; fax (404) 237–7841

Owner/Manager: Hamish Watson, general manager

Arrival/Departure: Arrangements can be made for transfer from the airport for a fee; it's included in package rates

Distance from Barbados International Airport: 18 miles (45 minutes)

Distance from Bridgetown: 12 miles (25 minutes)

Accommodations: 40 suites, including 2 multilevel luxury suites with pools

Best Room/Suite: The Colleton Suite and the Camelot Suite are to die for; otherwise go for the Sea View, second-story suites

Amenities: Air-conditioning, ceiling fans, direct-dial telephones, stocked mini-bar, hair dryer, bathrobes, drying racks, toiletries, ice service; in-room safes; radios and TV (can be arranged on request); room service from 8:00 A.M. to 9:00 P.M.

Electricity: 110/220 volts

Sports: Tennis, sailboarding, waterskiing, snorkeling, swimming at pool or beach, Sunfishes. Extra charge for deep-sea fishing and scuba diving.

Dress Code: Casually elegant; jeans, shorts, and swimwear not allowed in bar after 7:00 P.M.

Weddings: In the staff's own words, "We help arrange it all, the ceremony, the champagne, and the cheers."

Rates/Packages: Suites from $282, no meals, and from $457, with meals (April–September); from $347 and $522, respectively (October–December); packages from $2,500 per couple

Payment/Credit Cards: MasterCard, American Express

Deposit: 3-night deposit required in winter and spring; 1-night deposit, summer and fall

Government Taxes: 7.5 percent VAT on accommodations; 15 percent VAT on food and beverages

Service Charges: 10 percent

Entry requirements for U.S. Citizens: Return ticket and proof of citizenship required; passport best

BERMUDA

Cambridge Beaches

Location: On a twenty-five–acre peninsula on Bermuda's western coast, near Somerset Village.

Romantic Features: Dancing under the stars on the Mangrove Bay Terrace; boat ride to a private island for a picnic; five pink beaches to sink your toes into; privacy of your own cottage; couples' massage.

Cambridge Beaches, located on the western end of the island, has five Bermuda-pink pristine beaches and numerous little coves to discover that are tucked into the rocky ledges of the peninsula. With water on three sides, the resort's pink-and-white limestone cottages nestle into the nooks and crannies of the well-manicured tropical gardens above and along the shoreline. White roofs and louvers, mellow stone walls and steps that turn golden in the late-afternoon sun, and lush, flowering oleanders and hibiscus that have had many years to mature transform Cambridge Beaches into a magical world where dreams are made and fulfilled.

It's truly one of the world's premier hideaway resorts and one of Bermuda's most exclusive properties. There are a variety of rooms and suites, most with king-size beds and sitting areas, others with fireplaces, vaulted beamed ceilings, and French doors leading to large terraces and spectacular views of Long Bay, the Atlantic Ocean, or Mangrove Bay, dotted with sleek yachts riding at anchor, their stays slapping masts with low-pitched tings.

Rooms are individually decorated with cheerful English chintz fabrics in warm pinks, sunny golds, and blues; traditional Queen Anne furniture; and marble baths. Some of the larger suites feature charming antique pieces and extended grassy terraces; most have whirlpool tubs. Attractive scenes of Bermuda decorate the walls. You have your own terrace, where you can enjoy a cozy, private breakfast or dinner, and from your door it's only a short walk to the beaches.

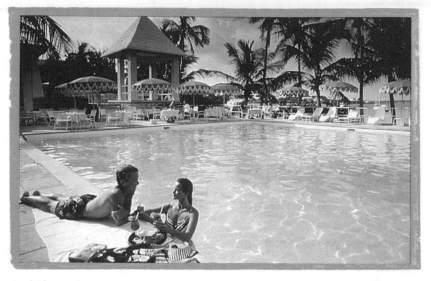

Cambridge Beaches, Bermuda

The 275-year-old Great House, overlooking Mangrove Bay, shelters a gracious lobby furnished with Bermuda and English antiques—it has that comfortable, "been here a long while" feel, yet decor is light and pleasant. An adjacent library is filled with books.

Downstairs you'll find the elegant Tamarisk Restaurant, where the food is a work of art. The chef, Jean-Claude Garzia, has won the prestigious MOF (Meilleurs Ouvriers de France), awarded to just eighteen French chefs worldwide every five years. Your plate may be decorated with fans of fresh fruit, delicate lacy butterflies of chocolate, or swirls of raspberry sauce in a pool of vanilla custard. The menu also includes island-style items such as baby shrimp curry pie with a light banana sauce, bouillabaisse, and pan-fried tenderloin with a Chambertin red wine and truffle sauce—all superb, as are the pastries, breads, and ice cream, which are made in Cambridge's own Pastry Shop.

The recently redecorated Port O'Call Bar, with its cozy fireplace, is a perfect spot to hide out when the weather is cool. A cable TV provides news and sports fans with the latest broadcasts.

For lunch and more casual dining, the Mangrove Bay Terrace invites you to dine and dance under trees and night sky. Wrought-iron chairs and tables are set on the stone terrace, where you can see the harbor from just about anywhere you sit. You can also take advantage of the resort's exchange dining program, which invites you to eat at five other properties at no extra charge.

You can also grab a casual bite to eat at the indoor/outdoor cafe located next to the spa. Here, in addition to some basics, you can get "all sport energy drinks" and a whole-grain "pita delight." Although giant chocolate chip cookies and spa cuisine might seem to be an oxymoron, I had no trouble diving into the gourmet pizza.

Another restaurant is planned near the main house, looking west to the sunsets.

Water sports activities and the marina are down at the end of the beach. Rent a boat and explore the private islands just off the coast or head to nearby Turtle Cove beach, pick up the phone at the bottom of the steps, and order "room service." The resort has a number of boats you can use, including canoes, sailboats, and motorboats. Cruise on a luxurious yacht, and watch the sunset while sipping a Sea Breeze.

Want to be pampered? Then treat yourself to a massage or facial at the European Spa, where you can indulge in a choice of more than one hundred massages and treatments. There's even a special session designed for couples who wish to learn the art of massage. Or relax by the lovely Ocean Spa pool, which is built under a retractable glass room—perfect for those cooler days. You can also swim against the current in the new swim spa.

If you can bear to leave the beach, check out the shops, art galleries and other attractions in Hamilton. A free Cambridge Beaches ferry shuttles you to the city three times a week. You can also explore the dockyard, located at this end of the island, or take a romantic horse-and-buggy ride in the nearby town of Somerset. Rent a moped or bicycle and ride off to discover the beauty of Bermuda. The speed limit on the island is about 15 to 20 miles per hour, so you can really enjoy an easy, carefree spin.

At Cambridge Beaches entertainment is not forgotten. There is music for listening and dancing most evenings and special evening cruises. Apparently, the magic works. A big red board is filled with names of repeat guests. One couple came to Cambridge on their honeymoon in 1947 and have been coming back ever since; in all they've returned seventy-six times.

Address/Phone: 30 Kings Point Road, Somerset, MA 02, Bermuda; (441) 234–0331; fax (441) 234–3352

E-mail: cambeach@abl.com

Web Site: www.CambridgeBeaches.com

U.S. Reservations: (800) 468–7300

Owner/Manager: Michael J. Winfield, president; Jean Christophe Nager, operations manager

Arrival/Departure: A 45-minute taxi ride from the airport costs approximately $44

Distance from Bermuda International Airport: 18 miles

Distance from Somerset: 1 mile

Accommodations: 81 rooms and suites in cottages, all refurbished within the past five years

Best Room/Suite: Cambridge Suites, which have a bedroom and separate living room with panoramic water views; suites with water views also good. Sunset Suite is superb.

Amenities: Air-conditioning, ceiling fans, toiletries, telephones, bathrobes, hair dryer; whirlpools in some baths; umbrella, toaster, safe, mending kit; room service; free shuttle to Hamilton; TV on request

Electricity: 110 volts

Sports and Facilities: 3 tennis courts (one lighted for night play), croquet, swimming in heated saltwater pool, indoor freshwater pool, or beaches; snorkeling, scuba diving, sailing, canoeing, sailboarding, kayaking, fishing, motorboating; spa, Universal gym, sauna, whirlpool, aerobics; yacht for special cruises; putting green, golf can be played at nearby Robert Trent Jones and on all Bermuda, Port Royal, and Mid Ocean Club courses; moped and bicycle rentals

Dress Code: In the dining room three evenings are smart casual; four evenings jackets are requested (no tie required); informal dining around the pool

Weddings: Can be arranged

Rates/Packages: Rates are per couple per night, including breakfast, dinner, tea, use of tennis courts, putting green, and ferry service to Hamilton. $365–$595 (April 16–November 15); $305–$500 (March 1–April 15); $245–$400 (mid November–end February). Honeymoon Package from $2,750 per couple, includes waterview rooms, breakfast, dinner, tea, "His 'N' Hers" massage, one day double moped, champagne, sunset sail, transfers, and photograph.

Payment/Credit Cards: Most major

Deposit: 2-night deposit at time of booking to cover first and last nights' accommodations; cancel 28 days or more prior to arrival for refund.

Government Taxes: 7 percent room tax; energy surcharge 4.25 percent

Service Charges: $13.50 per person per night

Entry requirements for U.S. Citizens: Proof of citizenship; return ticket; passport best

≈≈≈

The Reefs

Location: In Southampton, on the south shore of Bermuda.

Romantic Features: Hillside rooms overlooking the sea; room service breakfast on your private balcony; private pink beach with hidden coves to explore.

The Reefs is one of Bermuda's most romantic honeymoon resorts and has been consistently rated as one of the best on the island for a number of years. Sitting high above the beautiful pink beach and coral reefs below, the salmon-hued low-rise lanai cottages ramble over the landscaped, terraced grounds. All have great views of the sea from the balconies.

Rooms are attractively furnished with rattan chairs, sofas, tables, and bed; bright tropical prints; area rugs on red-tiled floors; and cheery prints of Bermuda scenes. The upper-level Lanai Suites have a king-size bed, a sitting area, and a private terrace where you can enjoy breakfast served on your table overlooking the sea.

The reception building houses an attractive lobby, comfortable lounge-bar, dining room, and tropical conservatory, where you dine under a glass roof. In the warmer months, you can enjoy a candlelit dinner outside on the terrace under the stars, and there is often music for dining and dancing. The Reefs' delicious international cuisine is included in your room rate.

If you want to dine outside while the surf rolls in nearby, try eating at the casual, thatched-roof Coconuts, the beach-level restaurant (warmer months only). You'll find the staff friendly and efficient.

The Reefs has a heated pool that overlooks the water and two all-weather tennis courts. There's a wonderful pink beach—one of Bermuda's best—and more to discover if you walk around the big black boulders that lie at the ends of the beach. Here you'll come upon more delightful small beaches tucked into coves, which continue along the shoreline. And, yes, the sand is really tinged pink from the bits of pulverized coral that have been mixed in over the years.

The Reefs is located within walking distance of the Sonesta Beach Hotel, so if you are in the mood for an evening show or some lively entertainment, simply walk next door. You can also rent a moped or go by bus or taxi to nearby Hamilton for some serious shopping.

The Reefs' traditions, such as serving tea each afternoon, are grounded in the British way of doing things, but the hotel is more informal than many other Bermuda hotels. Although the resort certainly appeals to a solid group of over-fifties who come back year after year, its lively mix of nightly entertainment, water sports, and fresh tropical decor attracts a large number of well-heeled young couples, as well.

Address/Phone: 56 South Road, Southampton SN 02, Bermuda; (441) 238–0222; fax (441) 238–8372

E-mail: reefsbda@ibl.bm

U.S. Reservations: Islands Resorts Reservations Ltd., (800) 742–2008

Owner/Manager: David Dodwell, managing director; Neal Stephens, general manager

Arrival/Departure: A 25-minute taxi ride from the airport costs approximately $26 weekdays, $28 weekends

Distance from Bermuda International Airport: 11 miles

Distance from Hamilton: 7 miles

Accommodations: 67 rooms and 8 one- and two-bedroom cottages

Best Room/Suite: Deluxe or premier lanais; Number 316, a premier lanai, has wraparound views

Amenities: King-size bed, refrigerator, bathrobes, hair dryer, in-room safe, umbrella, toiletries, air-conditioning; daily newspaper, rum swizzle on arrival, in-room beverages, iron and board

Electricity: 110 volts

Sports and Facilities: 2 tennis courts, pool, beach, fitness center, shuffleboard, croquet, cycle rentals, snorkeling, scuba diving; helmet diving and glass-bottom boats nearby; golf at nearby courses; fishing and sailing can be arranged

Dress Code: Casual during day; men required to wear jackets in restaurant except for Sunday, Monday, and Thursday, which are casual; beach restaurant and bar also casual

Weddings: Can be arranged

Rates/Packages: Rates are $244–$1,000 per couple per night and include breakfast and dinner, local phone calls, in-room beverages on arrival, and use of sports facilities. Honeymoon Package, $1,800–$4,100, includes 6 nights' accommodations, all the above inclusions, plus champagne, special dinner for two, airport transfers, 3-day bus and ferry pass, picnic lunch for two, taxes and service charges, special gift. Rates are 20 to 35 percent less during the colder months.

Payment/Credit Cards: Most major

Deposit: 2-night deposit at time of booking to cover first and last nights' accommodations; fully refundable if canceled 21 days prior to arrival

Government Taxes: 7.25 percent of nightly rate; included in Honeymoon Package

Service Charges: 10 percent; included in Honeymoon Package

Entry requirements for U.S. Citizens: Proof of citizenship; return ticket; passport best

BRITISH VIRGIN ISLANDS

≋

VIRGIN GORDA

The Bitter End Yacht Club

Location: Covers twenty-five acres, stretching along a mile of beach and waterfront on the North Sound of Virgin Gorda—the most protected and secluded deepwater harbor in the Caribbean.

Romantic Features: Magnificent sailing; thatched-roof bungalows on the beach; opportunity to combine a yacht cruise with an island stay; sunset sail; hammocks for two on your porch or balcony.

Don't let the name turn you off. This "Bitter End" could be your "Sweet Beginning." Artfully tucked into a cove on the northernmost tip of Virgin Gorda, one of the most picturesque of the British Virgin Islands, the Bitter End Yacht Club (BEYC) is a perfect place for newlyweds who love to sail. You can combine your passion for a romantic setting with a few days' cruise aboard a bare boat or crewed yacht, exploring the neighboring islands. Or you can spend all your nights at the resort and venture out onto the gentle seas during the day.

World-class yachtsmen have known about this place for many years, and people like Jean-Michel Cousteau and Mel Fisher have rendezvoused often at this unique tropical haven, which has seventy deepwater moorings, two restaurants, and a host of water sports activities—all first-class from beginning to end.

Protected by coral reefs and beach-fringed cays, this secluded, idyllic spot can most easily be reached by boat. The white sand beach, fringed by gnarled sea grape shrubs and palms, frames a lagoon that seems more like a large, clear, turquoise lake dashed with flashes of the bright-colored sails of sailboarders.

From the time of your arrival at Virgin Gorda's tiny airport—hardly large enough to hold your luggage—everything is handled by the Bitter End staff with great style. After you've gathered your luggage, you're whisked up and over the steep hills to a landing area about twenty minutes away. Then it's a five-minute boat ride across a brilliant Caribbean-blue lagoon, where you are met by a smiling staff member at the dock. (Those landing at Tortola come to the BEYC via high-speed water taxi.)

Native stone lines the walkways and roads, and flowers and tropical plants, including fragrant frangipani, bougainvillea, hibiscus, oleander, and sea grape, wind along the paths and up the hillside. Colorful nautical flags fly from the

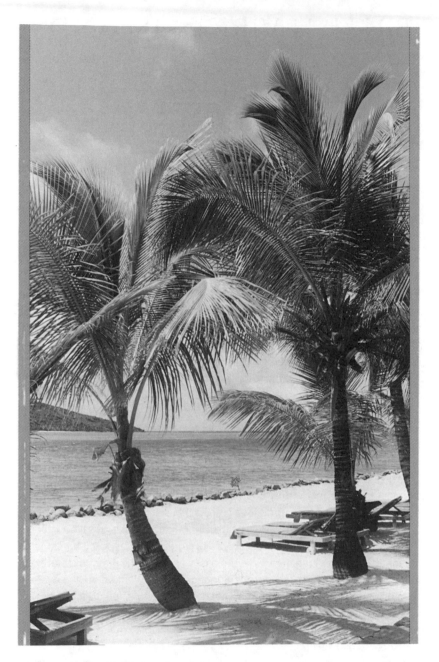

The Bitter End Yacht Club, British Virgin Islands

rafters of the bar, from poles along the walkways, and just about everywhere. Buildings are decorated with whimsical gingerbread trim and iron grillwork and are connected by a series of garden courtyards. Blue-and-white-painted wrought-iron tables and chairs sit on brick-paved patios accented by tiered fountains and flowering plants. All very Mediterranean.

As the sun sets, you'll soon become aware that the lighting throughout the resort is seductively low. (Can this be due to the Caribbean-style electrical power or is it planned for romantics like you?) As you walk along the seaside paths to the dining room, you'll find the tiny flashlight you got at check-in extremely useful.

Because BEYC is actually the marriage of two different resorts, the styles of accommodations are quite different. There are rustic beachfront bungalows that blend into the hills, with their thatched roofs and weathered wood exteriors, and there are more contemporary hillside chalets. The bungalows are much closer to the water than the chalets—some are right on the beach—and are very Caribbean in feeling. You won't have a room key, because there are no locks. Nor are they needed. Open wraparound, palm-thatched verandas, ceiling fans, large walk-in showers, bamboo furniture, a tiled dressing area, and native art and quaint knickknacks lend a homey island feeling to the bungalows. Since most come with twin beds, request ahead to have them put together.

The deluxe 600-square-foot chalets, perched high over the water, are more spacious and luxurious, with vaulted ceilings, balconies, air-conditioning, two queen-size beds, and a very large marble inside/outside garden shower room. Connected by wooden walkways much like jungle catwalks, the chalets have wood peaked ceilings and glass doors leading out to balconies, and they are attractively decorated in rich fabrics, native art, and grass-cloth walls.

The chalets and bungalows come equipped with a refrigerator and coffeemaker, and each has telephone service to the front desk and a comfortable sitting area. The choice is yours: Lie in luxury overlooking the harbor or pick a casual, native-style beachfront villa.

When it comes to water sports, you're in sailing heaven. There are enough Mistral sailboards, Sunfish, Lasers, Laser IIs, Rhodes 19s, J-24s, and outboard-powered skiffs to get the whole guest population of the resort out on the water at the same time.

A glass-bottom boat is available for touring the underwater world, and there are daily escorted snorkeling trips, scuba lessons, dive trips, and lots of regattas. There is also the Nick Trotter Sailing School, a great way for new sailors to learn how to tell a *jib* from a *ready-about*. If you want to explore nearby shores, you can take one of the skiffs and chug over to other parts of the island for a picnic or a visit. For landlubbers a lovely pool and patio area is located on the eastern end of the resort, near the chalets.

Well worth seeing is Anegada, known as Shipwreck Island. Also be sure to visit The Baths, giant granitelike boulders on the southwest coast. Take your bathing suit and swim in the pools located in, under, and around the huge rocks, some as high as 40 feet.

If you want the best of both worlds, you can live aboard one of the resort's Freedom 30s, fully outfitted, luxurious yachts that you can sail into the sunset for a few days or a few hours, returning to your home base for the evening. All meals are included, whether you eat onboard or ashore.

The BEYC has two restaurants. The Clubhouse, on the shore, serves breakfast, lunch, and dinner. You can eat inside, on the tree-shaded terrace, or on the veranda. The terrace bar, poised on the edge of the water, is a popular gathering place for guests to enjoy morning coffee or a late-afternoon cocktail.

Nearer the chalets is the Pavilion Dining Room of the English Carvery, which is open four nights a week for intimate candlelight dinners and dancing. You can also grab a quick snack or a light lunch at the English Pub at the Emporium, which serves pizza.

The BEYC attracts some big-name entertainers, and there is also entertainment in the piano bar, jazz club, and lounge. Bitter End's steel band plays several nights a week, and there are beach barbecues and sunset and moonlight cruises.

With close to 200 staff for just ninety rooms, the Bitter End gives you all the attention you want and need, but one of the best things of all is that it's done in a totally unobtrusive manner. You can wash your hair, take a walk on the beach, and when you return find a fresh towel in your room. Beds are turned down every night, and the beaches are raked every morning.

Although you will be surrounded by tempting things to do, you can find your own quiet spot on one of the secluded beaches and just sit back under a palm tree and watch a yellow finch eat sugar from your outstretched hand.

Author's note: The Bitter End Yacht Club was closed for extensive renovations, reopening after publication. The dining rooms and guest rooms were renovated and a new telecommunications system installed. Also new, a Yachtsman's Bathhouse and Lounge.

Address/Phone: North Sound, Virgin Gorda, B.V.I.; (809) 494–2746; fax (809) 494–4756

E-mail: binfo@beyc.com

Web Site: www.beyc.com

U.S. Reservations: (800) USA–BEYC, (800) 872–2392, or (312) 944–5855; fax (312) 944–2860

Owner/Manager: Owned by the Hokin family for over 25 years; Dana Hokin, managing director

Arrival/Departure: Transfers from Beef Island Airport, Tortola, or Virgin Gorda Airport included in 7-day package; otherwise $20 per couple charge for transfer

Distance from Virgin Island Airport: 30-minute drive or bus ride plus 10-minute boat ride

Distance from Spanish Town: 30 minutes

Accommodations: 95 rooms and suites, ranging from beachfront villas to Commodore Suites and live-aboard Freedom 30 yachts.

Best Room/Suite: Beachfront bungalows for beach lovers; hillside chalets for those who prefer luxury and a bird's-eye view of the water

Amenities: Air-conditioning (chalets only), ceiling fans, garden showers, hair dryer, coffeemaker, refrigerator, VCRs (in suites); turndown service; shops and convenience store

Electricity: 110 volts

Sports and Facilities: Water sports galore; Mistral sailboards, Sunfish, Lasers, Laser IIs, Rhodes 19s, J-24s, and outboard-powered skiffs; snorkeling, scuba diving; swimming pool, 3 beaches, fitness trail; marina; Blue Water Excursions

Dress Code: Very casual. Leave your cocktail dresses and sports jackets at home

Weddings: Can be arranged

Rates/Packages: From $360 per couple per night (spring–fall); $520 (winter); includes 3 meals and use of water sports equipment. A Honeymoon Package, 8 days/7 nights, is $3,850–$4,500 per couple. For honeymooning sailors there is the Admiral's Package; an 8-day/7-night plan, priced from $2,520 per couple (spring–fall) and from $3,640 (winter); includes accommodations, all meals, excursions, water sports, and unlimited use of the Bitter End's fleet of boats. A package combining 5 nights on a yacht and 4 nights in the resort is priced from $3,450 per couple.

Payment/Credit Cards: Most major

Deposit: 3 nights; cancel 30 days prior to arrival date for refund (by October 1 for Christmas season)

Government Taxes: 7 percent

Service Charges: $14 per person per day

Entry Requirements for U.S. Citizens: Proof of citizenship; passport best

Little Dix Bay

Location: Northwest corner of Virgin Gorda, just off the Sir Francis Drake Channel.

Romantic Features: Beautiful beachfront setting; romantic dining and dancing under the stars; hammocks for two; picnics on secluded beaches.

One of the most consistently appealing Caribbean resorts, Little Dix Bay was established over thirty years ago by Laurance S. Rockefeller, who visualized an ecological preserve and wilderness resort where privacy and solitude were paramount. Today Little Dix remains extremely romantic and seductive. It sits on 500 acres and has a lovely ½-mile crescent-shaped beach. The rooms and public areas are designed to blend into the surrounding gardens of flowering shrubs, sea grapes, and palms. Cottages containing two to eight rooms all face the sea. Some are on stilts and have cone-shaped roofs; others are more conventional. All have louvered-window walls designed to catch the cooling trade winds.

Coral reefs and a cove create a calm, safe "harbor" for swimming and water sports. In 1993 Rosewood Hotels & Resorts took over the operation of the resort, giving the property a major facelift, with new furniture and custom-designed fabrics, new lighting, telephones, redesigned bathrooms, and the addition of air-conditioning to about half the rooms. To lend a Polynesian ambience, bamboo beds and other interesting furniture pieces were imported from Asia, and unique touches were added, such as wicker baskets and artwork. Throughout the renovation, great care and sensitivity were taken to preserve the harmonious pact Little Dix has had with nature.

Cottages are constructed of native wood and stone with peaked wooden ceilings, circulating fans, and tile floors. Bamboo king-size beds; rattan furniture, including chaises roomy enough to hold two; and natural fiber area rugs are low-key yet elegant enough to satisfy the most discerning of guests. Rooms are located in clusters of cottages, some on ground level.

With more than 300 on staff, the hotel provides excellent, yet not overpowering, service. They pay attention to the little things, like replenishing your ice bucket daily and providing an abundant supply of fresh towels.

Little Dix has three restaurants. The open-air Pavilion, which has four dramatic Polynesian-style pyramid roofs and a stone terrace, offers international and Caribbean specialties, lunch buffets, afternoon teas, and candlelight dinners. Rack of lamb, fresh salmon, red snapper, and grouper are served grilled or with wonderful light sauces. Guests often gather on the terrace early in the evening for cocktails as the sun sets. After dinner a band plays music for dancing under the open skies. This is your chance to get dressed up for a really lovely evening of good food, wine, and romance—the kind of night you always dreamed about.

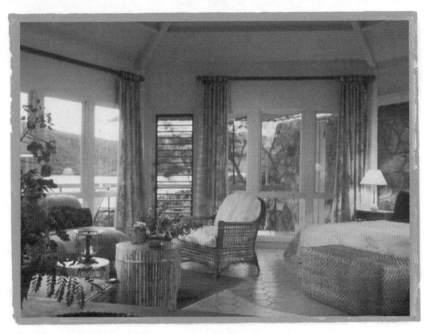

Little Dix Bay, British Virgin Islands

The more casual seaside Sugar Mill, its roof and terraces splashed by the reds and oranges of bougainvillea, is a good place to enjoy dinner featuring Mediterranean-inspired cuisine such as pastas, pizzas, paella, quesadillas, salads, fresh grilled fish, lobster, and steaks.

The Beach Grill serves light lunches and dinner; at night you eat at candlelit tables overlooking the beach, alive with the glow of blazing torches. Try the lobster dishes and steak specialties.

At Little Dix the beach is right in your "front yard." Float the afternoon away on a rubber raft, or sit under an umbrella of palm fronds. Take a box lunch and umbrella and climb aboard the resort's water taxi, which will shuttle you to a secluded beach. Snorkel in Devil's Bay and explore Mosquito Island. Ask the boatman to drop you near the famous Baths, and spend a few hours climbing above, under, and around the huge boulders that create this unique natural phenomenon. Swim in the grotto pools and climb the path that leads from the beach to a hilltop restaurant/bar.

Guided snorkel tours are offered four times a week, and you can take Sunfish lessons, aerobic exercise, and even a tour of the gardens with the resident horticulturist. The tennis center offers complimentary clinics and round-robins twice a week, and movies are shown every evening in the large, open-air lounge.

Your honeymoon package includes a sunset cocktail sail on the resort's trimaran *Pond Bay* and a ride on a Boston Whaler to Spring Bay for a picnic. Full-day sails to nearby areas as well as scuba diving, fishing charters, and beauty treatments are also available as optional choices.

Well-heeled guests have been coming here for years, appreciating the easy ambience and the excellent service—they treat it rather like their personal island club. During the winter months the guests tend to be on the more mature side. But in the spring—honeymoon season—the resort is popular with newly married young couples, many of whom have learned about the resort from their parents. (But beware: Christmas and Easter attract families.) Spring, summer, and fall are great times to come to Little Dix. Prices are lower, and the weather is great.

Address/Phone: P.O. Box 720, St. John U.S.V.I. 00831-0720; (284) 495–5555; fax (284) 495–5661

U.S. Reservations: (800) 928–3000; fax (214) 758–6640

Owner/Manager: Managed by Rosewood Hotels & Resorts; Peter Shaindlin, general manager

Arrival/Departure: Virgin Gorda can be reached via San Juan, Puerto Rico, and St. Thomas, U.S. Virgin Islands. Scheduled shuttles are also available to and from St. Thomas and Caneel Bay. Those arriving at Tortola International Airport are met by a Little Dix Bay representative and taken by private boat launch on a 20-minute ride to the resort.

Distance from Virgin Gorda Airport: 1 mile

Distance from Spanish Town: 2 miles

Accommodations: 98 rooms and 4 one-bedroom suites all facing the sea. Some rooms are set on stilts, and all have patios or balconies. Rooms on west side overlook gardens and sea beyond; rooms on east side are closer to beach.

Best Room/Suite: Newly created beachfront suites with oversize soaking tubs and showers and separate bedroom and living room, or the elevated hexagonal rooms on the west side, near the beach

Amenities: Air-conditioning (about half), king-size bed, ceiling fans, hair dryer, generous kits of lotions and shampoo, telephones (can be removed at guest's request), clock radios, TVs, minibars, in-room safes, robes, iron and board, refrigerator

Electricity: 110 volts

Sports and Facilities: Tennis day or night, scuba diving, snorkeling, sailboarding, sailing, Sunfish, kayaking, waterskiing, aerobics, fitness room

Dress Code: Informal during day; although jacket and tie are not required, most guests usually wear elegant attire when dining at Pavilion and long pants are required for men.

Weddings: Can be arranged

Rates/Packages: $550–$1,300 per couple (winter); $325–$900 (spring and fall); $250–$700 (summer); 7-night honeymoon package (per couple): $3,200-$6,500 (summer); $3,800-$8,000 (spring and fall); $5,500-$10,750 (winter); includes accommodations, meals, trimaran day sail, sunset cocktail cruise, Spring Bay afternoon picnic, champagne and fruit on arrival, transfers to and from Tortola, tennis, water sports, afternoon tea, water taxis to nearby beaches, guided snorkeling tour, Sunfish lessons, aerobic exercise, and massage for two

Payment/Credit Cards: Most major

Deposit: 50 percent of package, due 14 days from date reservations made. If booking 30 days prior to arrival, credit card deposit required within 24 hours of booking. A full deposit will be refunded if notice of cancellation is received at least 28 days in advance of arrival. For those traveling from April 1 to December 19, the full deposit will be refunded if reservation canceled at least 14 days prior to arrival date.

Government Taxes/Service Charges: 7 percent room tax and 5 percent service charge. Meal plans, food, and beverages are subject to a 15 percent service charge.

Entry Requirements for U.S. Citizens: A valid passport, authenticated birth certificate, or voter's registration card with a photo ID accepted as proof of citizenship

≈≈≈

PETER ISLAND

Peter Island Resort and Yacht Harbour

Location: A private, 1,800-acre island in the British Virgin Islands.

Romantic Features: Private honeymoon beach; deserted beaches to explore on your own; hammocks under the palms; dining and dancing under the stars.

Peter Island is an easy, twenty-minute boat ride from the Beef Island Airport, just long enough for you to stretch travel-weary limbs and bask in the warm sun and fresh salt air. As you pull up to the resort's pier, you'll see deserted white sandy beaches, coconut groves, and low hills covered with cactus and bougainvillea.

There aren't a lot of buildings here, and what structures do exist are so unobtrusive, you have to look hard to find them. There are only fifty-two rooms and three villas (Hawks' Nest I and II and Crow's Nest), along with two restaurants, a lounge, library, reception area, fitness center, and dive shop, on the entire 1,800-acre island. You'll find no Club Med sorts of "playmakers," no casino, no disco. What you will find is the opportunity to do pretty much what you want when you want to do it. If you like beaches, sun, and water sports, this island can be your nirvana. Like to sail? You can choose from a 42-foot yacht, Hobie Cats, 19-foot Squibs and Zumas along with kayaks and sailboarders. There are also power boats that can be chartered for deepsea fishing.

If you feel a little green about sailing a Sunfish by yourself, don't worry. The instructor keeps an eye on everyone. "I've never lost anyone yet," he'll tell you with a smile as he helps you push your boat into the water.

Peter Island is an excellent place for snorkeling and scuba diving as well as sailing. Snorkeling gear is free to guests, and just offshore the main swimming beach is a reef where you can see a wonderful assortment of colorful fish, shellfish, corals, and aquatic plants. All you have to do is to wade out, don your mask and fins, and paddle off.

Scuba lessons and dives are available for all levels. One of the most popular dive sites is the wreck of the *Rhone,* a nineteenth-century British mail ship and the site of the filming of Peter Benchley's *The Deep.*

If you like to go exploring, you can climb the rocks at the end of the main beach, follow the fitness trail and see who is the most flexible and the strongest, and walk to the really isolated Reef Bay Beach around the corner, where you can find lots of shells, coral, and bits of sea glass. Take along a blanket and a picnic lunch and enjoy a few hours on your own.

Peter Island has four Tru-flex tennis courts along with a small tennis center. A pro is available (high season) to give you lessons or arrange partners if you're

Peter Island, British Virgin Islands

looking for a set of doubles. Also located at the tennis center is a paperback book exchange library.

One of my criteria for a great beach resort is a place where you can go from your room to the beach in twenty paces and walk on that beach (and others) for miles. Peter Island passes the sand test. But there's more: king-size beds, attractive decor in the island mode, plenty of thirsty towels, lights bright enough for night reading, and a great view of the sea. You also have a minibar, a sitting area, a shower that looks into a small private garden, a double sink, a large walk-in closet, and lots of louvers that you can open to let in the breezes and the sounds of waves. Patios or balconies are furnished with beautiful teak lounge chairs. There are CD players in all rooms, but if you want to watch TV, you'll have to head to the library, tucked between the pool and the sea.

The resort's most recent renovation included guest rooms, restaurant, and outdoor areas and the addition of an outdoor pergola and bar for casual dining and drinking next to the pool.

For entertainment there is music by local bands for dancing or listening almost nightly on the open-air patio. Excursions to neighboring islands such as St. Thomas, Jost Van Dyke, and Tortola are also offered.

Peter Island gets its fish daily from local fishermen, and the chef knows how to cook it! Especially good is the grilled tuna served with a homemade pineapple chutney. The resort also makes its own desserts and pastries. Fresh muffins in the mornings, great cookies with white chocolate chunks and macadamia nuts, and Key lime pie made the traditional way are all delicious.

The resort's rates include breakfast, lunch, and dinner, a good thing since Peter Island's two restaurants are the only game in town.

Peter Island is for those who love beautiful beaches and water sports and don't need a lot of high-level activity. You're on your own here, with all the toys at your disposal.

Address/Phone: P.O. Box 211, Road Town, Tortola, B.V.I.; or P.O. Box 9409, St. Thomas, U.S.V.I. 00801; (284) 495 2000; fax (284) 495–2500

Web Site: www.peterisland.com

U.S. Reservations: (800) 346–4451; fax (616) 776–6467; Preferred Hotels and Resorts, (800) 323–7500

Owner/Manager: Wayne Kafcsak, general manager

Arrival/Departure: Those arriving at the Beef Island Airport are met by a Peter Island representative, escorted to a pier right next to the airport, and taken by private launch to Peter Island, about a 20-minute cruise. The resort also operates free round-trip ferry service several times a day to its dock at Baughers Bay, in Tortola. Helicopter transfers can be arranged from St. Thomas, San Juan, or several other islands. Peter Island has its own lighted helipad.

Distance from Beef Island Airport: About 4 miles by sea

Distance from Tortola: 4 miles

Accommodations: 52 rooms and suites: 32 with ocean or harbor view, 20 junior suites on beach

Best Room/Suite: Go for the beachfront suites

Amenities: Air-conditioning, ceiling fans, minibar, coffeemaker, double sinks, hair dryer, bathrobes, and umbrellas

Electricity: 110 volts

Sports and Facilities: Sunfish, sailboard, kayaks, floaters, snorkeling gear, dive center, and fleet of boats for fishing charters; 4 Tru-flex tennis courts (2 lighted) and tennis equipment; fitness trail with several "shape-up" stops and hiking trails; pool

Dress Code: Casual by day; casually elegant by night. No tie required at dinner, but collared shirts, pants, and shoes are required for dinner.

Weddings: Can be arranged. Good locations include the Crow's Nest, a spectacular villa on the highest part of the island; a lookout gazebo at the top of a hill; Honeymoon Beach, and the dining terrace.

Rates/Packages: $450–$930 per couple per night, including meals, transfers, water sports, bicycles, tennis, and ferry transportation to Tortola. Hawks Nest $870–$1,085; Crow's Nest: $3,000. If you want to combine your stay on Peter Island with 1 or 2 overnights at sea on the resort's yacht with guide, cook, and crew, 7-night packages are available from $4,970, including meals. Scuba and romance packages available.

Payment/Credit Cards: Visa, Mastercard, American Express

Deposit: 3 nights, due 10 days after reservations are made. Packages require full amount due 20 days after reservations; cancel 4 weeks prior to arrival date for refund.

Government Taxes: 7 percent

Service Charges: 10 percent

Entry Requirements for U.S. Citizens: Proof of citizenship necessary. Passport best, but an authenticated birth certificate, a citizenship certificate, or a voter's registration card with photo ID is acceptable.

≈≈≈

CAYMAN ISLANDS

≈≈≈

GRAND CAYMAN

Hyatt Regency Grand Cayman

Location: Directly across from Seven Mile Beach.

Romantic Features: Seven Mile Beach at sunset; tropical walkways laced through the property; sunset sail on the 65-foot *Spirit of Ppalu* catamaran.

B asking in the sun, playing golf on a unique championship course, and enjoying a side order of super scuba and snorkeling are all part of the honeymoon experience at the Hyatt Regency Grand Cayman. Entering the resort's palm-lined driveway, you quickly leave the hubbub of life back home far behind. The Hyatt's British-inspired, low-rise colonial buildings are surrounded by lush green foliage and a rainbow of tropical flowers. The Caribbean is just across the way, where the Hyatt recently built 53 new beachfront suites.

The pastel colors of the buildings, all offset by the brilliant blue sky, set the mood. After checking in, couples who have requested the Honeymoon Package are escorted out of the reception area past a stunning reflecting pool and tropical garden—the centerpiece of the Hyatt's courtyard—to a luxurious guest room, where a chilled bottle of champagne awaits. Rooms are typically Hyatt with a light tropical twist, but every amenity you could wish for is there, including, for some, a garden Jacuzzi. Regency Club rooms, located in a separate building, are extra special and offer more amenities, a private concierge, and complimentary continental breakfast and evening cocktails. The new suites are smack on the beach.

As you walk through the courtyard and gardens, all beautifully manicured, at every turn along the path you'll find romantic little enclaves. Whether it's a bench set in an alcove by a pond or a bridge over a stream running through the property, the setting seems designed for couples in love. The one-third-acre free-form pool has a great swim-up bar, which serves some fabulous frozen drinks.

The Britannia Beach Club will be high on your exploration list. Located across the street, on Hyatt's pearl-white sand strip of Seven Mile Beach, it is here where you may encounter your toughest dilemma. What to do? Lie back and relax at the edge of the crystal-clear Caribbean with a dark rum and orange juice from the Britannia Beach Club's bar, or choose from the almost overwhelming number of activities available through Red Sail Sports—sailboarding, parasailing, Waverunners, and more.

After unwinding for a few days, if you crave some adventure, try scuba diving. Not certified? No problem. A resort course is available for beginners. You'll learn to dive in one day, and at the end of it all, you'll understand why the Grand Cayman is called the underwater capital of the Caribbean.

For a unique experience, don't miss the 20-foot dive to Stingray City, where you'll feed the stingrays and perhaps catch a glimpse of Psycho, the dive master's "friendly" pet eel! Even if you don't dive, take the trip with your snorkeling gear and watch the scene from on top of the water. But don't think you'll avoid an encounter with the stingrays, as the dive master usually coaxes the rays to the top for a closer look at guess who? You.

A dive along the famous North Wall is a fascinating Cayman exclusive—one sure to provide scuba enthusiasts with new thrills. For those nondivers who don't want to miss the sights, Atlantis Submarines offers several unique services. Choose from a personal submarine trip for two (with a captain) or a voyage aboard one of its larger subs. Both submerge to depths of over 100 feet. Through the Cayman's crystal-clear waters (there's a minimum $500,000 fine for dumping anything into the water), you'll see every type of tropical fish you've ever seen in an aquarium and then some. The corals and underwater "road" systems may even give you that needed push to try the one-day resort scuba course to get a closer look at this magnificent underwater world. Look carefully and you may spot some sea turtles!

After the excitement of Stingray City, all you may be up for is finding a lounge chair and watching the sun sink in the horizon while Calypso music plays in the background.

By this time you've probably worked up quite an appetite. The award-winning Hemingway's, located at the Britannia Beach Club directly on Seven Mile Beach, provides a wonderful setting for a romantic dinner for two. With some of the best cuisine on the Island, Hemingway's specialty is, of course, Caribbean cuisine, including fresh fish and seafood. The swordfish and crab cakes are a must-try!

If you have any time left for other activities, try golf. The Hyatt offers a unique Jack Nicklaus–designed layout. Says Victor Lopez, divisional vice-president for Hyatt Hotels & Resorts, "The course configuration varies depending upon where the tees are located, so the forty-acre course can be played three ways: regulation golf, executive course golf, or Cayman ball." It's a challenge any way you play it.

For pure luxury in a tropical setting, with appealing activities and dining options, the Hyatt Grand Cayman delivers.

Address/Phone: Hyatt Regency Grand Cayman, Seven Mile Beach, Grand Cayman, B.W.I.; (345) 949–1234; fax (345) 949–8528

U.S. Reservations: Hyatt Resorts, (800) 55–HYATT

Owner/Manager: Ellesmere Britannia of Canada, owner; Hyatt Hotels & Resorts, operator; Doug Sears, general manager

Arrival/Departure: Taxis available at airport; transfers can be arranged (are not included in the Honeymoon Package)

Distance from Owens Roberts Airport: 5 miles (8 minutes)

Distance from Georgetown: 2 miles

Accommodations: 289 rooms and suites in 6 buildings; 53 new beachfront suites on Seven Mile Beach (9 2-bedroom suites and 44 1-bedroom junior suites) 44 Regency Club rooms, 2 bilevel suites, and 50 villas offering one to four bedrooms with kitchen and laundry facilities. Villas overlook the Hyatt's private waterway to the Caribbean or the golf course.

Best Room/Suite: Bilevel Governor's and Georgetown Suites

Amenities: Air-conditioning, minibar, satellite TV, direct-dial telephone, in-room safe, hair dryer, 24-hour room service, lotions, shampoos, and bath gels

Electricity: 110 volts

Sports and Facilities: Red Sail Sports has two locations on the Hyatt property and offers every water sport imaginable. Special activities include scuba/snorkeling trips to Stingray City and parasailing over Seven Mile Beach. The resort's golf course is designed by Jack Nicklaus.

Dress Code: Beach attire during the day; casual attire for evenings

Weddings: Arranged easily with the newly relaxed government regulations. A popular spot on the Hyatt property is the reflecting pool in the center courtyard. Weddings can also be arranged aboard the *Spirit of Ppalu* catamaran or for the adventurous couple—underwater. Advance notice is needed for all weddings.

Rates/Packages: $325–$455 per couple per night for a double room; $540 for a Regency Club room (winter); double $195–$345, Regency Club $420 (spring and fall); double $190–$310, Regency Club $380 (summer). For full breakfast and dinner daily, add $65 per person per day. Honeymoon Package includes accommodations, champagne, special Britannia honeymoon breakfast for two delivered to your room on the first morning (when meal plan is purchased), jeep rental for 1 day (minimum age, 25), sunset sail on the *Spirit of Ppalu,* massage for two, and a complimentary round of golf. Rates per couple: 4 days/3 nights from $1,039, 8 days/7 nights from $2,115.

Payment/Credit Cards: Most major

Deposit: One to two nights' room rate required 14 days after verbal confirmation; refundable on advance cancellation received in writing no later than October 1 for arrivals during the Christmas season, or 14 days in advance for all other periods

Government Taxes: 10 percent

Service Charges: 10 percent

Entry Requirements for U.S. Citizens: Proof of citizenship is required for U.S. and Canadian citizens. Birth certificate, voter's registration, and passport accepted.

DOMINICAN REPUBLIC

≈≈≈

Casa de Campo

Location: The resort sits on 7,000 acres, on the southeastern coast of the island.
Romantic Features: Moonlit horseback rides; vast tropical areas to explore.

Casa de Campo! It's big. Very big and most of it has been completely renovated and redecorated following a hit by Hurricane George in 1998. There are new rooms, new restaurants, and new features.

Casa de Campo offers a mind-boggling list of things to do, and it's got all the ingredients those looking for sun, sand, and sea require: pools galore, a private beach, and lots of water toys, plus thirteen tennis courts, an equestrian center, a fitness center, plenty of places to eat and drink, thousands of acres, a world-class shooting facility, splendid accommodations, and room service. What more could a body ask?

Want privacy? You've got it. There are 300 newly redecorated rooms and 150 villas, which may sound like a lot, but when they're spread out over 7,000 acres planted with all sorts of tropical things, you can be assured of finding your own very special private places.

There are shuttle buses running regularly throughout the property, but you may want to pay $27 to $35 a day and rent your own golf cart. It's a great way to get around.

Casa de Campo, which is Spanish for "house in the country," has a variety of rooms and suites. Within the mix of accommodations are hotel rooms and haciendalike villas. The super-spacious hotel rooms are located in one- and two-story clusters overlooking the golf links, which wind through the property. Stone and adobe rooms come with balconies, tile floors, louvered shutters, and designer furnishings. Two-, three-, and four-bedroom villas each have a living room, dining room, kitchen, terrace, gardens, and maid service. They may also come with private pools or Jacuzzis. All are exquisitely furnished.

Golfers will think they died and went to heaven, given the thirty-six magnificent holes to tee off on. This includes the world-class Teeth of the Dog course, which has been consistently ranked by *Golf Digest* in the "Top 100 in the World." Designed by Pete Dye, the course has eight holes that hug the rugged coastline, offering smashing views and teeth-rattling shots. Wait until you get those sand bunkers in your sights: Overshoot the bunkers and you're likely to hit either the rocks or more sand—the beach.

And speaking of beaches, "lounge lizards" will be blissfully happy. There are three beaches, including the lovely, private Minitas Beach. Coconut palms and thatched umbrellas provide shade on the wide, white stretch of sand. Water sports include just about anything you can think of, from sailboarding to scuba diving. Package rates include some sports, but you may have to pay extra for things like scuba and deep-sea fishing.

Each of the fourteen pools is unique in design and patio landscaping; all are so inviting you'll want to plant yourself in a different one each day.

Play tennis and you won't wear yourself out chasing an errant ball. Casa de Campo's tennis staff includes a number of people who will run and fetch for the players. The pro will give you private lessons, or you can participate in the clinics and round-robins that are routinely scheduled.

Also located on the grounds is a shooting center, the finest of its kind outside England. It has a 110-foot tower and a variety of sport-shooting options.

There is an extensive equestrian center where you can learn to ride or practice skills you already have. There are also an active polo operation, dude ranch, and rodeo arena.

Sitting atop some cliffs above the winding Chavon River is a must- see—the Altos de Chavon. This replica of a sixteenth-century Italian village, designed by the Italian filmmaker Roberto Copa, was constructed entirely by hand by local craftsmen. Cobblestone paths, stone carvings, arches, plant-shaded walks, and weathered stone buildings with red-tile roofs look very Old World, indeed. Although you might think it all a bit contrived, somehow it works.

Here you'll find a church, a museum of archaeology, an art gallery, an art school, craft shops, boutiques, and four restaurants. There is a large outdoor Roman amphitheater, which has been the venue for a number of name-brand concerts and performances, drawing stars like Frank Sinatra and Julio Iglesias.

When you stay at Casa de Campo, you'll have a choice of restaurants, running the gamut from gourmet candlelight dinners to barefoot-casual. Go Italian at La Piazzetta and Cafe del Sol; Mexican at El Sombrero; Dominican specialties at Café el Patio. Fresh fish like grouper, tuna, and red snapper along with quality meats and locally produced vegetables and fruits are artfully prepared. Try the banana milkshakes in the open-air, thatched Lago Grill. Enjoy the peerless views and gourmet cuisine from the cliff-hugging Casa del Rio restaurant. Or have dinner prepared for you in the privacy of your villa. So many options.

Your best bet is to choose the Honeymoon Inclusive package, providing you with accommodations, sports, food, and beverages. Villas are very pricey, and who needs to pay for an extra bedroom!

Address/Phone: P.O. Box 140, La Romana, Dominican Republic; (809) 523–3333; fax (809) 523–8548

E-mail: res@pwmonline.com

U.S. Reservations: (800) 877–3643 or (305) 856–5405; fax (305) 858–4677

Owner/Manager: Ana Lisa Brache, managing director

Arrival/Departure: Transfers can be arranged; Excel Club (a premium accommodations category) guests receive complimentary transportation from airport to resort

Distance from Santo Domingo Airport: 1½ hours; La Romana Airport 5 minutes

Distance from Santo Domingo: 1½ hours

Accommodations: 300 rooms, 150 two-, three-, and four-bedroom villas

Best Room/Suite: Go for a room nearest the location of your interests, such as a golf course or the beach

Amenities: Air-conditioning, ceiling fans, minibars, coffeemaker, TV, clock radio, in-room safe, hair dryer. Excel Club guests also get private maid service, breakfast, Dominican Bar, and more.

Electricity: 110 volts

Sports and Facilities: 3 championship 18-hole golf courses (1 for members only), Tennis Center with 13 Har-Tru courts (10 lighted); free weights and exercise equipment; shooting center; 14 pools; equestrian center, polo, marina, hiking, full range of water sports, fishing

Dress Code: Casual smart

Weddings: Can be arranged

Rates/Packages: $155–$499 per couple per night (summer and fall); $255–$745 (winter).

Payment/Credit Cards: Most major

Deposit: Secure with credit card

Government Taxes: Rooms, 13 percent; food, 8 percent

Service Charges: 10 percent

Entry Requirements for U.S. Citizens: Proof of citizenship; passport best

GRENADA
≈≈≈

Spice Island Beach Resort

Location: On Grand Anse Beach.

Romantic Features: Private garden patios with pools; Jacuzzis for two; patio a step away from the sand.

Sure it's on the quiet side—it doesn't have a disco or a casino. It also doesn't have activity leaders. But if being smack on a great beach, having your own private pool in a walled garden courtyard, and enjoying a large

Jacuzzi tub for two interests you, then you should definitely check out the Spice Island Beach Resort. Here the white towels are thick and fluffy, the king-size bed is dressed in high-thread-count linens, and the beach chairs under the wind-sculpted sea grape trees are just too inviting to pass by.

Spice is a well-seasoned beach resort that has been honed and perfected by its Grenadian owners, headed by Royston Hopkin, CMG, and his brother, Arnold. The Hopkin family has been in the hotel business for many years and really knows how to do it right. The resort has a high repeat guest business, and heaven help the Hopkins if they decide to make any major changes: They'll really hear it from their guests, who are happy with things just as they are. And who can complain?

Set on 1,600 feet of wide, white beachfront are two meandering rows of one- and two-story cottages huddled under palms and sea grapes. The one-story beachfront cottages, where you literally step from your patio right into the sand, have large Jacuzzis illuminated by a skylight, a sitting area, a bath with super-size shower, and two twin or double beds. There is also a terrace where you get unobstructed views of the water and the picturesque capital of St. George's in the distance. If being on the beach is a top priority, these rooms should do it. But you will have to put up with guests walking back and forth right in your "front yard," as they go to, from, and along the beach.

The private pool suites are much more secluded, especially the older ones on the northern end of the property, which have larger pools (about 16 feet by 20 feet) and raised garden terraces that give you excellent views of the sea through wide breaks in the row of beachfront cottages. The pool, the terrace, and a large garden are all enclosed by an 8-foot wall that ensures your privacy. Your terrace comes with two lounges, an umbrella, a round table, and two chairs. Walls are draped with passion flowers, bougainvillea, hibiscus, and other flowering plants.

The private pool suites on the other side of the reception area are newer and perhaps even a bit more private. They are also smaller, and when you sit on your terrace, although the beach is only twenty steps away, you really can't see it. You can also choose one of the garden-view suites. These are located on the second story over the newer pool suites and have vaulted ceilings and wide, tiled terraces. Water views and sea breezes are superb from here.

All rooms have whirlpool bath; some have full-size hot tubs with all the bells and whistles. Most baths have bidets, and rooms are furnished with rattan furniture, original paintings by Grenadian artists, and tropical print fabrics. Floors are ceramic tile, and there are lots of louvers to open for cross-ventilation, unless you want to crank up the mother of all air-conditioners; it's a big one. Spice's new Royal Pool Suites are not only very private, they're the most luxurious accommodations of all. A private sundeck, a canopied fitness area with a sauna and exercise bike, lush gardens, and a pool set the mood outside, while inside you can enjoy your marble bath, king-size bed, minibar, TV, music center, and lots of other amenities.

The property is well landscaped with a variety of tropical flowers and palms. Trellises, walls, and wood-slat roofs support lush vines, many covered with flowers like the showy, yellow buttercups.

The open-air bar and restaurant are adjacent to the beach, and entertainment is provided in the bar or courtyard several nights a week. Cuisine includes fresh local specialties and international dishes.

At the water sports center, you can arrange for complimentary snorkeling, kayaking, and Hobie-Cats, and there is a tennis court that provides racquets if you need them. Lessons are extra. A boutique is also located on the property.

Spice is located near St. George's and is thus close to "the action," but Grenada is not a place you come to for a lively nightlife. There are a couple of local clubs, such as Fantasia 2001 and Le Sucrier, nearby, and a weekly Rhum Runner Cruise, where it is party time big time, but in general you will have to be content with dancing to Spice's band, walking in the moonlight on the beach, sitting on your patio as the sun sets, and taking midnight swims in the sea or your own pool.

Grenada has a lot to offer in the way of hiking, scuba diving, and just sheer beauty. Its people couldn't be friendlier; its waters, more inviting. Still relatively undiscovered by Americans, Grenada gives you a lot for your money. For those who love the beach and privacy, Spice is a real winner.

Address/Phone: P.O. Box 6, Grand Anse Beach, Grenada, W.I.; (473) 444–4258; fax (473) 444–4807

E-mail: spiceis@caribsurf.com

Web Site: www.spicebeachresort.com

U.S. Reservations: (800) 223–9815 or (212) 476–9444

Owner/Manager: Royston Hopkin, CMG, chairman and managing director; Arnold Hopkin, deputy chairman and deputy managing director; Augustus Cruickshank, general manager

Arrival/Departure: 10-minute taxi ride from the airport (about $15)

Distance from Point Salines International Airport: 3 miles

Distance from St. George's: 6 miles (10 minutes)

Accommodations: 13 private pool suites; 39 whirlpool suites (beachfront and garden-view); 4 royal private pool suites

Best Room/Suite: Private Royal Pool Suites

Amenities: Whirlpool tub for two or hot tub, bidet, hair dryer, air-conditioning, ceiling fan, shampoo and conditioner, telephone, AM/FM clock radio, coffee and tea bar, minibar, room service, in-room safe; nightly turndown service

Electricity: 220 volts

Sports and Facilities: Swimming at beach, snorkeling, sailing a Sunfish, sailboarding; tennis court (lit for night play); gym; scuba diving nearby at Spice Island Diving, a full-service water-sports operator on Grand Anse Beach

Dress Code: Casual elegance (no shorts at dinner)

Weddings: Wedding coordinator on premises; wedding package available.

Rates/Packages: $395–$750 per couple per night (winter); $315–$575 (spring–fall), including breakfast and dinner. All-Inclusive Package rates, $405–$835, include all meals, bar service, wines, and sports. Passion in Paradise, from $3,200 per couple, includes 7 nights' private pool suite accommodations with whirlpool tub, all meals and drinks (except wine and champagne), water sports, bicycles, tennis, use of fitness center, a basket of spice-scented oils, snorkeling trip, greens fees, bottle of champagne, taxes, service charges, and sunset cruise.

Payment/Credit Cards: Most major

Deposit: 1-night deposit during summer months; 3-night deposit in winter. Cancel 14 days or more (summer) and within 30 days (winter) before arrival date for full refund.

Government Taxes: 8 percent; included in Passion in Paradise Package; $15 departure tax at airport

Service Charges: 10 percent; included in Passion in Paradise and All-Inclusive packages

Entry Requirements for U.S. Citizens: Proof of citizenship; passport best

JAMAICA

Grand Lido Sans Souci

Location: Ocho Rios, on Jamaica's north shore.

Romantic Features: Adults-only resort; private Jacuzzi; dancing under the stars alongside the beach.

According to legend, the natural mineral springs located on the grounds of Grand Lido Sans Souci will fill the hearts of couples who take a dip with the power of the forbidden, passionate love secretly shared by an English admiral and a Spanish maiden. All this aside, you won't need much inducement to feel the romance at this seaside property, which combines the elegance of a bygone era with the comforts you look for today.

After going through several ownership and management changes over the years, Grand Lido Sans Souci is now part of the all-inclusive SuperClubs family.

At this upscale and quietly elegant resort, you can now enjoy the benefits of package pricing. Everything—even name-brand liquors, meals, golf fees, and scuba-diving instruction—is all rolled into one price, paid before you come. Even weddings are complimentary.

Grand Lido Sans Souci enjoys a wonderful beachfront setting; part of it is tucked into the cliff at one end of the property, which drops to a white sand beach where the newest suites are located. The resort's pinky beige, three-story buildings are cheerfully accented with white gingerbread trim and terraces. One of the oldest resorts in Jamaica, it has been drawing people since the 1700s to partake in the curative powers of the natural mineral springs, which still flow down the rocks to the sea.

In the 1960s Sans Souci established itself as a holiday residential community for wealthy Brits who purchased apartments on the grounds. In the 1980s new owners renovated the entire place, turning the apartments into guest quarters. Recently an entire new group of buildings was constructed on the 400-foot beach at the west end of the property.

Over the years the gardens, one of the most charming aspects of Grand Lido Sans Souci, have had plenty of time to grow and mature. Follow the winding walks, which eventually lead to the spa, pool, and beach, and take in the beauty of the hibiscus, bougainvillea, red tulip trees, palms, and exotic flowering shrubs planted all along the way. In addition to the main beach, there is a clothes-optional beach.

Rooms and suites that overlook the ocean are spacious; most have separate sitting areas and large balconies. The newer suites on the beach are decorated in soft, light colors and have French doors that separate the bedroom from the living room area. Baths are natural-colored tile and marble with double sinks, and many have Jacuzzis.

You have a choice of three restaurants, including the casual Ristorante Palazzina, an indoor/outdoor eatery serving breakfast, lunch, and dinner; Casanova featuring gourmet cuisine and the most formal of the restaurants, perfect for romantic dining under the stars; and the Beach Grill offering snacks and local specialties.

If you want to be active, there are plenty of water sports as well as tennis, golf, croquet—you name it. You can also relax at Charlie's Spa: Get a massage, facial, manicure, pedicure, body scrub, and reflexology. At night there is music for dancing under the stars, and local entertainers often perform on the Terrace.

In French Sans Souci means "carefree." Once you spend a few days here, you'll understand why the name is so apt.

Address/Phone: P.O. Box 103, Ocho Rios, Jamaica, W.I.; (876) 994–1353; fax (876) 994–1544

E-mail: sslido@cws.com

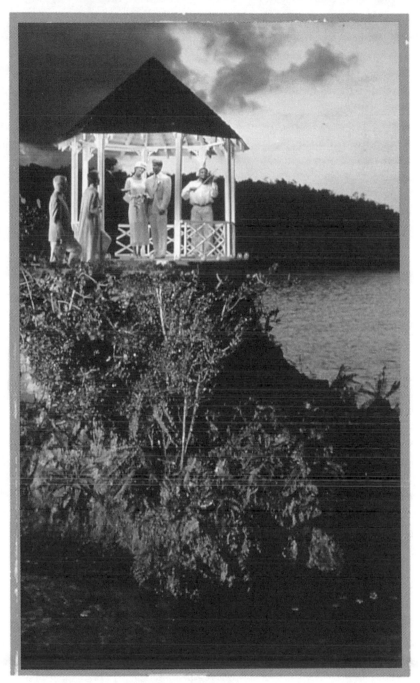

Wedding Gazebo at Grand Lido Sans Souci, Jamaica

Web Site: www.superclubs.com

U.S. Reservations: (800) GO–SUPER

Owner/Manager: John J. Issa, chairman; Pierre Battaglia, general manager

Arrival/Departure: Transfers included in rate

Distance from Donald Sangster International Airport, Montego Bay: 70 miles (1¾ hours)

Distance from Ocho Rios: 2 miles (5 minutes)

Accommodations: 146 suites

Best Room/Suite: Beachfront suite with Jacuzzi

Amenities: Air-conditioning, hair dryer, double vanities, whirlpool tubs (most), direct-dial telephones, TV, AM/FM clock radio/CD player, minirefrigerator, in-room coffee and tea; 24-hour room service; laundry, valet, and dry-cleaning services

Electricity: 110 volts

Sports and Facilities: 4 tennis courts (lit for night play), 4 pools, 2 Jacuzzis, 2 beaches; sailboarding, Sunfish sailing, waterskiing, snorkeling, kayaking, glass-bottom boat rides, scuba diving with resort certification; Hobie-Cats, watertrikes; mineral whirlpool tub, natural mineral spring pool, beach; Ping-Pong, basketball, volleyball, shuffleboard, bocce ball, darts, croquet; bicycling, morning walks, golf, aerobics, aquacize, fitness center

Dress Code: Tropically casual

Weddings: "Super-Inclusive" weddings are complimentary and include marriage license, minister, witnesses, flowers, music, champagne, and cake. The ceremony can take place in the seaside gazebo, on the beach, or in the gardens.

Rates/Packages: 3-night package, $1,640–$2,900 per couple; 7-night package, $3,520–$6,000 per couple (summer); 3 nights, $1,760–$2,900; 7 nights, $3,700–$6,220 (spring–fall)

Payment/Credit Cards: Most major

Deposit: Guarantee with credit card

Government Taxes: Included

Service Charges: Included

Entry Requirements for U.S. Citizens: Proof of citizenship; passport best

≈≈≈

Half Moon Golf, Tennis, and Beach Club

Location: Set on 400 beachfront acres in Montego Bay.

Romantic Features: Clusters of villas and suites, some with private pools; a wonderful beach; beautiful sunrises; candlelight dining and dancing under the stars.

Half Moon Golf, Tennis, and Beach Club enjoys one of the most romantic settings in the Caribbean. Put this together with one of the best managers in the Caribbean, Heinz Simonitsch, part owner and managing director of Half Moon since 1963, and it's no wonder that this resort attracts a sophisticated, international clientele, including Sean Connery, the Beatles, Prince Charles, and George Bush. Set on 400 acres of manicured gardens bordering a mile-long, white crescent beach, most of Half Moon's stark-white, two-story, plantation villas and beach houses are quietly arranged along the edge of a lovely, palm-fringed beach. Gardens are interspersed among the buildings, which serve as a brilliant backdrop for the red and orange bougainvillea that climbs up the walls and hugs the arches. Some of the rooms open onto wrought-iron balconies; first-floor rooms have arched Palladian windows with French doors that open onto a seaside terrace. The villas are really superb, with private pools and gardens.

Golfing couples will enjoy the excellent par 72 championship golf course designed by Robert Trent Jones, and racquet players can challenge their partners on the squash or tennis courts and meet other couples at the tennis pavilion. There is a full-service health center with Nautilus and life fitness equipment as well as aerobics classes, and there are biking, horseback riding, and paths for walking. Swimmers and sunbathers have a choice of several freshwater pools, located throughout the grounds, or they can head to the beach. You don't even have to get up when you want a drink poolside or on the beach. Waiters will scurry to bring drinks and refreshments right to your chair. Snorkeling, scuba diving, sailing, sailboarding, and deep-sea fishing are readily available, and if you want to totally relax you can try a sauna, a massage, or even an herbal wrap.

Your choice of accommodations includes deluxe rooms, suites, and villas, most strung along the beach and some set in the gardens. Rooms are airy and spacious, and most have sitting areas. They are furnished with white wicker and Queen Anne–inspired pieces made out of Jamaican mahogany. Black-and-white-tiled floors, sisal throw rugs and Oriental carpets, English flowered chintz, and authentic Jamaican art create an elegant yet exuberant mood, somewhat different from the usual Caribbean style. Worth considering are the Royal Beachfront Suites, which are enclosed in their own garden courtyard with two pools and a central lounge reserved exclusively for Royal Suite guests, where continental breakfast and evening cocktails are served each day.

Half Moon has six outstanding restaurants, the open-air Seagrape Terrace, the Sugarmill Restaurant, the Il Giardino, La Baguette, Sakura, and the Royal Stocks. Guests can select over one hundred different kinds of wines from several countries at any of the restaurants. The Seagrape specializes in Caribbean cuisine, and diners can sit on the tree-shaded seaside patio and enjoy dining by candlelight under the starry skies. If you're in the mood for chicken marinated

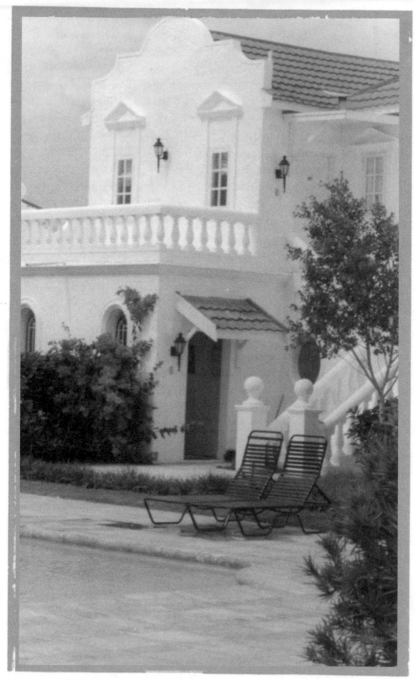

Half Moon Golf, Tennis, and Beach Club, Jamaica

in lime and fresh herbs, *duckanoo* (sweet potato dessert), or breadfruit vichyssoise, this is the place to come. During and after dinner there are a resident band for dancing well into the evening and a discotheque for late-night fun.

Under the direction of the French chef, Frederick Wagnon, the Victorian-style Sugarmill Restaurant is located on the grounds of—surprise—a sugar plantation, where you'll find the remains of a 200-year-old water-powered mill. Here diners are treated to dishes such as freshly made pastas, prime rib, flambéed entrees, and shrimp stuffed with ripe bananas and cooked in coconut batter. You can dine on the open-air terrace or inside while enjoying live music for listening and dancing.

For a change of pace, you can order room service and indulge in a lazy morning with breakfast in bed. Try the coconut waffles, fresh fruits, and Blue Mountain coffee. A Night Owl menu is available from 10:00 P.M. to 1:00 A.M. Beach parties, floor shows with native entertainers, and steel drum bands are scheduled on various days. As if there weren't enough places to hang out, there is also the breezy, beachside bar.

Since the choices and quality of food at Half Moon are among the best in Jamaica, if not the Caribbean, take one of the plans that includes food as well as the various sports activities. The Imperial Plan is the most comprehensive, followed by the Platinum Plan. There are also programs that allow you to dine around at sister properties (Round Hill, Plantation Inn, Coyaba, and Good Hope).

Address/Phone: Montego Bay, Jamaica, W.I.; (876) 953–2211; fax (876) 953–2731

E-mail: hmoonres@infochan.com

Web Site: www.halfmoon.com.jm

U.S. Reservations: Charms, (800) 742–4276; Utell, (800) 223–6510; Elegant Resorts International, (800) 237–3237

Owner/Manager: Heinz W. Simonitsch, managing director

Arrival/Departure: Transfer complimentary with Imperial, Golf, Spa, and Platinum Plans

Distance from Donald Sangster International Airport, Montego Bay: 6 miles

Distance from Montego Bay: 7 miles

Accommodations: 419, including rooms, suites, cottages, and villas; many with private pools

Best Room/Suite: Imperial Suites, Royal Suites, or beachfront cottages

Amenities: Air-conditioning, ceiling fans, hair dryer, minibar, toiletries, cable TV, radio, double sinks (villas and Royal Suites), in-room safe deposit box, shopping arcade with small grocery store, ironing board/iron

Electricity: 110 volts

Sports and Facilities: 18-hole championship golf course, putting green; 9 Laykold tennis courts (4 Omnicourts, lit for night play), 4 squash courts; scuba diving, snorkeling, sailboarding, sailing; paddleboats, glass-bottom boat; deep-sea fishing; horseback riding, bicycles; saunas; aerobics classes; 2 large pools and 5 smaller ones

Dress Code: Smartly casual

Weddings: A special wedding package, priced at $750, includes marriage officer, witnesses, flowers, champagne, video, cake, and photos. Allow one month to set it up. The fairy-tale gazebo, which sits at the end of a sliver of land that juts into the water, is a popular place to hold the ceremony.

Rates/Packages: The Platinum Plan, $345–$745 per person per night (winter), $270–$545 (summer); includes airport transfers, champagne on arrival, all meals, afternoon tea, bar drinks, minibar drinks, room service bar, dine- and lunch-around program, tennis, golf, sailing, sailboarding, glass-bottom boat ride, scuba diving, snorkeling, sauna, use of gym, bicycles, beach chairs and towels, squash, horseback riding, government tax, and 10 percent service charge. Imperial Plan, $420–$820 per person per night (winter), $345–$620 (summer); includes everything in the Platinum Plan plus private car transfers, sight-seeing tours, room service, bottles of wine and champagne, golf cart, caddy fees, golf gift, club and shoe storage, club rental, golf clinic, spa service and health programs, massage, aerobics and fitness classes. European Plan (no meals) packages are also available as well as spa and golf packages. (Don't try to figure out what you are going to have to pay from their rate card; Half Moon wins the prize for having the most confusing published rate information. Call your travel agent or ask one of the reservation representatives.)

Payment/Credit Cards: Most major

Deposit: 3 nights required for confirmation; cancel within 14 days (summer), 30 days (winter), or 45 days (Christmas) to avoid late charge of 1 night's room rate

Government Taxes: Included

Service Charges: Included

Entry Requirements for U.S. Citizens: Valid passport, or birth certificate with raised seal along with two recent photo IDs

≈≈≈

Sandals Resorts

Sandals Dunn's River, Sandals Montego Bay, Sandals Negril, Sandals Ocho Rios, Sandals Royal Jamaican

Location: Montego Bay, Negril, Ocho Rios.

Romantic Features: Couples only; nonstop activities and quiet hideaway places; romantic restaurants; Stay at One, Enjoy All program—use all the Sandals resorts at no extra charge.

S andals Resorts packages romance with a capital "R." Starting in Montego Bay, Jamaica, with the first property, Sandals now has more than a dozen (and growing) spread out over several other islands, including St. Lucia, Antigua, and the Bahamas. The resort company's all-inclusive, couples-only concept continues to score a "ten" with honeymooners for a number of reasons.

For starters, their ultra-inclusive plan, whereby you pay one price up front for virtually everything, is a real winner. Accommodations, meals, snacks, bar beverages including name-brand liquors, water sports, tennis, golf, tips, and just about anything else you can think of are all rolled into the package. Since many young couples have a set amount to spend, knowing there will be no surprises when they check out provides a high level of emotional comfort. It also eliminates the "Do we have enough cash to eat here tonight?" kind of discussion. But no matter how good an idea, this wouldn't work unless the resorts themselves were really romantic and special. They are.

Guided all along the way by its dynamic founder and chairman, Gordon "Butch" Stewart, Sandals has attained a well-deserved reputation for consistently delivering what it promises: a "no problem" romantic holiday with all the bells and whistles. Standard with Sandals are king-size beds, beautiful decor, a whole range of sports and fitness facilities, every water sport you can think of, including scuba diving, and a staff that radiates as much good cheer as kids on their first day of summer vacation.

The fact that you can walk up to any of the bars and order a drink or food at will without having to sign a chit or pull out your wallet is a big plus. This also goes for the restaurants. You can eat at the same one every night or eat around. You can order anything on the menu—wine, beer, mixed drinks—whatever you're in the mood for, and it's all part of the package.

There is a huge list of activities available to guests, all complimentary. On hand to keep the mood upbeat and arrange special activities and parties are the energetic Playmakers. If you like to be on the go from dawn to dusk waterskiing, hiking, or playing tennis or golf at the Sandals Golf and Country Club, you can pig out on the vast array of activities on tap at any of the Sandals properties. And if you tire of the scenery where you're staying, you can hop on a shuttle and spend the day or evening at one of the other Sandals resorts as part of their Stay at One, Play at Six, Enjoy All concept.

You'll find many other young newlyweds to exchange wedding stories with on your honeymoon at Sandals, and since the resorts operate exclusively for couples, you won't have to share your pool space with any kids. Many couples marry here and go on to make friendships that may last a lifetime.

Each of the Sandals properties offers the same quality of services and amenities. Where you choose to stay, however, will depend on what is really important to you. Each place has its own unique allure.

Sandals Montego Bay, the oldest of the properties and one of the most intimate, enjoys a wonderful beach. Its 244 rooms and suites are located in two-story buildings and two-unit cottages that are literally a stone's throw from the sand. The lobby is not as elegant as those of the other properties, and the resort's location close to the airport can be a distraction. However, the staff and guests cheerfully make light of the occasional jets that zoom in and out by waving to them—a Montego Bay tradition. And being so close to the airport means you can land, clear customs, and be on the beach inside about a half-hour. The beachfront suite with separate sitting room, marble bath, four-poster bed, and patio with a private pool is wonderful. And especially good here are the restaurants.

The 190-room Sandals Royal Jamaican is also close to the airport and is set on seventeen acres fringed by a series of six white, sandy beaches. The rooms, which are located in two- and three-story pink and white buildings, are designed in the spirit of a traditional Georgian great house and are elegantly furnished with four-poster beds, English flowered chintz drapes and bedspreads, and classic mahogany furniture. The buildings, arranged around three nice little pools, are named after homes owned by British royalty and look to the sea.

If you love white sandy beaches and don't mind being a bit out of the way, try the 219-room Sandals Negril Beach Resort & Spa. Ask for the loft suites, which are set into the palms and gardens along a 7-mile, powdery, white sand beach. It's about a ninety-minute ride from the airport and has a more laid-back ambience than the other Sandals resorts.

Set in a virtual Garden of Eden, Sandals Ocho Rios Resort & Golf Club is a botanical wonderland of flowers, trees, and shrubs. Hammocks are hidden in little glades, small streams bubble through the ferns and grasses, and bridges span the waterways. Two pools are action centers for high-energy sports like water volleyball and swimming races. There is also a smaller pool, hidden in the dense "jungle," where you can escape and simply loll around. If you're looking for a long stretch of white sand beach, you may be disappointed; the beach here is small. The views from your oceanside room are great, though, and the satisfaction level of the property's guests is high.

Sandals Dunn's River Golf Resort & Spa, one of Sandal's newest resorts in Jamaica, resembles a posh establishment on the Italian Riviera. Rooms are located in two large, red-roofed, two- and six-story buildings facing the sea. Here the grounds have been sculpted, molded, and planted to the nines, creating a playground of pleasure. The largest pool in Jamaica, with its own waterfall—a replica of Dunn's River Falls—and swim-up bar, along with seaside gazebos, Jacuzzis, bridges, and a piano bar are spread out over a large area. Rooms are elegantly furnished, and the beach is good.

You might assume, since the food is already included and paid for, that a place like Sandals could get away with providing rather average restaurants. Not so. At Sandals the restaurant side of the resort operation is first-rate. Dinners feature a la carte menus, and couples can dine alone or with other couples. Breakfast and lunch are buffets, but a nice Sandals touch is the "white glove" service—a waiter carries your tray to your table. Each resort averages four restaurants, and all offer a distinctly different dining experience, ranging from informal to elegantly casual. Most of the restaurants are oriented to the sea, and the Bali Hai restaurant at Sandals Royal Jamaican is actually on its own little island.

If you like Italian food, you can head to Cucina Romana, at Sandals Montego Bay, where you can dine on a freshly made pasta of your choice while enjoying the sunset view from your table on the open-air deck. Next door, at Sandals Royal Jamaican, the Courtyard treats its diners to fresh-grilled specialties. If the flair and flourish of a teppanyaki Japanese restaurant is tempting, you can try Kimonos at Sandals Negril. Here you'll dine on exotic Oriental entrees prepared right in front of you.

Sandals went all the way to Holland to find an authentic Indonesian chef for Bali Hai. Since the restaurant is located just offshore from Sandals Royal Jamaican, getting there via the resort's private launch is part of the fun. Once you arrive at the entrance of the ornate, carved-wood building, a hostess wraps a colorful silk scarf around you, your "costume" for the evening. Diners sit at long tables where hot and spicy as well as mild dishes (for more timid palates) are placed in the center for everyone to sample.

In the elegant category, Sandals Montego Bay's Oleander Room, brainchild of Horace Peterkin, the resort's enterprising general manager, has stenciling on the ceiling and a warm coral decor accented with brass lamps, chandeliers, and Palladian windows overlooking the sea. Most romantic. This is your chance to try some tasty Jamaican specialties.

Get hungry between meals? Each Sandals resort has an "anytime grill," open well into the night, offering snacks as well as made-to-order meals.

Dollar for dollar, the Sandals resorts offer a lot of value and a lot more unexpected pleasures.

Address/Phone: In Jamaica, W.I.: Sandals Dunn's River, P.O. Box 51, Ocho Rios, St. Ann; (876) 972–1610; fax (876) 972–1611; Sandals Montego Bay, P.O. Box 100, Kent Avenue, Montego Bay, St. James; (876) 952–5510 or 952–5515; fax (876) 952–0816; Sandals Negril, P.O. Box 12, Negril; (876) 957–5216 or 957–4217; fax (876) 957–5338; Sandals Ocho Rios, P.O. Box 771, Ocho Rios, St. Ann; (876) 974–5691; fax (809) 974–5700; Sandal's Royal Jamaican, Mahoe Bay, Box 167, Montego Bay, St. James; (876) 953–2231 or 953–2232; fax (876) 953–2788

U.S. Reservations: (800) SANDALS

Owner/Manager: Gordon "Butch" Stewart, chairman of the board; Louis Grant, general manager, Sandals Dunn's River; Horace Peterkin, general manager, Sandals Montego Bay; Baldwin Powell, general manager, Sandals Negril; Michael Darby, general manager, Sandals Ocho Rios; Carl Hendricks, general manager, Sandals Royal Jamaican

Arrival/Departure: Sandals guests are met at the airport and escorted to their resort.

Distance from Donald Sangster International Airport, Montego Bay: Driving time: Montego Bay 5 minutes; Ocho Rios 1¾ hours; Negril 1½ hours

Accommodations: Rooms, suites, bungalows: Sandals Dunn's River, 256 rooms and suites in five categories; Sandals Montego Bay, 244 rooms and suites in nine categories; Sandals Ocho Rios, 237 rooms in five categories; Sandals Negril, 219 rooms in six categories, including loft suites; Sandals Royal Jamaican, 190 rooms in six categories

Best Room/Suite: At Sandals Dunn's River, ask for the Penthouse Honeymoon Suite or the one-bedroom Oceanfront Suite; Sandals Montego Bay, the Presidential or Prime Minister Suites or the beachfront suite with the private pool (shared only with adjacent suite); Sandals Negril, Beachfront Honeymoon Suite or Beachfront Honeymoon One-Bedroom Loft Suites; Sandals Ocho Rios, Penthouse Honeymoon Ocean-View Suite; Sandals Royal Jamaican, Grand Luxe Honeymoon Beachfront or Beachfront Royal Suites. These accommodations will run you approximately $500 more (for 7 nights) than the most inexpensive room but are worth it if you care to splurge a bit.

Amenities: Air-conditioning, king-size beds, ceiling fans, hair dryer, generous kits of lotions and shampoo, telephones, clock radios, TV, minibar, and safe deposit box

Electricity: 110 volts

Sports and Facilities: Tennis day or night, scuba diving, snorkeling, sailboarding, sailing; Hobie-Cats, paddleboats, canoes, kayaks; racquetball, golf, pitch-and-putt golf, volleyball, basketball; pool tables, shuffleboard, horseshoes, croquet, Ping-Pong, aquatriking, squash, and waterskiing (except Ocho Rios). Also "Fit-Shape" program, exercise rooms, aerobics classes

Dress Code: Casual

Weddings: Over 500 weddings are performed annually at the various Sandals properties. On-site wedding coordinators arrange all the details, including taking care of the paperwork, leading the couple through the process of getting the marriage license, flowers, music, and reception. "WeddingMoons"—Sandals's term—can be as intimate as a couple getting married at the beach or under a gazebo with a best man and attendant "borrowed" from the Sandals staff. Or it can be a more elaborate affair held at one of the Sandals villas with a reception for the couple's family and friends.

A Sandals wedding costs $750 (or is free with a stay of five nights). The package includes preparation of documents, best man/maid of honor (if needed), wedding announcement cards, services of a justice of the peace or clergy, tropical flowers, wedding cake, champagne, personalized candlelight dinner, and wedding video. Options include special treats such as sunset cruise, reception, gift baskets, and upgraded villa accommodations.

There are many places a couple can choose to be married. Most popular are places like the gazebo at Sandals Montego Bay and the beach or the gardens in Sandals Ocho Rios. Brides can bring their own dresses or use one provided by Sandals. One bride who got married in Sandals Dunn's River wore a white, two-piece swimsuit with her veil, gloves, and garter. The groom wore a pair of white shorts, a bow tie, a cummerbund, and a boutonniere attached to one of his shirt garters. Taking a quick dip in the Caribbean after the ceremony was "no problem."

Rates/Packages: All-inclusive rates for 7 nights start at $1,715 per person

Payment/Credit Cards: Most major

Deposit: Guarantee with credit card

Government Taxes: Included

Service Charges: Included

Entry Requirements for U.S. Citizens: Proof of citizenship; passport best

≋≋≋

Swept Away Negril

Location: Located on twenty acres on Long Bay in Negril, at the western tip of Jamaica.

Romantic Features: Superb sports and fitness complex; white sand beach.

Swept Away's romantic beachfront setting, gardens, and spacious veranda suites along with its exceptional health and fitness complex have been wooing romantics ever since the resort opened just a few years ago. The luxurious suites, which sit amid tropical gardens overlooking the turquoise sea, are as tastefully decorated as they are comfortable. Jamaican in style and character, the decor is designed to complement the natural colors of the outdoors with the use of local woods, rattan chaises and chairs with puffy cushions, king-size beds, red-tile floors, and upbeat, pink and white fabrics. Your bedroom opens onto a very large veranda where you can enjoy the views of the gardens and sea. Rooms are air-conditioned, but you will probably find that the louvered-window walls along with a gently turning ceiling fan will keep you cool.

You might be tempted just to chill out on your veranda, but you'll find it hard to resist the wide array of tempting things to do. Tennis buffs won't have to line up at the tennis courts to wait to play: There are ten courts, five of them clay, unusual in the Caribbean, where courts are most often of the hard-surface variety. Swept away has a 25-meter pool, complete with lap lanes, air-conditioned racquetball and squash courts, an easy-on-your-feet aerobics floor, a parcourse fitness circuit, and even a basketball court. If you want to work out, you can head to the gym, which has all the latest equipment. Unlimited golf at the Negril Hills Golf Club, five minutes away, is included in your package.

Sitting on a twenty-acre piece of pristine beachfront on the western end of Jamaica, Swept Away has a boatload of water sports, such as sailing, kayaking, sailboarding, and waterskiing. Certified scuba divers get two free dives daily, and you can join others for a game of beach volleyball—always a good way to meet other guests.

Swept Away earns kudos for its cuisine, which tastes as good as it looks. Since the resort stresses a healthy lifestyle, you'll find a lot of choices on the menu that are low in fat, yet very tasty. There are a fruit and veggie bar on the grounds and a beachside grill where you can get things like fresh fruit and vegetable juice concoctions, pita sandwiches, and fish sandwiches. When it comes to serious eating, you can dine in either the alfresco Sea Grape beachside restaurant, featuring Jamaican specialties, or Feathers Restaurant, which offers gourmet cuisine. Be sure to try the pumpkin soup and fresh red snapper.

When night falls, you can dance under the stars to the music of a resident band or you can sit back and relax in the piano lounge.

Newlyweds are invited to a special party just for honeymooners, where they can win a one-week return stay at the resort, a dinner for two at a nearby restaurant, a catamaran cruise, horseback rides, or a 30 percent discount at the boutique.

You can be as active—or as lazy—as you want to be. No one coaxes you to do anything. One of the most difficult choices you may have to make is just what you want to do first. Do you want to dawdle in bed in the early morning and have room service bring you breakfast? Do you want to settle into a comfy chaise on the beach or by the smaller seaside pool, or do you feel up to the early morning beachfront power walk?

Swept Away packs a lot of value in its all-inclusive package, even a special massage class, where you can learn techniques to reduce and relieve stress in your mate. Just about the only thing you'll have to pay extra for are the services provided by the new full-service spa and salon facility, where you can get massages and beauty treatments.

Address/Phone: Long Bay, Negril, Jamaica, W.I.; (876) 957–4061; fax (876) 957–4060; U.S. address: 4944 LeJeune Road South, Coral Gables, FL 33146
E-mail: sweptaway@infochan.com
Web Site: www.sweptaway.com
U.S. Reservations: (800) 545–7937

Owner/Manager: Paul Pennicook, president and CEO, Issa Hotels and Resorts

Arrival/Departure: A representative from the resort will meet you at the airport for transfer to the resort

Distance from Donald Sangster International Airport, Montego Bay: 60 miles (1½ hours by car); 2 miles (5 minutes) from Negril Airport

Distance from Negril Center: 5 minutes

Accommodations: 134 Caribbean-style veranda suites in three categories: garden, atrium, and beachfront, most with king-size beds

Best Room/Suite: Beachfront suites

Amenities: Hair dryer, telephone, in-room safe, ceiling fan, toiletries, air-conditioning; room service for continental breakfast

Electricity: 110 volts

Sports and Facilities: 10 lighted tennis courts (5 hard, 5 clay), pool tables, 2 pools, bicycles, jogging track, golf course, basketball court; sailing, kayaking, waterskiing, sailboarding, snorkeling, scuba diving; fully equipped gym; aerobics; racquetball, squash, volleyball; saunas, Jacuzzis

Dress Code: For daytime dining women are requested to wear coverups and men, shirts; resort casual in Main Dining Room; in Feathers men required to wear collared shirt

Weddings: Swept Away averages six weddings a week. Complimentary with any package are minister's fee, marriage license, flowers, wedding cake, and champagne. Popular places to wed include a thatched-roof gazebo and seaside at sunset.

Rates/Packages: All-inclusive packages are priced per person per night and include accommodations, transfers, all meals, unlimited drinks, wine with lunch and dinner, late-night snacks, water sports and use of fitness facilities, afternoon tea, nightly entertainment, classes and clinics, two daily dives for certified divers, unlimited golf, and glass-bottom boat rides. 7 nights from $1,666; 6 nights from $1,428; 5 nights from $1,190; 4 nights from $1,047; and 3 nights from $785.

Payment/Credit Cards: Most major

Deposit: 1-night deposit for 3- to 7-night stay, 3-night deposit for stays over 7 nights; deposit due within 1 week of booking; balance due 30 days prior to arrival. Cancel 8 to 21 days prior to arrival date for full refund; 3-night charge if you cancel 7 days or less prior to arrival date.

Government Taxes: $27 departure tax

Service Charges: Included

Entry Requirements for U.S Citizens: Proof of citizenship required; passport best

NEVIS

Four Seasons Resort Nevis

Location: Set on 2,000 feet of beachfront on Nevis's leeward coast.

Romantic Features: Catamaran cruise to private beach; candlelight dinners on your veranda; a pristine setting amid palms, sand, and sea.

O nce you hear the rustle of the swaying palms, feel the gentle breezes crossing the beach, and see the flourishing tropical rain forest from your private veranda, you will no doubt believe that you have landed in paradise.

Four Seasons Resort Nevis, which is part of the Four Seasons group of prestigious, upscale resorts in exotic locations around the world, lives up to its reputation for providing a bundle of services and luxurious appointments, such as the large marble baths and the Evian water sprayed gently on your face by attendants to cool you while you lounge on the beach or by the pool. But beware: This resort also delivers high prices and can make a serious dent in your budget.

One of the best things Four Seasons has going for it is its location—really spectacular, with a long, golden sand beach lined by what seem to be hundreds of tall, graceful palm trees that blend into the hillside beyond.

It also has an impressive, 6,725-yard, eighteen-hole Robert Trent Jones II golf course that climbs from sea level up the volcanic slopes of Mt. Nevis to the fifteenth hole, where, from your perch at about 1,000 feet above sea level, you will see some incredible views of the sea and craggy hills. The course takes you up and down the mountainside, over deep ravines, and along the ocean. What more could a golfer want! Perhaps a pro shop? Of course. Nothing is left to chance here.

Tennis players have a fancy complex of ten courts, a pro shop, and organized lessons and clinics. And if this isn't enough, there is a fully equipped health club, a complete water sports center, two pools, Ping-Pong, croquet, hiking paths, and myriad other activities that may pull you away from your lounge on one of the most beautiful beaches in the Caribbean.

Occasionally even those with a passion for *plein air* find it necessary to come inside. Because the restaurants and lounges have been designed to ensure maximum exposure to the outdoor environment, even when you are technically indoors at the resort you can still enjoy a magnificent view, trade-wind breezes, and the sound of lapping waves.

Most of the public rooms are located in the sumptuous Great House, the heart of the resort. Many public rooms are open-air, with patios and terraces leading to gardens of tropical Nevisian flowers. The Library Bar is enclosed, cozy, and could have come straight from England—it even has a fireplace and paintings of tall ships. On the rare occasions when the sun is not shining, this is a wonderful place for cocktails before and after dinner.

The two-story bungalow buildings that stretch along the beach have rather uninspired architectural designs, but the interiors of the rooms and suites are spacious and decorated to the nines. Deep chestnut brown armoires, carved headboards, brass lamps, and botanical prints contribute to the British ambience. The use of rattan chairs, tropical-colored fabrics and prints, and tile floors keep the rooms from looking too heavy. Fresh flowers and potted palms also help lighten it all up.

The bathrooms will really knock your socks off. They're simply superb, with lots of marble, double vanities, attractive lighting, and plenty of fluffy towels. The Four Seasons toiletries are especially fine.

There are two gourmet restaurants that serve Caribbean-inspired meat, fish, and seafood dishes and fresh fruits and vegetables: the more formal Dining Room, with its French doors, high ceiling and chandeliers; and the casual, open-air Grill Room La Cabana, serves Mediterranean specialties and brick-oven pizzas. The Ocean Terrace overlooks the pool and the beach, and there is the Tap Room, with a game area and entertainment lounge, a pool cabana, and a sports pavilion.

Evenings you will be able to enjoy dancing and listening to local bands, including a steel drum group.

So if you don't mind blowing a lot of cash, be prepared to revel in one of the most ultraluxurious mega-resorts in the islands.

Address/Phone: P.O. Box 565, Pinney's Beach, Charlestown, Nevis, W.I.; (869) 469–1111; fax (869) 469–1112

U.S. Reservations: (800) 332–3442

Owner/Manager: Brian Parmelee, general manager

Arrival/Departure: Most fly to Antigua, San Juan, or St. Martin for quick flight to St. Kitts, where guests are met by a hotel representative and whisked to the private dock in Basseterre to board a boat for the 30-minute ride to the resort. While onboard you complete check-in formalities and enjoy some refreshments.

Distance from St. Kitts Airport: 20 minutes by boat; 6 miles by land

Distance from Charlestown: 1 1/2 miles

Accommodations: 196 rooms and suites, each with a large veranda ranging from 120 to 160 square feet, overlooking the ocean, Nevis Peak, or the golf course. There are also 20 exquisite villas and homes for rent.

Best Room/Suite: The oceanfront Nelson and Hamilton Suites

Amenities: Air-conditioning, ceiling fan, toiletries, telephone, TV, VCR, clock radio, ice maker, minibar, hair dryer, twin vanities, separate shower and tub, magnifying mirror, bathrobes, bath scale; 24-hour room service

Electricity: 110 volts

Sports and Facilities: 10 tennis courts (3 lighted), 18-hole championship golf course, health club with saunas, whirlpool baths, gym with Nautilus equipment; fitness program, aerobics, massage therapies; beach, pool, snorkeling equipment, sailboards, kayaks, sailboats, sea cycles, catamarans; waterskiing, fishing, scuba diving, croquet, volleyball, shuffleboard, and hiking

Dress Code: Casual elegance

Weddings: Wedding coordinator on premises can arrange all the legalities as well as the ceremony, reception, wedding cake, music, photography, and flowers.

Rates/Packages: Romance in Paradise package, $4,040–$6,885 per couple, includes 7 nights in deluxe oceanfront accommodations, flowers, champagne, and truffles, candlelight dinners, unlimited golf and tennis, massage for two, transfers, and half-day catamaran cruise to private beach. Tax and service charges are extra.

Payment/Credit Cards: Most major

Deposit: 3-night deposit applied toward first and last nights' stay (if staying for a week); refundable if canceled 3 weeks or more prior to arrival date.

Government Taxes: 9 percent

Service Charges: 10 percent

Entry Requirements for U.S. Citizens: Proof of citizenship; passport best

≋

Nisbet Plantation Beach Club

Location: On the island's reef-protected north shore.

Romantic Features: Private cottage steps away from the beach; dining in a historic Great House; hammocks for two strung between palms; in-room massages.

You come here for the peace and the waves washing up on shore, the sound of which mingles with the rustling coconut palms. Cone-shaped mountain peaks rise like soft-pointed hats into the mist; a few lazy cows trespass across manicured rolling lawns; you walk barefoot in the sand as the sun sets. Isn't this what the Caribbean is all about? You expect an island of just 36 square miles with a population of about 9,000 to be quiet and laid back. It is.

If you want to experience the "real" Caribbean, try Nisbet Plantation Beach Club. It all starts with your arrival at the little island airport just barely large enough for a small counter and desk. Already the warm tropical air is blowing away the travel kinks.

I arrived at Nisbet just in time for tea accompanied by thinly sliced salmon sandwiches, pumpkin bread, and chocolate chip cookies. Sitting at an umbrella-shaded table on the outdoor patio of the Great House, I had an unobstructed view right down to the sea, a promise of things to come.

Staggered from the Great House along either side of a wide, grassy, palm-studded way leading to the sea are one- and two-story yellow cottages with four-sided, pointed roofs (Nevis, by law, has no buildings more than two stories). Hibiscus, oleanders, crotons, and a variety of other brilliant tropical flowers and shrubs hug the buildings and walkways. A tennis courts is tucked into a corner of the property, and an open-air beachfront restaurant and bar sits at the water's edge.

Cottages are airy and beautifully appointed with tropical fabrics, rattan chairs, white-tile floors, and plump cushions. Most have high ceilings, walk-in closets, screened porch, and king-size beds. All have patios or balconies. If air-conditioning is a must, you can request it: Not all rooms have it, nor is it really needed. Louvered windows, fans, and constant ocean breezes guarantee to keep you cool.

What surprises at Nisbet are the details. There's a faucet to rinse the sand off your feet just outside your entrance, reading lamps by your bed at just the right height, a drying bar for wet suits, a minibar, a full-length mirror, double vanities, straw carpets in the screened sitting area, plenty of tables and chairs, a coffeemaker, umbrellas, and even a flashlight and a can of bug spray. (Yes, the Caribbean does have an occasional bug or two.) Cool blue-and-white seersucker bathrobes are a refreshing change from the traditional terry. Half shutters between the two rooms in the suites allow air and light to come into the bedroom without sacrificing privacy.

At night the property is lit not with neon-colored floods into the trees, but naturally, softly. It feels like a plantation (which it was in its former life). There are few concrete walkways, mostly you walk on grassy or gravel paths (leave your heels at home). There are rows of palms heavy with clusters of coconuts, banana trees, and room to play croquet.

The beach is wide and long and there are plenty of chaises to go around. Hammocks are strung between palms, and there is a seaside pool and terrace.

What makes it all work is the husband-and-wife management team, Kathie and Don Johnson. They're young and energetic but certainly not inexperienced. Each has more than twenty years in the hotel industry. And it shows.

From ensuring that their guests are met at the airport to being on hand to make sure everything runs smoothly—from a guest who requests a fan to coffee being served promptly at the beachfront restaurant—they oversee every detail. Kathie and Don are "people people." They like to talk to their guests to hear how things are going. To make sure they are happy.

Nisbet has two restaurants: the romantic, candlelit Great House, with its open terrace, high tray ceiling, and arched windows, and Coconuts, the casual poolside restaurant open for breakfast and lunch. The food does not disappoint. Executive Chef Klaus Ryborz uses as much fresh local ingredients as he can get his hands on. The menu changes each night, revolving around what he can get that morning: fresh fish, poultry, meat, vegetables, and fruits are skillfully and creatively cooked into dishes that combine the flavors of the Caribbean and more traditional tastes. There is always a vegetarian dish.

Chilled avocado and passion fruit soup, fresh mahi mahi fillet with almond and banana crust served with a lemongrass sauce and steamed purple potatoes; smoked butternut squash ravioli served with artichokes and shiitake mushrooms in a sun-dried red pepper cream sauce with fresh Parmesan cheese; and chocolate truffle torte are typical choices.

In the evening Kathie and Don greet their guests with complimentary hors d'oeuvres in the Great House lounge before dinner. Once a week, Nisbet's popular beach barbecue features an array of fresh fish and other items. Local bands play in the lounge most evenings.

Nisbet is not a place to come if you want to party all night, ride madly on Jet Skis, or play volleyball in the pool. Rather, you come to soak up the enticing aromas of the flowers and the views of the sea and hills, poke down roads overgrown with grasses to an abandoned sugar mill, pack a picnic and drive to a secluded beach for lunch, or just hang out on the beach with a piña colada.

Above, the palms' feathery fronds gently nudge the sea breezes. Cooling and soothing. Peace.

Address/Phone: St. James Parish, Nevis, West Indies; (869) 469–9325; fax (869) 469–9864

E-mail: nisbetbc@caribsurf.com

Web Site: www.NisbetPlantation.com

U.S. Reservations: (800) 742–6008; e-mail: irr@worldnet.att.net

Owner/Manager: Kathie and Don Johnson, managers

Arrival/Departure: Round-trip transfers provided from St. Kitts

Distance from St. Kitts: About 5 minutes by Nevis Express; 45 minutes by ferry; Puerto Rico about 1 hour by air

Distance from Charlestown: 10 miles; distance from St. Martin about 25 minutes by Winair or Nevis Express

Accommodations: 38 rooms and suites in plantation-style cottages

Best Rooms/Suites: Deluxe Suite with a separate living room; Premier Suites with living room, wet bar, and open patio

Amenities: Hair dryer, fans, minibar, TV, coffee bar, toiletries, umbrella, robes, flashlight, *New York Times* fax, some rooms with air-conditioning

Electricity: 110 volts

Sports and Facilities: Pool; walking, hiking, boating, tennis, snorkeling, massages; golf, horseback riding, plantation tours, ecotours, guided hikes, scuba diving, biking, deep-sea fishing nearby. Try a soothing massage for two in the privacy of your room. Roosevelt Browne, LMT, NCMT, can provide a 50-minute Aveda aroma wrap and massage, a salt glow and massage or other fabulous treatments.

Dress Code: Resort casual. About the only one who wears a tie around here is Patterson, the maître d' who claims to own more than 700 unique ties.

Weddings: Can be arranged; Wedding package $895 for ceremony, champagne, flowers, cake, photographer, wedding coordinator, license, registration and minister's fee, and transportation to and from authorities as necessary

Rates/Packages: $275–$345 per room per night (summer), $470–$590 (winter), including breakfast and dinner, tea, use of tennis courts, snorkeling equipment, laundry service, transfers from Nevis Airport, local telephone calls, and postage. Romance Package: from $3,400 per couple, including 6 nights' accommodations, breakfasts, dinners, tea, champagne, car rental for two days, service charges, taxes, transfers, and $100 bar credit.

Payment/Credit Cards: Most major

Deposit: Three nights' deposit at time of booking. Cancel within 28 days prior to arrival date for refund in winter; 14 days in summer; 60 days holidays.

Government Taxes: 9 percent

Service Charges: 10 percent

Entry Requirements for U.S. Citizens: Proof of citizenship; passport best

PUERTO RICO
≈≈≈

Horned Dorset Primavera Hotel

Location: On four acres, tucked away on the west coast of Puerto Rico.

Romantic Features: Small, intimate inn by the sea; cocktails on seaside veranda as the sun sets.

The elegant Horned Dorset Primavera Hotel, which is hidden away on Puerto Rico's western shore, focuses more on relaxation than recreation and offers only a few facilities. The resort attracts solitude-seeking guests who want a small hotel with plush European standards. Located 2½ hours from San Juan, the Horned Dorset isn't the easiest of places to find. But once you do, you may never want to leave. And that is just part of its mystique.

Its name sounds like a weird kind of English pasta, but the hotel, directly on the pounding surf, is named after a breed of sheep raised on the grounds of the owner's upstate New York inn. No sheep are in sight; still, the setting is bucolic.

The grounds are lavishly landscaped with exotic plants. A recently built Spanish colonial hacienda with a curving split staircase brings you to the stunning, tiled-floor breezeway/lobby and an open porch cantilevered over to catch the sea spray. Below is a courtyard with a gigantic fountain, and beyond that is a large swimming pool with a wide lounging deck set up with Japanese umbrellas.

Off the lobby is a smaller, open dining terrace for breakfasts of warm banana bread, local fresh-ground coffee, finger bananas, papaya, and pineapple from local fields. Light lunches might feature fresh, grilled fish and a yummy salad. Drinks are served in the charming, wicker-furnished library, home to Pompideau, a pampered macaw in a huge cage.

The walk up the hacienda's stairway to dinner, with the tree frogs chirping a chorus, brings you to the second-floor dining room, where you are served a six-course prix-fixe dinner by candlelight. A member of the elite Relais & Chateaux group, the resort serves fine, French-inspired cuisine. A typical dinner might include Carrot Soup, Lobster and Grilled Vegetable Salad, Passion Fruit Granité, Roasted Sierra with Red Wine Sauce, Radicchio and Celery Salad, Cheeses, and Papaya Soufflé with Lemon Sauce.

As you dine, romantic ballads are softly played in the background by a classical guitarist. You can sit by French doors that open onto a balcony overlooking the ocean and the tiny beach.

The tropical grounds are extremely quiet. No pets, no TVs, no radios, and no children are allowed on the property. What to do? How about lazing by the pool or reading a novel from the library? Fishing, whale watching, and golf are only thirty minutes away and can be easily arranged. Or walk along an almost deserted beach for a couple of miles past a small fishing settlement.

Temptation in this languorous, lush bit of paradise lurks behind the mahogany-shuttered windows of well-appointed suites that match the plush public rooms in quality. There are hand-woven rugs over tile floors, louvered and mullioned windows, roomy armoires, and large, lavish European baths with quirky features like big, old-fashioned tubs and brass antique shower fixtures.

Woodwork is from island artisans, and four-poster beds, claw-footed tubs, and some of the only bidets on the island are unexpected amenities. All units have individual air-conditioning, queen-size sofa beds in sitting areas, and furnished balconies looking out on the water and beach.

An ultraluxurious unit housing eight suites with plunge pools was finished in 1995, and these, along with the new Mirador Villa, are the most superb accommodations. Coming soon are twenty-two two-storied villas, each with its own pool.

The Horned Dorset is located in a part of Puerto Rico you may not even have a clue exists: quiet, quiet, and, yes, quiet. No casinos, no discos, no glitz. Just the Straits of Mona separating you from another island far across the water.

Address/Phone: Rincon, Puerto Rico 00677; (787) 823–4030; fax (787) 823–5580

E-mail: PGH@coqui.net

Web Site: www.horneddorset.com

U.S. Reservations: (800) 633–1857

Owners: Harold Davies and Kingsley Wratten

Arrival/Departure: Transfers can be arranged from the San Juan or Mayaguez Airports

Distance from San Juan International Airport: 120 miles (2½ hours); Mayaguez Airport, 6 miles (10 minutes)

Distance from Rincon: 5 miles

Accommodations: 30 suites and 1 new, one-bedroom Mirador Villa

Best Room/Suite: New suites with plunge pools

Amenities: Air-conditioning, hair dryer, marble bath, toiletries, ceiling fans, ice service, room service (breakfast)

Electricity: 110 volts

Sports and Facilities: Pool, water sports, golf nearby, scuba and deep-sea fishing can be arranged

Dress Code: Semiformal, evenings

Weddings: Can be arranged

Rates/Packages: $190–$270 per person per night (winter), $140–$210 (summer); Mirador Villa, $400 per person per night (winter), $325 per person (summer), $71.25 per person includes breakfast, dinner, and gratuity; Romance package, $2,900–$3,750 per couple (summer), includes 7 nights' accommodations, breakfast, dinner, transfers, and champagne.

Payment/Credit Cards: All major

Deposit: Credit card deposit for 4 nights (winter); 1 night (summer); for refund cancel within 45 days of arrival date (winter); 15 days (summer)

Government Taxes: 9 percent

Service Charges: 15 percent on food and beverages; 3 percent for general service

≈≈≈

Hyatt Regency Dorado Beach

Location: Twenty-two miles west of San Juan on the north shore of Puerto Rico.

Romantic Features: Beachside casitas; long walks amid lushly planted gardens.

Formerly a grapefruit and coconut plantation, the classic Hyatt Regency Dorado Beach, which sits, along with its sister hotel, the Cerromar Beach, on 1,000 beautifully landscaped acres by the sea, gives you lots of room to spread out. Both properties have recently completed a $55 million renovation program inside and out. This sprawling, former private playground of the Rockefellers was designed and built to respect the ecosystem surrounding it long before it became a cliché to do so. Lushly planted, the hotel supplies maps to guests interested in knowing more about the tropical trees and exotic plants; many are clearly labeled for identification. Long walks here can be educational as well as romantic.

To blend in with its environs, the Dorado's clean, modern lines are partially hidden in a cloak of palms; the resort overlooks two championship golf courses and the pounding surf. The main building, a modernized plantation house, looks to the Atlantic. It features a trilevel terrace restaurant aptly named the Surf Room, where Caribbean and continental cookery is accompanied by the sound of crashing waves. Service is excellent, and the nightly menu changes to reflect international themes. Big windows and a breezy walkway outside give this Hyatt restaurant added panache.

Another charming restaurant, housed in an original 1900 hacienda, combines Caribbean and Mediterranean menus, while a more prosaic clubhouse restaurant sells snacks to golfers. Food prices are high, and if you have to ask, you should probably choose another resort.

Drinks are poured at various bars and lounges, some offering live entertainment and dancing. Two pools will keep you cool, one Olympic-size with wide patios. Other diversions, all shared with the neighboring Hyatt Regency Cerromar Beach, include a casino, seven tennis courts, two championship Robert Trent Jones eighteen-hole golf courses, and a complete water sports program—including a certified sailboarding course. The surging surf here is tamed by a breakwater, but the steep, curving beach is more suitable for sunning or sailboarding than for swimming.

If you like water play as well as swimming, a shuttle runs continuously to the Cerromar, 1 mile away, where one of the world's longest "river" swimming pools offers splashy fun. Rent a bike and pedal along trails laced through the grounds, which are planted with citrus, wild orchids, and over 600 varieties of native plants.

If you want to explore the area around the Dorado, you can head into Old San Juan and enjoy the pleasures of this old Spanish colonial city. It has some great shops with real bargains in jewelry and handcrafted items. You can also take a horse-and-buggy ride along the cobbled streets.

Completely refurbished accommodations in the fourteen two-story buildings that flank the central section are designed to take advantage of views and ventilation. The spacious, air-conditioned units have earth-toned and pastel furnishings, terra-cotta tile floors, safes, minibars, telephones, TVs, jalousies, and terraces or balconies. Separate dressing areas and marble combination baths add a deluxe spin. Ground-floor units have double beds; upper rooms have four-poster kings. The three-story, pool-view wing, which overlooks the beach and is linked to the lobby by elevator, houses balconied superior rooms.

For privacy there are better choices. Two- and three-story golf-view buildings have private verandas facing the fairways and are set in a cool coconut grove near the lobby and dining area. Most special are the casitas on the beach. With tile floors, ceiling fans, baths with skylighted showers, and terraces on the lawn sweeping down to the beach, these are the most romantic accommodations of the resort—a perfect place to hang out a do not disturb sign, order room service, and watch the sun set.

Address/Phone: Road 693, Dorado, Puerto Rico 00646; (787) 796–1234; fax (787) 796–2022

U.S. Reservations: Hyatt Hotels, (800) 55–HYATT

Owner/Manager: Hyatt Hotels & Resorts

Arrival/Departure: You might want to fly in to the private airstrip, or, as most mortals do, drive in from the San Juan Airport. Taxis available at airport. Transfers arranged for a fee.

Distance from San Juan International Airport: 31 miles; Dorado Airport, 1 mile

Distance from San Juan: 22 miles west

Accommodations: 298 rooms, including 17 casitas and 1 two-bedroom suite

Best Room/Suite: Upper oceanfront rooms, which have four-poster king-size beds; or casitas, which have showers with skylights and king-size beds and are located between the beach and the pool

Amenities: Air-conditioning, climate control, ceiling fans, hair dryer, bathrobes, minibar, coffeemaker, in-room safe, iron and ironing board, TV, clock radio, telephone, toiletries; nightly turndown service, 24-hour room service

Electricity: 110 volts

Sports and Facilities: 7 tennis courts, pool, 2 golf courses; water sports, jogging and biking trails, sailboarding school, health spa, computerized exercise room, aerobics, in-line skating, Ping-Pong, casino

Dress Code: Casually elegant; jackets required for men for dining in winter

Weddings: Can be arranged

Rates/Packages: $175–$375 per couple per night (summer); $250–$350 (spring and fall); $375–$550 (winter); Honeymoon package, including accommodations, champagne, a honeymoon breakfast, a candlelight dinner with wine, and transfers, from $1,139 per couple for 3 nights; $2,135 per couple for 7 nights

Payment/Credit Cards: All major

Deposit: 3 nights; cancellation 14 days prior to arrival date for refund

Government Taxes: 11 percent

Service Charges: 15 percent on food and beverages suggested

Entry Requirements for U.S. Citizens: U.S. Commonwealth; none required for U.S. citizens

ST. KITTS

The Golden Lemon Inn & Villas

Location: On Dieppe Bay, on the northeast coast of St. Kitts.

Romantic Features: Private sunning areas; intimate inn; a moonlight dip in your own villa pool.

This special, small resort got its name when owner Arthur Leaman's friends told him he had bought a "lemon" when he purchased the seventeenth-century stone and wood former Huguenot warehouse on Dieppe Bay. Leaman, a former editor at *House & Garden*, decided to make this lemon into more than lemonade. He created the glorious Golden Lemon, bathed by light that filters through the graceful coconut palms surrounding it.

Staying at this stylish, one-of-a-kind country inn in St. Kitts is like being a guest at a private home. The main building has been renovated to look like a plantation house, but with sophisticated pizzazz only a designer like Leaman could pull off: vivid, lemon-hued walls trimmed with white, painted floors, whimsical and offbeat mixes of old and new, mainland and local bibelots. All highly creative.

Breakfast can be taken in your villa by the pool, in the garden, or on the gallery outside your great house room. Lunch is served outdoors on a stone terrace, and afternoon tea is presented on the garden patio, ringed with lush, tropical foliage. Guests often gather on the lower gallery for a convivial cocktail hour with the scent of night-blooming flowers all around.

Dinner is served in the main dining room, on the back patio by the pool, or in the front gallery. You can also ask to have your dinner served in your suite or at a private table—the staff enjoys catering to honeymooners. The menu, which changes daily, is graciously served and usually includes a soup, fresh fish or continental dish, local produce, and a grand dessert and coffee. Choices include items like braised Cornish hen with tropical fruit, grilled shrimp-and-fish kabob, and pasta with lobster sauce.

Exceptional guest rooms in the great house are filled with fun, style, and fantasy and have names such as Parrot, Victoria, and Paisley. All are unique. The two-story villa accommodations of the Lemon Court and Lemon Grove are spacious and eclectically furnished with a combination of antiques, Oriental rugs, four-poster beds, wicker, wrought iron, island artifacts, and objets d'art. Many have walled gardens and private pools right off the living areas. There are no TVs, radios, or air-conditioning here, and they aren't missed.

The Golden Lemon sits on a rather plain black sand beach behind a lava stone wall. Industrious fishermen mend nets nearby, for the everyday life of the islanders goes on just outside the resort's boundaries. A reef located just offshore is great for snorkeling, and a tennis court offers a chance for further exercise. But this is not a resort for the hyperactive. Lazing around the main pool, reading a book, getting a massage, and sipping an island drink are popular activities. Or, as Leaman will tell you, the Golden Lemon is for those who are good at doing nothing in grand style.

Address/Phone: Dieppe Bay, St. Kitts, W.I.; (869) 465–7260; fax (869) 465–4019

E-mail: info@goldenlemon.com

Web Site: www.goldenlemon.com

U.S. Reservations: Caribbean Inns, Ltd., (800) 633–7411

Owner/Manager: Arthur Leaman, owner; Joy Bradish and Martin Kreiner, managers

Arrival/Departure: Guests are met on arrival at Golden Rock Airport and transported to the hotel; taxis are available at the airport. Round-trip transfers cost $40 per couple unless guests are staying on a package.

Distance from Golden Rock Airport: 14 miles (30 minutes)

Distance from Basseterre: 14 miles (30 minutes)

Accommodations: 24 rooms and suites: 8 in main building; 6 in Golden Lemon Court, with pools; 10 in villa cottages, with pools and terraces

Best Room/Suite: Lemon Grove villas, cottages with walled gardens and private pools

Amenities: Ceiling fans, telephones, hair dryer, toiletries, room service

Electricity: 110 volts

Sports and Facilities: Pool, tennis court, snorkeling; scuba diving and hiking can be arranged

Dress Code: Casual

Weddings: $650 wedding package includes ceremony, flowers, cake, witnesses, and dinner

Rates/Packages: $300–$500 (winter); $245–$390 (summer) including breakfast per couple per night, Dinner Plan add $35 per person per night. For Lovers Only, $2,188–$3,178 for 6 nights, including breakfasts, 2 nights' dinner for two, transfers, sight-seeing tour, champagne, rain forest walk/volcano climb or massage, T-shirts, and catamaran trip to Nevis with lunch.

Payment/Credit Cards: Most major

Deposit: 3 nights; cancel 21 days prior to arrival date for refund (winter), 14 days (summer), and 45 days (Christmas/New Year's)

Government Taxes: 7 percent

Service Charges: 10 percent

Entry Requirements for U.S. Citizens: Proof of citizenship; passport best

ST. LUCIA

≈≈≈

Anse Chastanet

Location: Sits on 500 hillside acres on the southwestern coast of the island.

Romantic Features: Dramatic open rooms with spectacular views of the Pitons on the edge of the sea; huge open showers (one with a tree growing right through it); candlelight dining and dancing in the Treetops Restaurant.

There are no televisions, no room phones, nothing really to break the spell of tropical moonlight, refreshing sea breezes, and the scent of frangipani in this dense, green, jungly paradise that is the idyllic setting for Anse Chastanet. Your room may be wide open to lofty views of the blue-green pyramidlike peaks of the Pitons and the variegated blue sea. And this is exactly what Nick Troubetzkoy had in mind when he created Anse Chastanet.

Nick, an architect, and his wife, Karolin, have carved into the thick tropical forests on this remote hillside one of the most unique and romantic resorts you'll find anywhere in the world. This is the way you imagine a resort in the Caribbean should be—and better. Cooled by the sea breezes, not by air-conditioners; open louvers, and in the premium rooms, no walls at all, so that you can hear the birds, the waves, and the rustling of palms; and a view from your balcony that looks through the tops of the trees out to the mountains and sea beyond. Waking up to see the cones of the two Pitons framed by the arches of your octagonal "tree house" can blow you away. It's that good.

There are only forty-nine cottages, partially camouflaged by the lush, tropical foliage that rises like a thick green carpet from a lovely, coconut-palm-fringed beach. Thirty-seven of the cottages are staggered up the hillside, and twelve are located at the beach level; most have views of the two Pitons—Gros and Petit—that distinguish St. Lucia. As you walk up the hillside to your cottage, you may wonder if the climb is worth it. It is. The higher you are, the better the view and the privacy.

Each room is fun and dramatically different not only in decor but in shape. Standard hillside rooms are rectangular and slightly smaller than the superior rooms, which are octagonal or rectangular in shape and feature two twins or one king-size bed. Beachside rooms are quite spacious, with either two double or one king-size bed, a bath with two sinks, a shower, and a large balcony or patio. Although these are just steps from the beach and probably the best choice for those who can't or don't want to climb the hill, they have garden, not ocean, views.

It is the premium rooms located high up the hill that are so spectacular. Many guests have grumbled on their first climb up to their suite and asked to be transferred to a beachfront room. But after one night would they move? No way. These rooms are just too special.

Even the showers are worth writing home about; many are as large as a garage. Ginger (number 14B) has a gommier tree growing right through it. Some open onto gardens, others to the sea. Most have no curtains or doors. "There is a fan club for every room!" exclaims Karolin. "Even the original octagonal rooms have a loyal following."

It's not just that the rooms are super-spacious—7B is roughly 30 feet by 30 feet—it's the way they blend into the surroundings. Mahoe (number 14A), for example, is totally open on two sides. The only creatures that will share your private moments are the birds (which you'd expect would fly in and out, but they don't). You have mosquito netting to drape around your bed, but unless you want it for the romantic effect, you really don't need it.

The Troubetzkoys have carried their good taste and creativity into the decor of the resort, as well. Furniture, designed by Nick and constructed from local woods, has been made locally. Thick, puffy cushions covered in a cheerful plaid madras sit on the chair frames and beds. The madras theme is also carried throughout the property: tablecloths, staff uniforms, napkins, and bedspreads are made out of this traditional island fabric by local seamstresses.

Red-tile or wood floors, original art by Reina Nieland, a Dutch-Canadian artist who works in burlap and mixed media to create superb abstract collage, and woodcarvings by Lawrence Deligny, a St. Lucian artist, are located throughout the rooms and public areas. Simple but effective basket lamp shades with yellow insect repellent bulbs hang around the perimeters of the rooms, balconies, and restaurants.

If you can tear yourself away from your room, you'll find there's plenty to do here if you like water sports, hiking, or relaxing with a soothing massage. The resort has its own minispa, Kai Belté ("house of beauty"in patois). Professionally trained therapists offer a variety of massage treatments and reflexology at the spa or in your room. Also available at the spa are other beauty and body treatments, including body polishes, waxing, facials, pedicures, and manicures. Charges range from $15 to $80, the latter for a fifty-minute massage for two.

Among the resort's new toys are fifty Cannondale bikes with all the accessories, which can be rented for a half or full day. Several trails have been made lacing the 500-acre property. There is a palm tree or palm-roofed umbrella for every guest who wants some shade on the picturesque, volcanic sand beach, which seems to sparkle with diamond dust in the sun. At one end of the beach, you'll find the casual Trou-au-Diable restaurant and bar, two boutiques, and the scuba center.

Two more restaurants, a bar, and a reception area are located midway up the hill. Dining up here in the Tree House Restaurant is literally dining in the treetops. You look through leafy green foliage and the feathery branches of the flamboyant trees down to the beach and the turquoise waters, which slowly roll onto the shore. Breakfast is served at the Piton Restaurant, on the same level as the Tree House.

Food is excellent, especially the fresh-grilled catch of the day, which might be red snapper or grouper. Fresh fruits and vegetables such as breadfruit and christophine (tastes and looks a bit like a potato) as well as curries are very tasty. Soups are a meal in themselves. And be sure to try the banana pancakes, a house specialty.

There are live entertainment six nights a week, a manager's rum punch party on Mondays, and an underwater slide show on Wednesdays. One of the Troubetzkoys' major commitments is to the crafts of St. Lucia. Already a woodcarver has his own workshop area at the northern end of the beach, and a pottery shop has been established on the grounds. Many of the articles these craftspeople make, such as the carved wood fish, can be purchased at the boutiques. The work of several local and international artists is represented in many of the rooms. Some rooms are actually dedicated to a particular artist.

In the Trouhet, Karolin's continuing effort to promote art, a gallery is in the works.

For scuba enthusiasts Anse Chastanet is a dream come true. The waters off the beach are brilliantly clean and clear. A reef on the southern end of the beach, which is known for its excellent underwater plant and fish life, was recently declared a marine preserve.

Michael and Karyn Allard, managers of the Scuba St. Lucia Dive Center, maintain a staff of seven fully qualified dive instructors and offer a complete range of courses and facilities for beginners up to experts. Dive trips operate daily to sites around the island. If you ever wanted to learn to scuba, this is the place to do it. After some basic instruction, you can actually take your first dive right off the beach, where the reef falls from 20 to 140 feet.

Whether you're diving or snorkeling, you'll find the reef alive with corals, sponges, black spiny sea urchins, chromis, sea cucumbers, and schools of fish in wonderful bright colors. A resort course perfect for beginners is priced at $75; the open-water certification course is $425.

A must-do while you're here is an excursion with Menau, Anse's resident horticultural guide. Menau knows a lot about the flora and fauna of the island. One of the most interesting tours is a trip with him to the ruins of an eighteenth-century French sugar plantation located off the resort's Anse Mamin Beach.

A complimentary water taxi, *Peace on Earth,* takes you to Anse Mamin and Soufrière, just around the corner, the first capital of St. Lucia and now a sleepy fishing village. In Soufrière you'll find some well-weathered houses, shops, and a crafts market.

If you want to explore the many beautiful coves and small islands that ring St. Lucia, you can charter the resort's 37-foot yacht for a half- or full-day sail and snorkeling tour. The trip costs between $200 and $300.

Anse Chastanet is not for everyone. There are more than one hundred steps leading from the beach to the hillside rooms. So if steps are out for you, you probably should go elsewhere. Anse Chastanet is also not for those who need ready access to phones, TVs, and faxes. The only public phones are found in the reception area midway up the hill. There's a fax machine in the office, and that's it.

But if living well in spacious accommodations amid the stunning sights, sounds, and sweet fragrances of nature appeals to you, then think Anse Chastanet. There's no better place to be.

Address/Phone: P.O. Box 7000, Soufrière, St. Lucia, W.I.; (758) 459–7000 or (758) 459–7554; fax (758) 459–7700

U.S. Reservations: Ralph Locke Islands, (800) 223–1108 or (310) 440–4225; fax (310) 440–4220

Owner/Manager: Nick Troubetzkoy, owner and managing director; Karolin Guler Troubetzkoy, director of marketing and operations

Arrival/Departure: Pickup can be arranged at the airport; the fare is approximately $45 per car (four people) from Hewanorra Airport; $75 per car from Virgie Airport

Distance from Hewanorra International Airport: 18 miles (1 hour); Virgie Airport, 30 miles (1¾ hours)

Distance from Soufrière: 1½ miles

Accommodations: 49 rooms: 4 spacious, open-style, Premium rooms on hillside, with dramatic Piton views; 12 large, open Deluxe hillside rooms with Piton or ocean views; 12 deluxe beachside rooms with a garden view; 17 Superior hillside rooms with wraparound balconies; 4 Standard hillside rooms (smaller with queen- or king-size bed)

Best Room/Suite: Room 7F, huge and totally open on two sides; 14B, another wide-open room with a tree growing through the shower; 14A, with a giant, four-poster bed and wide-open vistas

Amenities: Hair dryer (a really good one), refrigerator, tea and coffee bar, ceiling fans, super-size baths (most), bidets (some), louvered walls, toiletries; boutique

Electricity: 220 volts

Sports and Facilities: Scuba diving with Scuba St. Lucia; snorkeling, ocean kayaking, sailboarding, Sunfish sailing, hiking, swimming at beach; mini spa; tennis, table tennis; mountain biking; half- and full-day yacht charters aboard a 37-foot O-Day craft; plantation tour

Dress Code: Men requested to wear long slacks or long-cut Bermuda shorts at Tree House Restaurant

Weddings: Can be arranged; popular sites are the Tree House Restaurant or the beach; each wedding is treated as a unique affair. Wedding package priced at $695, with a number of options, such as private boat charter, live entertainment, and video available.

Rates/Packages: Double room, including breakfast and dinner, $415–$695 (winter); the breakfast and dinner plan is optional in the shoulder and summer seasons and is available at $60 per person per day; double room $220–$460, meals not included (spring and fall); $180–$420 (summer); drinks packages to stock refrigerator can be prebooked or booked on arrival. Escape package includes 7 nights' accommodations, transfers, volcano tour, drinks package, fruit, and resort scuba course; plus breakfasts and dinners, winter season only; $2,150–$2,970 (winter); $1,278–$2,022 (no meals), $1,758–$2,500 (breakfast and dinner) (spring and fall); $1,102–$1,846 (no meals), $1,582–$2,326 (breakfast and dinner) (summer). Honeymoon, spa, scuba packages and Total Romance packages available, including such extras as champagne, massages, snorkeling trip, diving course, scenic boat shopping trip, and more.

Payment/Credit Cards: Most major

Deposit: 3 nights in winter; 2 nights in summer and shoulder seasons; all weekly packages must be prebooked and prepaid in full. Cancellations subject to 3 nights' fee (winter) or 2 nights' (summer and shoulder) if notification is not received 21 days prior to arrival date (winter), 55 days (Christmas), or 14 days (summer and shoulder).

Government Taxes: 8 percent

Service Charges: 10 percent

Entry Requirements for U.S. Citizens: Proof of citizenship; passport best

≈≈≈

Le Sport

Location: On the northernmost tip of the island.

Romantic Features: Sunsets from your seaside terrace; body massages for two; hilltop Oasis spa.

L ooking for a tropical sun destination that offers sports and activities geared to help you shape up your body and feed your spirit? Then try Le Sport. Tucked into a secluded cove between a high outcropping of rocks, Le Sport lets you really unwind and be pampered with soothing treatments like Swedish massages, seaweed wraps, facials, and salt loofah body buffs.

Want more action? There are tennis, aerobics, jogging, golf, water sports, scuba diving, snorkeling, Ping-Pong, wake-up walks, and a whole bulletin board of activities. You can do it all or do nothing at all.

Since the resort is all-inclusive, you don't have to reach for your wallet every time you want to have a drink or meal, indulge in a massage, or try the sailboarder. Instruction, ranging from scuba and golf lessons to fencing and archery, is also included. Couples can even take part in a private one-hour honeymoon massage class to learn massage techniques with their partners.

The stunning $3.5 million temple of pleasure, called the Oasis, sits at the top of the hill, overlooking the sea and the hotel, and was modeled after the Alhambra in Granada, Spain. It's a bit of a long walk up the hill to the Oasis, but what a view. Resembling an old cloister, the Oasis is built around an open courtyard. In the middle is a beautiful, serene, dark-water pool bordered by a grassy apron and several lounges set under low palm trees. Guests come up here for total peace and quiet. Even the pool aerobics, which takes place here once a day, doesn't upset the mood; music is not part of the program. Just about the only sounds you hear are the bubbling fountains that flow into pools. And from just about anywhere you sit, you can see the turquoise sea framed through the stark white arches and columns of the building.

There are more than thirty small treatment rooms housed in the Oasis, designed for such earthly indulgences as reflexology, aromatherapy, and Thai massage. Many guests bring a book, suntan lotion, and towels and come up here to spend the day, leaving their lounge only long enough to keep their appointments.

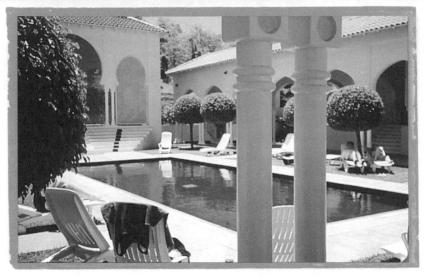

Le Sport, St. Lucia

Upon arrival, after filling out a health questionnaire, you'll meet with the medical staff. Then you'll get a printout of your appointments. From here it's on to days of pampering and playing.

Down at the beach you can waterski, snorkel, or swim. Sit under one of the thatched umbrellas and no one will intrude on your privacy unless, of course, you want a cool drink. Then all you have to do is to plant your orange flag in the sand, and an attendant will come to take your order.

There are plenty of activities for those who want to keep busy, starting with the power walk at 7:00 A.M. You can play tennis day or night, play Ping-Pong, take the resort scuba course, or go on an excursion to see St. Lucia's volcano and working cocoa and coconut plantation.

There are three pools at Le Sport, including a water volleyball pool; the Oasis pool, which is a lap and exercise pool; and a full-size swimming pool. Golf greens fees and transportation are all included in the daily rate, and there is a golf practice area with two instructors, nets, a putting green, and a sand trap.

There are two restaurants, including the new Tao, specializing in East/West fusion cuisine, and the Cariblue, an open-air beachfront restaurant. Dinner is served by candlelight, and you can choose from a regular gourmet menu, which changes nightly; lighter options are available. Monday nights there is a Caribbean buffet featuring a wide variety of local dishes, and Thursday is barbecue night.

Later the beat heats up at the disco in the Terrace Bar and Theater, where there is often entertainment, with various local performers and an exceptionally good staff show.

Afternoon tea is served from 4:00 to 5:30 P.M. and includes finger sandwiches, light cakes, and scones. The air-conditioned piano bar is a popular spot to meet friends or just stop for a cocktail. After dinner Le Sport's resident pianist plays from 7:00 P.M. until the last guest retires.

Rooms and suites are located in two-, three-, and four-story buildings and include fifty-three new rooms and suites. The most desirable are the luxury oceanfront rooms and suites, which have balconies overlooking the water and come with white rattan furniture, upholstered in soft pink, peach, and mint fabric, and marble floors. The bathrooms are white Italian and rose-salmon Portuguese marble. Most rooms and suites have king-size four-poster beds, and the newest rooms have mahogany beds and large balconies.

For those who are active and fit enough to want every imaginable exercise and treatment facility available along with a wide variety of sports activities, yet also want a relaxing, romantic Caribbean vacation, Le Sport offers this unique combination. And with everything included, it's one of the best values around

Address/Phone: Cariblue Beach, P.O. Box 437, Castries, St. Lucia, W.I.; (758) 450–8551; fax (758) 450–0368

Web Site: www.lesport.com.lc

U.S. Reservations: Tropical Holidays (800) 544–2883

Owner/Manager: Michael Bryant, general manager

Arrival/Departure: Transfers included to/from airport

Distance from Virgie Airport: 7 miles (20 minutes); Hewanorra International Airport, 28 miles (1½ hours)

Distance from Castries: 8 miles

Accommodations: 155 rooms in two buildings. All rooms feature ocean views and individual terraces or patios.

Best Room/Suite: Luxury oceanfront rooms or Luxury oceanfront suites

Amenities: Hair dryer, bathrobe, telephones, air-conditioning, ceiling fans, refrigerators, (luxury deluxe ocean-view and oceanfront rooms only); room service for continental breakfast and fresh fruit; beauty salon on premises (extra charge)

Electricity: 220/110 volts

Sports: Snorkeling, sailboarding, Sunfish sailing, scuba diving, waterskiing, tennis, hiking, swimming at beach or in pools, golf, bicycling, fencing, archery, volleyball, Ping-Pong, stretch classes and yoga classes, variety of body treatments, weight training with personal trainer, aerobics, sauna, Swiss needle showers, stress management, meditation, mixology classes, and dance classes

Dress Code: Casual

Weddings: Can be arranged with a week's notice

Rates/Packages: All-inclusive per person per night rates include accommodations, sports, treatments, meals, beverages, classes, tips, taxes, and service charges: $195–$390 per person per night, double occupancy

Payment/Credit Cards: Most major

Deposit: $300 per person deposit; cancel 21 days prior to arrival for refund.

Government Taxes: Included

Service Charges: Included

Entry Requirements for U.S. Citizens: Proof of citizenship; passport best

≋≋

Sandals St. Lucia Golf Resort & Spa

Location: On a ½-mile stretch of white sandy beach in Castries on the island's northwestern coast.

Romantic Features: Couples only, all-inclusive plan, nonstop activities and quiet hideaway places, romantic restaurants, secluded villas with private plunge pools; Stay at One, Play at Two program gives you use of Sandals Halcyon St. Lucia Beach restaurants and facilities at no extra charge.

Sandals has brought its ultra-all-inclusive, couples-only concept to St. Lucia, with Sandals St. Lucia Golf Resort & Spa. Getting to the resort can be an interesting experience depending on the airport you fly into. Coming into the Hewanorra, the larger airport, guarantees you a one-hour trip through winding mountain roads. It allows you views of banana plantations, the rainforest, the Pitons, and the island's volcanic attraction. For a closer look you can book tours of the island through the resort. The trip from the airport may be enough, however, since the resort offers plenty of things to keep you busy.

The first thing one couple I spoke to said you should do when you get to the resort—"even before the obvious honeymooner thing"—is to make dinner reservations. Said this newly married couple, who spent their June honeymoon there, "While we certainly never experienced a shortage of food at the resort, we found that there was limited seating at the specialty restaurants, especially the French place, La Toc, and Mario's, the Italian restaurant at the Halcyon resort." (At Sandal's St. Lucia you're allowed full access to the other resort on the island, Sandals Halcyon St. Lucia; a free hourly shuttle runs between the resorts.)

Author's Note: Please see description of Sandals Resorts all-inclusive features covered in Jamaica section.

They said they loved Sandals St. Lucia for a number of reasons: "Here you don't have to deal with kids and singles. If you do feel like socializing with others, you have something instantly in common with the other guests—you share the same wedding date. So not only is everyone in the best mood of their lives, but you can feel free to trade wedding stories from what went perfectly right to where Uncle Ralph's hairpiece flew during the Electric Slide." They added, "If you feel like making a party out of it, you can join others with the Sandals' 'Playmakers,' who organize everything from aqua aerobics to beer-chugging contests."

The couple added, "One extra that we did indulge in was a sunset cruise. It's one of the few things you have to pay extra for, arranged through Sandals. It was a three-hour cruise on a large catamaran fully equipped with a stocked bar, a guitarist you can sing along with if you choose to, and a breathtaking view of the island at sundown. It turned out to be one of the most memorable parts of our honeymoon."

The larger and more luxurious of the company's two properties on the island, Sandals St. Lucia sits on 155 acres and boasts a huge, sprawling pool (the largest on the island), with waterfalls, a swim-up bar, whirlpool baths, bridges, and a pavilion. The property has 329 rooms, offering twelve categories in various locations and configurations including 56 new villas on Sunset Bluff. Two-story town houses, with a living room and patio upstairs and a bedroom downstairs, are set high along a bluff at one end of the property and come with marble baths, minibars, four-poster beds, and sitting areas; some also come with private plunge pools. Other rooms and suites are located closer to the ½-mile beach and near the golf course. Some of the villas are two-story; some also have plunge pools. Although the villas are more private, if you want to be near the action, go for the Grande Luxe Beachfront rooms and suites.

Sandals St. Lucia has several restaurants and bars, two pools, a fitness center, and a whole boatload of sports options, including golf on the premises, as well as a disco and nonstop other activities.

With five restaurants on the property and the opportunity to use three more at the second Sandals property, you can stay a week and dine at a new place every night. You can choose from the elegant La Toc restaurant, where the emphasis is on French cuisine, or try Japanese food at Kimonos, steak and ribs at Arizona, or Caribbean and Creole items at the Pitons Restaurant. You can eat inside by candlelight; outside, under the stars by the sea or by the pool. At night entertainment kicks in with theme parties, disco dancing, billiards, and a piano bar.

Although you may find little impetus to leave the property, if you do decide to explore, there's much to see. St. Lucia, with its starkly beautiful Pitons, reminiscent of upside-down ice cream cones, is blessed with more than 19,000 acres of verdant rain forest. Reminiscent of Fiji or Kauai, with its steep hills and valleys carpeted with rich tapestries woven of palms, banana trees, bamboo, flowering plants, and other tropical foliage, St. Lucia is cut by streams and waterfalls plunging into deep pools curtained with giant ferns and fringed by golden sand. Dark volcanic-grained beaches sparkle like diamonds in the sun.

Most visitors make a trip to the famous La Soufrière volcano and Sulphur Spring. The last eruption here took place 200 years ago, leaving a smoking crater with more than twenty-one bubbling black pools of water that resemble liquid tar. Hydrogen sulfide, a stinky but nonpoisonous gas smelling like rotten eggs, continually rises from somewhere deep in the earth, creating these boiling pools that are thought by some to have health benefits (when cooled down sufficiently, of course).

The whole scene is like a set from *Star Wars*. As you peer over the top of the rim and look down over this most inhospitable landscape, you can occasionally see someone bravely trekking over the grayish ground and rocks. (Don't try it—that stuff is hot.)

At Morne Coubaril Estate, a fifty-acre working plantation and museum, you can stroll through the attractive gardens and see reconstructed houses similar to those the original plantation workers lived in, small cramped affairs with mud floors and walls papered with newspaper. Here you can see how cocoa is harvested, dried, pulverized, and molded into chocolate sticks; you can also watch workers at the coconut "factory," where coconuts are processed and every part is put to some practical use, including the fiber of the shell, which is used in mattresses.

Address/Phone: P.O. Box 399, Castries, St. Lucia, W.I.; (758) 452–3081; fax (758) 452–1012

U.S. Reservations: (800) SANDALS

Owner/Manager: Konrad Wagner, general manager

Arrival/Departure: Sandals guests are met at the airport and escorted to their resort.

Distance from Virgie International Airport: 10 minutes; Hewanorra International Airport, 75 minutes

Accommodations: 329 rooms, suites, villas in 12 categories

Best Room/Suite: One-Bedroom Sunset Oceanview Suites (with private pools) and Grande Luxe Beachfront Suites

Amenities: Air-conditioning, king-size beds, ceiling fans, hair dryer, generous kits of lotions and shampoo, telephones, clock radios, color TVs, safes; suite concierge service also includes terry robes, upgraded amenity kit, fully stocked wet bar, sitting area, mahogany four-poster bed, daily *New York Times* fax and services of dedicated suite concierge

Electricity: 110 volts

Sports and Facilities: 3 freshwater pools, 3 whirlpools, fitness center, tennis, scuba diving, snorkeling, sailboarding, sailing, Hobie-Cats, aquatriking, waterskiing, paddleboats, kayaks, golf, pool, volleyball, darts, shuffleboard, table tennis, lawn chess

Dress Code: Casual

Weddings: On-site wedding coordinators arrange all the details, including taking care of the paperwork, leading the couple through the process of getting the marriage license, flowers, music, and reception. "WeddingMoons"—Sandals's term—can be as intimate as a couple getting married at the beach or under a gazebo with a best man and attendant "borrowed" from the Sandals staff.

Rates/Packages: All-inclusive rates for 7 nights start at $2,170 per person

Payment/Credit Cards: Most major

Deposit: Guarantee with credit card

Government Included

Service Charges: Included

Entry Requirements for U.S. Citizens: Proof of citizenship; passport best

≋≋

Windjammer Landing

Location: Set on a hillside on Labrelotte Bay, on the northwestern coast of St. Lucia.

Romantic Features: Private dinner on your garden terrace overlooking the sea; your own plunge pool.

You can reach Windjammer by land or by sea. Either way, you'll be impressed with this little seaside "village" of white villas with red roofs and white adobe turrets and arches reminiscent of Mykonos in the Greek islands. Narrow, winding brick paths, which meander up the hillside to the villas, are lined with a profusion of flowering bougainvillea, hibiscus, and oleander. Since the villas are clustered together comfortably, there is room on this 55-acre resort to explore: to poke around the nooks and crannies defined by the villas, gardens, pools, restaurants, and beaches.

An open-air car with a fringed top shuttles you up and down the hill to and from your villa to the beach, pools, and restaurants. But you'll find it tempting to laze away the day at your own private plunge pool, which is set in a tiled courtyard surrounded by flowers. From here the views of the sea and the hills in the distance are magnificent.

The one-bedroom villas, with 1,200 to 1,300 square feet of space, are a perfect choice for a romantic hideaway. The living rooms are large and airy, furnished with wicker furniture with pastel fabric cushions that contrast nicely with the red-tile floors and thick, round arches and windows. Cocoa straw mats, hand-painted tiles, and original art along with fresh flower arrangements add splashes of color to the white plaster walls, and lofty ceilings are light, pickled pine. There is a lovely tiled terrace with a dining area as well as a good-size kitchen.

Water sports on the grounds are complimentary, including an introductory scuba lesson. You can join in the aerobics, participate in the waterskiing contest, go on a snorkeling trip, or take part in a sailing regatta. There are fashion shows, games in the main pool, beach volleyball, water polo, and calypso lessons. Tennis courts are lighted for night play.

Windjammer has four restaurants and two cocktail lounges, along with a minimart, boutique, and on-site car-rental office. One of the most popular restaurants, Jammers, carries you into the world of the South Seas with its Polynesian decor. Its sprawling, open-air veranda, covered with a thatched roof, is a great place to enjoy breakfast, lunch, and dinner. Seafood, grilled fish, and fresh island vegetables are superbly prepared by the resident chef. Try a cocktail of mango shrimps dressed in honey and ginger vinaigrette.

Dine at Josephine's, and you'll be able to savor dishes that reflect the Caribbean culture. Here you are served by staff dressed in traditional costume. The Conch & Bandshell is made up of gazebos, pavilions, and terraces where you will have a variety of dining options from 11:00 A.M. until late evening.

A wood-fired oven set into the wall is a feature of Papa Don's, where you can get pizza, pasta, and other good things. (You can also order a pizza and have it delivered to your room.)

Want a very private dinner for just the two of you? Just ask the kitchen staff to prepare and serve a special meal on your terrace. Start with Chilled Breadfruit Vichyssoise and follow it up with a Mille-Feuille of Fresh Mahi Mahi with a Saffron Cream Sauce and a Panache of Vegetables.

Address/Phone: P.O. Box 1504, Labrelotte, Castries, St. Lucia, W.I.; (758) 452–0913; fax (758) 452–9454

E-mail: www.windjammer@canow.lc

Web Site: windjammer-landing.com

U.S. Reservations: (800) 743–9609; L.R.I. (Loews Representation International), (800) 223–0888

Owner/Manager: Lawrence Samuel, general manager

Arrival/Departure: Round-trip transfers included in Honeymoon package

Distance from Hewanorra International Airport: 32 miles (1¾ hours); 5 miles (20 minutes) from George Charles Airport

Distance from Castries: 5 miles

Accommodations: 227 rooms in 114 villas: 21 deluxe; 21 superior; 35 one-bedroom villas; 27 two-bedroom villas; 28 three-bedroom villas; 3 four-bedroom villas

Best Room/Suite: One-bedroom villas (two have private Jacuzzis overlooking the bay)

Amenities: Hair dryer, air-conditioning, sun terrace, cable TV, ceiling fans, toiletries, bathrobes, in-room safe, cassette players, golf umbrellas, VCRs on request; closets are roomy; villas have fully equipped kitchen, microwave, blender, and coffeemaker

Electricity: 110 volts

Sports and Facilities: 4 pools, beach, PADI scuba program, snorkeling, waterskiing, sailboarding, fitness center, aerobics, golf nearby; deep-sea fishing can be arranged, 42-foot cruiser available for charter

Dress Code: Casually elegant

Weddings: Windjammer's wedding package is priced at $650 per couple and includes the ceremony, marriage license, certificate, fees, cake, champagne, photographer, sunset cruise, candlelight dinner served in your villa, taxi to and from the lawyer's office, and upgrade to villa with private plunge pool (based on availability). Options include a video, live music, and special flowers.

Rates/Packages: $330–$1,070 per couple per night (Christmas); $240–$790 (winter); $160–$540 (spring, summer, and fall). Lovers' Paradise, $2,150–$3,800 includes 7 nights' accommodations, candlelight dinner in your suite, sparkling wine and fruit plate, sunset cruise or day's car rental with gourmet picnic basket, windjammer polo shirts, complimentary tennis, Sunfish sailing, waterskiing, and transfers.

Payment/Credit Cards: Most major

Deposit: 3-night deposit at time of booking; for full refund, cancel 14 days or more prior to arrival date (winter); 7 days (spring, summer, and fall); 45 days (Christmas)

Government Taxes: 8 percent

Service Charges: 10 percent

Entry Requirements for U.S. Citizens: Passport

ST. MARTIN

≈≈≈

La Samanna

Location: Sits on fifty-five acres of beachfront property on the French side of the island.

Romantic Features: Spectacular ocean views; private terraces opening onto a pristine, white sand beach.

After setting a standard for the ultimate in luxury resorts in the Caribbean since the mid-seventies La Samanna went through a period of decline in the late eighties. In 1996 Orient Express Hotels reopened the hotel after a multimillion-dollar renovation.

The decor is light, elegant, and airy with lots of wicker, bamboo, and wood. Furniture upholstery and cushions are covered in pretty fabrics in blues, greens, and coral. Custom-designed wood and natural hemp headboards, large hand-carved bedside chests, limestone-topped dining tables on bamboo bases, and majavey-wood director's chairs for dining on the terrace provide guests with a comfortable, attractive environment. Appointments include hand-blown glass candle cylinders and a unique collection of contemporary artwork. Suites have oversize sofas, mahogany desks and chairs, and tiled kitchen counters.

The stark, white buildings, softened by the brilliant colors of bougainvillea, hibiscus, and other tropical flowers and the cerulean blue doors, stand at one end of a pristine beach, which you can see from just about every spot on the property. Very Mediterranean in style, with white arched windows and doors and terra-cotta tile floors, your room's terrace or patio opens onto the beach. The twisted shapes of wind-sculpted sea grape trees frame patches of bright turquoise sea just outside your room.

While at La Samanna you'll be pampered with a number of special services. For example, you can opt for express checkout service, whereby your exit documents are processed quickly—no long lines to deal with.

Cuisine is French-inspired, although you will also find some regional Caribbean dishes on the menu. You can dine in the main restaurant or al fresco on the terrace. The bar, with its multihued Indian wedding tent ceiling, is furnished with comfortable cushioned wicker chairs—a lovely place to sip a chilled glass of champagne while you enjoy the cooling sea breezes.

There is also a new rotisserie grill located at the poolside bar where you can order lunch and beverages. Want to take a picnic and have lunch at a secluded beach? All you have to do is ask and everything will be arranged.

The pool is a serene haven for those who simply want to lie back on their cushioned teak lounges and enjoy the sun.

Water sports available at La Samanna include sailing, sailboarding, snorkeling, waterskiing, and swimming. You can also play tennis, exercise in the Fitness Pavilion, or go deep-sea fishing.

The library is a quiet place to relax, read, or play a game. Browse through the books and find something for the beach. Or indulge in a little shopping spree in the picturesque seaside village of Marigot, just ten minutes away. Here you'll find a number of upscale designer boutiques along with some trendy restaurants. La Samanna has recently added a boutique and three new suites and has redecorated other accommodations.

Address/Phone: P.O. Box 4077, 97064 St. Martin CEDEX, F.W.I.; 011–590–87–64–00; fax 011–590–87–87–86

U.S. Reservations: Orient-Express Hotels, (800) 237–1236

Owner/Manager: John Volponi, general manager

Arrival/Departure: A La Samanna representative greets guests at the airport and has a prearranged taxi service waiting for a prompt transfer to the resort. Transfer is included with package; others pay $15 each way.

Distance from Juliana International Airport: 6 miles (10 minutes)

Distance from Marigot: 5 minutes

Accommodations: 83 ocean-view accommodations include traditional guest rooms, one- and two-bedroom suites, and three-bedroom villas, all with living rooms, dining areas, and private patios or terraces. Recently second-floor balconies were added to some units; stairs give direct access to the beach.

Best Room/Suite: Beachfront villas

Amenities: Hair dryer, air-conditioning, robes, ceiling fan, toiletries, telephone, AM/FM clock radio, minibar, vanity mirrors; nightly turndown service, 24-hour room service; daily newspaper, welcome gift; VCR players and video library available, including all Academy Award–winning films

Electricity: 220 volts

Sports and Facilities: 3 tennis courts, infinity pool, snorkeling, sailboarding, waterskiing, fishing; deep-sea dive boat and sailboat rental; fitness center; massages and beauty treatments

Dress Code: Casual elegance

Weddings: Can be arranged

Rates/Packages: Passion in Paradise package 7-nights, $2,705–$11,590 includes accommodations, transfers, dinner for two, massages, and picnic cruise to private island

Payment/Credit Cards: Most major

Deposit: Three-night deposit; balance due 30 days prior to arrival. Full refund if canceled 30 days or more prior to arrival date; less than 30 days, forfeit 3-night deposit.

Government Taxes: 5 percent

Service Charges: Not included

Entry Requirements for U.S. Citizens: Proof of citizenship; passport best

≈≈≈

U.S. VIRGIN ISLANDS
≈≈≈

ST. JOHN

Caneel Bay

Location: Situated on a private, 170-acre peninsula on St. John.

Romantic Features: A different beach for each day; natural splendor of 6,500 acres of national park surrounding the resort; candlelit dining amid the flower-bedecked ruins of a sugar plantation.

With 5,000 acres of tropical jungle around you, there is plenty of room to spread out on Caneel Bay, one of Laurance Rockefeller's most beautiful creations. He discovered this pristine, jungle-covered island in 1952 when he was on a sailing trip. After purchasing a good portion of the island, he set about to personally oversee the building of Caneel Bay, insisting that it be a low-key, ideal vacation resort for those who wanted to escape to a peaceful, natural retreat.

Over the years many couples have started their married lives here, and their children have come after them on *their* honeymoons. It's traditionally been ranked as one of the best honeymoon resorts in the world, the kind of place "old money" likes—elegance without the glitz or bells and whistles.

In 1993, the upscale Rosewood Hotels & Resorts took on its management and undertook a multimillion-dollar renovation project, redecorating just about everything except the scenery.

The cottages, which are constructed of natural stone and weathered wood, are spread out along the fringes of the beaches and in the gardens and manicured lawns. Designed to blend into the lush tropical plants and trees that surround them, the cottages have louvered windows that let in the cooling sea breezes and wonderful views of the beaches or gardens. For those who prefer a more controlled environment, air-conditioning has recently been installed in all cottages. The new decor emphasizes a palette brought in from the outdoors, including corals, blues, and greens. Accessories and furniture also echo nature's design in clay, cane, bamboo, and local hardwood. There are six categories of rooms: courtside, tennis garden, ocean-view, beachfront, and premium as well as Cottage 7, a luxury villa popular with visiting bigwigs.

On the whole, the rooms are not super luxurious, nor are the baths mega-marble marvels. But with Caneel's setting and amazing natural assets, who can complain?

If you come here for a week's honeymoon, you will be able to plunk your-self on a different beach every day, but the alluring Honeymoon Beach may seem most appropriate. At Caneel your day spreads out before you like a sybaritic feast of wonderful things to do and see. If you love nature, you'll have miles of trails to follow that wind through the 5,000-acre Virgin Islands National Park. At night you can take walks along the pathways, which are softly lit with low mushroom lights to aid hikers, joggers, and strollers.

Feel adventurous? Then take a jeep or boat to other islands or to Caneel's sister property, Little Dix Bay on Virgin Gorda. Ask Caneel to pack a picnic lunch for you, and spend a relaxing day on your own. You can also head to Cruz Bay for shopping and browsing. There are several excellent shops in this little town along with some good restaurants.

Tennis players will be in racquet heaven, with eleven courts surrounded by tropical gardens in the terraced Tennis Park. The resort offers complimentary clinics and private lessons, and there is an on staff pro and a fully stocked shop

Water sports abound. Stop at the Beach Hut and get a Sunfish or sail-boarder and sail off into the calm waters in the bay. You can go snorkeling either by yourself or with a guide or charter a boat for deep-sea fishing. The best snorkeling is off the north end of Caneel Beach, where you can see bright green parrot fish, funny-looking needlefish, and sinister moray eels tucked into crevices of coral. The brilliant world underwater also comes to life through the eyes of Lucy Portlock, the staff marine biologist, who personally escorts guests on weekly snorkel tours through the island's undersea treasures.

More than 1,400 different kinds of plants and trees flourish on Caneel's property. The resort's horticulturist, Eleanor Gibney, will take you on a tour of the grounds.

Caneel's three restaurants and terrace lounge look out over the sea. Turtle Bay, a gourmet restaurant reminiscent of a grand plantation house, invites you to enjoy open-air all-day dining while looking out over gardens to the deep turquoise sea beyond. At the Caneel Beach Terrace, a casual, open dining room along the beach, you can indulge in a sumptuous lunch buffet every day. From your table in The Equator, which is set in the ruins of an ancient sugar planta-tion, you can see the twinkling lights of St. Thomas across the water; the Breezeway and Terrace provide a casual, comfortable place to meet friends and relax with a cool rum punch.

Meals are included in the romance and other packages. Those on daily rates should budget for the meal plan: $65 per person per day for breakfast and din-ner; $85 for all meals.

At night there is live music for dancing under the stars while the torches set in the lush foliage turn the resort into a tropical wonderland.

Address/Phone: P.O. Box 720, Cruz Bay, St. John, U.S.V.I. 00831-0720; (340) 776–6111; fax (340) 693–8280

Web Site: www.rosewood-hotels.com

U.S. Reservations: Rosewood Hotels & Resorts, (800) 928–8889; fax (212) 758–6640

Owner/Manager: Rosewood Hotels & Resorts, management company; Brian Young, general manager

Arrival/Departure: Caneel Bay can be reached via San Juan, Puerto Rico, and St. Thomas, U.S.V.I. St. John and St. Thomas are served by frequent flights from major U.S. gateways. Caneel Bay's regular ferry service operates between downtown St. Thomas and Caneel Bay several times each day. The resort also operates regular ferry service three times each week to its sister resort, Little Dix Bay, on Virgin Gorda, B.V.I. Look for the Caneel Bay desk at the Cyril E. King Airport, St. Thomas.

Distance from Cyril E. King Airport: 12 nautical miles (40 minutes)

Distance from Cruz Bay: 3 miles

Accommodations: 166 rooms and cottages. All have terraces; many have king-size beds.

Best Room/Suite: Secluded Cottage Point area

Amenities: Ceiling fans, air-conditioning, direct-dial telephones, minibar, hair dryer, bathrobes, TV, toiletries, in-room safes; ice service; room service

Electricity: 110 volts

Sports and Facilities: 11 tennis courts (5 lighted), pool, boating, sailing, snorkeling, and swimming; scuba diving can be arranged

Dress Code: Casual during the day; men required to wear slacks, collared shirts, and closed-in footwear in evening; jackets required during height of winter season for dinner in Turtle Bay restaurant.

Weddings: Can be arranged

Rates/Packages: Per couple per night rates include use of nonmotorized boats, snorkeling gear, shopping trip to St. Thomas, tennis and weekly clinics, introductory scuba clinic, feature movie presentations, rum tasting, and garden walk. $350–$850 (winter); $325–$575 (spring and fall); $250–$475 (summer). Pure Romance package includes all the above plus 7 nights' accommodations, champagne on arrival, all meals, unlimited half-day "ensign" sails, day trips to Little Dix Bay, sunset cocktail cruise, transfers to and from St. Thomas, massage for two. $4,100–$7,600 per couple (winter); $3,800–$5,600 (spring and fall); $3,200–$4,800 (summer). Tennis, Island Hopper, and other packages also available. Meal plans: $80 (breakfast and dinner), $100 (breakfast, lunch, and dinner); per person.

Payment/Credit Cards: Most major

Deposit: 3-night deposit; balance due 30 days prior to arrival. Full refund if canceled 21 days or more prior to arrival date (winter); 7 days (summer); otherwise forfeit deposit. $1,000 deposit for packages, due 14 days from date of booking; remainder due at checkout.

Government Taxes: 8 percent on room rate only; packages are subject to a 15 percent surcharge, which covers all room tax, service charges, and meal-plan gratuities

Service Charges: 7.5 percent

Entry requirements for U.S. Citizens: Proof of citizenship required when traveling between the United States and British Virgin Islands

LATIN AMERICA
AND MEXICO

Caribbean Sea

PANAMA

Barcelo Playa
Tambor

COSTA RICA

NICARAGUA

Ritz-Carlton, Cancun

★ Maroma

HONDURAS

★
Hacienda
Katanchel

BELIZE

GUATEMALA

EL SALVADOR

*Gulf
of
Mexico*

U. S. A.

Westin Brisas Ixtapa

La Casa
Que Canta

Hotel Villa del Sol

MEXICO

Las Hadas

★

Pacific Ocean

COSTA RICA

≈≈≈

Barcelo Playa Tambor

Location: Located on Tambor Beach 10 miles from Paquera, Pun Tarenas Province, in Ballena Bay on the west coast of Costa Rica, on the southern tip of the Nicoya Peninsula.

Romantic Features: Loving and lazing in the lap of luxury at an all-inclusive resort; primordial excursions to the nearby, world-famous rain forests and biological reserves of Costa Rica.

You are not planning to have an ordinary marriage, so why should you choose an ordinary honeymoon? Stay at the five-star Barcelo Playa Tambor and you can have all the fun and amenities of an all-inclusive resort and still indulge your interests in things natural and environmental—like the wonders of pristine rain forests. Uniquely located in one of the most beautiful areas of Costa Rica, with its long stretches of unspoiled Pacific Ocean beaches, Barcelo Playa Tambor is set in the midst of one of the most important systems of national parks and biological reserves in the world. The resort itself has private, parklike grounds and is blessed with its own sandy cove, shady woods, streams, and a rich variety of exotic subtropical flora and fauna including toucans, parrots, and lizards.

On arrival you are welcomed with a cool drink at the large open-air reception and lounge area, which is filled with tropical plants. In the distance you can see a huge, free-form pool, swim up bar, poolside bar and grill, and, beyond that, the palm trees that, you will soon discover, fringe a private crescent of golden sand beach, where you can try out one of the sea kayaks or sailboarders.

Large, rolling lawns are interspersed with colorful bushes and flower beds, which are spread throughout the beautifully landscaped grounds, where the white-balconied, pastel-colored accommodations are located. Easygoing yet tropically elegant, this bright and cheerful resort was built on what was once a cattle ranch. None of the buildings is higher than two stories, and all rooms, which are decorated in a bright, tropical style, come with a balcony or terrace.

You never have to go beyond the Playa's boundaries if you don't want to. Days can be spent in the sun lying by the pool or at the beach, or wandering down the many paths of lush, natural forest greenery. Like all good all-inclusive resorts, Playa Tambor has many planned activities during the day—such as

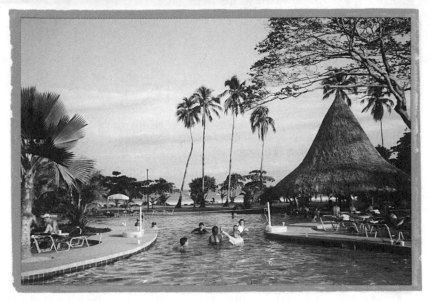

* Barcelo Playa Tambor, Costa Rica

water polo, dancing lessons, and aerobics classes. Special nightly entertainment is always planned, the disco pulses with Latin rhythms, and your luck can be tested in the casino. You can choose to eat at the a la carte restaurant, the sumptuous buffet spread, or the beach grill. On the nights when a full moon coincides with low tide, a rollicking Pirate's Party is held on the beach.

But there is more. One of the reasons you may have come here is to explore Costa Rica. This amazing little country is home to more than 4 percent of the world's total flora and fauna, and about 25 percent of its national territory is protected. Whether you walk along the water's edge to the nearby fishing village (at low tide!) or sign up for an excursion farther afield to one of the country's volcanoes, biological reserves, or national parks, you will come away with a strong sense of how dependent we are on nature for enrichment, beauty, and balance in our lives. Not a bad honeymoon gift to take home!

The resort is very helpful in setting up these adventures. One nearby excursion takes you to Cabo Blanco National Rain Forest on the tip of the Nicoya Peninsula. You can wander with a guide in the marine bird sanctuary and catch glimpses of pelicans, brown boobies, and magnificent frigate birds, not to mention howler monkeys, kinkajous, anteaters, and collared peccaries. There are also more than 119 tree species.

Playa Tambor is for those with a keen sense of adventure and a desire for an exotic, tropical vacation. The fact that it's all-inclusive makes it even better.

Address/Phone: (Puntarenas, Costa Rica), c/o Edificio Palacio Hotel, San Jose, Costa Rica; 011–506–683–0303; fax 011–506–683–0304

E-mail: tambor@sol.rasca.co.cr

U.S. Reservations: (800) 858–0606

Owner/Manager: Guillenmo Cabrer, Barcelo Hotels, General Manager

Arrival/Departure: Land transfers from San Jose Airport via bus, ferry, and another bus take about 3½ hours; air transfers take about 25 minutes' flying time. If you have to stay overnight in the capital city of San Jose because of international flight connections to transfers, arrangements will be made for accommodations at a sister hotel, the elegant, five-star Barcelo San Jose Palacio (about 20 minutes by taxi from the airport). You are entitled to all-inclusive privileges during your stay there, with certain restrictions.

Distance from San Jose Airport: 3½ hours by buses and ferry; 25 minutes by charter airplane

Distance from Tambor: 10 minutes; the nearest large town is Puntarenas, about 1 hour by ferry

Accommodations: 402 doubles. Each room has two European double beds (close to the familiar queen-size bed) and en-suite bathrooms with deep tubs.

Best Room/Suite: All rooms are in the same deluxe category and are priced as such

Amenities: Air-conditioning, telephone, satellite TV, direct-dial phone, and in-room safe deposit box

Electricity: 110/220 volts, 60 Hz. Two-pin plugs are standard. (These are U.S. equivalents.)

Sports and Facilities: 3 tennis courts, 2 multipurpose courts (football, basketball, volleyball); water polo, aerobics, fitness center; scuba diving, sailing, catamarans, sailboarding, kayaking, deep-sea fishing; horseback riding; nearby golf course, Monster-Truck tours, ATV tours

Dress Code: Casual

Rates/Packages: $65–$120 per person per night (April–December); $65–$156 (December–April). Price includes all meals, local-brand beverages, nonmotorized water sports, nightly entertainment, daily activities. Air/land packages are available. A 3-night package from Miami is $589. Call for most recent promotions.

Payment/Credit Cards: Most major

Deposit: $150 per person upon booking and full payment 7 days prior to arrival.

Government Taxes: Departure tax, $6.00

Service Charges: Included in room rate

Entry Requirements for U.S. Citizens: Valid passport

MEXICO

~~~

Hacienda Katanchel

Location: Built on the grounds of an ancient Mayan settlement near Merida in the heart of the Yucatan west of Cancun.

Romantic Features: Private pavilions surrounded by exotic jungle flowers and foliage; personal plunge pools; swimming in jungle pools; guided hikes to archeological sites.

The clackety-clack of wheels rolling over the corrugated-like path announces the arrival of guests brought to the front door of their suite in a small cart pulled by Margarit, the horse. So begins another memorable stay at one of Mexico's most unique resorts, the Hacienda Kantanchel.

Much like Sleeping Beauty was awakened after a long deep sleep, so, too, was Hacienda Katanchel, a restored seventeenth-century, 741-acre country estate in the heart of Mexico's Yucatan. When Monica Hernandez and her architect husband, Anibal Gonzalez, were looking for a vacation home near Merida, the jumping-off point for those visiting ancient Mayan archeological sites, their broker told them about a special place in the jungle a few miles east of town. Driving onto the property thick with rampaging jungle vegetation, they knew they had arrived at the main house when the bumper of their Suburban hit the bottom step of the staircase leading up to the front door. It was no wonder the building was hard to see. It was covered with a tangle of thick vines. Monica said they ducked under the vines that were held up by chicken wire, walked up the stairs, and were met by a caretaker and four dogs. Incredibly they walked into a sparkling-clean room. Although the wealthy owner had not visited the eight-room Hacienda for more than thirty-five years due to ill health, the caretaker had maintained the living quarters in case the owner were to return.

"We knew immediately this was for us," said Monica, awed by the beauty of the rooms. Spanish colonial in style, the Hacienda seemed perfect for them. As they set about cleaning and restoring the building and grounds, they discovered more buildings, small houses also covered in rampant jungle growth that had once been residences for the local workers. It was a bit overwhelming. So many houses, thirty-three in all, were discovered hidden in the tall underbrush that had grown unchecked for more than thirty years.

Later, when one of the Gonzalez's guests remarked that this complex would make a wonderful hotel, it sparked the beginning of a new venture for the couple, who admitted they knew absolutely nothing about running such a place. But why not?

Monica and Anibal plunged into the venture, restoring and transforming the small houses into guest cottages they called pavilions. They furnished the rooms with all their favorite things bringing in interesting furniture pieces from everywhere—many antiques—Ralph Lauren damask bed linens, thick expensive towels, and pillows Monica personally head tested. "I love good pillows and always travel with mine," she said.

Six more guest accommodations were created from rooms in the original Hacienda. Banana trees, papaya, and other fruit trees were planted. Each pavilion got its own plunge pool filled with invigorating mineral water pumped in by turn-of-the-century windmills from the seventeen wells also found on the property. Terraces were added to the pavilions and furnished with hammocks and comfortable lounges. Gardens were planted for every cottage, themed around four types of plants: decorative, fragrant, eatable, and medicinal.

Rooms are quietly dramatic, decorated in the elegant minimalist style. Lots of white. White iron king-size beds, white sheets, white blankets, towels, linens, Egyptian cottons, and furniture fabrics—all set against a backdrop of rich jewel-like wall colors in peaches, melons, and reds. Rooms are spacious with brilliant Mexican tile floors. Each item used in the decor, from the art work on the walls to the antiques and lamps, is carefully placed. Nothing in these rooms is superfluous.

The lofty Casa de Maquinas, with its polished hardwood floors, high arches, and fine wood tables and chairs, is a perfect setting for elegant dining. Those who prefer more casual dining can sit on the open-air terrace. Much of the food is prepared using produce grown right on the property. Meals, which can best be described as light cuisine with a touch of Mayan or "Mayan Novelle," is delicious. Fresh seafood is a specialty.

There is a lovely lounge, a library, an office, and a boutique located in the Tienda de Raya, once an on-premise general store. The grand salon (as well as the stunning dining room) was once part of a large nineteenth-century factory that processed sisal for exportation. A large swimming pool is also on the grounds.

Even the toiletries are special, natural: papaya shampoo, handmade soaps, and a citrus-based insect repellant that smells good to everyone but the bugs. Highly sensitive to maintaining the integrity of the ecological balance, Monica and Anibal have created a chemical-free environment; everything is organically grown.

There is no TV, no radio, no clock. Yet you do have a phone and even a fax hookup. There is no air-conditioning, nor is it needed. Anibal designed the pavilions to take full advantage of the cool jungle breezes. Ceiling fans help things along.

With all this natural beauty, there is no need to do anything beyond relax in the gardens, get a soothing massage, and swim in the pool. However, there is much to do for those who love nature. Guided walks are richly rewarding. Maybe you'll spot a rare white-fronted parrot or Green Breasted Mango. The region is filled with a huge number of exotic birds, animals, and plants. Pink clouds of flamingos can be found in a wildlife preserve on the coast.

There are archeological sites few know about to be discovered and better known places like Chichen Itza, Uxmal, and the ancient city of Ak to visit. You can bike along trails and swim in the crystalline waters of the jungle's cenotes, deep sinkholes that are blue, blue, blue. If you're daring enough, you can swim through the underground caves carved into the cavernous limestone.

Certainly you will want to visit nearby villages, which seem to belong to another century, places where people work in crafts passed down for generations. Some work in "henequn" (sisal and hemp) and Jipijapa making straw hats, baskets, and other items; some weave hammocks and embroider table-cloths and *hipile* (traditional smocks). Hand-painted pottery is also locally made. The resort's vans are available to take you to visit charming pastel-colored colonial villages and historic haciendas located in the area.

Hacienda Katanchel is a place for those who love nature and quiet and things from another time. And luxury. And don't miss, Cairo, the Azahuac (a kind of greyhound). He is usually close by to greet and say goodbye to the Hacienda's guests.

Address/Phone: Km. 26, Highway 180 (Merida-Cancun), CP 97470 Mexico; 011–52–99–234–020; fax (888) 882-9470

E-mail: hacienda@mail.mda.com.mx

Web Site: www.hacienda-katanchel.com

U.S. Reservations: Fax hotel directly at toll-free number above, or call Small Luxury Hotels, (800) 525–4800

Owner/Manager: Monica Hernandez and Anibal Gonzalez

Arrival/Departure: Arrangements can be made for pickup at airports in Merida and Cancun.

Distance from Merida Airport: 15 miles

Distance from Merida: 15 miles; 2½ hour drive from Cancun

Accommodations: 39 rooms and suites

Best Room/Suite: Honeymoon Suite with king-size bed and whirlpool bath

Amenities: Hair dryer, telephone, toiletries, ceiling fans

Electricity: 110 volts

Sports and Facilities: Large main pool, several plunge pools; hiking, swimming, aerobics, yoga, massage therapy

Dress Code: Casual smart

Weddings: Can be arranged

Rates/Packages: Room rates from $250; Honeymoon Suite $300

Payment/Credit Cards: Most major

Deposit: Guarantee with credit card

Government Taxes: 17 percent

Service Charges: 10 percent

Entry Requirements for U.S. Citizens: Proof of citizenship; passport best

≈≈≈

Hotel Villa del Sol

Location: On palm-lined La Ropa Beach in the quaint village of Zihuatanejo, 150 miles northwest of Acapulco on the Pacific Coast.

Romantic Features: Lovely white crescent-shaped private beach.

It's only 6 miles from Ixtapa, but this small gem is quite different, indeed, from Ixtapa's large chain of hotels. It has a beauty of a beach sheltered by a dense canopy of palms and framed by a carpet of tropical foliage that begins at the edge of the beach, rising up into the hills behind. Nestled in this greenery are fifty-four suites in adobelike two-story casitas. Six new luxury Lagoon Suites and a two-bedroom Presidential Suite were added in 1999. Winding stone walkways lead from the cottages to the two palapa-roofed bar/restaurants and the beach. Water runs in a meandering channel from the main fountain, along the paths, and into the pool.

Once you've had time to let the magic of Villa del Sol sink in, you'll be hooked. From the time you step up into the rather unpretentious yet charming tiled reception area and pass through to the gardens just beyond, you've entered the Mexican version of the Garden of Eden, and in this garden everything works: from the high-tech faucets that glide open like butter to the attractive lights that line the walkways. Created by Helmut Leins, who came to Mexico several years ago from Germany, Villa del Sol combines the casual and colorful ambience of Mexico with the superb service-oriented traditions of Europe.

Passionate about details, Helmut says he makes sure that he sleeps in every room at least once a year. This way he knows if everything is as it should be. It's only when you stay here that you notice how well thought out it all is—subtle things like soap dishes, towel bars, and shelves are all perfectly placed.

Helmut's charming French wife, Muriel, oversees the room decor and goes to great lengths to get just the right accessories and furnishings. Each of the fifty-four suites is unique and appointed with authentic Mexican artifacts, such as wooden masks, terra-cotta pots, and ceramic birds. One-bedroom suites have king-size beds; two-bedroom suites have one king-size and one-queen-size bed. Suites come with separate sitting areas, terraces or balconies, and luxurious baths with large walk-in showers. Rooms are decorated in rich, Mexican-loomed fabrics and enhanced by colorful handmade Mexican tiles. Terra-cotta and white ceramic tile floors are accented by area rugs; beds are draped in filmy white gauze; and a hammock is strung in a corner of each patio, providing a pleasant retreat for an afternoon siesta.

Villa del Sol's beachfront suites are about as romantic as it gets. The problem is, once you've seen them, you'll not want to leave. These suites are pure Mexican magic at its best. Each has a large patio smack on the beach with a hammock for two as well as a table and chairs; you can wake up slowly there to fresh coffee and croissants each morning. Sitting areas open onto a wide deck with a blue-tiled plunge pool. A lounge for two, padded and comfortable, is the perfect place to catch a snooze. King-size canopied beds and extra-large baths and views of orange-flamed sunsets take the romance level up another notch. Red-tile floors, fresh flowers, shelves, and roomy closets all add to the wonderful ambience.

If one wants to nitpick (and that's all it is): Some of the bungalows are a bit on the dark side, especially those that front the gardens. The heavy tropical vegetation overhanging the roofs tends to keep sunlight at bay. But this is a minor thing and will soon be forgotten once you settle in. The newer casitas, some with private plunge pools, are more open and spacious.

A large round palapa-thatched roof, which looks much like a giant sombrero, houses an open-air bar and restaurant. Orlando's Bar, named after the affable master of the bar, whose wit and diplomacy are legendary, is also housed under its own thatched roof. Repeat guests always look forward to swapping stories with Orlando, who will serve you exotic drinks such as coco loco.

The white sand beach, shaded by palms and palm-frond umbrellas, is set up with comfortable lounges with thick cushions, where you can crash and snooze. Want a frosty margarita and some freshly made guacamole and tortilla chips? Just signal the beach attendant, and it will be brought to you in speedy fashion. Generally the waters off La Ropa, unlike the rougher beach areas in neighboring Ixtapa, are very swimmable. When the surf kicks up, however, you can cool off in one of the resort's four pools including a stunning new infinity pool overlooking the beach.

There are two tennis courts, which, like everything else on the property, are well maintained. If you're looking for a game of tennis and your spouse isn't up to it, ask Helmut if he'd like a set or two.

Dining at the Villa del Sol under the palapa roof is just about everything you could want: excellent, well-prepared food, candlelit tables by the sea, and warm smiles from those who serve you. Just outside the resort entrance lies the picturesque village of Zihuatanejo. Still very much a sleepy fishing village in spite of the tourism influx at nearby Ixtapa, here you can still watch the fishermen bring in their daily catch, and you can stroll down decorative brick-paved streets past small shops and cozy little restaurants. If you crave a bit of lively nightlife, you can head to one of the large hotels on Ixtapa's Palmar Beach. But then, who really wants to leave the Villa del Sol for very long?

Address/Phone: P.O. Box 84, Playa La Ropa, 40880 Zihuatanejo, Gro., Mexico; 011–52–755–42239 or 011–52–755–42758; fax 011–52–755–4258 or 011–52–755–44066

E-mail: hotel@villasol.com.mx

Web Site: www.villasol.com.mx

U.S. Reservations: (888) 389–2645

Owner/Manager: Helmut and Muriel Leins, owners; Peter M. Koehler, general manager

Arrival/Departure: Taxis are available at the airport (about $7.00 each way per car)

Distance from Ixtapa-Zihuatanejo International Airport: 15 minutes

Distance from Zihuatanejo: 5 minutes; from Ixtapa, 10 minutes

Accommodations: 54 individually designed rooms and suites, including 18 luxury suites

Best Room/Suite: Beachfront suites

Amenities: Air-conditioning, ceiling fans, king-size beds, toiletries, in-room safe, TV, refrigerator, terrace, hammock, telephone, laundry and valet service. Suites have a living room area, minibars, cotton bathrobes, electronic safes, private fax, satellite TV, stereo, and CD player. Some have whirlpool or minipool.

Electricity: 110 volts

Sports and Facilities: Beach, waterskiing, snorkeling, sailboarding, sailing, 4 freshwater pools; 2 lighted tennis courts; two 18-hole golf courses 10 minutes away; scuba diving, deep-sea fishing, and horseback riding can be arranged

Dress Code: Casual; casually elegant for dinner

Weddings: Can be arranged

Rates/Packages: From $160 (summer); from $230 (winter). During winter the meal plan for breakfast and dinner is mandatory ($50 per person per day in summer). No children under 14 during winter months.

Payment/Credit Cards: Most major

Deposit: 2 nights' deposit; cancel 7 days before arrival for full refund

Government Taxes: 15 percent

Service Charges: 10 percent suggested

Entry Requirements for U.S. Citizens: Proof of citizenship; passport best

La Casa Que Canta

Location: On a cliff above Zihuatanejo Bay adjacent to Playa La Ropa, near the center of Zihuatanejo.

Romantic Features: Views, view, views; intimate suites with private plunge pools; wonderful small terraced places where you can drink or dine.

L a Casa Que Canta, "the house that sings," is one of those rare finds in Mexico, a small, intimate, five-star inn perched atop a cliff overlooking the Pacific. The clusters of pink-hued adobe-like casitas with terraces and thatched roofs that look like giant mops atop little blockhouses are staggered down the hillside so that you get a great view of the sea from each room.

Eclectically and creatively furnished with authentic Mexican artifacts and furniture, the suites have chairs with arms that are brightly painted to resemble birds and legs carved like feathers. A large, colorful striped animal (could it be a pig or a tapir?) sits on the floor balancing a carved bird on its back. A large terra-cotta bird with real, brightly colored feathers sits on a table, one of the many cleverly designed lamps scattered here and there in the public areas and suites. Furniture painted by well-known Mexican artists such as Frida Kahlo and Diego Rivera, mermaids, and ceramic angels along with tons of plants and Mexican tapestries and paintings add beauty and a sense of fun to La Casa Que Canta.

Your suite, with its bedroom, sitting room, and separate patio, is home to a number of valuable and whimsical art pieces: hand-painted desks, folk art from Erongaricuaro and *equipale* chairs. All these wonderful things are set against a background of creamy white walls and bed linens and red-tile floors edged with shiny, polished pebbles. Wood louvered doors open out to the terraces, which are partially thatched and have two extra-long lounge chairs, colorfully painted wrought-iron tables and chairs, a cushioned sitting area, lamps, and hammocks. In the harbor below you'll see a scattering of beautiful yachts—picture-postcard stuff. Don't look for a TV: There isn't one—but who needs it, with such views? (If you really need a quick catch-up on the world outside, there's a TV in the "theater room.") Your bath has a granite counter with double vanity, a pink-marble walk-in shower, a walk-in closet, separate toilet with bidet, and oversize bath towels.

Other resorts might be able to duplicate the decor (although I doubt it, unless the designers are prepared to spend years searching for interesting Mexican art and furniture pieces), but a better setting would be hard to find. Your terrace, the pool, the dining room, the various terraced rooms tucked into the descending hillside—everything—sits over the sea, which continually crashes into the wet, dark, jagged rocks at the base of the cliff. There is a saltwater pool as well as a Jacuzzi cut into the rocks near the bottom of the cliff. The freshwater pool, near the top of the cliff, is constructed so that the water seems to simply slip over the side of the pool down to the sea. You can quite happily while away the entire day sitting on the patio here, enjoying the scenery and sun.

La Casa Que Canta, Mexico

In the evening when you come into your room, you'll find a floral surprise waiting for you: an elaborate pattern of flower petals on your bed, perhaps shaped into a heart. You also might find flowers tucked into washcloths, in soap trays, and on your bedside table.

La Casa Que Canta is but a two-minute walk to Playa La Ropa, a lovely white sandy beach with good swimming.

Meals are served outdoors overlooking the bay or in a palapa-palm-frond–thatched structure, where you'll also find a reception area, lounge, and bar. Dining hours are relaxed. You can eat anytime after 8:00 A.M., and Mexican specialties, salads, and grilled items are offered at both pool terraces. Like tequila? The resort features twelve different brands. Try a frosty and yummy quanabana margarita, or go for a cold Corona, the local beer, which goes great with the bar's new selection of Mexican tapas at the Terrace Bar.

Enjoying cocktails and dinner on the terrace at night is about as romantic as it gets: The soft, yellow lights play on the lofty, palm-thatched ceilings, and endless views of the sea are punctuated by the winking lights of Zihuatanejo in the distance. Light peeks through the holes of large round terra-cotta pots and gently glows from hanging wicker shades; there are enough private cozy sitting areas tucked here and there for every couple who wants their own space.

Just five minutes away is Zihuatanejo, a charming fishing village nestled into the curve of a bay cut sharply into the hills. Small white houses with red-tile roofs, a variety of fishing vessels anchored in the bay or pulled up on the shore, and a small population of happy, easygoing people make this a fun place to visit. If you crave some modern-day action, the beach resort area, Ixtapa, is just a ten-minute drive around the corner.

This all may seem familiar if you saw the movie *When a Man Loves a Woman,* starring Meg Ryan and Andy Garcia, which was filmed here. A glance at the guest book says it all: A honeymoon couple writes, "La Casa Que Canta was the best place to start the first day of the rest of our lives." Another says simply, "Wow! Pure magic."

Address/Phone: Camino Escenico a la Playa la Ropa, 40880 Zihuatanejo, Gro., Mexico; 011–52–755–47030; (888) 523–5050; fax 011–52–755–47040

E-mail: casaquecanta@podernet.com.mx

Web Site: www.casaquecanta.com.mx

U.S. Reservations: (888) 523–5050 or Small Luxury Hotels, (800) 525–4800

Owner/Manager: Jacques Baldassari, owner; Marcela Mier y Concha, general manager

Arrival/Departure: Transfers from Ixtapa/Zihuatanejo Airport can be arranged

Distance from Ixtapa-Zihuatanejo International Airport: 12 miles (20 minutes) 35-minute flight from Mexico City

Distance from Zihuatanejo center: 5 minutes

Accommodations: 24 suites, each with its own living room and terrace; suites range in size from 800 to 1,733 square feet; 10 suites have private pools

Best Room/Suite: Private pool suites

Amenities: Air-conditioning, fans, bidet, large walk-in shower, magnifying mirror, toiletries, hair dryer, telephones, in-room safe, minibar, bathrobes; room service, massages available

Electricity: 110 volts

Sports and Facilities: 2 pools (1 freshwater "infinity" pool, 1 saltwater), saltwater Jacuzzi, most water sports, horseback riding; golf and tennis nearby

Dress Code: Casually elegant

Weddings: Can be arranged

Rates/Packages: $260–$295 per couple per night for a grand suite, $365–$400 for a private pool suite (low season); $345 for a grand suite, $485–$525 for a pool suite (high season)

Payment/Credit Cards: Most major

Deposit: 2-night deposit; refund if canceled 30 days prior to arrival date (60 days for Christmas and Easter)

Government Taxes: 17 percent

Service Charges: 10 to 15 percent suggested

Entry Requirements for U.S. Citizens: Proof of identity; passport best

≈≈≈

Las Hadas

Location: Sits on 650 acres on Santiago Peninsula, about three hours south of Puerto Vallarta on Mexico's Pacific Coast.

Romantic Features: Private tented cabanas; Moorish fantasy suites overlooking the Pacific; suites with private pools.

The beach isn't the most spectacular in the world—actually rather small as beaches go—but that didn't stop Bo Derek and Dudley Moore from having a romantic fling there in the classic movie *10*. They ate in the El Terral restaurant, with the Pacific surf and night skies as a backdrop, and indulged in a friendly frolic in their posh suite. The setting was Las Hadas, on Mexico's picturesque Pacific Coast.

When architect Jose Luis Ezquerra applied his audacious creative powers to designing Las Hadas (which means "the fairies" in Spanish), he conjured up a Moorish fantasyland composed of dazzling white towers, domes, minarets, arches, and spires. The resort is terraced up the green-foliage–carpeted hillside, looking much like an elaborate, tiered wedding cake. Bright clouds of bougainvillea cascade over walls and into courtyards; brilliant blossoms of hibiscus and mimosa, palms, and many varieties of cactus paint beautiful patterns against the white adobe walls.

Moorish tented white cabanas on the beach provide private retreats from the hot sun, and another tented outdoor "room" shelters a poolside bar. All these fanciful structures are linked by a network of cobblestone walkways, edged in marble and lined by tropical plants.

In addition to the beach, Las Hadas has two pools. One is quiet and secluded; the other is more like a sprawling lagoon, with waterfalls, flower-covered little islands, and a rope bridge. You don't have to look very hard to spot a lazy iguana catching some sun on one of the islands. Pick a red hibiscus blossom, and he (or she) will eat it right from your fingers.

There are several kinds of rooms and suites, ranging from standard right up to the Presidential Suite, which is very private, with a living room, a large walk-in closet, a private pool and Jacuzzi, an upstairs dining terrace, and a private entrance. The Las Hadas Suite is another luxurious accommodation. All rooms have marble floors, air-conditioning, balcony or terrace, and a number of amenities.

The Camino Club rooms give you more privacy as well as the use of a private pool. Fantasia Suites are larger, with king-size beds. Some have living rooms, more than one terrace or balcony, a bathroom, a wet bar, and spacious terraces. The decor is in keeping with the Moorish theme, and colorful artwork and fresh flowers are used to pep up the white walls.

Las Hadas has several restaurants, including the elegant Legazpi, open November to April, which serves classic international cuisine; El Terral, a more

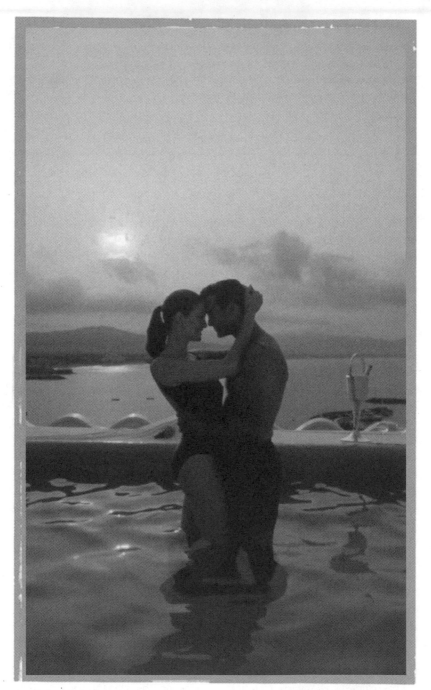

Las Hadas, Mexico

informal, open-air restaurant, where you can try some excellent Mexican dishes along with grilled meats; Los Delfines, a thatched-roof, seaside eatery serving lunch and beverages and specializing in fresh seafood; and El Palmar, an informal restaurant overlooking the main pool, where you can have breakfast, lunch, and dinner.

There are also a popular swim-up pool bar, a piano lounge, and a tented beach bar.

You'll find plenty to do if you like water sports, and when the day cools down, you can head to the tennis courts. If you want to see what lies outside the gates of Las Hadas, hop aboard the resort's trimaran, which runs daily excursions to Manzanillo, and take a romantic Sunset Bay cruise.

As sensual as Las Hadas is during the day, it really turns up the steam when night falls: Golden lights dance in and around the pointed spiral roof towers, scalloped tiers of open balconies, and arched windows, creating a magical wonderland designed for romance.

Address/Phone: Rincor de las Hadas, P.O. Box 158, 28200 Manzanillo, Colima, Mexico; 011–52–333–4–00–00; fax 011–52–333–4–19–50

E-mail: zlo@caminoreal.com

Web Site: www.caminoreal.com.manzanillo

U.S. Reservations: (800) 7–CAMINO or Leading Hotels of the World, (800) 223–6800

Owner/Manager: Michel Beuffe, general manager

Arrival/Departure: Regular air service to Playa de Oro Airport; private transfers, at $50 per couple round-trip, can be arranged; shuttle service and taxis available at $15 per person each way.

Distance from Playa de Oro Airport: 30 minutes

Distance from Manzanillo: 15 minutes

Accommodations: 233 rooms and 41 suites grouped in multistory towers and terraced rows; some suites are set apart with their own pools

Best Room/Suite: If you want the one where Derek and Moore cavorted to Ravel's *Bolero,* ask for the Las Hadas Suite. It has two living rooms, two bathrooms, a private pool with terrace, a wet bar, an upstairs dining terrace, and great views of the sea. For more modest budgets a room in the Camino Real Club or a Fantasia Suite is recommended. The higher up, the more privacy and the better the view.

Amenities: Air-conditioning, satellite TV, minibar, toiletries, marble baths, telephone; room service

Electricity: 110 volts

Sports and Facilities: 10 tennis courts lit for night play, 2 of them clay, ($9.00–$15.00 per court per hour); La Mantarraya 18-hole golf course ($66

greens fees with caddy, $90 with cart), club rentals ($25); marina, beach, 2 pools; water sports, including snorkeling, sailing, swimming, waterskiing, sailboarding, Sunfish sailing, speedboat rides, and deep-sea fishing

Dress Code: Tropical elegance

Weddings: Can be arranged

Rates/Packages: $252–$386 per couple per night for a room; $360–$927 for suites; breakfast and dinner, $30 per person

Payment/Credit Cards: Most major

Deposit: 1-night deposit due 15 days before arrival; cancel 3 days or more before arrival date for full refund

Government Taxes: 17 percent

Service Charges: 15 percent

Entry Requirements for U.S. Citizens: Proof of citizenship; passport best

≈≈≈

Maroma

Location: On the east coast of the Yucatán Peninsula, 20 miles south of Cancun.

Romantic Features: Small, intimate property with 520 acres (much of it jungle); a secluded beach; king-size beds draped with silky netting; private terrace with hammock; candlelit dinners with piano music.

From the time you arrive at the small, elegant Maroma, you are completely pampered and left alone. Yet the Maroma "family" makes you feel as though anything is possible; all you have to do is ask. And for the most part, it's true!

Marked by a plain wooden gate off the Yucatán Peninsula's main corridor, a rutted, single-lane path winds through jungle, past flowering trees and around iguanas sunning themselves. In a small clearing is a cobblestone driveway, at the end of which is an elegant whitewashed hacienda. A small reflecting pool and an assortment of honking geese and ducks greet you.

Upon entering the open-air, tiled foyer, you are welcomed by a charming hostess and a frosty Maroma margarita (with a delicious secret ingredient). The hostess asks if you have any special requests and tastes: When would you like your fresh coffee, juice, and pastries to arrive in the morning? What are your favorite foods and drinks? What special activities would you like arranged?

A quiet, secluded estate of loosely linked suites and elegantly lighted walkways set around a pretty blue-tiled swimming pool fed by a gurgling fountain, Maroma is a collection of one- and two-story buildings, some topped by thatched palapa roofs made of native palm fronds.

Past the pool is the large, breezy main building, El Sol, with high ceilings, winding staircases and terra-cotta tile floors. Inside are a small bar and a casually elegant dining room, flanked by a slate terrace with a large Jacuzzi and steps leading to a beach of fine, soft white sand.

Your room, designed to appeal to the senses, is furnished with handsome Mexican colonial furniture, rich fabrics, and original artwork. A silky, translucent netting cascades from the ceiling and flows over the bed to a floor of large, honey-colored tiles. Thick cloth curtains frame the entrance to a room-size sunken tub and a shower made of golden ceramic tiles.

The beach is quiet and mostly deserted. At one end of the mile-wide cove is a secret sulphur spring that feeds into the shallows. Find it by digging your toes in the talc-soft sediment. You'll know you're there when you smell the pungent sulphur. The jungle that surrounds Maroma is home to monkeys, anteaters, possum, foxes, and a variety of exotic birds.

Maroma, Spanish for "somersault," is named for the swirling currents beyond the offshore reef, a mixing of tidal currents and upwellings that first bedeviled Mayan seafarers trading along the coast and at the nearby island of Cozumel. It's funny that such a quiet, serene place like this should be named after a turbulent waterway.

La Maroma, the namesake ocean current, however, poses no problem for the snorkeler or swimmer. The water sports concession is run by Jean-Claude, a Frenchman, and Michael, his teenage son. They are expert guides to the local waters and are both full of exuberant French charm and a love of this area.

Charles, the relaxed restaurant host, chats easily with all the guests, recommending things to do and telling stories about Maroma. Under his laid-back but attentive eye operate a cast of smiling, expert servers. Not quite an employee but surely part of the Maroma family is Pierre, a small, beautiful jungle cat that Charles raised from a kitten. Pierre spends his afternoons lounging on the wood beams under the palapa roof of the beachfront bar.

The menu at Maroma clearly caters to an international crowd. The elegant but pricey fare includes appetizers like lobster in filo on balsamic-perfumed tomato compote and duck mousse with green peppercorns and entrees such as mosaic of fish and shellfish with caviar, beef tenderloin medallions with Roquefort, and an array of chicken, pork, lamb, and duck dishes. If you have a taste for heat, ask for the *chnee-pek,* Mayan for "dog's nose." This salsa—a combination of onions, habañero chiles, and tomatoes, will spice up any meal.

Charles and the servers will encourage you to use your imagination and ask for whatever dish you're in the mood for. If the ingredients are in the kitchen, they'll be happy to make you a custom meal. Another tip: When it's not busy, ask to have a flambéed coffee drink prepared for you and taken up to the Mirador, a private rooftop alcove with sweeping views of the moonlit beach. For lunch the strip steak with Oaxaca cheese and roasted poblano chilies is hearty and delicious. Breakfast is leisurely and lovely and offers all kinds of choices, ranging from the compote of pineapple marmalade, dripping with honey and spiked with cinnamon, to custom egg dishes and pancakes with bananas and pecans. As the sun is fading on the beach, order margaritas, chips, and the incredible guacamole.

If you're looking for a real traditional Mexican meal, you're best off heading to a restaurant in nearby Playa del Carmen. About twenty minutes south on the main strip, this is the shopping and nightlife hub of the area. Playa's shopping district is filled with roaming European backpackers and tourist couples from the occasional cruise ships that dock there. Along the main drag, wall-to-wall shops sell jewelry, clothes, hammocks, and all manner of gifts and souvenirs. Music trickles out from bars and eateries. Several of the restaurants have mariachi bands that wander through the outdoor tables—a Mexican-vacation must.

But some guests never feel the urge to leave Maroma. And it's not hard to understand why. Like the peacocks that roam the walkways prowling for bugs, like the ducks and geese that have made their home at Maroma, and like little Pierre taking his afternoon naps at the Beach Bar, honeymooners at Maroma may find that it's really quite pleasant to stay just where they are.

Address/Phone: P.O. Box 51, Cancun, Quintana Roo, 77500, Mexico; 011–52–987–44730; fax 011–52–988–42115

Web Site: www.Maroma.net

U.S. Reservations: Contact the hotel directly

Owner/Manager: Jose Luis and Sally Moreno

Arrival/Departure: Complimentary transfers are provided in a comfortable, air-conditioned Maroma car

Distance from Cancun Airport: 30 minutes

Accommodations: 7 Garden View rooms; 25 Ocean View rooms; 2 junior suites; 1 one-bedroom suite; 1 two-bedroom suite

Best Room/Suite: Rooms on the upper levels have the best views; however, each room is special in its own way

Amenities: Hair dryer, toiletries, beach towels, telephones; 24-hour room service, daily delivery of bottled water, safe in the office for valuables, Jacuzzi, massage; on-call hairdresser, manicurist, and medical assistance

Electricity: 110 volts

Sports and Facilities: Snorkeling, Hobie-Cat sailing, sailboarding, scuba diving, deep-sea fishing, horseback riding; book and video library with TV and VCR; boutique; beach bar; golf courses nearby. Also nearby and easily arranged are visits to Tulum, Cozumel Island, and Xcaret theme park and day and overnight excursions to Chichen Itza, Sian Ka'an Biosphere Reserve, Merida, and Tikal.

Dress Code: Casually elegant

Weddings: Will be happily arranged, from filling out the paperwork to arranging flowers and special surprises

Rates/Packages: Garden View rooms, $225–$405; Ocean View, $288–$450; Deluxe Ocean View, $324–$486; Junior Suite, $360–$540; 1-bedroom suite, $513–$666; 2-bedroom suites and villas, $630–$1,035. Rates include full breakfast daily, round-trip airport transfers, and one snorkeling trip. Honeymoon Package, $1,422–$2,015, including 3 nights' accommodations, breakfast, transfers, champagne, flowers, special dinner, snorkeling, sunset cruise, gift, tax, and service.

Payment/Credit Cards: Most major

Deposit: Guarantee with credit card; cancel within 7 days of arrival to avoid a 1-night penalty charge in low season. In high season 15 days are required and the penalty is 2 nights. At Christmas, New Year's, and Easter, a 21 day cancellation is required and the penalty is 2 nights.

Government Taxes: 10 percent IVA, 2 percent hospitality tax

Service Charges: 10 percent, rooms; 15 percent, restaurant

Entry Requirements for U.S. Citizens: Passport or original birth certificate

≈≈≈

Westin Brisas Ixtapa

Location: 120 miles northwest of Acapulco, on Mexico's western coast.
Romantic Features: The only large hotel in Ixtapa on its own beach; magnificent suites; lobby bar is the place to be for sunset.

I t creeps up on you. At first this monolithic structure of high ceilings and ochre-colored concrete walls pierced by patterns of square and rectangular openings, which let in light and air, seems strangely stark. Plain. Even ugly, to some. The reception area is softened only by a few pieces of simple, sturdy, varnished wood tables and a long bench reminding one of the sitting area in a railroad station. Look up and see geometric splashes of bright canary yellow and magenta. Clay pots, looking much like relics from an archaeological dig, sit in clusters on the pitted quarry tile floor. Giant stone marbles of various sizes sit in a corner of the lobby. Strange place, this.

Then, just about the time you're pulling out your credit card, you start to feel the breezes. No matter how hot it is just outside in the glaring Mexican sun, you are cooled and soothed. The architect, Ricardo Legorreta, who designed the hotel, built it without actual windows—just open spaces to take full advantage of the building's cliffside location on the edge of the sea. Unless you actually get out on the water, you can't really see the entire structure, which is constructed in the shape of a pyramid, its balconies climbing up the receding sides. All rooms have spectacular views and capture the refreshing breezes coming in from the Pacific.

At the base of the resort is a lovely cove beach that belongs exclusively to the Westin Ixtapa; unlike the other resorts just around the bend, which are lined up side by side along the 2-mile stretch of Palmar Beach, guests at the Westin need not share their sand with anyone else. You get down to the beach by elevator, or you can take an ecowalk along paths lined with rain forest–like tropical foliage.

When he created this hotel, Legorreta, one of Mexico's most renowned architects, produced an excellent example of the minimalist style of Mexican architecture. Corridors are lit by open squares cut into the ceiling; large-scale contemporary art hangs on walls in both the public areas and guest rooms. Nothing is frivolous here.

The most romantic accommodations are the junior suites, located on the top (twenty-second) floor. You have a sitting room, a bedroom, a roomy marble bath with granite-topped vanities, and two patios, one with a Jacuzzi. You can sit in the Jacuzzi under the stars and gaze out at the sea or relax in your hammock.

Furnishings are understated and very classy: cobalt-blue-glass–based lamps, three-dimensional wall murals, Mexican red-tile floors, blue-tiled headboards, flowers in wonderful pots and vases, and lots of space. Beds are covered with brightly colored cotton spreads and pillows.

These are not suites you want to leave. Sofas have double-thick cushions covered in brilliant Mexican woven fabrics in magenta, yellow, and turquoise. Closets, in keeping with the natural look, have nets instead of doors.

There are four pools, one just for adults; all sit on a hill overlooking the sea. The adjacent solarium serves light meals, including fresh seafood, and Les Fuentes is the place to go for drinks.

Westin's restaurants include El Mexicano, a romantic, haciendalike eatery with an inner garden courtyard; the Portofino, serving Italian cuisine; and Bellavista, where you eat outdoors on a covered terrace looking out over the Pacific.

At dusk the Westin Ixtapa glows warmly as the golden rays of the sinking sun turn the hotel into a temple of gold.

Address/Phone: Playa Vista Hermosa 40880, Ixtapa Zihuatanejo, Gro., Mexico; 011–52–755–321–21; fax 011–52–755–307–51

E-mail: wesixt@zihuatanejo.podernet.com.mx

U.S. Reservations: (800) 228–3000

Owner/Manager: Rafael Millan, general manager

Arrival/Departure: The Ixtapa-Zihuatanejo Airport is 20 minutes away by taxi (56 pesos, about $7.00); transfers by van can be arranged.

Distance from Ixtapa-Zihuatanejo International Airport: 20 minutes

Distance from Ixtapa Center: 3 minutes

Accommodations: 428 rooms and suites, each with patio

Best Room/Suite: Go for the junior suites on the top floor, or the master suites, which have private pools

Amenities: Air-conditioning, ceiling fans, king- or queen-size beds, toiletries, TV, radio, cotton bathrobes, real hangers, hammocks; hair dryer in suites; refrigerator and telephones in master suites, some have whirlpools or minipools; laundry and valet service, 24-hour room service

Electricity: 110 volts

Sports and Facilities: 4 lighted tennis courts, gym, 4 pools, beach, Jacuzzis, most water sports; golf 5 minutes away

Dress Code: Casual

Weddings: Can be arranged

Rates/Packages: $180–$945 per couple per night; Honeymoon Package $737 (4 nights) includes junior suite with Jacuzzi, champagne, fruit basket, and breakfast daily.

Payment/Credit Cards: Most major

Deposit: 2-night deposit; cancel 7 to 14 days prior to arrival date (depending on season) for refund.

Government Taxes: 15 percent plus 2 percent state tax

Service Charges: 15 percent suggested

Entry Requirements for U.S. Citizens: Proof of citizenship; passport best

≋≋≋

The Ritz-Carlton, Cancun

Location: It rests on 7½ acres on the Caribbean Sea on the tip of the Yucatan Peninsula in Cancun.

Romantic Features: Private candlelight dinner on the beach or poolside; massage on the beach; private patios overlooking the sea.

Cancun, with its very large hotels and booming commercial areas, may not be everyone's margarita, but anyone who appreciates luxury, pampering, and just the finest in accommodations and service can totally "get into" this superb resort. Once you step onto the marble floors of the elegant lobby, check in and see where you'll be spending the next few nights, you may find you'll have little desire to do much more than lounge on the beach or by the two sparkling pools. You could take a day to visit the Mayan ruins at Chichen-Itza or Tulum. And you could go shopping. That is if you can drag yourself away from all the good things at the Ritz.

The Ritz-Carlton, Cancun has received a lot of awards for everything from service to overall excellence since its opening more than six years ago. You really can't go anywhere on the property without feeling special. In addition to soft corals and golds, sparkling chandeliers, sweeping drapes, Oriental carpets, and highly polished traditional furniture, there are flowers everywhere.

Rooms are beautifully furnished in traditional French furniture upholstered in light brocades and prints. They come with marble baths and full length French doors lead to spacious balconies overlooking the sea.

On the patios and dining terrace, the cobalt-blue market umbrellas are offset by red-tile floors and white chairs and lounges. The cobalt theme is subtly repeated in the crystal water goblets in the dining room, where plushly upholstered chairs in coral fabrics and beautiful appointments such as Chinese vases and original art help create a quietly elegant place for that special dinner.

The coral and cream hotel may have 365 guest rooms and suites; still its design, roughly in the shape of a "U" facing the sea, with the public areas in the center, makes it feel like an intimate boutique hotel. You can get from your room to the beach in no time at all. The elevators are zippy; everything works.

There are four restaurants: The Caribe Bar & Grill, offering light meals and tropical drinks; The Club Grill, featuring regional specialties; El Cafe Mexicano, for casual dining including meals on the oceanfront terrace; and the elegant Fantino, the most formal of the four places to eat. Fantino's white-and-gold–brocade chairs and beautiful china and crystal set the mood. The Lobby Lounge with its white wicker chairs, puffy cushions, potted palms and ornate marble floors, almost Moroccan in style, provides a pleasant place for cocktails, and entertainment.

At the Ritz, you'll find yourself looking forward to your next meal. Everything is so good, so beautifully presented—starting with breakfast, where you may choose, for starters, fresh papaya, oranges, berries, mango, and pineapple served in a half shell of coconut or the Papaya Smoothie, a meal in itself.

For dinner you might have risotto of lobster, apple and foie gras Napoleon with black pepper and honey vinegar, savory bread soufflé with tequilla sauce, and porcini with white truffle butter. Certainly a dessert like warm black and white chocolate almond cake will satisfy the most demanding sweet tooth.

For those who want to get in on the latest craze, check out the new Cigar Lounge which by the way is as popular with women as with men. Here you can select your smoke from a fine selection of Cuban cigars as well as sip a variety of tequilas, ports and cognacs. The decor—burgundy leather chairs, wood paneling and original oil paintings—simply adds a bit of humph, humph to the whole scene.

If tequila is one of your passions, you'll have plenty of opportunity to indulge. Thirty of Mexico's finest tequilas can be found at the Lobby Lounge, many quite rare. Want to learn more about this national beverage? The Ritz's "tequiller" holds daily tasting sessions where you can get the scoop on its history and production.

The Ritz-Carlton, Cancun is a perfect setting for romance. You can arrange a private candlelight dinner for two on the beach or on your terrace; wake up late and have breakfast in bed; or sit under a beach cabana and enjoy some quiet time. But be warned: you may never want to leave.

Address/Phone: Retorno del Rey #36, Zona Hotelera, Cancun, Quintana Roo, Mexico; 011–52–9881–0808; fax 011–52–9885–1015

U.S. Reservations: (800) 241–3333

Owner/Manager: Luis Marc, general manager

Arrival/Departure: Arrangements can be made for pickup at the Cancun Airport

Distance from Cancun: In the hotel zone

Distance from Cancun International Airport: 15 minutes

Accommodations: 365 rooms including 50 suites and 57 Ritz-Carlton Club rooms.

Best Room/Suite: A suite on the Ritz-Carlton Club floor; Executive Oceanfront Suite also great

Amenities: Air-conditioning, hair dryer, telephone, toiletries, ceiling fans, 24-hour room service, two-line telephones with fax connection, TV, minibar

Electricity: 110 volts

Sports and Facilities: Two outdoor pools and whirlpools; three tennis courts, health center, saunas, watersports, massage therapy, gym, golf nearby

Dress Code: Casually elegant

Weddings: Can be arranged

Rates/Packages: $249–$550 per room per night; 3-night honeymoon package from $1,224

Payment/Credit Cards: Most major

Deposit: Guarantee with credit card

Government Taxes: 10 percent Federal tax; 2 percent lodging tax

Service Charges: Not included

Entry Requirements for U.S. Citizens: Proof of citizenship

EUROPE

Black Sea

North Sea

Aegean

Ionian Sea

Adriatic

Tyrrhenian Sea

Mediterranean Sea

Bay of Biscay

English Channel

NORWAY

SWEDEN

DENMARK

LATVIA

LITHUANIA

BYELARUS

UKRAINE

NETHERLANDS

GERMANY

LUXEMBURG

BELGIUM

POLAND

CZECH

SLOVAKIA

AUSTRIA

HUNGARY

SLOVENIA

CROATIA

BOSNIA

SERBIA

ROMANIA

BULGARIA

MACEDONIA

ALBANIA

GREECE

SWITZER-LAND

FRANCE

ITALY

CORSICA

SARDINIA

SICILY

MALTA

SPAIN

PORTUGAL

BALEARIC ISLANDS

U.K.

IRELAND

Akti Myrina Hotel ★

Hotel Goldener Hirsch ★

Schlosshotel Lerbach ★

Hotel Danieli ★

Villa D'Este ★

Excelsior Palace Hotel ★

Negresco ★

Château du Domaine Saint-Martin ★ ★ ★

Château Eza ★ ★

Grand Hotel Punta Molino Terme ★

Reid's Palace ★

Gleneagles ★

Radisson Edwardian Hampshire Hotel

Le Manoir aux Quat' Saisons

Hartwell House

The Lygon Arms

The Feathers Hotel

U. K.

AUSTRIA
≈≈≈

Hotel Goldener Hirsch

Location: In the heart of Salzburg, on elegant Getreidegasse.
Romantic Features: Antique beds; Old World charm in fifteenth-century inn, the magic of Salzburg just outside your door.

T
he Hotel Goldener Hirsch is pure Austrian, from the puffy duvets to the quaint, wrought-iron folk art lamps that decorate the rooms. If you are coming to Austria for your honeymoon and want a historic inn in the heart of Salzburg, try this one. You'll know you're there when you spot among the many beautifully wrought hanging signs along the narrow street the one with a gold deer atop an ornate golden circle Goldener Hirsch stands for "gold deer." From the time you check in at the elaborately carved front reception desk and follow the bellman to your room on a rather circuitous route, you'll begin to realize that this is indeed a unique place.

The Goldener Hirsch is not just one building but a combination of interconnected buildings that stand smack on one of the most elegant streets in the baroque, historic heart of Salzburg. The Getreidegasse is lined with trendy boutiques and antiques shops, and just down the street is Mozart's birthplace; close by is the Festspielhaus (Theater).

Each of the seventy-three rooms and suites is individually furnished with cozy sitting areas, a conglomeration of antiques, and masterpieces of rural art. On the beds are those wonderful creations of European refinement—goosedown duvets and fine, soft linens. Headboards, desks, tables, and bureaus are likely to be mellowed orange pine. The baths are modern, and rooms come with comfortable amenities such as telephones, a TV, a radio, and a minibar.

There is no way you can spend a night here and not be touched in some way by the rich heritage of this fine old inn. Its character and place in the world are due in part to the work of a very special lady, Countess Walderdorff. She is the one who rescued the centuries-old structure from its sad state of disrepair and began its reconstruction during the difficult years following World War II. During the renovations the countess supervised every detail of the hotel's rebirth, from the hand-wrought iron light fixtures to the specially made china.

Almost from the first day it opened its doors, the Goldener Hirsch became known as the "in" place for notables to stay and be seen when they came to Salzburg. Heads of state and the elite of the world have come to overnight and sup at this famous hostelry, among them the Duke and Duchess of Windsor, Herbert von Karajan, and Leonard Bernstein.

Hotel Goldener Hirsch, Austria

Today it's the lady's son, Count Johannes Walderdorff, who heartily welcomes guests from near and far places. Enjoy a quiet cocktail at the bar before sitting down to dinner. You can try local specialties and delicious draught beer in the rustic Herzl-Taverne, with its attractive inner courtyard. Indulge in all kinds of good things at the hotel's Goldener Hirsch restaurant, one of the best in Austria. Ask Count Walderdorff to recommend his favorite dishes and he may suggest that you try the goose liver and *tafelspitz* (a boiled beef dish). Top it all off with a delectable caramel soufflé and caramel and walnut pancakes. "I tried twenty-eight versions of this recipe until I got it right," said the Count.

The Goldener Hirsch is not a particularly elegant place, nor is it one that offers much in the way of entertainment or activities. It doesn't need to. It's friendly and charming, and imagine: The whole wonderful city of Salzburg is right outside your door, with just about everything within easy walking distance. There are museums to explore, concert performances to attend, romantic little restaurants to try out, shops to browse, and endless, interesting streets to discover.

Address/Phone: Getreidegasse 37, A–5020, Salzburg, Austria; 011–43–662–80840; fax 011–43–662–843–349

E-mail: goldhirsch@alpin.or.at

U.S. Reservations: (800) 325–3535; fax (800) 325–3589; Leading Hotels of the World (LHW), (800) 223–6800

Owner/Manager: Johannes Walderdorff, director

Arrival/Departure: Taxi from airport or train station

Distance from Munich International Airport: Approximately 84 miles (2 hours); 3 miles (10 minutes) from Salzburg Airport

Distance from Salzburg: Located in heart of town

Accommodations: 66 rooms, 4 suites

Best Room/Suite: Room 23 with its antique painted bed is charming; suites are roomier

Amenities: Hair dryer, telephone, radio, toiletries, air-conditioning, minibar, TV; room service, valet service

Electricity: 110 volts

Sports and Facilities: Guest privileges at Gut Altentann Golf & Country Club with payment of greens fees; other sports nearby include tennis, swimming, skiing, squash, and horseback riding

Dress Code: Informal by day; jacket and tie for men appreciated for dinner

Weddings: Can be arranged

Rates/Packages: From $382 per couple per night, including taxes; Luxury Romance Package, $459 per couple per night, includes breakfast, taxes, service charges, champagne, and late checkout.

Payment/Credit Cards: Most major

Deposit: Guarantee with credit card

Government Taxes: Included

Service Charges: Included

Entry Requirements for U.S. Citizens: Passport

ENGLAND

The Feathers Hotel

Location: In a small market town on the edge of the Cotswolds near Oxford.
Romantic Features: Fireplaces; elegant town house–style rooms; intimate candlelit restaurant.

At the bottom hem of the Cotswolds, in the backyard of Blenheim Palace, birthplace of Sir Winston Churchill, is the small market town of Woodstock. The first time I was in Woodstock, I was with a tour en route to visit a number of gardens and homes in the region. We zipped right through town, bypassing the village center and barely hesitating long enough for the driver to shift gears. This is not unusual. Except for those who go directly to Blenheim, Woodstock is not a usual stop on the tourist route. Which makes Woodstock all the more desirable to any who want to explore the Cotswolds but escape at the end of the day to a more serene place than its more famous neighbors over the hills.

Still, Woodstock has to be one of England's prettiest towns. Many of its buildings, which are constructed largely of mellow Cotswold stone, date back to the twelfth century.

In the center of this historic village, within walking distance of the Triumphal Arch leading into the palace grounds and just down the street from Chaucer's house and some wonderful old pubs, is the seventeenth-century Feathers Hotel. The Feathers Hotel, composed of four adjacent but separate houses, is grand without being pretentious. Thanks to the congenial general manager, Martin Godward, and his staff, you feel relaxed, welcome.

Richly furnished rooms, filled with antiques, gilded mirrors, original paintings, leather, and fabrics, all contribute to an ambience of timeless tradition and privilege. Yet, whether you're staying for one night or one week, it doesn't take very long for you to feel quite at home.

Sofas and chairs are so comfortable, you're tempted to put your feet up on the highly polished coffee table (wouldn't suggest it however) and sink into the plump cushions for a snooze or read one of the books or magazines provided in the library (by all means).

Tea is served in late afternoon in the study; after dinner, coffee and cordials are offered. On cooler evenings a log fire radiates good cheer and warmth. The holidays are a particularly cheery time; the public rooms are decorated with Christmas trees and hot mulled wine is served.

In summer the Courtyard Garden, filled with flowers and shrubbery, is a perfect place for a light lunch, tea, or a drink. There is also the Whinchat Bar, a cozy place to unwind and perhaps sip a Pimms or brandy. A unique feature of the Whinchat is its display of stuffed birds in glass boxes: During the Victorian period these pieces were very much in vogue and today are collector's items.

Each of the rooms and suites is different, starting with the names. Continuing the "feathers" theme, each room is named after a bird; e.g. partridge, barn owl, peacock. Canopied beds, carved mahogany headboards, flower bedspreads, flowing drapes, balloon curtains, traditional wallpapers, and a mix of period reproductions and antique furniture are skillfully incorporated into the decor. One room decorated in navy blue and white has a high pitched ceiling with the original heavy beams; another with a king-size bed is decorated in deep reds, beautifully setting off the mahogany armoire and headboard. In still another room, French doors lead out to a private courtyard.

Some rooms have fireplaces; suites come with sitting rooms and a second TV. The rooms are continually being redecorated and updated—you'll certainly not find these accommodations stuffy or tired.

The Feathers Hotel, England

Antique paneling and walls of bookshelves create a unique setting for the restaurant. The cuisine, prepared by Mark Treasure (who lives up to his name), is beautifully presented and served. As much as possible, Chef Treasure uses local produce, meats and fish, successfully marrying classical cuisine with innovative touches.

In addition to an a la carte menu, there is a table d'hôte lunch menu of two or three courses. More than 180 kinds of wines in a variety of price ranges are offered to complement the meal.

The Feathers Hotel is an excellent base for exploring the Cotswolds. It is also close to many walking paths and the river, where you can try punting (with a chauffeur). Other leisure pursuits available locally include helicopter lessons, rally driving, golf, shooting, fishing, horseback riding, walking, and ballooning!

Address/Phone: Market Street, Woodstock, Oxfordshire OX20 1SX, England; 011–44–1993–812–291; fax 011–44–1993–813–158

E-mail: enquiries@feathers.co.uk

Web Site: www.feathers.co.uk

U.S. Reservations: Josephine Barr, (800) 323–5463

Owner/Manager: Martin Godward, general manager

Arrival/Departure: Car rentals available at London's Heathrow and Gatwick Airport; transportation can be arranged by the hotel

Distance from London Heathrow International Airport: 60 miles (1¼ hours)

Distance from Oxford: 8 miles

Accommodations: 22 rooms and suites

Best Room/Suite: The Peacock, a spacious suite with a garden patio and separate sitting area; Goldcrest Suite, with two baths (one with a power steam shower)

Amenities: Hair dryers, phones, TVs, toiletries; some have air-conditioning, fax machine

Electricity: 240 volts

Sports and Facilities: Walking, hiking, golf, shooting, fishing, horseback riding, and ballooning nearby

Dress Code: Informal, but no jeans or shorts please

Weddings: Can be arranged for up to 60 people

Rates/Packages: £105–£295 per couple per night including continental breakfast, early morning tea, newspaper, and VAT

Payment/Credit Cards: Most major

Deposit: Guarantee reservation with credit card

Government Taxes: Included

Service Charges: Included

≈≈≈

Hartwell House

Location: Set on ninety acres in the Vale of Aylesbury, Buckinghamshire, 50 miles northwest of London.

Romantic Features: Gracious country estate; fireplaces; elegant dining; gardens; serpentine walkways; lake; wonderful spa.

Just because it looks like it would cost a king's ransom doesn't mean it actually does. In fact, Hartwell House, though certainly appealing to the well-heeled, is one of the more reasonably priced Grand Estate–style hotels I've come across. Apparently King Louis XVIII thought so, too. Exiled from France when Napoleon was flexing his muscles, King Louis leased the estate in 1809 at a grand sum of £500 per year.

Large enough to accommodate more than 130 people who came with him to keep him company, Louis made Hartwell House his residence for the next five years. Since that time Hartwell House has been altered by three architects, damaged by fire, and used as a school. Today, after a meticulous restoration by Historic House Hotels, Hartwell House stands as one of Europe's most gracious country house hotels.

Located about an hour's drive from London's Heathrow Airport, Hartwell House lolls in contented splendor amid rolling manicured lawns accented by topiary. Beyond these grounds cows graze peacefully, held back from nibbling the lush lawns by a ha-ha, an "invisible," ditchlike barrier.

Rooms and suites are located in the main building as well as in Hartwell Court, a group of charming eighteenth-century coach houses that also contain the Hartwell Spa and a series of meeting rooms.

Although every room is different, each has a sitting area. Some rooms have four-poster canopy beds. Some have fireplaces. All have marvelous bathrooms with all the expected amenities.

Louis's former bedroom, now called the King's Room, looks out over the south lawns and pastures and is almost too opulent to leave. You can perch on the sofa, pour two glasses of sherry from the decanter on the coffee table, sit back, and gaze out over the bucolic scene just outside your high bay windows. Cows find shelter from the sun under groves of trees; two children dash across the lawns to hide behind one of the tall, chipped yew hedges—probably not unlike the scene Louis himself viewed when he had time to muse.

History permeates this room, for peering down on you from their lofty perches on the walls are the life-size oil paintings of some very important-looking aristocrats from King Louis's days.

Although Hartwell's Georgian interiors date from the 1740s, with much use of the ornate rococo style, I did not find the house to be dark or imposing. Decorators have lightened the look with soft pastel colors.

Large mullioned windows let in plenty of light, and ceilings and walls are high. Superb plasterwork details include leaves and flowers in ivory against pale pastel backgrounds on walls and ceilings, and balusters on the unique Jacobean staircase create interest with their wood-carved, not-so-flattering figures of influential people.

The Great Hall, a masterpiece of English baroque design, features an elaborate carved fireplace. Just a few steps away is the oak-paneled bar, where you can sip your Pimms while gazing at original paintings of the eighteenth-century gardens of Hartwell by Spanish painter Balthazar Nebot.

There are three dining rooms, decorated in soft golds and greens, with artfully designed ceilings, chandeliers, and draperies. The library at Hartwell is appointed with many antiques and period pieces, including some objects that were in the original house.

Though I have often found the dining staff in some of these more elegant European manor house properties to be on the pretentious side, I did not find it so here. The wait staff certainly knew all the proper things to do but at the same time was friendly and not at all stuffy.

Cuisine, created by Chef Roger Barstow, includes imaginative dishes such as layered terrine of home-smoked duck and chicken with globe artichokes and truffle dressing; filet of Scottish beef with creamed spinach and celeriac, confit shallots and garlic, a parsley puree, and a Cabernet Sauvignon jus; and three apple puddings: tarte tatin, apple and cider mousse, and crispy apple dishes with sorbet served on lemon custard.

For something more casual there are the Spa Buttery, open for breakfast, lunch, and afternoon tea, and the Spa Bar, open daily until 7:00 P.M.

At Hartwell there is plenty to keep you busy without leaving the grounds. Take time to stroll through their lovely park. It features a number of pavilions and monuments, including a statue of Hercules and an obelisk. Garden mavens who know the pristine reputation of Capability Brown, who landscaped some of the finest properties in Britain, will appreciate the fact that one of his pupils created the beautifully sculpted grounds that guests enjoy today.

The Hartwell Spa, modeled after an orangery, is just 100 yards from the main building. The spa is indeed a good place to hang out. It has a swimming pool, a steam room, a whirlpool bath, saunas, and a gym, along with the bar and small restaurant—a great place to settle down with coffee, breads, and the London *Times* after an early morning workout. The pool is surrounded by an arcade furnished with comfortable lounges. Sink back in the thick cushions and admire the beauty of the gardens just outside the windows. Or indulge in one or more of the many soothing treatments offered, such as a facial, a massage, reflexology, aromatherapy, and a detoxifying algae wrap.

There are also other places you can go to relax in the grand style: the rococo-style Morning Room, the Drawing Room, and the Library. All overlook the gardens. You can also escape to the sunny roof terrace, once used by King Louis's buddies for growing vegetables and keeping rabbits and chickens. Or on a cool day, after a brisk walk or a few hours of touring, you can retreat to the warmth of the Great Hall and the comfort of the highly plumped couches in front of a crackling fire while you sip a glass of brandy or sherry or a cup of tea. Highly civilized.

Hartwell House makes an excellent base for exploring the English country-side. Within easy driving distance are places like Blenheim Palace, Waddesdon Manor, Claydon House, Windsor Castle, and Stowe Landscape Gardens. The Vale of Aylesbury is picnic country. Ask the hotel staff to pack a picnic lunch for you. They can pack your hamper with good things like smoked salmon and lemon, avocado and prawns, fruits, lobster salad, strawberries and cream, scones, and wines and champagne.

Lord Byron, thinking Louis a bit foolish to leave Hartwell, even if it was to assume his throne, wrote, "Why wouldst thou leave calm Hartwell's green abode . . . Apician table and Horatian Ode?" And the spa wasn't yet built in Louis's day!

Address/Phone: Oxford Road near Aylesbury, Buckinghamshire HP17 8NL, England; 011–44–1296–747–444; fax 011–44–1296–747–450

U.S. Reservations: (800) 260–8338; Relais & Chateaux, (212) 856–0115

E-mail: resarc@relaischateaux.fr

Owner/Manager: C. A. Jonathan Thompson, director and general manager

Arrival/Departure: Guests can be met by prior arrangement at London Heathrow Airport; nearest rail stations are Aylesbury and Thame & Haddenham Parkway

Distance from London Heathrow Airport: 35 miles

Distance from London: 50 miles

Accommodations: 30 rooms and suites in the main house; 16 rooms and suites in Hartwell Court

Best Room/Suite: King's Room (Number 15); Queen's Room; in Hartwell Court one of the ground-floor suites opens onto a private garden

Amenities: Hair dryer, telephone, TV, bathrobe, toiletries, magnifying mirror, pants presser

Electricity: 240 volts

Sports and Facilities: The Hartwell Spa with pool, whirlpool spa bath, steam room, sauna, treatment rooms, and gym; 2 tennis courts; jogging track

Dress Code: Gentlemen requested to wear jacket and tie evenings in the dining room

Weddings: Small wedding receptions can be arranged

Rates/Packages: Room rates from £205 per couple with early morning tea, service and VAT. Winter and Spring Champagne Breaks, £290 to £410 per couple per night (minimum 2 nights), including room, early morning tea, breakfast, dinner, champagne, service, and VAT; Historic House Summer Breaks from £290 per couple, including all of the above plus admission to one of the historic properties in the area, such as Blenheim Palace. Spa packages also available. (The hotel welcomes children 8 years of age and older.)

Payment/Credit Cards: Visa, Mastercard

Deposit: Guarantee with credit card

Government Taxes: Included

Entry Requirement for U.S. Citizens: Passport

≋

Le Manoir aux Quat' Saisons

Location: In a small country village between the Chilterns and the Cotswolds.

Romantic Features: Cocktails on the terrace overlooking the meadows and gardens; a stroll through the tranquil Japanese gardens; sleeping in a round stone, medieval dovecote.

Those who dream of honeymooning in a centuries-old stone manor house and have the wherewithal to pay the bill should head to Le Manoir aux Quat' Saisons. England has a lot of wonderful castles and estate hotels, but you'd have to look far and wide to find a place with as much going for it as this one: romantic rooms, idyllic setting, superb service, convenient location near the Cotswolds and London, plus one of the best restaurants in all the kingdom.

Once a favorite country retreat of Lord Coventry, trusted servant of James I, and a refuge for public officials in high standing, this magnificent estate became a hotel in 1984 when Raymond Blanc opened Le Manoir. During the past few years, the property has been totally refurbished, and a garden wing and two glass conservatory dining rooms have been added.

One of the most unique accommodations, the Michael Priest Suite, is located in the fifteenth-century dovecote, a round stone tower with a conical pointed roof. The bathroom has a huge antique tub on feet that has been painted with fanciful pink and white doves and flowers. A great shower gives you the option of steam super jets coming at you from all sides. A wide, soft pink–carpeted staircase winds up to the second level, where a queen-size bed is topped by "garlands" of white and pink fabric swags held aloft by white doves suspended from the ceiling by invisible wires. The thick walls of the tower are painted in a warm yellow and decorated with pretty pictures hanging from wide pink ribbons. There are also a skirted dressing table, a cabanalike pink-and-white–striped tented "closet," and a small leaded window opening onto the gardens. The only downside of this blissful romantic bower is its size—it's a bit tight; other suites are roomier. But for sheer romance this is a honeymoon favorite.

Hollyhocks is in the main building and was the bedroom of one of the former owners of the estate. It is extremely spacious, furnished with a couch, chairs, dressing table, desk, coffee table, and large, canopied bed. A number of leaded windows open onto the courtyard. Also popular are the two-story garden suites, which have a sitting room on the lower level along with a furnished patio; the bedroom is upstairs. All are exquisitely decorated with a combination of traditional English furniture, antiques, artwork, chintz, and French accents.

New rooms arranged around a garden courtyard combine clean contemporary lines with antique-accents. Broad bands of off-white textures wrap around walls; mirrored tables and twentieth-century artwork complement hand-hewn beams and geometrical tapestry carpets.

Flowers are lavishly spread through the public areas and guest rooms. An in-house florist has her own cutting garden and flower house tucked into the corner of the property. A recent addition to the hotel, a Japanese garden, may seem a bit out of sync with the English gardens, but somehow it fits. A delicate mist of water falls from hidden places between the trees that overhang the

Le Manoir aux Quat' Saisons, England

pond, and a teahouse welcomes those who want to stop and be soothed.

Throughout the grounds you'll find a number of original sculptures. A bronze work of birds rising through the reeds is particularly appealing. Many are for sale, as the gardens serve as an excellent showcase for artists such as Judith Holmes Drewry and Lloyd Le Blanc. Prices range from about $300 to over $50,000.

Walk through the three acres of vegetable gardens and you'll begin to understand why the food here is so good. The thirty or so chefs who prepare the meals each day use only the freshest of ingredients. Baby zucchini picked just minutes before serving, with blossoms still attached (to stuff with crabmeat and truffles); beetroot, runner beans, artichokes, leek, spinach, tomatoes—more than one hundred varieties of vegetables, herbs, and fruits planted here supply the hotel with most of its produce. Meat comes from a local butcher just down the road. Recently the hotel expanded its kitchen and restaurant facilities, adding a patisserie and bakery, a new cookery school, and a cocktail bar. Take a peek in the kitchen, and on the shelves you'll see huge glass jars filled with plums, cherries, raspberries, and other fruits.

But having the right ingredients is just the beginning of the road leading to a Michelin two-star rating. It takes a great chef like Raymond Blanc to complete the picture: Blanc's list of credits fill a page and more. Each of his creations not only looks like a work of art; it titillates taste sensations you never knew you had. Your meal may also seem to be priced like an art object (hors d'oeuvres such as pressed duck confit and foie gras in a truffle gelée costs about $36;

entrees such as pan-fried wild salmon fillet on a sorrel sabayon will set you back about $47; homemade sorbets on a waffle "painter's palette" cost around $23), but look at it this way: Sure it costs a lot, but here you're not just paying for dinner, you're investing in a delectable memory guaranteed to last a lifetime. If you come to the hotel and can't afford to try the restaurant, you might as well go somewhere else.

Meals are served in three different dining rooms: the original one and two new conservatory rooms, which are pleasant and pretty year-round.

Lest you be tempted to simply loll on the grounds and take in the never-ending vistas of pure English countryside, there is a croquet court and a garden courtyard, enclosed by hedges. You can go biking, walking, or fishing or arrange with the concierge to play golf or go horseback riding. And Le Manoir is in a great location for exploring the Cotswolds, Oxford, and other historic and interesting places, such as Blenheim Palace, the Royal Shakespeare Theatre, and Windsor Castle.

Le Manoir Quat' Saisons combines the country charm of merry old England, the cuisine of France, and the technical expertise of today's engineering: a real winner! Now if the price of a room here in 1474—about 95 cents for a week—could be matched today, you'd really be in heaven.

Address/Phone: Church Road, Great Milton, Oxford OX44 7PD England; 011–44–1184–427–881; fax 011–44–0184–427–8847

E-mail: lemanoir@blanc.co.uk

Web Site: www.manoir.co.uk

U.S. Reservations: Relais & Chateaux, (800) RELAIS–8

Owner/Manager: Raymond Blanc, chef-patron; Philip Newman-Hall, general manager

Arrival/Departure: Pickup at London's airports can be arranged; from Heathrow via private limousine (about $135 per car); from Gatwick Airport (about $235); helipad on grounds

Distance from Heathrow International Airport: 40 miles (under 1 hour); Gatwick, 55 miles (1½ hours)

Distance from Oxford: 8 miles south

Accommodations: 32 rooms and suites

Best Room/Suite: The two-story Michael Priest Suite, built in a fifteenth-century dovecote; Hollyhocks, a spacious room with a four-poster bed in the main building; and the two-story suites in the new garden wing

Amenities: Hair dryer, TV, telephone, radio, terry robes, sewing kit, heated towel bar, bidet, double sinks, toiletries, magnifying mirror, full-length mirror, padded hangers, trouser press; daily newspaper, fresh fruit, Madeira, mineral water, 24-hour room service, fresh flowers, VCRs on request

Electricity: 220/240 volts

Sports and Facilities: Latex tennis court, croquet, pool, bicycles, walking trails, fishing; riding and golf nearby

Dress Code: Country elegant

Weddings: Can be arranged; gardens and terraces make lovely setting

Rates/Packages: £395–£550 per couple per night for a suite; £230–£340 for a room; rates include breakfast.

Payment/Credit Cards: Most major

Deposit: $150 per couple per night; cancel 2 weeks prior to arrival date for full refund

Government Taxes: Included

Service Charges: Included

Entry Requirements for U.S. Citizens: Passport

The Lygon Arms

Location: In the center of the town of Broadway in the Cotswolds.
Romantic Features: Canopy beds and fireplaces; garden lunches.

You couldn't ask for a better base from which to explore the beautiful Cotswolds. Located right on the main street in the heart of Broadway (one of the Cotswolds' most charming towns), The Lygon Arms is steeped in Old English charm and character, from its hand-hewn rafters to its massive stone fireplaces and antique four-poster canopy beds. A member of the Savoy Group of hotels, The Lygon Arms has a history of welcoming travelers for more than 470 years.

The sixteenth-century front doorway is believed to have been built in the year the *Mayflower* sailed for the New World, and in 1651 Oliver Cromwell was a guest at the inn the night before the Battle of Worcester (the final battle of the Civil War between Charles II and his Cavaliers and the Parliament's Roundheads). The room where Cromwell slept contains a handsome Elizabethan fireplace, original oil paintings, antique Jacobean-style furniture, and an ornate seventeenth-century plaster ceiling frieze. An ancient staircase used by King Charles II and original oak paneling can be found in the cozy first-floor sitting room.

The hotel's accommodations are divided between the old, original structure and a relatively new (1960s) east wing. Although I would choose the older rooms, with their uneven floors, plastered walls, exposed beams, and antique furniture, the newer rooms are also quite charming and are decorated in softer, lighter colors. They can also be quieter. Some of the rooms located at the front of the building have windows that open over the main street and are noisy at times.

Because the Cotswolds is one of England's most popular tourism destinations, this area is often teeming with tourists during the warmer months. Nevertheless, when I visited in August I found The Lygon Arms to be a wonderful haven from the browsers and shoppers just outside the entrance.

The hotel has a lovely inner courtyard where you can sit at an umbrella table and have a cup of tea or lunch, and in the lounge areas there are a lot of nooks and crannies where you can settle into a comfortable chair and read a paper, sip a cocktail, or just watch the world go by.

A new $3 million country club was added in 1991 and is connected to the hotel so that guests can walk from their rooms to the facilities without going outside. The club has a large, attractive, Roman-style indoor pool with a retractable glass roof that opens (weather permitting), a jogging track, a spa bath, a fully equipped fitness room, solaria, a steam room, saunas, and a billiards room. A floodlit tennis court is also on the premises, and a croquet lawn is located in the gardens.

The truly adventurous can take off from the hotel in the early morning or evening for a balloon ride over the rolling countryside or get a bird's-eye view of the area from a helicopter—The Lygon Arms has its own helipad. Other activities, such as golf, fishing, riding, and sight-seeing, can be arranged through the concierge.

Elegant dining takes place in the Great Hall, which boasts a seventeenth-century minstrel's gallery, stags' heads, heraldic friezes, and a barrel-vaulted ceiling. Gourmet meals are created by the hotel's award-winning chef, Graeme Nesbitt, who turns out dishes such as salad of lobster and mango with yogurt-and-lime dressing and canon of Cotswold lamb with tomato linguini and watercress mousseline. He uses fresh, locally grown produce when in season. A three-course vegetarian menu is also offered. Oliver's Brasserie is popular with guests who want to eat in a more casual atmosphere, and light lunches are served in the cocktail bar.

There is lots to see in the area, including Blenheim Palace (Churchill's birthplace); Stratford, Sudeley, and Warwick Castles; Cambridge; and Hidcote Garden. Quaint Cotswolds villages such as Chipping Campden, Burton-on-the-Water, and Upper and Lower Slaughter are also great fun to explore.

In one of the lounges, you'll find inscribed on the wall, "The hay is so good, the dog so fat," an old saying meaning, "The beds are good, the food is delicious." So it was when it was written many years ago; so it is today at The Lygon Arms.

Address/Phone: Broadway, Worcestershire WR12 7DU England; 011–44–138–685–2255; fax 011–44–138–685–8611

E-mail: info@the-lygon-arms.co.uk

Web Site: www.savoy-group.co.uk

U.S. Reservations: Leading Hotels of the World, (800) 223–6800

Owner/Manager: Kirk Ritchie, managing director and general manager; Barry Hancox, hotel manager

Arrival/Departure: Taxi and chauffeur-driven car transportation can be arranged to The Lygon Arms from London's airports and local stations. A complimentary meet-and-greet service at Heathrow will help you get on your way. A private car transfer costs £140 (about $210) per car from Heathrow. The hotel also has a helipad.

Distance from London Heathrow Airport: About 75 miles (2 hours)

Distance from London: 75 miles

Accommodations: 58 rooms and 5 suites, some with four-poster beds; most have queen-size beds; 6 rooms have patios

Best Room/Suite: Four-poster rooms; The Great Bedchamber has a vaulted Tudor beamed ceiling and a marvelous, heavy mahogany four-poster bed; Room 5 in the old section is located directly across from the Cromwell Room. If the Cromwell Room is not being used for a private party, you can use it at no extra charge and enjoy a candlelight dinner for two in front of the fireplace.

Amenities: Hair dryer, radio, TV, telephone, in-room safe, toiletries

Electricity: 240 volts

Sports and Facilities: The country club has a fitness center, billiards room, beauty treatment facilities, table tennis, indoor pool, steam bath, sauna, and spa bath. There are also a tennis court (lit for night play) and a croquet lawn. Golf, horseback riding, squash, fishing, and hot air ballooning can be arranged.

Dress Code: Casual by day; dressier for dinner in the Great Hall restaurant

Weddings: Can be arranged

Rates/Packages: From £175 per couple per night, including accommodations, continental breakfast, and newspaper. A special midweek package priced at £275 per person includes two nights' accommodations, breakfast, use of the country club, VAT, newspaper, and dinner each evening. A Champagne Break package includes two nights' accommodations, champagne breakfast each morning, use of the country club, VAT, and dinner one evening (extra nights are available).

Payment/Credit Cards: Most major

Deposit: Guarantee with credit card

Government Taxes: 17.5 percent VAT

Service Charges: Not included

Entry Requirements for U.S. Citizens: Valid passport

Radisson Edwardian Hampshire Hotel

Location: In the heart of the West End, London, on the south side of Leicester Square.

Romantic Features: Four-poster beds; one-way arched windows overlooking Leicester Square let you see out, but those you're looking at cannot see you.

You couldn't be more in the middle of all the London action if you pitched a tent in the center of Leicester Square. The Radisson Edwardian Hampshire Hotel sits right on the square and is within easy walking distance of theaters, Covent Garden, Piccadilly Circus, Chinatown, the National Gallery, SoHo, and many trendy restaurants and nightclubs; the Hampshire's Penthouse overlooks Trafalgar Square. Elegant and intimate, the Hampshire stands on ground once occupied by seven private houses built in the late 1600s by the Earl of Leicester, who saw this area as a great social center for his wealthy country friends.

All you have to do is walk through Leicester Square on a warm, balmy day and see that this part of London is still a beehive of activity. Street entertainers draw crowds around them, people stand in small groups talking, and many come and go, in and out of the restaurants and stores surrounding the square. The entrance to the tube is steps away. It's a happening place.

The building that is today the Hampshire started life as the Royal Dental Hospital around 1900. In 1987 Radisson Edwardian Hotels bought the structure and, after an expensive and expansive redo, opened the Hampshire in 1989 as a five-star hotel. Furnished in the style of English country houses, each of the 124 guest rooms is different.

The decor recalls the Edwardian period, a bit difficult to define, since this "style" is actually a mixture of many cultures. This style was fashionable during the Edwardian period (1901 until the death of King Edward VII, in 1910). At this time wealthy travelers returned to England with furniture and artifacts from their grand trips to faraway places like the Orient and the Middle East. They used their money garnered from the booming Industrial Revolution to fill their homes with things like Persian carpets, Chinese porcelain, Indian tapestries, Japanese paintings, and delicately carved wood pieces.

It is this eclectic mix of English fabrics and wood paneling accented by selected pieces and colors of other countries that makes each of the 124 rooms in the Hampshire so unique. Yet everything works splendidly together, the decor sending out a message of elegance with soft creams, light greens, and corals. Beds have romantic canopies, fabric crowns, or other interesting treatments— the decorators used yards and yards of material both for the beds and for the drapes. Many rooms have built-in armoires, and lovely moldings accent the ceilings, windows, and doors throughout the hotel.

Little touches like a chandelier in the elevator and the glimpse of an inviting lounge let you know before you even enter your room that your accommodations will be special. The Lynhurst Suite (Number 705) for example, decorated in light creams and greens, has a beautiful four-poster bed and a sitting room. The Winchester Suite is very roomy, with a wonderful shower. And Number 116 is especially appealing. You can check out all the activity in Leicester Square through your huge arched windows, but no one from the outside can see you, for the window glass is one-way.

The Hampshire "Hallmark" rooms, though designed to appeal to business travelers since they feature work areas, fax machines, and two telephones, still have amenities that would be welcome to those on a romantic getaway: bathrobes and slippers, king-size beds, and express check-in and checkout. These rooms also tend to be larger, with sitting areas.

The Hampshire's Apex Restaurant serves modern British food; the Apex Bar is cozy, comfortable, and a good place to unwind any time of the day or evening. For lighter meals try the Terrace Brasserie, an informal eatery right on Leicester Square. All restaurants serve pre- and posttheater menus. You can even eat dinner early, see a show, and come back for dessert and coffee, then sit quietly by the fire or in a private alcove or brush shoulders with the locals in Oscars Wine Bar.

The Hampshire is a great base for those who love theater and lots of things to do, all within shouting distance.

Address/Phone: Leicester Square, London WC2H 7LH England; 011–44–171–839–9399; fax 011–44–171–930–8122

U.S. Reservations: Radisson Edwardian Hotels, (800) 333–3333

Owner/Manager: David Batts, director of operations

Arrival/Departure: Limousine service available from airport; Underground from Heathrow or Gatwick takes you within 1 block of the hotel (take Piccadilly Line to Leicester Square)

Distance from Heathrow and Gatwick Airports: About 15 miles

Accommodations: 124 rooms and suites

Best Room/Suite: Junior suites, such as Number 111, a Four-Poster suite; Hallmark rooms also good choices; Number 116 has a king-size bed

Amenities: Air-conditioning, TV, minibar, tea- and coffeemaker, hair dryer, toiletries, room service, no-smoking rooms, 24-hour room service, trouser press, fax machines, terry robes and slippers (some rooms); in-room safes in deluxe rooms

Electricity: 220 volts

Sports and Facilities: New fitness studio; golf can be arranged through the concierge

Dress Code: Informal; jacket requested for dinner at the main restaurant

Weddings: Can be arranged; Penthouse provides beautiful setting overlooking London

Rates/Packages: £350 per couple per night for Hallmark room accommodations, including breakfast, champagne, red roses, and chocolates; supplement for suites

Payment/Credit Cards: Most major

Deposit: Guarantee with credit card 1-night deposit

Government Taxes: 17.5 percent VAT

Service Charges: Included

Entry Requirements for U.S. Citizens: Valid passport

FRANCE

≈≈≈

Château du Domaine Saint-Martin

Location: Centrally located in the center of the French Riviera in a thirty-two-acre park overlooking the Mediterranean and the quaint village of Vence.

Romantic Features: Cottages with private terraces looking out to the sea; serene setting steeped in history.

A s you approach the unassuming entrance to the Château du Domaine Saint-Martin after a rather heady ride through narrow, loopy roads, a break in a lush, thick, clipped hedgerow takes you into the quaint complex of charming old buildings with roots dating back to A.D. 350. Once the residence of the Knights Templar, this serene place is a haven for those who love history and peace, graciousness and good food.

Several rooms in the château itself are beautifully appointed with antique furniture, Persian and Flemish carpets, original art, and fresh flowers that set a mood of timeless elegance. There are also six *bastides* randomly placed on the wooded estate. Each of these bastides has its own sitting room, bedroom, and bath and a whole lot of privacy. Enjoy the sunset while sipping a glass of fine French champagne from your private terrace and look out over the tops of the trees and old stone houses staggered down the hill to the sea beyond. In the vivid late afternoon light, this shimmering vision conjures up a page from a romantic novel.

Wander into the gracefully landscaped lawns and gardens, where you'll find chairs and tables for relaxing; head to the tennis court for a bit of exercise or to the swimming pool, where there are lounges, umbrella tables, and chairs. During the summer months you'll also find a grill restaurant that serves beverages and light meals.

The restaurant is known for its fresh fish, which in all likelihood has been purchased by the chef the same morning from local fishermen. The skillful use of herbs and preparation of vegetables and fruits harvested from the Domaine's own gardens are what has given this restaurant a reputation as one of the best in the region. Homemade pasta and soups, rack of lamb, and superb soufflés are hard to resist. The hotel's selection of regional wines is also excellent.

The Domaine is ideally situated to serve as a base for exploring the excitement of Cannes and Nice as well as Monaco, not far away. Also nearby are some extraordinary art galleries, such as the Maeght Foundation, where you'll find Miró, Calder, Chagall, Kandinsky, and Matisse paintings and sculptures. Several large sculptures are also located on the beautiful, sprawling grounds.

A short drive away is the medieval town of Vence, which has preserved its old ramparts and has some wonderful little shops and streets. It is also home to the Matisse chapel. Not far from Vence is Cagnes-sur-Mer, where you'll find Les Collettes, once the home and studio of Renoir. It's with a sense of reverence that you see the chair he sat in when he painted, the brushes he used, the lounge with its fragile silk covering where his models lay, and the old shed and twisted old olive trees that appear in many of Renoir's best-known works.

Visit one of the loveliest fortified medieval towns in Europe, St. Paul de Vence, which sits high on a hilltop and is still partially ringed by ancient stone walls. Wander through the narrow, twisting, cobbled streets; watch the men play a game of *boules* in the village square; and browse through the many antiques shops. Among the prize souvenir items you'll find here are the miniature ceramic house "blocks" by Jean-Pierre Gault and other artists, which replicate the French houses in these medieval towns.

And after you've been out exploring the countryside and small villages, you can return to spend the rest of the day and evening amid the quiet elegance of Château du Domaine Saint-Martin. Magnifique!

Address/Phone: Avenue des Templiers-BP 102, 06140 Vence CEDEX, France; 011– 33–493–5802–02; fax 011–33–493–24–0891

E-mail: st-martin@webstore.fr

Web Site: www.chateau-st-martin.com

U.S. Reservations: Relais & Chateaux, (800) RELAIS–8

Owner/Manager: Andrée Brunet, general manager

Arrival/Departure: Rental cars available in Nice

Distance from Nice Côte d'Azur Airport: 12 miles (20 minutes)

Distance from Nice: 12 miles

Accommodations: 40 rooms and suites: 32 rooms in château; 8 suites in *bastides* with double bed, sitting room, and terrace

Best Room/Suite: Private *bastides;* junior suites with terraces

Amenities: Hair dryer, toiletries, air-conditioning, bathrobes, TV, telephones, balconies or terraces, room service

Electricity: 220 volts

Sports and Facilities: 2 tennis courts (clay), heated pool; golf nearby at Biot, Valbonne, and Mougins

Dress Code: Jacket and tie required for dinner

Weddings: Can be arranged

Rates/Packages: ff 1,500–ff 2,500 per couple per night (January–March); ff 2,500–ff 3,500 (April–October); ff 3,000–ff 4,500 (May–October 1). Wedding Escape, ff 18,500 per couple for 2 nights, includes suite accommodations, breakfast, 1 dinner for two, wedding ceremony, lunch for two, and transfers from Nice Airport.

Payment/Credit Cards: Most major

Deposit: 2 to 4 nights at time of booking; prepayment of balance due 1 month prior to arrival; credit card not accepted for payment of this part of account; cancel 1 month in advance in high season; 2 weeks in low season.

Government Taxes: Included

Service Charges: Included

Entry requirements for U.S. Citizens: Valid passport

Closed: Mid-October–Christmas

≈≈≈

Château Eza

Location: Situated on the Moyenne Corniche between Nice and Monaco, on the Côte d'Azur.

Romantic Features: Dramatic setting on cliff overlooking the Mediterranean; elegant theme rooms, some with terraces.

Like the legendary Camelot, Château Eza stands in a medieval village awash in romance and mystery. But while King Arthur's domain was an invention of British folklore, this exquisite, intimate hotel tucked away in a 1,000-year-old fortress village is very real.

Modern-day Lancelots and Guineveres will love this castle of stone, the former summer residence of the Swedish royal family. Set on a narrow cobblestone street, it clings to the side of the ancient rock wall of Eze, more than 1,300 feet above the Mediterranean.

Situated midway between Nice and Monte Carlo, it is conveniently located on the Moyenne Corniche (the middle road running between the two cities), allowing guests easy access to the many attractions of the famous Côte d'Azur—provided they can tear themselves away from the breathtaking views of Cap Ferrat and the sea.

Stone passages and walkways lead to ten guest accommodations. All have modern conveniences such as air-conditioning and fine baths, and the rooms are enhanced by charming fireplaces, stone walls, beamed ceilings, balconies, and the pièces de résistance: the views.

Each room is thematically different: There is a quaint room perched on the cliff's edge overlooking the mountains, and there is an intimate, romantic room with a canopy bed, fireplace, and balcony as well as a very grand Louis XVI chamber with a separate dressing area fit for a queen. La Suite du Château, a three-room suite with a floral and ivy theme, has a bedroom with loft, sitting room, separate dressing room, private terrace with garden, and spectacular sea view. Another suite is especially dramatic, with high ceilings, arches, columns, and an enormous iron bed. Take your pick! All the rooms are elaborately furnished with Oriental rugs, antiques, upholstered chairs, and stunning accessories. Fresh flowers are replaced daily.

Although there are no sports facilities on the property, within the walled city of Eze there is the Jardin Exotique, filled with cacti as well as gift shops, art galleries, and restaurants.

Dinner at Château Eza is served in either the indoor glass dining room or outdoor terrace atop the cliffs. It is considered one of the most romantic dining spots in the world. Chef Thierry Bagnis shops each morning at the Nice market for fresh fruits, vegetables, and meats. His cooking style reflects his Provence and northern Italian origins. The risotto de gambas, frais aux poireaux frits, and darne de turbot poelee aux artichauts are excellent.

Château Eza, France

Desserts include wild strawberry tarts; a bitter-black concoction that is coffee liqueur heart with a cacao bean crust; and petals of zucchini flowers with vanilla ice cream flavored with apricot marmalade. The wine list is extensive. Although dinner for two with wine is on the high side of $200, the special lunch menu (without wine) is a bargain.

The staff at the hotel is efficient, friendly, and helpful; restaurant service, excellent.

You would need a time machine to travel back more than a thousand years to the medieval era—unless, of course, you chose to visit Château Eza. Here, on a spellbinding cliff overlooking the Mediterranean, all the romance and chivalry of King Arthur is yours, albeit for the modern-day equivalent of a king's ransom.

Address/Phone: 06360 Eze Village, Côte d'Azur, France; 011–33–493–411–224; fax 011–33–493–411–664

E-mail: chateza@webstore.fr

Web Site: www.slh.com

U.S. Reservations: (800) 507–8250

Owner/Manager: Mr. and Mrs. Terry Giles, owners; Jesper Jerrik, general manager

Arrival/Departure: By taxi, available at airport

Distance from Côte d'Azur Airport: 10 miles

Distance from Nice: 10 miles (15 minutes); inside the medieval village of Eze

Accommodations: 4 suites; 6 guest rooms

Best Room/Suite: Le Suite du Château

Amenities: Air-conditioning, safe, TV, video, telephone, hair dryer, toiletries, bathrobes, flowers, champagne, candy

Electricity: 220 volts

Sports and Facilities: Beach 10 minutes away

Dress Code: Men should wear a jacket at dinner.

Weddings: One of their specialties

Rates/Packages: Rates per couple: ff 2,000–ff 3,500; suites ff 3,500–ff 4,000; including breakfast, service charge, and taxes. (Hotel closed early November–early April.)

Payment/Credit Cards: Most major

Deposit: 1-night deposit; 15-day cancellation notice for full refund

Government Taxes: Included

Service Charges: Included

Entry Requirements for U.S. Citizens: Valid passport

Closed: November–April

Negresco

Location: Sits right on the famed French Riviera, on the Côte d'Azur, in Nice, which is cradled in a mountain range that plunges straight down to the sea.

Romantic Features: A veritable palace where guests are treated like the royalty who frequent the resort; four-poster beds, marble baths with gold sinks, and charming terraces facing the sea.

If you have ever dreamed of rubbing shoulders with royalty, Nice's Hotel Negresco may be as close as you will ever get to an invitation to Buckingham Palace.

The Negresco is a step back to La Belle Epoque, when crown princes and monarchs fled the harsh European winters and escaped southward to this jewel on the French Riviera.

Located in Nice on the legendary Côte d'Azur, the gilt-edged Negresco is the queen of the Riviera hotels. Staying here is an exercise in luxury and excess, and it is not surprising to find the hotel was inspired by the Palace of Versailles. Built in 1912 by Rumanian immigrant Henri Negresco, it was intended as a haven for the upper crust of Europe. It still is. Classified by the French government as a historic monument in 1974, the Negresco is frequented by movie stars, heads of state, and the world's beautiful people.

Unlike many of those venerable grandes dames that have fallen on hard times, the Negresco has not lost its luster. It has been polished and honed to a fare-thee-well. In fact when you walk through the various rooms—each one different from the other—you may be taken aback by the riot of bright colors, patterns, ornate accessories, and frivolities used in the decor. Only the Negresco can get away with bright blue flowered drapes, vivid red carpeting, gilt mirrors, and gold-flecked tubs. Walls are brocade, beds are huge (some are four-poster) with puffy down pillows and thick comforters, fur spreads, antique needlepoint chairs, and gold double sinks. These rooms are beyond elaborate! (A sense of humor helps.)

The hall porters and doormen are dressed in traditional French costumes, copies of the uniforms worn by the staffs of aristocratic homes during the eighteenth and nineteenth centuries. The reception hall, with its fine gold molding, is decorated with Louis XVI period furnishings. To the left is the Salon Massena, which is adorned in the Empire style with gold thread tapestries that are exact replicas of the fabrics of the throne room at the Château Fontainebleau. Straight ahead, under the world-famous glass dome made in the workshop of Gustave Eiffel, is the majestic Salon Royal. On the floor is the largest carpet ever made by the Savonnerie factory—so large that it took an oversize truck and a huge crane to handle it when it was sent out for cleaning.

The Baccarat chandelier, one of a pair ordered by the Tsar of Russia at the end of the nineteenth century, is a nice touch. Its mate hangs in the Kremlin.

Works by Picasso, Leger, and Cocteau hang on the walls, and everywhere you'll see period pieces, tapestries, and antique furniture. If you ever wanted to stay overnight in a museum, this is it.

Amid all this splendor there is something breezy and fun about the Negresco. Perhaps it is the impeccable staff, who are bent on providing each guest with every possible service and are never overbearing or stuffy.

There are two restaurants, the brasserie-style La Rotonde, with its cheerful merry-go-round decor, complete with painted wooden horses, and the well-known Chantecler. La Rotonde serves outstanding pasta, hors d'oeuvres, fish, and meats along with exemplary pastries. Prices are surprisingly moderate.

The Regency-style Chantecler restaurant, with its sumptuous wood paneling, flower-patterned silk curtains, Aubusson tapestry, red velvet chairs, and fine portraiture, is the setting for a trip to gastronomic heaven. Award-winning chef Alain Llorca favors regionally based cuisine from Provence and the Mediterranean, with taste the most important characteristic. Chantecler received two Michelin stars in 1997.

At the Negresco all you need is a crown and scepter for your royal honeymoon.

Address/Phone: 37 Promenade des Anglais, BP 1379, 06007 Nice CEDEX, France; 011–33–493–1664–00; fax 011–33–493–88–3568

E-mail: negresco@cote-dazur.com

U.S. Reservations: Leading Hotels of the World, (800) 223–6800

Owner/Manager: Mr. and Mrs. Paul Augier; Nicole Spitz, general manager; Guy Bellet, manager

Arrival/Departure: Taxis available at airport

Distance from Côte d'Azur Airport: 4 miles (10 minutes)

Distance from Nice: Is in the heart of Nice

Accommodations: 140 rooms; 18 suites

Best Room/Suite: Deluxe rooms and Presidential Suite

Amenities: Air-conditioning, bidet, radio, cable TV, minibar, direct-dial telephones, robes, toiletries; stereo on request

Electricity: 220 volts

Sports and Facilities: Swimming at beach, waterskiing; gym, hairdresser, fitness center, and tennis and golf nearby

Dress Code: Elegantly casual; jacket required in Chantecler restaurant in the evening

Weddings: Can be arranged

Rates/Packages: ff 1,300–ff 4,150, including service charges and VAT. Honeymoon package: ff 3,600–ff 4,420, including 2 nights' accommodations, breakfasts, fruit, discount in store, champagne, gift, taxes, and service.

Payment/Credit Cards: Most major

Deposit: 1-night deposit; 15-day cancellation notice for refund

Government Taxes: $1.00 per person per day city tax (high season)

Service Charges: Included

Entry Requirements for U.S. Citizens: Valid passport

GERMANY

Schlosshotel Lerbach

Location: 9 miles east of Cologne, in the wooded valleys of Bergischesland.

Romantic Features: Relaxing in quiet country setting; ballooning over the countryside.

When you stay at the ivy-covered Schlosshotel Lerbach, once a private castle, you feel much like you are visiting privileged friends in the country. The sprawling grounds, rooted in a setting of gently rolling green hills and meandering streams, are bucolic. Situated in Germany's Bergischesland, east of Cologne, the castle is surrounded by fine old trees, and double stone stairs lead down to a nice garden area and a glimmering fish pond. The Lerbach staff treat you as if you were privileged guests of an old friend, making it easy to settle in here very quickly.

Over the past 600 years, the hotel, once Burg Lerbach Castle, has gone through a lot of changes. Built around 1384, the castle was converted to the classic English manor house style in 1838. After serving as a private palace and later as headquarters for a film company, this magnificent estate was transformed into a stylish hotel just a few years ago.

Each of the fifty-four rooms and suites is individually decorated and distinguished by welcoming touches like books on the shelves and fresh flowers. Some have canopy beds, others brass beds. Many suites are multilevel with nice sitting areas with writing desks. Rooms are furnished with period furniture and artwork, tapestries, Oriental carpets, and interesting accessories like puffy throw pillows, porcelain pieces, and leatherbound books. Bathrooms are large and have tubs and showers.

The castle sits in a park of more than seventy acres. You have plenty of room to find your own private place. For a special treat arrange for a hot air balloon tour of the countryside. Your journey starts in the park and lifts you over the hills, valleys, vineyards, and lakes, which are so very beautiful here. Enjoy a delightful picnic later under the trees.

One of the most dreamy places to relax is on the pretty terrace, which is set up with wrought-iron tables and perky yellow umbrellas. In good weather you can have your breakfast, lunch, or tea here. For more active souls there is a red-clay tennis court on the grounds as well as a well-equipped health club, the Lancaster Beauty Farm.

Or how about a hiking trip in the Siebengebirge? You start out with a gourmet breakfast in the hotel, then it's off on a guided hike in the mountains, with a picnic lunch served in the countryside.

The hotel has two restaurants: the gourmet Restaurant Dieter Müller, featuring creative modern-French specialties such as Homard Rôti Parfumé aux Truffes Exotique Saint-Pierre and Sorbet au Champagne. Dieter Müller has earned a three-star Michelin rating as well as other honors. The more moderately priced but also excellent Restaurant Schloss-Schänke specializes in regionally influenced new-German cuisine. There are also the Hotelbar, showcasing original artwork by famous painters such as Salvador Dali and Max Ernst, a terrace overlooking the park, and a lounge featuring a large fireplace.

Schlosshotel Lerbach is an excellent base for exploring this exceptionally beautiful area of Germany. History buffs will want to visit nearby Cologne, where there is a lot to see besides the famous cathedral, such as an original Roman mosaic floor, museums, and art galleries. Have lunch in an old brewery or take a day cruise on the lovely Rhine River.

Address/Phone: Lerbacher Weg, D–51465, Bergisch Gladbach, Germany; 011–49–2202–2040; fax 011–49–2202–204940

E-mail: lerbach@T-online.de

Web Site: www.althoffhotels.de

U.S. Reservations: Relais & Chateaux, (800) RELAIS–8

Owner/Manager: Thomas H. Althoff, owner; Kurt Wagner, director

Arrival/Departure: Private transfers from airport can be arranged

Distance from airport (Cologne/Bonn): 15 miles

Distance from Cologne: 12 miles (20 minutes)

Accommodations: 47 rooms; 7 suites

Best Room/Suite: Each is different; ask for a room with a canopy bed.

Amenities: Hair dryer, minibar, TV, in-room safe, music system, telephones; portable fax machine on request; room service, fresh flowers, fruit basket

Electricity: 220 volts

Sports and Facilities: Archery, swimming pool, sauna, solarium, massages, fishing, hiking, jogging trails, tennis, horseback riding (in season), ballooning (arranged); golf nearby

Dress Code: Casual by day; jacket requested in Dieter Müller for dinner

Weddings: Can be arranged

Rates/Packages: DM 390–DM 700 per couple per night for a room; junior suite, DM 790; suite, DM 990–DM 1,300, including breakfast, parking, use of swimming pool and sauna, tax, and service
Payment/Credit Cards: Most major
Deposit: Credit card guarantee
Government Taxes: 15 percent VAT included
Service Charges: Included
Entry Requirements for U.S. Citizens: Valid passport

GREECE
≈≈≈

LEMNOS

Akti Myrina Hotel

Location: On west coast of Lemnos, in the northern Aegean Sea.
Romantic Features: Stone cottages with private terraces overlooking sea and private beach; unspoiled Greek island with aura of mythology; resort ferries guests to beaches so remote, there is no access by land.

Nestled into forty-one rolling acres filled with flowers and fruit trees, the weathered stone bungalows and cottages of Akti Myrina Hotel visually meld into the rugged stone hills of the island of Lemnos, serving as a dramatic backdrop for this unique hideaway. Lemnos, an island of about 182 square miles and home to only about 18,000 people, is where the ancient Greeks first staged their Hephaestian Games, sports contests from which the Olympics evolved.

The resort has been here for more than thirty years, building up in that time a loyal group of repeat guests, including celebrities, famous industrialists, authors, artists, and politicians who come here seeking a relaxed vacation in a serene and beautiful environment.

Akti Myrina is not a pretentious or particularly luxurious resort. That's not what it's all about. Rather it's valued for its traditions, its sheer natural beauty, its hospitality, and its sense of place on an island that has not yet been touched by mass tourism. It fulfills your dreams of what a Greek island is and should be. This is a place where you can have breakfast delivered to your garden terrace and linger over fresh breads and delicious coffee as you watch the sea roll in on the beach below.

The owner and on-site managing director, Helen G. Dalacouras, fell in love with the property many years ago when she came here with her husband, George, a Greek shipowner, and her family to vacation each summer. In 1988 the Delacourases bought the resort, and since then Mrs. Delacouras has put her heart and substantial financial resources into Akti to make sure her guests yearn to come back again. She sees to it that rooms and grounds are meticulously maintained, linens immaculate and fine, food fresh and beautifully presented, and the staff attentive and friendly.

It's like a wonderful little Greek village set on one of the prettiest sites you'll find anywhere. Bungalows and cottages climb gently up a small hill from the beach, connected by stone walls, walkways, and flower-filled courtyards. Terra-cotta pots filled with flowers sit on walls and along the paths and stone steps leading to the beach. The original cottages were built by a group of Greek businesspeople as holiday homes for themselves and were designed to carefully harmonize with the surrounding land.

Unlike the majority of Greek beaches, which are public, the Akti's strip of sand is private, a designation acquired at great expense and effort by the Delacourases.

The rooms are spacious, with native stone walls and floors; wood ceilings and trim are offset by the bold colors and patterns of the bedspreads and pillows. The chairs are well-designed caned pieces, and the tables and other furniture are simply designed out of wood as well. Twin beds are placed side by side and can be converted to king-size beds. French doors lead out to the patios, which are very private—many have wonderful old trees creating a green, leafy canopy. Here a garden table and chairs invite guests to order room service for an intimate breakfast or dinner. At night you can see the lights of the small village of Myrina twinkling in the distance, spreading their reflections over the water.

There are three restaurants on the grounds as well as a beach bar, pool bar, piano bar, and Hephaestos TV and playroom. A colorful buffet lunch is set up at the simple but pleasant restaurant by the beach. Tables covered with blue-and-white checkered tablecloths sit on the grassy area adjacent to the beach. At night you can dine at Taverna Castro, the Hephaistia, or Caviria restaurants, and you can choose to eat inside or on the open terrace overlooking the pool and sea. Enjoy fresh lobsters and fish such as gilthead bream and red mullet, which are caught locally, or try traditional Greek specialties such as *Dolmadakia Yalantzi* (stuffed grape leaves), *Moschari Stifado* (a sort of beef ragout), and *Taramossalata* (fish salad). Continental cuisine is also offered. A wide selection of Greek and French wines are featured, and locally produced honey, cheeses,. figs, raisins, and almonds are always available.

After a long trip you may decide simply to chill out under one of the blue and yellow umbrellas located along the beach or at one of the heated pools. If you're up for some exercise, challenge your partner to tennis or try out some of the water sports activities, such as waterskiing and sailboarding. There are also canoes and pedalboats available. Or discover the romance of the island's secluded bays by sailing with Captain Yannis aboard the resort's *caique* (a typical Greek sailing vessel).

From the air Lemnos looks like a giant butterfly resting on the water, its edges scalloped with deserted sandy beaches carved into rugged rocks. Though not a particularly lush island, a variety of flowers and plants have stubbornly survived and thrived, including the dense, carpetlike Burnet shrub, rock roses, thyme, wild olive trees, and oleander. Of particular interest are the fossilized forests that were created centuries ago. In addition to walking, one interesting way to see the island is to join one of the guided horseback trips that takes you along the hilly trails.

The capital and main town, Myrina, is a picture postcard harbor village of one-, two-, and occasionally three-story white buildings with red-tile roofs hugging a small harbor, where little fishing boats fight for space along the piers. These graceful craft are mostly white-trimmed with touches of blues and reds and greens, their bows and sterns swooping gracefully up to points.

It's only a fifteen-minute walk into town from the Akti, and once you get there you can browse in the shops, have a snack and a glass of retsina at a taverna, and take in the activity as the boats come and go. In the evening walk along the Romeikos Yalos road when everything takes on a hazy purple hue in the fading light.

On Lemnos you can explore some interesting archaeological sites, including the remains of prehistoric Poliochni, a Minoan civilization; the ruins of Pelagian walls, which date back to 551 B.C.; and the thirteenth-century Venetian fortress that once guarded the harbor. At night the ruins, which sprawl along the hill above the town, are floodlit and look like a golden, lacy fringe sitting atop the rocky cliffs below. It's all there to seduce you—the island, the people, the beaches, the mythology, and, of course, Akti.

Address/Phone: Myrina, 814 00 Lemnos, Greece (summer); 107 VAS, Pavlou Kastella, 185 33 Piraeus, Greece (winter); 011–30–1413–7907 (winter); fax 011–30–14137–639 (winter); 011–30–254–22681 (summer); fax 011–30–254–22352 (summer)

U.S. Reservations: None; book directly through hotel

Owner/Manager: Helen G. Dalacouras, owner and managing director

Arrival/Departure: Guests can be met at Lemnos Airport with prior arrangement

Distance from Lemnos Airport: 15 miles southeast; 1 mile west of marina

Distance from Myrina: 15-minute walk

Accommodations: 110 rooms in stone bungalows; 15 cottages

Best Room/Suite: Rooms 305 to 312 on end overlooking sea; also Cottages 214 and 215

Amenities: Air-conditioning, minibar, telephone, writing desk

Electricity: 220 volts

Sports and Facilities: Private beach, 2 heated pools, 3 floodlit tennis courts, fitness center, minigolf, table tennis, volleyball, fishing, swimming, water sports, billiards; private *caique* for trips to neighboring islands; Hephaestos TV and playroom

Dress Code: Casual

Weddings: Can be arranged

Rates/Packages: About $290–$440 per couple per night, including breakfast, dinner, taxes, and service charges

Payment/Credit Cards: All major

Closed: October–end of April

Deposit: 1-night deposit; cancel within 14 days for refund

Government Taxes: Included

Service Charges: Included

Entry Requirements for U.S. Citizens: Valid passport

ITALY

Excelsior Palace Hotel

Location: On the Portofino Coast overlooking the Mediterranean.

Romantic Features: Seaside balconies; boat trips along the coast; in-room massages for two; Old-World elegance.

The Excelsior Palace Hotel is a great find, offering excellent value and service in Rapallo, one of Italy's most popular resort areas. The grand turn-of-the-century Excelsior Palace, set on a piece of prime waterfront land on the Italian Riviera, has been restored and is now an excellent choice for those looking for romantic yet reasonably priced accommodations overlooking the Mediterranean. Once a popular gathering place for the international beau monde, it has welcomed Ernest Hemingway, Rita Hayworth, and Eleanora Duse.

Marble halls are punctuated with huge vases of fresh flowers; a grand health club features spacious granite baths; bedrooms and suites all boast balconies and a view of the sea through large sliding glass doors; rooms are more spacious than many of the pricier digs in the area. Furnishings are tasteful, understated, and upbeat, with light-colored print fabrics and white-painted French Provincial–style furniture.

The Yachting Bar and dining rooms flow out on the lovely terrace with its white balustrades, candlelit tables and wrought-iron tables and chairs—a perfect place to sip your Pelligrino or Campari while gazing out at the deep blue water and the yachts riding at anchor in Rapallo Bay. Enjoy traditional Italian cuisine in the Lord Byron restaurant and regional and Mediterranean dishes in the Eden Roc. Or venture into historic Rapallo and try one of the many delightfully intimate restaurants there such as La Sostra; dance the night away at Happening (a disco on the hills above the town) or Villa Porticciolo (a seafront disco); or savor delicious fresh fish at Ristorante Eden.

Hike the trails that wind along the coast and in the national park; take a boat from Rapallo around the peninsula to Camogli, passing Portofino and S. Fruttuoso, and instead of taking the boat back, hike through the park back to the hotel. Explore the caves at Isolona, visit the many shops and galleries in Rapallo and Portofino, and explore ancient castles. The beautiful Ligurian coastline, the Cinque Terre, and Genoa are not far away.

The oldest golf course in Italy is less than a mile from the hotel, and a variety of water sports including waterskiing and scuba diving can be arranged at the Beach Club. For those who want it both ways, you can stay a few days in the hotel and extend your vacation cruising on a chartered yacht stopping at such ports as Naples, Portofino, Capari, Ischia, and Venice.

Address/Phone: Via San Michele di Pagana, 8-16035 Rapallo (GE) Italy; 011–39–185–230–666; fax 011–39–185–230–214

E-mail: excelsior@thi.it

Web Site: www.thi.it

U.S. Reservations: Prima Hotels; (800) 44–PRIMA

Owner/Manager: Michele Zanconato, general manager

Arrival/Departure: Shuttle service available from Genova Airport

Distance from Genova Airport: 18 miles; Milan, 90 miles

Distance from Portofino: 3½ miles

Accommodations: 114 rooms; 17 suites; all with sea views

Best Rooms/Suites: Junior suites

Amenities: Air-conditioning, hair dryer, toiletries, in-room safe, minibar, turndown service, cable TV

Electricity: 220 volts

Sports and Facilities: Beach Club; health and fitness club with indoor heated pool, sauna, steam bath, Jacuzzi, gym, massages, thalassotherapy, beauty treatments, sunbed; beach, water sports; tennis, golf course, horseback riding, boat excursions, and hiking trails within 1 mile of hotel

Dress Code: Resort casual

Weddings: Can be arranged

Rates/Packages: Room rates from $223, including breakfast, taxes, and service charges. Sea, Beauty, and Relax and The Green Sea (for golf and tennis) packages available

Payment/Credit Cards: Most major

Deposit: By credit card

Government Taxes: Included

Service Charges: Included

Entry Requirements for U.S. Citizens: Valid passport

≋≋

Grand Hotel Punta Molino Terme

Location: On the northern coast of the island of Ischia, near Ischia Porto.

Romantic Features: Dancing under the moon, shining on the Bay of Naples; candlelight dinner on the seaside terrace.

I f the term *romantic* suggests a private hideaway, then the Grand Hotel Punta Molino Terme, overlooking the Bay of Naples, is about as romantic as it gets. This contoured, white-as-snow hotel sits in a vast pine woods park opposite the Aragonese Castle, on the little fisherman's island of Ischia.

The boat to the island takes a little over an hour from Naples and is slow, breezy, and dreamy. You pass the fabled Isle of Capri, and then Ischia appears in the distance, guarded by the picturesque castle on the cliffs.

Ischia (pronounced *Iskea*) is still undiscovered by tourists, and certainly few Americans know about it. Mention the name even to an Italy lover and he or she will probably say "God bless you." The island is just too peaceful and sleepy to be popular, but for some this is exactly what makes it such a find.

After a short drive from the dock, you reach the hotel, which is set among lush landscaping, and fronts on a beach walkway that runs along the coastline. The public rooms are cool and classically elegant, decorated with custom-made Italian tiles, traditional furniture, white walls, tapestries, and original paintings. Fresh flowers are everywhere, and the understated decor features a mix of antiques and art pieces.

The dining room, with lavender tablecloths and tapestry chairs, has picture windows overlooking the dark blue pool and aqua water beyond. You can eat outside, on the terrace, or on the roof garden to catch the breeze and enjoy the fishing boats going out for the catch.

The cuisine is Italian or international, featuring local seafood, of course, and it is graciously served. A pianist plays for the cocktail hour, through dinner, and on into the night, when couples can dance under a moon shimmering on the bay.

The cool, stylish guest rooms have ceramic tile floors, beds with antique headboards, minibars, TVs, and balconies with panoramic views of the sea. The dominant color is blue, reflecting the sea and sky. Mirrored bathrooms have showers or baths and amenities such as hair dryers, robes, and plants.

What to do here on this quiet island? You can swim in the stunning pool and relax on the little private beach, where topless bathing is an option, and you can participate in a variety of water sports. If you like to walk, you can go to the nearby woods and follow the footpaths. You can also take a four-hour boat ride around the island.

The most popular activities center on the hotel's well-equipped spa. Since ancient times the thermal waters here have been enjoyed by travelers seeking soothing treatments and relaxation. Today the hotel's spa still offers thermal baths, mud packs, saunas, hydromassage, and facials.

After an invigorating massage you can sunbathe and sip a Campari on the little jetty that juts into the lapping water. Watch the local children playing nearby on the rocky public beach, catch the distant sounds of family life coming from the fishermen's houses, or gaze at the beautiful castle just across a bridge. Or do all three. It's all part of soaking up the laid-back life in Ischia.

At twilight walk along the beach as the lights turn on in the small buildings in the distance. The peaceful serenity of this place can really creep up on you.

Address/Phone: Lungomare Cristoforo Colombo 23, Porto, Italy; 011–39–081–991–544; fax 011–39–081–991–562

U.S. Reservations: Leading Hotels of the World, (800) 223–6800

Owner/Manager: Eugenio Ossani, owner and general manager; Rosario Mazzella, managing director

Arrival/Departure: By boat from Naples seaport of Mollo Beverello: 40 minutes by hydrofoil, 1½ hours by ferry; transfers can be arranged on request

Distance from Naples Airport: 24 miles via ferry

Distance from Naples: 24 miles via ferry

Accommodations: 86 rooms; 10 suites

Best Room/Suite: Ocean-view suite

Amenities: Air-conditioning, minibar, telephone, radio, TV, bathrobe, toiletries, magnifying mirror, safe, hair dryer

Electricity: 220 volts

Sports and Facilities: 2 outdoor pools, 1 indoor pool; beach, spa, water sports; game room; tennis nearby

Dress Code: Casual

Weddings: Can be arranged

Rates/Packages: ITL 225,000–ITL 550,000 per night per couple, including breakfast, dinner, service charges, and taxes; spa packages available

Payment/Credit Cards: Most major

Deposit: Guarantee with credit card

Government Taxes: Included

Service Charges: Included

Entry Requirements for U.S. Citizens: Valid passport

≋

Hotel Danieli

Location: Prime location on Venice's famed lagoon next to the Doge's Palace and near the entrance to the Grand Canal. Situated right in the heart of the city, it is a two-minute walk to St. Mark's Square.

Romantic Features: Venice's opulence and history are combined in this authentically elegant Grand Hotel of the world, which once hosted visiting royalty and ambassadors (and continues to do so).

To stay at the super-deluxe Hotel Danieli is to embrace the romantic heart and soul of this unique city of gondolas and canals, flower boxes, and foot-bridges, cathedrals, and ancient architecture. As with every corner of Venice, every nook and cranny of the Danieli begs to be photographed. The fourteenth-century palace of the Doge Dandolo is the central building of three attached wings that house 231 restored rooms and suites of varying vintage, decor, and views, but all definitely in the deluxe category.

Arriving by private water taxi right to the doorstep of the hotel, you walk into what is now a covered courtyard foyer with a gorgeous, golden stairway leading up to the rooms (elevators, of course, are always there for the travel weary). The lobby is sublime, darkly opulent, and unforgettable, with its marble arches, ornate ceilings, breathtaking Venetian glass chandelier, and huge fireplace. The ghosts of such eminent and historic guests as George Sand, Charles Dickens, and Richard Wagner can easily be conjured up as you sip a drink in the Bar Danieli.

And right outside the front door is Venice itself. If you haven't already pre-arranged a package of sight-seeing and excursions, the concierge will be happy to help you arrange a gondola ride, a guided city sight-seeing tour, an excursion to the islands of the lagoon—Murano, Burano, and Torcello—to see the famed

Hotel Danieli, Italy

Venetian glass being made (with plenty of opportunity to shop), to visit the school of lace-making, and to tour the ancient cathedral of Torcello.

When you want to take a break from sight-seeing, you can spend the afternoon at the world-renowned Venice Lido (beach). A free water taxi takes you over to the Excelsior Lido Hotel to swim and sunbathe at the swimming pool or right on the beach, with its rows of cabanas. You can try your hand at the nearby casino or take in a round of golf.

On more than one morning, you may very well forgo a breakfast served in your room to eat at the hotel's open-air (in good weather) roof-top Terrace Restaurant to take in the early morning Venetian light and the breathtaking views of the lagoon.

Address/Phone: Riva degli Schiavoni, 4196, 30122 Venice, Italy; 011–39–041–522–6480, fax 011–39–041–520–0208

E-mail: claudiostaderini@sheraton.com

Web Site: www.luxurycollection.com/danieli

U.S. Reservations: (800) 325–3535

Owner/Manager: Giuliano Corsi, general manager

Arrival/Departure: By air to the Marco Polo Airport, just outside of Venice, and then by private water taxi from the airport to the hotel. By train (Santa Lucia Station), then 20 minutes by boat.

Distance from Marco Polo Airport: 35 minutes by boat

Distance from Venice Center: In the heart of the city

Accommodations: 235 deluxe rooms of varying vintage, decor, and views, including 11 suites and 190 double rooms

Best Room/Suite: 6 suites, 3 junior suites, and 51 double rooms are available with wonderful lagoon views

Amenities: Air-conditioning, hair dryer, minibar, shaver outlets, TV with international programs via satellite, direct-dial telephone, toiletries; robes in suites; room service

Electricity: 110/220 volts

Sports and Facilities: In season there are many sporting options on Venice Lido. The concierge can arrange tennis, horseback riding, golf, waterskiing, sailboarding, and yachting. Free boat service to the Lido is available.

Dress Code: Smart casual for daytime; dressier in the evening

Weddings: Can be arranged

Rates/Packages: From $400 per couple per night for a room. Special arrangements can be made for amenities such as champagne, breakfast in bed, fruit, and flowers.

Payment/Credit Cards: Most major

Deposit: Guarantee with credit card; cancel up to 24 hours in advance without penalty.

Government Taxes: 10 percent

Service Charges: Included (at client's discretion)

Entry Requirements for U.S. Citizens: Valid passport

≈≈≈

Villa D'Este

Location: Set on ten acres on the western shore of Lake Como.

Romantic Features: Spectacular lakeside setting; floating pool; dancing under age-old trees in the foothills of the Alps; watching the sun set over the lake and the mist waft down from the mountains.

The ultimate vacation resort on Lake Como, one of the loveliest lakes in the world, is Villa D'Este. Built by a cardinal as his personal home in the sixteenth century, this impressive, neoclassical pleasure palace sits amid ten acres of gardens, manicured lawns, magnolias, and towering trees. Once you pass through the elegant entrance, you will have everything you need to enjoy a relaxed, yet fun-filled honeymoon. In addition to the heart-stopping lakeside setting framed by the high ridges of the mountains, the resort boasts a full range of sports and fitness facilities, several restaurants, a night-club, and a cozy piano bar.

As you come into the palatial lobby, with its high, vaulted ceiling, graceful white columns, wide double marble staircase, and fine period furniture, you enter another world, where you will be pampered like royalty, but not so much so that it becomes overbearing. The staff here strikes just the right note between service and respect for your privacy.

Each of the 110 spacious rooms and 56 suites is different, and many, including those rooms located in the Queen's Pavilion, have balconies overlooking the lake. Rooms are elaborately decorated with rich, jewel-like fabrics and colors. Chandeliers, comfortable upholstered chairs and sofas, luxurious full drapes pulled back with golden cords and brocade ties, Renaissance-style artwork, and plush carpets give you accommodations fit for a king and queen.

Clark Gable, Paul McCartney, Ali McGraw, Woody Allen, Arnold Schwarzenegger, John Cleese, and Carly Simon have all stayed here, along with other notables. It's a good place to unwind and fall in love all over again with the person you care most about.

In 1875 Franz Liszt remarked, "When you write of two happy lovers, let the story be set on the banks of Lake Como." No doubt he had in mind strolls along the shore in the moonlight and serene afternoons lying on the banks when he

Villa D'Este, Italy

wrote this. But today this is only part of what you can do here. For active couples there are plenty of options. One of the resort's useful novelties is its large, freshwater pool, which actually floats in the water on its own island, just off the water's edge. There are also an indoor pool and a children's pool as well.

There are eight tennis courts as well as a squash court, waterskiing, sailing, and even hanggliding, along with various sports lessons and clinics scheduled throughout the week. Take a canoe and spend a peaceful afternoon paddling along the waters. If staying fit is on your agenda, you'll find the gym well equipped with the latest exercise and weight-lifting equipment. Or relax in the Turkish baths or saunas and get a soothing massage. Golf enthusiasts can practice their putting on the special green located on the villa grounds and later get in a game at a course just down the road.

All the dining facilities are oriented toward the lake. In good weather meals are served outdoors either on the open-air Verandah, which is covered by bright yellow awnings, or at the large, open Grill Room, set under a canopy of leafy, ancient plane trees; the walls are dense, green hedges, and the views are of the shimmering lake. At breakfast you can order a specially prepared omelet from the trolley and watch it being cooked or you can ponder your choices from the lavish breakfast buffet. Head to the terrace or sit poolside for lunch and enjoy a selection of fresh fruits, salads, fish, and pastas.

At night the Verandah lowers its glass walls to shelter diners from the night breezes and turns up the romance factor with candles, lots of fresh flowers, and soft lights. The presentation of food is a work of art: Grilled salmon is served with red, green, and yellow peppers in the shape of leaves, and a lemon tartlet arrives in a pool of vanilla custard laced by a delicate pinwheel pattern of chocolate and strawberry sauce. You almost hate to stick your spoon into it and disturb the fragile beauty of that confection. But when you do, you'll scrape every last drop from your plate. It's just too good. After dinner, mellow out at the piano bar or dance the night away at the disco.

If you should wish to venture out, you can visit the nearby quaint medieval villages with red-roofed buildings and narrow, winding streets and explore ruins of centuries-old castles and fortresses. One of the best ways to see the area is to take a boat ride around the lake, where you will see spectacular villas.

Address/Phone: Via Regina 40, 22012 Cernobbio, Lake Como, Italy; 011–39–031–3481; fax 011–39–031–348844

E-mail: info@villadeste.it

Web Site: www.villadeste.it

U.S. Reservations: Leading Hotels of the World, (800) 223–6800 or (212) 838–3110; fax (212) 758–7367

Owner/Manager: Jean-Marc Droulers, chairman and CEO; Claudio Ceccherelli, general manager

Arrival/Departure: You can arrange for pickup by the hotel at the airport, but check rates. The resort is easily accessible by car (car rental at airport); helipad at hotel.

Distance from Airport: 27 miles (45 minutes) from Malpensa and Linate, Milan's two airports

Distance from Como: 3 miles; Cernobbio is less than 1 mile; Milan, 35 miles

Accommodations: 110 rooms; 56 suites. Many have balconies overlooking the water; others face gardens

Best Room/Suite: Rooms in the nineteenth-century Queen's Pavilion and suites in the main building overlooking lake

Amenities: Hair dryers, telephone, in-room safe, toiletries, air-conditioning, whirlpool tub, minibar, TV; room service; foreign newspapers

Electricity: 220 volts

Sports and Facilities: 8 tennis courts (6 clay, 2 manteco), squash court, gym, putting green, jogging route with 15 checkpoints, sauna, Turkish bath, 3 pools (2 outdoor, 1 indoor); waterskiing, sailing; canoeing; sailboarding; golf 20 minutes away; spa with health and beauty treatments

Dress Code: Casual sports clothes during day; evening: jacket and ties required for men in the dining room

Weddings: Can be arranged; outside terrace popular

Rates/Packages: ITL 860–ITL 989 per couple per night, including buffet breakfast. "Romantic Stay" from ITL 3,320 per couple per night, includes 3 nights' accommodations, breakfasts, 3 dinners or lunches per person, one beauty treatment or massage per person, flowers, plus use of most of the sports facilities

Payment/Credit Cards: Most major

Deposit: Depending on season

Government Taxes: Included

Service Charges: Included

Entry Requirements for U.S. Citizens: Valid passport

Closed: December–February

PORTUGAL

≋

Pousadas

Author's Note: I have treated Portugal's pousadas as a group: To profile just one would be doing the concept a disservice, as each is completely unique. Since rooms are limited, be sure to make reservations well in advance.

Locations: If you want to explore Portugal by car, to travel at your own pace, and experience a very special place to stay and dine each evening, try plotting your itinerary through the countryside from pousada to pousada. Some are in or on the edge of town; others are in the middle of nowhere (or so it seems).

Romantic Features: Red-tile roofs and clusters of white houses in the green-clad moors glimpsed through rectangular spaces between the crenelated walls; huge silk-draped beds; fireplaces; gardens; history, history, history.

If you ever wondered what it would be like to live like a duke or countess or even a king or queen; to dine in a baronial stone hall, walls hung with priceless tapestries; to gaze from your hilltop terrace over the red-tiled roofs and fields of the world below; or to sleep in a bed topped by a crown of gold and crimson–velvet drapes, then catch the next jet to Portugal and check into a pousada. Dotting the countryside are forty-four pousadas, a network of unique places to stay, created in some of the country's most historic castles, palaces, monasteries, and regional structures. Most occupy the highest sites in their area and boast exceptional views of hills, mountains, lakes, and rivers.

From the Pousada de Sao Teotoio in the north which is built inside the thirteenth century fortress town of Valenca, to the cliff-top Pousada do Infanta on the southern coast, the pousadas range from the very opulent, including former castles and convents to much simpler places chosen for their exceptional location—perhaps on a lake or overlooking a river valley. Government owned and operated by Enatur, most pousadas average fifteen rooms. Many have swimming pools, some are located in the middle of medieval walled villages; others peer out over the sea.

Pousadas (derived from the Portuguese verb "pousar," to lodge or repose) were created not only to save some of these wonderful buildings but to provide places to stay where travelers are treated as honored guests. For example, there is the small riverside regional Pousada de Vale do Gaio, a modest, peaceful place where you wake to the sound of a cock's crowing and have breakfast on an outdoor terrace overlooking a shimmering river. Then there is the grand Pousada de D. Joao IV, with its age-burnished walls, once a royal convent. Original frescos and wall paintings have been beautifully preserved; rooms are arranged around the interior courtyard gardens.

There is nothing shabby or slipshod about any of the places in the furnishings, linens, toiletries, or service. Everywhere I went I was impressed by the consistency of the amenities and the cuisine, all the more remarkable when you consider that converting a thick-walled monastery to a first-rate hotel could not have been easy. It is obvious that a great deal of money has been spent to do the job right.

I was very impressed with the quality of the cuisine served in the pousada restaurants. A combination of regional specialties and continental dishes were presented with flair and creativity. Fresh fish, cataplana de mariscos (seafood cooked in a special pan), steamed lobster, fish stew, frango na pucara (chicken cooked in a clay pot), and cozido a portuguesa (meat stew) were particularly tasty. Meals were accompanied by locally grown vegetables and fruits.

Here are details about a few of Portugal's pousadas:

≋ Castelo Obidos, Obidos (north of Lisbon). Hugging the edge of the thirteenth-century walled town, with just nine rooms, this is the smallest of the pousadas and perhaps the most romantic. Three rooms are in tower suites with dramatic views of the countryside. Here your knight in shining armor may have competition: A model dressed in full armor stands sentry in the sitting room. Tapestries, dark wood antique furniture, candles (electrified), and thick stone walls provide the proper medieval ambience. The cobbled town just down the street, although no stranger to tourists, is fun to browse.

≋ Pousada D. Maria I, Queluz (5 miles from Lisbon). This posh pink-and-white confection was once a residence for the king's court. For a peek at what life was like in the eighteenth century among the rich and titled, just across the street is the Queluz National Palace, with its splendid gardens and museum. The pousada is perfect for those who want to enjoy Lisbon during the day but prefer to escape the hustle-bustle of the city in the evening. The excellent restaurant, Cozinha Velha, is housed in the former royal kitchens. Rooms are spacious and furnished with handsome wood furniture and rich brocades. 24 rooms; 2 suites.

≋ Pousada de Santa Luzia, Elvas (on the border of Spain and Portugal). With its airy and comfortable rooms decorated in light pastel colors and cheery painted furniture, this pousada is a good stopover location for those crossing the Caia border. See the 843-arch Amoreiras aquaduct nearby. Good restaurant and large pool and deck. 25 rooms.

≋ Pousada de Sao Francisco, Beja (southeast of Lisbon). A converted thirteenth-century monastery with a lovely swimming pool, gardens, and tennis court. Restaurant has a deserved reputation for superb fish dishes. 37 rooms.

≋ Pousada de D. Joao IV, Vila Vicosa (east of Lisbon). In the sixteenth-century this richly endowed complex was the Royal Convent of Chagas de Cristo. Many of the original altars, tiling, and artwork have been preserved and incorporated into the public and private rooms. Theme rooms include the Astronomy Room and the Painter's Room. Exceptional fresco of the Last Supper in dining room; after dinner fun in the billiard room. 33 rooms; 3 suites.

≋ Pousada de Rainha Santa Isabel, Estremoz (east of Lisbon close to Spanish border). D. Dinis once lived in this thirteenth-century palace with his wife, Queen Isabel. Today a fine pool with a generous-sized terrace and gardens tempt guests to laze the day away, yet there is a lot to see in this walled town. The dining room with its vaulted ceiling has been the setting for many royal meals. 23 rooms; 3 suites.

≋ Pousada de Palmela, Palmela (south of Lisbon). This converted hilltop fortress with stunning views of Lisbon served as the headquarters of the Portuguese Knights of St. James in the thirteenth century. In modern times it has hosted such dignitaries as the President of France and the Queen of Denmark. Glassed-in cloisters overlook a wisteria-clad courtyard. Thick walls and smallish windows create interesting window seats in many of the guest rooms. Some furnishings date back to fifteenth century. Imaginative cuisine. 27 rooms; 1 suite.

≋ Pousada D. Afonso II, Alcacer do Sal (south of Lisbon). Storks nest on poles just outside the entrance to this restored castle, which sits high above the Sado River. Guests enjoy fine views from their balconies of the countryside and red-roofed houses. Interesting mix of antiques and modern furnishings and artifacts. Beautiful gardens, pool, and archaeological museum on grounds. Very good restaurant. 31 rooms; 4 suites.

Address/Phone: Portuguese National Tourist Office, 590 Fifth Avenue, Fourth Floor, New York, NY 10036-4707; (212) 354–4403; fax (212) 764–6137; 011–351–1–8442000 (8442001 for reservations); fax 01–351–1–8442085/7

Web Site: www.Portugal.org, or log onto www.pousadas.pt

U.S. Reservations: Marketing Ahead, (800) 223–1356

Owner/Manager: Enatur

Arrival/Departure: Most guests fly into Lisbon and rent a car

Distance from Airports: Varies

Accommodations: 9 to 51

Best Room/Suite: Some favorites: The Terrace Suite at Pousada de Evora, where jasmine winds over the wrought-iron balcony; a Tower Suite at Castelo Obidos; Room 108 at Pousada de Rainha Santa Isabel, a kingly room with a blue-and-gold canopy bed; Painter's Suite at the Pousada de D. Joao IV

Amenities: Hair dryer, telephone, radio, laundry service, toiletries; most have satellite TV; minibar, restaurants; some have air-conditioning, fireplaces, whirlpool tubs

Electricity: 220 volts

Sports and Facilities: Most have swimming pools and gardens

Dress Code: Casual smart

Weddings: Can be arranged

Rates/Packages: From $90 to $195 per room (high season); $68 to $145 (low season); suites $85 to $285. Special interest packages available.

Payment/Credit Cards: Most major

Deposit: Guarantee with credit card

Government Taxes: Included

Service Charges: Included

Entry Requirements for U.S. Citizen: Valid passport

≈≈≈

MADEIRA

Reid's Palace

Location: Perched atop a cliff overlooking the Bay of Funchal.

Romantic Features: Wrought-iron balconies overlooking sea; Old World elegance.

Madeira has been called a floating garden. Indeed, this 287-square-mile island plunked about 600 miles off the coast of Lisbon, Portugal, in the middle of the North Atlantic, is exuberantly lush with flowers and tropical vegetation. Its volcanic origins have created an island of contrasts: dramatic green mountains; coastal plantations of sugarcane, bananas, and other crops terraced up the hillsides; deepwater bays and clear mountain streams. It's not really a place you come for beaches: It has few. But because of its charm, its beauty, and its subtropical climate, Madeira has been attracting sun seekers from the damper climes in northern Europe for more than one hundred years.

The oldie but goodie grandee of Madeira's many resorts is Reid's Palace. Sitting high on its own promontory on the southern coast near the center of Funchal, Madeira's principal city, Reid's enjoys a commanding view of the Atlantic and the bay. What it lacks in beaches it makes up for in views and service. After all, Reid's has had more than a century to get it right, and it has.

From the time you arrive, you don't have to sniff it out—you know it at once. Reid's is a place "old money" likes to come to. The British-style hotel's guest list amassed over the years reads like a *Who's Who:* Sir Winston Churchill, Prince Edward, George Bernard Shaw, Gregory Peck, Queen Ingrid of Denmark, and Roger Moore, to name a few.

With its clubby bars, polished antique furniture mellowed with lemon oil, crystal chandeliers, silk brocades, and cushioned wicker terrace furniture as well as contemporary amenities like air-conditioning and modern baths, Reid's continues to be *the* place to stay in Madeira.

There are 162 rooms and suites located in the main Victoria building and in the newer wings. Most have balconies facing the sea. Those on the upper floors of the main building are preferred for their views and their character, aged like fine wine over the years.

There's no beach, but there are plenty of sports and activities to keep you as busy as you want to be. There are two large heated saltwater pools with ample lounging space on the patio and lawn; a nifty jetty at the base of the cliff for private swimming and sunbathing, sailboarding, sailing, scuba diving, and game fishing; two all-weather courts for tennis; and lots of hiking trails. Boat trips around the island are available, and there are two golf courses on the island: Santo da Serra (forty-minute drive); and Palheiro Golf Club (twenty-minute drive).

The health center offers a variety of massages and treatments with specially priced spa packages; the saunas are free of charge to guests.

There is no skimping on service or food at the various restaurants. They're simply superb. The casual Garden Restaurant looks over the pools and sea—a great place to have breakfast and lunch; chandeliers, gleaming crystal, Palladian windows, and Old World elegance characterize the Main Dining Room; regional cuisine and fresh fish are featured at the informal Villa Cliff Restaurant; outdoor dining is offered seasonally at Brisa do Mar Restaurant; gourmet fare is offered at Les Faunes; and a buffet lunch is served on the pool terrace.

A pianist plays every evening in the main dining room and Les Faunes, and there is dancing to a live band nightly in the cocktail bar.

Most rooms in the hotel have recently been redecorated, lightening up the whole look. Fortunately, the redo has incorporated the best of the characteristics of the original guest room decor, which made these rooms unique and special.

You'll want to take time to explore the island and perhaps walk along some of the many trails that wind through the hills. Squeaky clean like Bermuda, scenic like Hawaii, it's a beautiful place to be.

Address/Phone: P-9000 Funchal, Madeira, Portugal; 011–354–291–717171; fax 011–354–291–717177

E-mail: reidshtl@mail.telepac.pt

Web Site: www.orient-expresshotels.com

U.S. Reservations: Leading Hotels of the World, (800) 223–6800; fax (212) 758–7367; Orient Express Hotels, (800) 524–2420

Owner/Manager: Anton Küeng, general manager

Arrival/Departure: Transfers to and from Funchal Airport included in honeymoon package; otherwise can be arranged for a fee ($50 for private transfer per car); approximately $25 per carload for taxi

Distance from Funchal Airport: 30 minutes; 75 minutes by air from Lisbon

Distance from Funchal Center: 10 minutes

Accommodations: 167 rooms and suites

Best Room/Suite: Deluxe rooms or suites on higher floors of main building and Garden Wing

Amenities: Air conditioning, hair dryer, minibar (free soft drinks), toiletries, TV, radio, telephone; personal safes, 24-hour room service

Electricity: 220 volts

Sports and Facilities: 2 heated saltwater pools, seaside terrace/swimming area, 2 all-weather tennis courts, Ping-Pong, billiards, health center with sauna and massage, waterskiing, scuba diving; golf at Santo da Serra and Palheiro Golf Club courses; hiking trails nearby; deep-sea fishing

Dress Code: Casual during day; jacket and tie for men for dinner in more formal restaurants

Weddings: Can be arranged

Rates/Packages: PTE 48,500–PTE 98,000; suites PTE 110,000–PTE 510,000 per couple per room; including breakfast, use of tennis courts and watersports, shuttle, minibar (soft drinks and beer), service charges, and taxes. Meal plans available. Honeymoon package (not available high season), PTE 130,000–PTE 140,000 per couple; includes 3 nights' accommodations; breakfasts; gourmet meal in Les Faunes, island tour; vineyard tour; gift; wine; flowers and fruit; transfers; free use of tennis court, pools, and sauna; taxes and service charges; 7 nights, PTE 220,000–PTE 270,000; includes all of above features plus visit to Monte, island tour in private limousine with picnic, and half-day boat excursion.

Payment/Credit Cards: Major credit cards

Deposit: Credit card deposit; cancel 14 days or more before date of arrival for full refund

Government Taxes: Included

Service Charges: Included

Entry Requirements for U.S. Citizens: Valid passport

SCOTLAND
≈≈≈

Gleneagles

Location: On 830 acres north of Edinburgh in Perthshire, the gateway to the Highlands.

Romantic Features: Walks into the heather-covered hills; fireside cocktails after a brisk horseback ride; four-poster beds.

When it first opened, people titled and/or ridiculously rich flocked to this venerable estate in the Scottish countryside. The golf courses quickly gained an international reputation as the finest in the realm. Today Gleneagles is a first-rate resort appealing particularly to those who love to be active, for there is a lot to do here on this sprawling property. Three golf courses plus the "wee" nine-hole course, a full-blown equestrian center, tennis courts, a falconry school, a spa, even an off-road driving school, plus a number of other sports and activities, ensure that those with an itch to see and do are blissfully happy.

The setting in the wild and wonderful heather-clad Perthshire Hills is magnificent, a perfect venue for those who love to hike, ride, and enjoy the outdoors. Shimmering lochs and rivers invite anglers to fish in the fresh, cool waters. Equestrians will find some of the most spectacular riding country in Europe at their doorstep. And with a complete riding school and forty-five horses, there is instruction for every level.

Ever wanted to learn the fine art of falconry, one of the world's most aristocratic sports? At Gleneagles you'll find the British School of Falconry right on the grounds; you can try handling and flying Harris hawks. Or what about popping a clay pigeon out of the sky? At Gleneagles Jackie Stewart Shooting School, set smack on a grouse moor, you can learn how to master this unique sport.

Golfers can't help but love Gleneagles. Besides the original King's and Queen's Courses, there is the Monarch's Course, an eighteen-hole layout designed by Jack Nicklaus, opened in 1993. And for those who want to brush up on their game or even learn how to play, there is a superb golf school. Tuition is included in some of the package plans.

Other activities are located in the resort's leisure club. Here you'll find a pool, Jacuzzi, hot tubs, sauna, Turkish baths, gym, squash courts, snooker tables, croquet, bowls, pitch-and-putt course, tennis court, and bicycles. All these things are free to Gleneagles guests. Within the club there is also the spa, where you can enjoy a wide number of therapies and treatments, such as aromatherapy and massages. Except for those on a special package, these treatments cost extra.

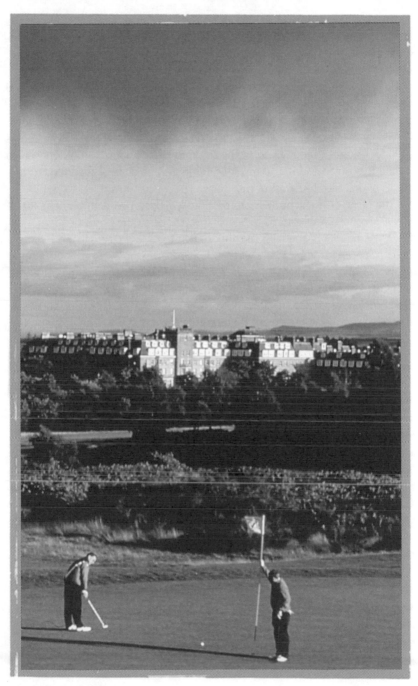

Gleneagles, Scotland

Lest you think Gleneagles is all about fun and games, there is more. Guests have a choice of six places to eat and drink and can choose from a wide assortment of cuisines, ranging from Scottish specialties to Continental. Try grouse, salmon, kippers, venison, and scones and cream.

Rooms and suites are furnished traditionally with chintz bedspreads and draperies; comfortable upholstered chairs and sofas are covered in rich greens, golds, blues, and reds. You'll find highly polished wood tables and desks, brass lamps, leather stools, silk-lined walls, and handwoven carpets; some rooms have four-poster canopy beds. In the summer French doors can be opened to let the fresh breezes in. In the colder months some suites have working fireplaces guaranteed to banish winter chills.

The grounds of Gleneagles are beautifully landscaped with gardens, trees, and lawns. Take your camera and walk or cycle along the paths or venture farther over the moors and hills. Ask the kitchen to pack a picnic for you and discover a special glade by a lake where you can have lunch.

In the summer daylight hours are long and can last until 10:00 or 11:00 P.M., giving you plenty of time to explore the countryside, where you can see hundreds of castles. For some local flavor attend the local Highland Games or sheepdog trials. And remember, if you can tear yourself away for a day or two, Glasgow and Edinburgh are only an hour away and well worth a visit.

Address/Phone: Auchterarder, Perthshire, Scotland, PH3 1NF; 011–44–1764–662–231; fax 011–44–1764–662–134

E-mail: resortsales@gleneagles.com

Web Site: www.gleneagles.com

Reservations: Leading Hotels of the World, (800) 223–6800

Owner/Manager: Peter J. Lederer, managing director

Arrival/Departure: Arrangements can be made for private transfer to the hotel. The charge for a chauffeur-driven car is about $100. Gleneagles train station is 1 mile from the resort, and all trains are met by the hotel's minibus (no charge). Free transfer to Edinburgh Airport on Monday morning for those staying Sunday night.

Distance from Edinburgh or Glasgow Airport: 45 miles (1 hour's drive); taxi about $80, limousine $110

Distance from Perth or Stirling: 20 miles

Accommodations: 214 rooms plus 15 suites

Best Room/Suite: Suites are ideal; the Royal Lochnagar is the best and costs a king's ransom.

Amenities: Hair dryer, TV, minibar, toiletries, telephones, terry bathrobes, trouser press

Electricity: 220/240 volts

Sports and Facilities: 5 tennis courts (4 all-weather, 1 grass), 3 championship 18-hole golf courses, 1 nine-hole course, squash court; riding, shooting, gym, spa, pool, falconry, fishing, mountain biking, snooker, jogging, hiking (it's a good idea to book sports activities such as golf at the time you make your reservation)

Dress Code: Smart casual

Weddings: Can be arranged; garden weddings are particularly lovely; bagpipers serenade newlyweds

Rates/Packages: from £235 per couple per night for a room, £315–£1,300 for a suite (November to April); £345 for a room and £395–£1,350 for a suite (May to October), including accommodations, full Scottish breakfast, and VAT. Honeymoon at Gleneagles £520–£630 per couple per night, includes suite accommodations, flowers, chocolates, carriage drive, champagne breakfast in suite, chauffeur transfers, and dinner for two on first anniversary. Ask about special-interest packages, such as golf, spa, and riding.

Payment/Credit Cards: Most major

Deposit: Guarantee with credit card

Government Taxes: Included

Service Charges: Not included

Entry Requirement for U.S. Citizens: Valid passport

≋

ASIA AND THE PACIFIC

AUSTRALIA

≋

Bedarra Island

Location: On Bedarra Island, 3 miles off the tropical northern Queensland coast.

Romantic Features: Very, very quiet private island; lovely beaches.

W hen you hear an Australian say, "Going troppo, mate," he or she could be heading to Bedarra Island, a sunny tropical bit of paradise located just off the northern coast of Queensland—Great Barrier Reef territory. For this cheery saying means you're going to a place guaranteed to provide lots of hot sun, sand, and sea. Bedarra offers all this and more—or less, depending on how you look at it. It's secluded; it's quiet. Very quiet. Here there are no schedules to follow and very little in the way of nightlife.

A white, sandy oasis in the middle of a brilliant turquoise sea, Bedarra Island is a small, intimate resort. Staying here is much like staying at the home of a wealthy relative who just happens to be out of town: Members of the staff are in attendance and have been told to do everything in their power to keep you happy. And they do!

At this sybaritic destination, besides being waited on, you're quite welcome to help yourself to anything you desire, at any time. If you want something

Bedarra Island, Australia

special, all you have to do is ask. Caviar? They'll bring it. An omelet at three in the afternoon? They'll cook it. Want to go over to Dunk Island for some action? They'll get the boat fired up. You just name it.

Your multilevel villa is yours alone. Crafted from native timbers, it sits on stilts amid lush gardens. Ceilings are high, with exposed beams; floors are made of highly polished wood. The bright, airy decor reflects the colors from outside. Linens are smooth and lovely; pillows are puffy, soft down. (If you want something different, just ask.) Towels are thick and thirsty and are changed often.

Each villa has a balcony, a good place to enjoy your welcome bottle of champagne while gazing out at the sea. Only a few steps from the beach, each villa comes with a king-size bed and a separate lounge area with CD stereo system, TV, video, and fully stocked complimentary minibar.

Since Bedarra is a very private island, you'll have no trouble finding innumerable places to be alone. Discover hidden coves; walk in the lush rain forest, which flourishes alongside the beaches; or float side by side on rubber rafts. Swing gently in one of the hammocks slung between palms on the beach, or ask for a picnic hamper filled with delicious food and champagne to take with you to a secluded spot.

Although Bedarra's chefs find new ways to tempt you daily, they also make a point of asking if you have any personal requests. The open bar, which is available to you twenty-four hours a day, is stocked with domestic and imported beers, champagnes, fine vintage red and white wines, spirits, and liqueurs.

The restaurant, which is round and constructed of local woods, overlooks the gardens and turquoise lagoons, a perfect setting for that special romantic dinner. Enjoy the excellent cuisine and be sure to top it all off by indulging in a delectable Pavlova (a meringue dessert). There are only fourteen other couples at most, so if you're looking for a lively nightlife with lots of socializing, this might not be the place for you to come. If, however, a serene, beautiful natural setting and lots of pampering by an extremely competent and caring staff appeal, then Bedarra is worth the trip.

Address/Phone: P.O. Box 1033, Bedarra Island via Townsville, Queensland, Australia 4810; 011–61–7–4068–8233; fax 011–61–7–4068–8215

E-mail: resorts_reservations@poaustralia.com

Web Site: www.poresorts.com

U.S. Reservations: P&O Australian Resorts, (800) 225–9849

Owner/Manager: P&O Australian Resorts, owner; Shane McNally, general manager

Arrival/Departure: Private resort launch to and from Dunk Island airstrip

Distance from Airport: 15-minute launch ride from Dunk Island airstrip

Distance from Cairns: About 150 miles

Accommodations: 15 private, two-level and split-level villas crafted from native timbers

Best Room/Suite: Villa Number 1 is most secluded.

Amenities: Hair dryer, toiletries, air-conditioning, ceiling fans, ISD telephones, radio, ironing facilities, TV, VCR, bathrobes, CD stereo system

Electricity: 240 volts

Sports and Facilities: Tennis, use of motorized dinghies, island hiking, paddleskis, sailing, swimming, snorkeling, fishing, sailboarding. Guests may use sporting facilities at nearby Dunk Island, just 15 minutes away, at no extra charge.

Dress Code: Casual

Weddings: Can be arranged

Rates/Packages: All-inclusive rates, approximately AU$680 per person per night, includes accommodations, 3 meals daily, open bar, snacks, tennis, water sports, and laundry. Rate for 3-night package, approximately AU$2,040 per person, includes villa accommodations, meals, beverages, champagne, picnic lunch for two, transfers, and gift.

Payment/Credit Most major

Deposit: Credit card guarantee; no charge for cancellation made 30 days prior to arrival date; less than 30 days, a 1-night charge

Government Taxes: Included

Service Charges: None

Entry Requirements for U.S. Citizens: Valid passport

≈≈≈

Hayman

Location: 20 miles from the Australian mainland, on 960 acres of one of the Whitsunday Islands, considered to be the most beautiful of all the Barrier Reef Islands.

Romantic Features: Private dinners for two on beach or in tropical gardens; themed penthouses filled with antiques; island picnics and snorkeling on Bali Hai and Langford Reef.

Hayman, a long, low, sprawling property with reflecting pools filled with swans, tropical gardens, waterfalls, and palm-lined beaches, is designed for romance. The Great Barrier Reef is close by, but you may find it hard to tear yourself away from your Hayman Island paradise. Situated at the tip of the Whitsunday Islands, this luxurious 214-room resort is the only place on the 960-acre island. And what a place!

It takes a bit of doing to get here, but it's worth it. First you have to get to Australia; then you can fly from Sydney or Brisbane to Hamilton Island, where you board a sleek yacht for the forty-five–minute cruise to Hayman. While onboard, you enjoy complimentary flutes of champagne and get all the registration formalities out of the way so that you can head right to your room on arrival.

The resort, which stretches along a cove on the southern part of Hayman Island, fronts two lovely beaches. Some say the waters around this island offer some of the finest sailing in the world. Hayman Island, 3 miles in length and a mile wide, is shaped like a crescent with mountains running along its spine, punctuated by a tall peak standing 820 feet above sea level. The island is covered with a dense blanket of native eucalyptus trees, and the Australian bushland goes right to the edge of the white beaches.

All rooms and suites have either private balconies or terraces with views of the pools, lagoons, and beaches or gardens. Rooms are low-key but elegant, decorated in soft pastels and florals that complement the tropical setting. Your room or suite comes with large glass patio doors, white sliding louvers, handwoven rugs and dhurries, original paintings and sculpture, comfortable upholstered chairs and sofas, and lavish marble baths. The one-, two-, and three-bedroom penthouses on the top floor of the East Wing are each decorated in a different style, accented with a stunning selection of furnishings and objets d'art. You can choose from a variety of themes including Greek, Japanese, Italian palazzo, Moroccan, South Seas, contemporary, North Queensland, California, Art Deco, and French provincial.

You don't have to be water-oriented to be enraptured by the dazzling freshwater pool floating in the midst of a huge saltwater lagoon—it's seven times larger than an Olympic pool. There is also an intimate pool surrounded by palms, tropical gardens, and fish ponds. Here you'll have as much privacy as you want. Wander through exotic gardens and along the beaches and never see another soul.

In addition to a full range of water sports facilities and six tennis courts, Hayman has an excellent health club equipped with Hydragym computerized workout equipment, such as rowing machines, aerobicycles, and treadmills, along with spas, saunas, and steam rooms. Want to be pampered? Indulge in a Swedish or aromatherapy body massage.

Many things make Hayman an exceptional resort, but its proximity to the Great Barrier Reef really sets it apart. This incredible natural wonder is more than 1,200 miles long and is made up of 2,000 individual reefs and 71 coral-based islands. Snorkelers and scuba divers universally classify the reef as the ultimate underwater experience. The waters around Hayman churn with fish of all shapes and colors, and even for a rank novice it is a thrill to glide above and through their world. If you prefer to stay dry, you can opt for a glass-bottom boat ride or a helicopter or seaplane excursion, which will take you directly over the reef.

Hayman has its own marina and offers chartered fishing excursions aboard the *Sun Aura*, a 40-foot game-fishing boat. Since these waters offer some of the finest fishing in the world, you might get lucky and catch some dinner, which the Hayman chefs will be happy to prepare for you.

In all there are six restaurants, each one featuring its own unique fare. There is also an extensive wine cellar of more than 35,000 bottles. La Fontaine, the resort's signature restaurant, is the most formal, with Waterford chandeliers and Louis XVI furniture. Its "cuisine moderne" is outstanding and beautifully presented. There is also the Oriental Seafood Restaurant, where you can try Moreton Bay "bugs," a cross between lobster and crab, served in an outstanding black bean sauce. The menu includes food selections from China, Malaysia, Thailand, and Japan. Fresh herbs from the resort's gardens are used in preparation of the meals. Hayman bakes its own breads and makes chocolates and ice creams. La Trattoria is a lively, informal, indoor/outdoor Italian bistro featuring pastas, salads, and antipastos at moderate prices. Planters is your ultimate Australian-style bar and grill, and you can also eat at the Coffee House, a casual beachfront restaurant serving buffet breakfasts, lunches, and pastries throughout the day. The Beach Pavilion offers daily blackboard specials, barbecues, snacks, and drinks. And there is always room service, available at any hour.

After dinner you can enjoy nightly performances by resident and guest artists, and you can dance the night away in the island's nightspot, Hernando's.

Hayman's guests give the staff high marks for professionalism, friendliness, courtesy, and dedication. These, combined with an idyllic setting and superb facilities, add up to a top-notch honeymoon resort.

Address/Phone: Great Barrier Reef, North Queensland, Australia 4801; 011–61749–401–234; fax 011–61749–401–567

E-mail: reserve@hayman.com.au

Web Site: www.hayman.com.au

U.S. Reservations: Leading Hotels of the World, (800) 223–6800; Ansett Airlines, (800) 4–HAYMAN

Owner/Manager: BT Hotels Ltd., owners; Jolyon Bulley, general manager

Arrival/Departure: Fly Ansett or Qantas to Hamilton Island, where guests board one of Hayman's three luxury yachts for the 45-minute trip to the island. A minibus will pick you up at the wharf for the 5-minute ride to the resort complex.

Distance from Hamilton Island Airport: 45 minutes by boat plus 5 minutes by minibus

Distance from Hamilton Island: 25 miles (approximately 50 minutes)

Accommodations: 203 rooms and 11 penthouse suites

Best Room/Suite: Beachfront rooms or suites, which allow you to walk from private terrace onto beach

Amenities: Air-conditioning, TV, Movielink, telephones, ceiling fan, minibar, in-room safe, refrigerator, tea/coffeemaker; hair dryer, toiletries, robe and slippers

Electricity: 240 volts

Sports and Facilities: No charge for snorkeling, Hobie-Cats, sailboarding, paddle skiing; use of 6 tennis courts, golf target range, putting green; playing billiards, table tennis, and badminton; hiking trails lace the island. Activities incurring charges include parasailing, water sleigh, yacht charter, reef trips, dinghy hire, snorkeling excursions, aerobics; tennis lessons, full diving services with instruction and equipment, diving trips.

Dress Code: Casual during the day; jacket required for dinner at La Fontaine; elegantly casual at other five restaurants

Weddings: Exquisite setting for garden weddings. Choice locations: gardens or in front of sparkling waterfall. A new wedding chapel sits on a hillside, with the beautiful Whitsundays providing a perfect backdrop for couples exchanging wedding vows.

Rates/Packages: Rates per couple per night range from AU$490, including breakfast, for a garden-view room to AU$1,500 for an East Wing suite overlooking the Whitsunday Passage. Penthouses are priced from AU$1,700, including breakfast. Honeymoon package, priced at AU$485 per couple when purchased with any other Hayman package, includes chilled wine and chocolates, private dinner, Hayman momento, massage for two, and tax.

Payment/Credit Cards: Most major

Deposit: 1 night; cancellation 1 week prior to arrival for full refund.

Government Taxes: 10 percent

Service Charges: Included

Entry Requirements for U.S. Citizens: Valid passport

≈≈≈

Silky Oaks Lodge

Location: Adjoins the Daintree Rain Forest National Park, on the northern bank of the Mossman River Gorge, near Port Douglas and Cairns.

Romantic Features: Very private wilderness chalets.

This one is definitely for the adventurous couple. Located on the edge of the Daintree Rain Forest National Park, Silky Oaks gives you the wilderness experience without the bugs and the cold showers. If you were to look up into the treetops from the Mossman River as the night darkness arrives, you would see the twinkling lights and windows of cottages glowing through the leafy canopy of the forest. Silky Oaks chalets are built on stilts to sit high in the dense tropical foliage and constructed of wood inside and outside. Large sliding glass doors open onto a veranda with a hammock for two, giving you a marvelous perch from which to view the world below. Tarzan and Jane would have loved it.

The chalets are spacious, comfortable, and very private with sitting areas, queen-size beds, and lots of windows. Although it's set in the Mossman River Gorge in a lush ancient rain forest, you'll find that your private "treetop" chalet has air-conditioning, an en-suite bath, a hair dryer, a telephone—even a mini-bar. From your veranda look carefully and you may be able to catch a glimpse of a platypus or tortoise. Or, most certainly, a resident bush turkey.

Winner of several tourism awards, the lodge features a superb open-air restaurant set high in the treetops overlooking the natural rock swimming pool and the river that flows below. The observation lounge and the guest lounge, which is ringed with large windows, are furnished with rattan chairs with comfortable cushions and Oriental carpets. The lodge, chalets, and rain forest are connected by a series of paths and boardwalks on stilts.

There is plenty to do at Silky Oaks. You can go kayaking, hiking, and swimming and even play tennis. The one thing you must absolutely do is visit the Wallaby Nursery located on the property. This is where orphaned wallabies, wallaroos, and kangaroos are nurtured and raised. Perhaps you'll even get to feed one of the babies from a bottle. It's not unusual to arrive at the restaurant for cocktails and find a wee guest: a baby roo hanging in a specially made pouch from the back of a chair.

Silky Oaks Lodge, Australia

Silky Oaks is only 75 minutes from Cairns, the jumping-off point for the Great Barrier Reef, which is really a must-see if you've come all this way. Stay three nights at the lodge and your excursion to the reef or a day-long Australian Wilderness Safari is on the house. You also get free guided rain forest walks and nighttime animal spotlight walks. On the shelves of the lodge's reference library is an impressive selection of books to help you understand the wilderness surrounding you.

Just outside your doorstep is a whole world of interesting flora and fauna to discover. After morning tea at the lodge's Tree House Restaurant, you can walk to the World Heritage–listed Daintree National Park, the oldest living rain forest in the world, where you will be surrounded by huge trees, primitive plants, and myriad collections of birds, butterflies, and little creatures such as lizards. Sling bridges take you over bubbling creeks, and marked paths show you the way to some spectacular sights—electric-blue butterflies, bright yellow-and-green birds, and tiny frogs.

Take a refreshing dip in the crystal-clear billabong, a natural pool surrounded by big boulders and lush tropical foliage. Take a picnic lunch (provided by the lodge) for a fun day on your own. Or explore the rain forest on horseback, retracing the steps of the old teamsters. Back at the lodge's bar, you can make new friends from all over the world.

The food is worth writing home about. This may look like a wilderness lodge, but there is nothing primitive about the cuisine served here. You may not be able to remember exactly what you ate, but you will remember that the food was some of the tastiest you've ever had—anywhere. Fresh tropical fruits and lots of great seafood from the nearby Barrier Reef along with Asian and Continental dishes are prepared with great skill. As one recent guest put it, "Every day we really looked forward to returning to the lodge for dinner. It got to be a habit."

There are several companies, such as Tauck Tours and Swain Australia, that take you to Australia and combine a wilderness adventure with a stay at Silky Oaks. A typical program takes in the Daintree Rain Forest, Cape Tribulation, and the Bloomfield Track and includes a Daintree River cruise. Maybe you'll catch a peek at an estuarine crocodile sunning on the riverbanks.

Address/Phone: Finlayvale Road, Mossman; P.O. Box 396, Mossman 4873, Australia; 011–61–7–4098–1666; fax 011–61–7–4098–1983

E-mail: resorts_reservations@poaustrailia.com

Web Site: www.poresorts.com.au

U.S. Reservations: P&O Australian Resorts, (800) 225–9849

Owner/Manager: Steve Anstey, manager

Arrival/Departure: From Cairns you can rent a car, take a limousine (seats up to 6), or go by bus (check at desk in airport; you'll go by coach to Mossman, where Silky Oaks Lodge will pick you up). Pickup can also be arranged at various Cairns hotels.

Distance from Cairns Airport: 1¼ hours by limousine (AU$220 round-trip per car or AU$55 per person each way for two passengers)

Distance from Cairns: 16 miles north (20 minutes) from Port Douglas; 51 miles (1¼ hours) from Cairns

Accommodations: 60 private "treehouse" chalets on stilts located near the lodge overlooking the lagoon or the treetop canopy or situated deeper in the rain forest itself.

Best Room/Suite: Chalets with Jacuzzis

Amenities: Air-conditioning, ceiling fan, minibar, tea/coffee facilities, hair dryer, toiletries, clock radio, telephones; massages available; nightly turndown service, laundry service, ironing board/iron, bath robes

Electricity: 220 volts

Sports and Facilities: Hiking in the rain forest, tennis, swimming, canoeing, river kayaking, horseback riding, wilderness safaris, bicycling; trips to the Great Barrier Reef; golf at the Mirage Country Club (20 minutes from Silky Oaks); fishing, night animal spotting, Aboriginal tours, river cruises, rain forest, picnics

Dress Code: Casual

Rates/Packages: AU$380 per couple per chalet per night. Three-night package, AU$680 per person, double occupancy, includes accommodations, breakfasts, guided rain forest walks, and a Great Barrier Reef Cruise or Australian Wilderness Safari, both full-day trips.

Payment/Credit Cards: Most major

Deposit: Credit card guarantee

Government Taxes: Included

Service Charges: None

Entry Requirements for U.S. Citizens: Valid passport

FIJI

Turtle Island

Location: 500-acre privately owned island in the South Pacific.

Romantic Features: Thatched beachfront cottages; fourteen beaches; dining by candlelight on the beach or on a mountaintop.

Some call it the most romantic place on earth. Apparently Columbia Pictures thought so, as it picked this island as the site for its 1980 movie *Blue Lagoon* starring Brooke Shields. The original 1949 version with Jean Simmons was also shot here.

Turtle Island, Fiji

One recent bride said they had to carry her off the island because she didn't want to leave. This is a true fantasy island, where you live in your own thatch-roofed beachfront *bure* (cottage), spend lazy barefoot days on the beach, and get to know, at the most, thirteen other couples (the whole place accommodates only fourteen couples).

When Turtle was simply a relatively unknown Fijian island located somewhere in the South Pacific, Richard Evanson, an American, came here to find a simpler life apart from the hectic world of television, where he had achieved success working on the West Coast. Evanson liked it so much, he stayed, eventually purchasing the island in 1972 and building a small resort with the help of Joe Naisali, a Fijian.

In constructing Turtle, Evanson was extremely careful not to upset the beauty and balance of the environment. He planted thousands of trees, including many Honduras mahoganies, carved a small road from the underbrush to go around the island, and protected the natural development of Turtle with a 500-year-old trust. Small and intimate, Turtle is a jewel not only because of its unspoiled physical beauty but also because of the interaction of its guests with the warm, loving Fijian people. Sitting under a banyan tree and singing with guests and staff in the late evening can be a spiritual experience.

When dinnertime rolls around, it's like one big house party. (Unless, of course, a couple wants to have a romantic dinner someplace on their own, such as on a lantern-lit beach or at the top of a mountain, all easily arranged.)

The minimum stay of six nights gives you time to relax, unwind, and explore Turtle's many pleasures. Turtle's all-inclusive fee frees you to go with the flow. No bills to sign. No need to wonder about additional charges, since everything is included—even deep-sea fishing and scuba diving.

A seaplane brings you to Turtle from Nadi, Fiji's main airport. As you approach, you'll see the brilliant colors of the Blue Lagoon and miles of white, powdery sand ringing the island. From the time you step from the boat to the shore, you are warmly attended to by a very hospitable staff who call you by your first name (only first names are used here). Your picture is taken when you arrive so that the staff will recognize you on sight. If you have any special requests or needs, they'll already know about them from the questionnaire you filled out before you came. Like a white omelet every morning? You'll get it. Don't eat meat? No problem. Get ready for some great vegetarian meals.

Here the sea is calm, with gently rolling waves, perfect for swimming and snorkeling. Perhaps you'd like to visit some Yasawa children on a neighboring island or escape to one of the fourteen beaches around Turtle and be totally alone.

Fourteen thatched-roof two-room *bures* built of coral stone are roomy, comfortable, and private with separate sitting areas, wet bars, "his and her" baths, four-poster beds, rattan furniture, rush mats, and louvered walls. Ten grand *bures* have private Jacuzzis, king-size beds, hardwood floors, outdoor lily ponds, and verandas. Vaulted ceilings are constructed in the traditional Fijian way, by hand shaping and lashing noko noko poles in a decorative pattern. And perhaps best of all, you have plenty of space around your *bure,* which is located directly on the beach of the Blue Lagoon.

Lali drums and guitar music announce that it's cocktail time. Food is fresh and delicious, with an emphasis on organically grown produce and fruits just picked from the trees. Turtle's three-acre garden provides plenty of food. Grilled lobster with lemongrass, all kinds of seafood, fresh fish caught earlier in the day by local fishermen, and wine from Turtle's extensive wine cellar are prepared with skill and flair. Try *Kokoda,* a Fijian dish of fish marinated in lime and coconut milk, or mud crabs dipped in vinaigrette sauce.

At Turtle you have so many choices: Go horseback riding or have a champagne picnic on the beach; take a nap in a hammock strung between two coconut palms; hike into the jungle hillsides; or visit the market on a nearby island. And participate in weekly *lovo* feasts and Fijian sing-alongs, where you share *kava,* the Fijian ceremonial drink.

You will probably find the most difficult thing about Turtle is leaving. After a week here, among some of the friendliest people you'll find anywhere, life for you will be just like a beautiful song—"*Vovosa malva mai vei au.*"

Address: P.O. Box 9317, Nadi, Fiji Islands 72921; 10906 NE Thirty-ninth Street, Suite A-1, Vancouver, WA 98682-6789

U.S. Reservations: (877) 2–TURTLE; fax (360) 253–3934

E-mail: usa@turtlefiji.com

Owner/Manager: Richard Evanson

Arrival/Departure: Fly from Los Angeles nonstop to Fiji with eight flights weekly. Round-trip transfer via seaplane from Nadi, Fiji, to Turtle Island is $380 per person, including tax (make arrangements when booking main flight).

Distance from Nadi International Airport: 30 minutes

Accommodations: 14 suites

Best Room/Suite: Grand Bures

Amenities: Ceiling fans, hair dryer, iron, ironing board, tea and coffee making facilities, CD players, toiletries, neck massager, beach bag, bathrobe, stocked refrigerator, snorkeling gear; next-day laundry service

Electricity: 240/110 volts

Sports and Facilities: Water sports such as boating, scuba diving, windsurfing, and snorkeling; deep-sea fishing; hiking on trails; horseback riding

Dress Code: Casual (you don't even need shoes); pack light, as you are limited to 33 pounds of luggage for the seaplane flight. Extra luggage can be stored at Turtle's facility in Nadi.

Weddings: Can be married in traditional Fijian ceremony held at sunset on the Blue Lagoon. Your wedding attire is hand-painted *tapa* cloth (you may look like pears, but who cares?) and you wear garlands of fresh flowers (that helps). Newlyweds are carried on a throne to their wedding feast. Wedding fee: $2,200 plus 10 percent tax, which includes the cost of the feast, choir, cake, kava ceremony, video, photos, flowers, and wedding attire. Private wedding package, $1,100.

Rates/Packages: $1,200–$1,598 per couple per night for everything, including accommodations, activities, meals, all beverages (even unlimited champagne), excursions to neighboring islands, use of boats and water sports equipment, all services, and 10 percent tax. Seven-night package $10,118–$11,718 per couple, includes all nightly rate inclusions plus airfare.

Payment/Credit Cards: Deposit by credit card; final payment by check

Deposit: $1,500 at booking. Balance due 45 days prior to your arrival. If you cancel, you can be rescheduled for another date within a 5-year period, but no refunds.

Government Taxes: 10 percent included

Service Charges: Not necessary. If you wish, you can contribute to staff Christmas fund when you leave.

Entry Requirements for U.S. Citizens: Valid passport

≈≈≈

FRENCH POLYNESIA

≋

Bora Bora Lagoon Resort

Location: Motu Toopua, a small, roadless coral island within the Bora Bora Lagoon.

Romantic Features: Tahitian-style *farés* (bungalows; pronounced fa-RAY; the Tahitian word for "home") built on stilts right over the lagoon; private island setting; magnificent views of the Bora Bora mountainscape; unusual adventures like shark-feeding expeditions.

A full moon rises over Mt. Otemanu, the crenellated peak that inspired the legends of Bali Hai. The moon's rays shimmer on the glassy lagoon like a king's ransom of silver. This is the vision that awaits when you step onto your *lanai* (terrace) at the Bora Bora Lagoon Resort, an exclusive enclave set on a private isle off Bora Bora. Many consider Bora Bora to be the loveliest island in French Polynesia, with its mountaintops soaring heavenward like the skyline of an emerald city. Here a necklace of barrier reef is clasped around a perfectly blue, perfectly clear lagoon.

The resort is located on Motu Toopua, an islet in the lagoon that's just five minutes by boat from Bora Bora's main town, Vaitape. There are no roads, no electricity (the hotel uses generators), no other businesses—just twelve acres of tropical gardens and views of the mountains, reefs, and fields. After arriving by private launch at the hotel's long pier, you're taken to the main building, constructed of lava stone and bamboo, with local *aito* logs supporting the roof. Here you're welcomed with a lei and refreshing drink of coconut water.

You'll stay in Tahitian-style *farés* (bungalows), with peaked roofs thatched with pandanus palm leaves. One wall is made up of louvered panels that you can slide open to the views and prevailing breezes. Each room offers a king-size bed and separate bath with a deep soaking tub and shower as well as a TV and VCR. The most romantic quarters are the over-water bungalows, built on stilts above the opalescent lagoon. A small stairway leads down to the water, so you can swim right from the deck.

Inside, the rooms reflect Polynesian chic, with tapa cloth hangings, coconut-shell inlays, and lovely floors of lustrous yucca wood streaked with a yellow and brown grain. Decorator fabrics come from French Polynesia and intertwine tones of ocean turquoise and sunset red. The most unusual piece of furniture is the glass coffee table: The top slides back so you can feed morsels of bread to the multicolored fish that gather below . . . an unusual twist on a "floor" show. The underwater spectacle is even illuminated at night!

The so-called beach bungalows are actually located in the gardens. Although they have the exact same decor as the over-water accommodations, they lack the magic of the sea-moored *farés*.

The resort has two different restaurants, including the Otemanu Room for formal dining. Once a week the resort schedules a Tahitian feast, with roast suckling pig and a folkloric dance show.

Bora Bora Lagoon offers plenty of activities—and delicious ways of doing nothing at all. A quarter of a mile of white-sand beach stretches alongside the transparent waters, and there's a marvelous pool that flows right to the edge of the tiles—the largest swimming pool in French Polynesia. Practice your strokes on the two lighted tennis courts (racquets and balls are available if you didn't bring your own). At the fitness center you'll find exercise machines and free weights. Learn to paddle an outrigger canoe, or opt for a massage in your own room or at the spa facility.

Feel adventurous? You can also choose from a roster of intriguing excursions (which cost extra) each day. Tops on your list should be a four-wheel-drive expedition around Bora Bora. Dauntless Land Rovers crash through jungle, revving up steep, rocky, muddy, pothole-wracked tracks to some dynamite scenic overlooks. For thrill seekers there are the shark feeds. Wearing snorkel gear, you watch safely from the shallows as dive masters serve up chunks of raw fish to black-tip sharks, which circle just a jaw's breadth away. Other activities include helicopter tours and snorkel excursions.

Exciting as these excursions are, your most vivid memories will be of the spectacular scenery in Bora Bora.

Address/Phone: Motu Toopua; B.P. 175, Vaitape, Bora Bora, French Polynesia; 011–689–60–40–00; fax 011–689–60–40–01

E-mail: bblr@mail.pf

Web Site: www.boraboralagoonresort.orient-express.com

U.S. Reservations: Orient Express Hotels, (800) 237–1236; Leading Hotels of the World, (800) 223–6800

Owner/Manager: Miguel Simões de Almeida, general manager

Arrival/Departure: From the moment you step off the airplane at Bora Bora Airport, you are welcomed with leis and whisked to the resort across the lagoon on a private motor launch

Distance from Bora Bora Airport: 15 minutes

Distance from Vaitape: 5 minutes by boat

Accommodations: 50 over-water bungalows; 16 beach bungalows; 12 garden bungalows; 2 suites

Best Room/Suites: Over-water bungalows

Amenities: In-room safe, minibar, electric ceiling fan (air-conditioning is not needed), hair dryer, telephone, in-house video system, TV, double sinks; in the over-water bungalows an illuminated glass-top coffee table gives a private view of the marine life; daily laundry service

Electricity: 220 volts

Sports and Facilities: Two tennis courts, swimming pool, Tahitian outrigger canoes, pedalboat, beach volleyball, snorkeling, sailboarding, sailing, fitness center. Deep-sea fishing, waterskiing, parasailing, jeep safaris, sunset sails, and scuba diving can be arranged.

Dress Code: Tropically casual

Weddings: The resort can arrange an authentic Tahitian wedding, including Tahitian dress for the couple, a waterfront ceremony with Polynesian music and dance, photos, sunset cruise on a pirogue canoe, and a candlelight dinner for two. (The ceremony, however, is not legally recognized in the U.S.)

Rates/Packages: $520–$770 per couple per night. Meal plans available. All-inclusive Total Experience Package for 4 days/3 nights, $3,200 per couple, includes accommodations in an over-water bungalow, floral greeting, American breakfast and lunch daily, dinner for two evenings, special picnic lunch, shark-feeding excursion for two, 4-wheel drive excursion, parasailing, half-day rental in a FunCar, transfers, use of tennis courts, fitness room, and all nonmotorized watersports—and more.

Payment/Credit Cards: Most major

Deposit: Guarantee with credit card

Government Taxes: 7 percent

Service Charges: Not included; not encouraged

Entry Requirements for U.S. Citizens: Valid passport and outbound ticket; if you're staying more than 1 month, you may need a visa.

≈≈≈

Hotel Bora Bora

Location: On the southwestern coast of the island of Bora Bora, 150 miles northwest of Tahiti in the Leeward Society Islands.

Romantic Features: Over-water thatched bungalows; king-size beds covered with clouds of gauzy net.

Remember those pictures of thatched huts perched on stilts over turquoise blue water? This is it. Bora Bora, the Grace Kelly of islands, flawlessly beautiful. Home to Hotel Bora Bora, a member of the prestigious Amanresorts group, this South Seas paradise appeals to sophisticates willing to go the extra mile to experience the exotic.

As your plane zooms in on this small island (only 4 miles long and 2½ miles wide), you'll spot palm-thatched bungalows half hidden in the greenery. Crystalline waters in blues, greens, and turquoise swirl around the white-fringed shoreline. Green volcanic peaks that run like a spine down the middle of the island soar toward the brilliant blue sky.

When you arrive, take off your watch, lie back, and soak in the scenery and seamless service. Many of those on the Polynesian staff have been working at the resort for over twenty years and truly know how to anticipate whatever it is you need.

Constructed of cedar, the individual bungalows and *farés* are spread over grounds that have had more than thirty years to grow lush and lovely. All have hand-tied, thatched pandanus (palm) roofs, private bars, radio/cassette players, and roomy tiled baths with freestanding, oval, wood-rimmed tubs and separate showers. Deluxe bungalows are located on the beach and have separate lounges and sundecks with steps leading to the water. Superior bungalows are also located on the beachfront and come with a small patio facing the sea and a hammock nearby. Bungalows have patios and are set in the gardens.

For the most fun opt for one of the bungalows over the water. Some are in the shallow lagoon waters; others are situated on a coral reef in a deeper section of the lagoon. Each of the over-water bungalows features an enormous room more than 750 square feet; a king-size, four-poster bed swathed in mosquito netting; sliding glass doors leading out to a deck with a pandanus shade overhang; and steps to a small platform, where you can sit on the edge and dangle your feet in the water. Floor-to-ceiling louvered panels allow the sea breezes to slide in, and you have a generous-size sitting area and dressing area with loads of storage space.

Farés, which are located on the beach and in the gardens, are very roomy and come with a living room; a bedroom with a king-size, four-poster bed; an en-suite sitting room; a bathroom; and a large sundeck. Eight *farés*—very spacious, with 1,200 square feet—have private swimming pools enclosed in courtyards furnished with cedar lounges and comfortable cotton cushions; three have outdoor Jacuzzis set into sundecks.

You can eat at the Matira Terrace restaurant overlooking the lagoon or at the Pofai Beach Bar. Both have lofty thatched roofs and are open on all sides to great views and cooling sea breezes. By the time you realize that your dinner and drink tab is heading skyward like the volcanoes, you really won't care much; but be prepared. Meals are not included in the rates (unless you get the Honeymoon package, which gives you some breaks). Entrees can range from $15 upward; a reasonable bottle of wine, $25 and up.

You are entertained nightly by local musicians; a Tahitian dance show is held twice a week.

Many of the activities center on the water: picnics to deserted islands, outrigger canoe rides, sunset cruises and sailing. You'll find the snorkeling very good just offshore—the fish will eat bread right out of your hand. If you want to explore the colorful underwater world farther out, you can take one of the reef trips.

Hotel Bora Bora, French Polynesia

There is a scuba-dive program for all levels of divers. Beginners can take a resort course or go all the way to certification. There are also catamaran sails, fishing excursions, deep-sea and saltwater fly fishing, moonlight horseback riding, helicopter tours, island tours, jeep excursions, shark-feeding expeditions, and a library with enough books to fill any extra hours you may have.

A special package combines three nights in a *faré* at Hotel Bora Bora and a private yacht charter for three nights with full crew service aboard *Tara Vana*, a 50-foot catamaran.

If you want to experience something really wild, for about $600 you can take part in the Warrior Ceremony, a colorful ritual performed by a Tahitian dance group leader with two Tahitian warriors standing in attendance, holding flaming torches. You drink champagne, nibble on canapés, and enjoy a mini dance show before boarding an authentic Tahitian sailing canoe for a forty-five-minute sunset cruise.

Hotel Bora Bora is restrained, in harmony with its graceful surroundings and the gentle, graceful people who live and work here. It will take you very little time to shrug off the jet lag, sink your toes in the sand, and get into the rhythm of a world that moves at a pace you can absorb.

Address/Phone: Point Raititi, Bora Bora, French Polynesia; 011–689–60–44–60; fax 011–689–60–44–66

E-mail: hbbresa@mail.pf

U.S. Reservations: Amanresorts, (800) 421–1490; fax (818) 710–0050

Owner/Manager: Peter Wynne, manager

Arrival/Departure: Transfers from Bora Bora Airport are complimentary; VIP airport express services available on request

Distance from Bora Bora Airport: 7 minutes; flying time between Tahiti and Bora Bora is 45 minutes

Distance from Vaitape: 3⁶/10 miles

Accommodations: 54 Polynesian-style bungalows and *farés* set amid the gardens, on the beach, or over the lagoon

Best Room/Suite: Over-water bungalows numbers 118 to 128 or a *faré* with in-deck Jacuzzi or private pool.

Amenities: Ceiling fans, freestanding bathtubs, separate showers, hair dryers, minibars, coffee and tea facilities, radio/cassette players, personal safes, telephones (optional), toiletries, bathrobes, and slippers; *New York Times* faxed daily

Electricity: 110/220 volts

Sports and Facilities: Complimentary activities include 2 tennis courts, snorkeling, outrigger paddles and sailing, canoes, billiards, table tennis, basketball, volleyball, and tennis; optional activities include jeep excursions, glass-bottom boat tours, sunset cruises, reef trips, deep-sea fishing, scuba diving, shark feeding, and sailing and hiking excursions

Dress Code: Casual chic

Weddings: Can be arranged, but marriage may not be legally recognized in the United States

Rates/Packages: From $480 per couple per night for a bungalow; from $650 for a *faré;* Honeymoon package for approximately $2,090 per couple includes round-trip transfers from airport, 3 nights' accommodations in a lagoon over-water bungalow, room tax, champagne and fruit, breakfasts, one candlelight dinner with wine served on the terrace of the bungalow, private sunset sail aboard an outrigger sailing canoe, and farewell gift

Payment/Credit Cards: Most major

Deposit: Guarantee with credit card deposit within 7 days of acknowledgment from the central reservations office; should a reservation be canceled within 7 days of arrival date or in the event of a no-show, the first night's charge along with transfer costs will be charged to the credit card or deducted from the prepayment

Government Taxes: 8 percent

Service Charges: Not included; not encouraged

Entry Requirements for U.S. Citizens: Valid passport and outbound ticket; if you're staying more than one month, you may need a visa

INDONESIA

≋

Amandari

Location: In Ubud, Bali, in the center of the Indonesian archipelago.

Romantic Features: Sunrise walk to the river; scent of frangipani; gamelan concert at sunset; private garden pools; swimming in a pool that seems suspended in midair.

If you believe that the best things come in small packages, Amandari is just further proof. You'll find this little jewel of a hotel perched dramatically on a cliff overlooking the Ayung River Gorge, on the exquisite island of Bali. Below are sweeping views of terraced rice paddies and tiny villages, palms and orchids, a dreamscape to savor in luxury. Designed as a Balinese village, Amandari, one of the very special Amanresorts properties, has thirty garden suites, some with private pools and garden courtyards.

What better place to go to celebrate your union than in Bali, which is legendary for its beauty. The graceful, sarong-clad people sway as they walk, balancing goods on their heads. The land is green and lush, with sinuous rice paddies, and the island is ringed by soft, white sand beaches and clear water.

Traditional dancers greet you at the open-air lobby, with its thatched-roof, templelike facade; floors of local marble; and carved teak furniture made on the island. The adjacent library/lounge offers comfortable chairs and a chance to learn about the surroundings and the gentle, artful Hindu culture.

The villages in the neighboring area each specialize in a different art form: Ubud is known for painting; Mas, for woodcarving; Celuk, for gold jewelry. The hotel can arrange to drive you around the island, where days can be spent bargaining for art and soaking in the rich culture. Each village also has its own distinctive dance, performed to the percussive music of the gamelan. Visitors can enjoy watching a new presentation each night at the open pavilions.

Dining here takes advantage of the views. The restaurant, overlooking the river, is dreamy with candlelight and soft music and serves fine international and Indonesian cuisine. The lounge offers spectacular views; a poolside bar features light meals.

Activities include tennis, hikes into the gorge, biking in the villages, and rafting on the Ayung River. But the loveliest activity of all has to be swimming in one of the most beautiful pools in the world. Contoured in the shape of a rice terrace, the pool appears to meld into the valley beyond. With the reflection of the clouds spreading out over the water, it seems as if you are swimming right up to the edge of the gorge. At one end is a pavilion, where at sunset the ringing sounds of the gamelan fills the air.

Suites are spectacular, some with private pools. Each is enclosed in its own garden courtyard and has a private entrance. Steep paths and stone steps lead to other bungalows and down to the river and the villages. Duplexes have spiral staircases that go up to the bedroom. All suites have polished marble floors, teak furnishings, four-poster beds with hand-painted canopies, and patios with sunken marble tubs hidden behind Balinese walls. Decorative sliding wall screens, creamy white walls accented by wood trim, and lovely paintings and sculpture further enhance the accommodations.

The high-pitched thatched roofs, oversize daybeds, elegant Asian furnishings accented with native art, flowers, glass walls overlooking the beauty of this island, and sarongs provided to each guest to wear to temple ceremonies—all are wondrously romantic things.

Amandari, which means "place of peaceful spirits," is aptly named.

Address/Phone: Ubud, Bali, Indonesia; 011–62–361–975–333; fax 011–62–361–975–335

E-mail: amanres@indosat.net.id

Web Site: www.amanresorts.com

U.S. Reservations: (800) 447–7462 or (800) 421–1490; (212) 223–2848 in New York or (818) 587–9650 in Los Angeles

Owner/Manager: Amanresorts Ltd.

Arrival/Departure: Complimentary transfers provided from airport

Distance from Bali Airport: 1 hour

Distance from Ubud: 5 minutes

Accommodations: 30 luxury suites enclosed in private courtyard, 11 with private pools; duplex suites have outdoor garden showers and queen-size beds. The Amandari Suite is available with 1 or 2 terrace-style bedrooms and a separate living room pavilion. The suite's 40-by-18-foot pool overlooks the gorge.

Best Room/Suite: Asmara Suite and Ayung Suite are duplex accommodations with private pools and views of the rice terraces and valley. The Amandari Suite has a separate living room pavilion, pool, and outdoor-dining bale of teak and bamboo.

Amenities: Hair dryer, toiletries, air-conditioning, ceiling fans, mosquito netting, twin vanities, minibar/refrigerator, garden patios, in-room safe, radio, sunken marble tub; 24-hour room service

Electricity: 220 volts

Sports and Facilities: Swimming in main or private pool, rafting, trekking, biking, tennis court, and a fully equipped health and fitness center

Dress Casual; shorts not allowed in temple areas of villages

Weddings: Can be arranged

Rates/Packages: $525–$1,050; $1,225–$2,300 suites; per couple per night

Payment/Credit Cards: Most major

Deposit: Guarantee with credit card deposit within 7 days of acknowledgment from the Bali Central Reservations Office; should a reservation be canceled within 7 days of arrival date or in the event of a no-show, the first night's charge along with transfer costs will be charged to the credit card or deducted from the prepayment

Government Taxes: 11 percent

Service Charges: 10 percent

Entry Requirements for U.S. Citizens: Valid passport

≈≈≈

Amanwana

Location: On island of Moyo, east of Lombok and Bali.

Romantic Features: A hideaway close to nature; luxury tented "villas."

Ever thought of spending your honeymoon in a tent on some exotic, almost deserted South Pacific island? If so, then Amanwana, on the island of Moyo in Indonesia, may be your ticket to romance. There are only about 2,000 inhabitants on the entire 120-square-mile bit of land, and it's not exactly easy to reach. You need to get to Bali, take a plane and then a boat, and after about two hours you should finally be pulling up to the jetty of the Amanwana resort. You'll have to look hard to see anything, for this little spot of heaven has been carefully placed in this dense, junglelike forest—no trees were cut down during its construction, and all the work was done by hand.

Amanwana, which means "peaceful forest," is part of the upscale Amanresorts group, which has created unique, very special small vacation places in harmony with nature. Amanwana, the first in the resort company's hideaway category, is like going camping and having your cake, too. Its clever design combines the sense of camping in the wild with the luxuries of modern-day conveniences such as air-conditioning, king-size beds, and double tile vanities.

Set on an island that is a wildlife reserve, the spacious tented rooms are more luxurious than many resort hotel accommodations. The canvas ceiling swoops to a peak in the center of the room over the bed, which is enveloped in an umbrella of filmy netting falling from a high round crown. The canvas, which extends over an outside veranda, is actually roped and pegged to the ground. Here the similarity between this accommodation and the tent you slept in at summer camp ends. The floor of your room is polished teak; there is a generous-size sitting area with two corner sofas covered in a natural, off-white fabric, and there are practical, well-designed, but simple tables and chairs as well as a desk.

Three sides of the tent are windows with off-white, cotton accordion shades, and there are beautiful straw mats on the floors. Native original sculpture, tapestries, and paintings decorate the off-white walls. The bathrooms are really an unexpected pleasure, boasting double vanities, beautiful twin mirrors in teakwood frames, teak louvered windows, a shower and toilet, plus baskets containing toiletries on the shelf. And the rooms are air-conditioned as well as cooled by ceiling fans.

The tents are randomly linked by paths that lead to the beach, the reception area, and the dining pavilion. Located in a bungalow, the reception area has a library stocked with lots of books, and the decor is pure Indonesian, with hand-hewn wooden tables and stools and original wall hangings, carvings, and paintings.

The open-air pavilion, where you find the bar, restaurant, and lounge, is located under a soaring ceiling of woven bamboo. Views are of the sea; food is basic, fresh, and good with choices from both Western and Asian cultures; and dinner is by candlelight. In fact, since the lighting tends to be less than bright even in your rooms, you'll find the mood can readily be called seductive anywhere you are in camp after the sun goes down.

There is a teak sundeck perched on the edge of the shoreline with coral steps leading to the water. Lounges, which are sturdy and constructed of wood and have upholstered cushions, provide a great inducement for those who want to lie back and relax in the sun. You can also have a private dinner on the deck or on the beach.

Activities are centered on the crystal-clear turquoise sea and the land. A guided trek into the tropical forest takes you to a beautiful inland waterfall, where you can swim in the pools created by the cascading waters. Walk under the wide tamarind, banyan, and native teak trees; catch a glimpse of monkeys, deer, and wild boar.

Or head out to sea for a late-afternoon sail and see the sun go down over the Flores Sea. Amanwana also has a fleet of nine vessels, including an outrigger canoe that can take you on a cruise of the area, stopping for a picnic on the beach along the way.

Scuba enthusiasts will love it here. The island is ringed with a wonderful coral reef, and a number of interesting dive sites are accessible right from the front of the camp as well as by boat. Beginner courses are $100; PADI International Certification and other instruction are also available.

Keep in mind that the rainy season is from December to March; the rest of the year is pretty dry.

For a real South Pacific experience, you might try combining a stay at Amanwana with two or three nights at one or more of the other Amanresorts. (Please see descriptions of Amanpuri and Amandari in this chapter.)

Address/Phone: Moyo Island, West Sumbawa Regency, Indonesia; 011–62–371–22233; fax 011–62–371–22288; Reservations: 011–62–361–771267; fax 011–62–361–771266

E-mail: amanres@indosat.net.id

Web Site: www.amanresorts.com

U.S. Reservations: (800) 447–7462 or (800) 421–1490; (212) 223–2848 in New York or (818) 587–9650 in Los Angeles

Owner/Manager: Amanresorts Ltd.

Arrival/Departure: Transfers to Moyo Island are by a Merpati Airlines flight from Bali to Sumbawa (about 1 hour with a stop in Lombok); from there it's a 1-hour cruise on Amanwana's *Aman XI* motor yacht to the camp. Total round-trip fare from Bali, $150; Amanwana also has a helipad. *Please note:* There is a strict limit of 30 pounds of luggage per person, soft-sided preferred. Guests staying at any of Aman's three resorts in Bali prior to or after Amanwana will be provided with complimentary transfers to the airport.

Distance from Denpasar Airport, Bali: About 3 hours total travel time from door to door

Accommodations: 20 luxury tents with king-size beds and en-suite bathrooms

Best Room/Suites: Open-front tents closest to the shoreline

Amenities: Hair dryer, toiletries, air-conditioning, ceiling fans, mosquito netting, twin vanities, minibar, veranda

Electricity: 220 volts

Sports and Facilities: Trekking excursions, boating, snorkeling, cruise excursions, sports fishing, massage; freshwater dipping pool; scuba diving can be arranged

Dress Code: Smart casual

Weddings: Can be arranged

Rates/Packages: $590–$725 per tent per couple; includes all meals, water sports, and nonalcoholic beverages

Payment/Credit Cards: Most major

Deposit: Guarantee with credit card deposit within 7 days of acknowledgment from the Bali Central Reservations Office; should a reservation be canceled within 7 days of arrival date or in the event of a no-show, the first night's charge along with transfer costs will be charged to the credit card or deducted from the prepayment

Government Taxes: 11 percent room tax

Service Charges: 10 percent

Entry Requirements for U.S. Citizens: Passport that is valid for duration of stay and ongoing or round-trip airline tickets. *Please note:* It is recommended that you start taking antimalaria medication (e.g., doxycycline) before you arrive.

Closed: January 15 to March 15

~~~

Kamandalu Resort & Spa

Location: In the highlands of central Bali, just north of Ubud.

Romantic Features: Showering in a private walled Balinese shower under the stars; your own thatched pavilion overlooking emerald-green paddy fields and the Petanu River.

If you have decided to go all the way to exotic Bali for your honeymoon, consider including a stay at the Kamandalu. Granted it's not on the beach, but for those who want to really soak up Balinese culture, this little gem of a place, set on a tropical forested hillside with green paddy fields spreading out below, would be an excellent choice. Enhanced by accommodations that have been designed to replicate a typical Balinese village, Kamandalu is located very near Ubud, home of many gifted artists from Indonesia and other parts of the world, who come to live and work in this serene environment.

Just a short shuttle ride from the resort, you'll find a bustling little town and the artists and craftspeople who live and work here.

At Kamandalu pavilion cottages with traditional thatched roofs hover just below the tall palms, which have been profusely planted on the hillside. Since the pavilions cling to the curved terraces of the hillside, you may find you have to walk many steps up (or down) a hill to get where you're going.

All pavilions and villas have garden showers, marble floors, modern baths with sunken marble tubs, and the villas have a *bale bengong* (sitting area). They come with modern amenities such as air-conditioning, minibar, TV, in-house movies, audio system, in-room safe, and garden showers.

The simplest and smallest of the pavilions features an outdoor garden shower; the deluxe pool villas are more spacious and have better views and outdoor Jacuzzis; the deluxe pavilions come with private sunbathing areas and pools and valley views; villas, designed in the typical thatched Lombok style *sasak* (house) each contain a courtyard garden and two separate rooms, including a *bale bengong;* deluxe villas are more spacious versions of the smaller villa.

Many pavilions have king-beds that are richly decorated with Balinese canopies and headboards. Furniture is simple yet elegantly styled in wood with traditional Balinese fabric cushions. Ceilings are lofty and show the intricate underside of the thatched roofs.

Kamandalu Resort & Spa, Indonesia

Meals are served in the Petulu Restaurant and highlight cuisine from Bali along with international specialties. There is also the Cempaka Bar and Lounge as well as a library bar with panoramic views of the rice terraces.

The resort has a large swimming pool, tennis courts, and hiking and jogging trails. If you feel adventurous, you can go whitewater rafting.

The Kamandalu Heritage Herbal Spa, a new addition to the property, offers health and beauty care treatments. Experience the soothing essences of selected *jamus,* herbal mixtures used in various treatments offered at the spa.

In its commitment to the local culture and people, Kamandalu has provided a nearby village with clean water and an easy access to the hotel temple, which is built into the hills. Villagers come here to present their offerings to God. While you're staying at the resort, you'll see the villagers quietly going about their business, tending the rice fields and driving their ducks to the paddy to eat.

Sometimes in the distance you may hear the music of a special festival or celebration. Kamandalu is a tranquil place located in close proximity to authentic villages, not to be mistaken for the hub of Bali's tourist nightlife. The main pool may have a swim-up bar and you may have twenty-four–hour room service, but if you want discos and nightclubs you'll have to go somewhere else. Here when the sun goes down, life slows. You relax; you enjoy.

Address/Phone: Jalan, Tegallalang, Banjar, Nagi, P.O. Box 77, Ubud Bali, 80571 Indonesia; 011–62–361–975–825 or 011–62–361–975–835; fax 011–62–361–975–851

E-mail: kamandalu@indo.net.id

U.S. Reservations: Contact hotel directly

Owner/Manager: D. Johan Wijaya, general manager

Arrival/Departure: Guests are picked up from the airport; cost is $25 one way.

Distance from Bali Airport: 1-hour drive

Distance from Ubud: 1 mile

Accommodations: 58 thatched-roof pavilions and villas set in private walled enclosures; each is designed as a typical Balinese house, some with *bale bengongs* (sitting areas) overlooking the rice paddies and hillside and outdoor showers; some have private pools and separate living rooms

Best Room/Suite: Jacuzzi or Pool Villas

Amenities: Air-conditioning; in-room safe; minibar; I.D.D. telephone, audio system; satellite TV; toiletries; coffee and tea maker; hair dryer; garden showers, some with Jacuzzis and private pools; in-house movies

Electricity: 220 volts

Sports and Facilities: Large swimming pool with swim-up pool bar and children's pool, tennis court, jogging track, hiking trails, nature walks; whitewater rafting can be arranged

Dress Code: Casual elegance

Weddings: A mock wedding in traditional rich red and gold Balinese costumes available to guests booking Balinese Wedding package

Rates/Packages: $200 per room per night for a pavilion; $300–$525 for a villa. A Romantic Indulgence package, $1,355–$1,973 per couple, includes 4 days/3 nights in Pool or Garden Villa, breakfasts either in your pavilion or in the Pudak Restaurant, transfers, fruit basket and welcome drink, spa treatment, candlelight dinner, and a barbecue dinner.

Payment/Credit Cards: Most major

Deposit: Credit card

Government Taxes: 11 percent

Service Charges: 10 percent

Entry Requirements for U.S. Citizens: Proof of citizenship; passport best

THAILAND
≈≈≈

Amanpuri

Location: On the island of Phuket, off the southern coast of Thailand.
Romantic Features: Private treetop pavilions; serene island retreat.

In Sanskrit *Amanpuri* means "place of peace." It is. No discos, no slot machines, no traffic noise. Amanpuri, the first of thirteen intimate Amanresorts, is a haven from the fast-paced world many of us live in. Once here you'll have plenty of time to unwind and soak in the tranquillity and beauty of Amanpuri. In fact, doing nothing in an exotic place is exactly what many come here for.

One thing for sure: You'll know you're in Thailand when you arrive in Amanpuri. Most of what has been built here has been created out of local materials made by local craftspeople.

The main roof of the Grand Sala, the centerpiece of Amanpuri, soars to 40 feet. Its multiple, pitched roofs and columns are reflected in the rectangular pool, which is filled to the brim with the clearest of water. The Grand Sala, simply yet elegantly decorated with live orchids and antique furniture, is where you are greeted when you arrive at Amanpuri. At that time a manager is assigned to look after you for the duration of your stay.

Built on three levels into the trees and tropical foliage of a former coconut plantation, forty pavilions are spread out over twenty acres. They stand on stilts linked by elevated walkways. The design of the resort is refined, with guest pavilions and the Grand Sala integrated into a harmonious whole. Steep-pitched roofs curve to a sharp peak—like Buddhist temples—and buildings are constructed of wood accented by earthy, red-hued trim.

You'll find a well-equipped gym with treatment rooms where you can be pampered with massages, facials, and other soothing delights. The Grand Sala, a huge open-air reception area with a lounge and pool, is found on the second level.

A lot of natural materials such as bamboo, stone, and teak are used throughout the resort. You'll find caned chairs, baskets, stone walls, and teak floors.

Pavilions are very spacious, containing 1,200 square feet including the bedroom, dressing area, bath and shower, outdoor *sala* (sitting area), and sundeck. Each bedroom is quietly elegant. Decor doesn't jump out and hit you with a resounding "wow!" Rather it seduces with creamy, white walls; floor-to-ceiling decorative wood panels; fiber rugs; carved furniture; soft, handwoven cottons and silks; pottery; plants; and Thai sculpture. Bathrooms are enormous, designed for two; closets have enough drawers to hold an entire winter wardrobe.

Although some rooms have good ocean views, most are located in the dense palm groves overlooking the gardens. When Amanpuri was built, the integrity of the land was respected.

The Terrace Restaurant features fresh seafood and Continental and Thai specialties daily; and surprise, there is also an Italian restaurant where you can dine by candlelight on the veranda overlooking the sea. Musicians will serenade you as the moon rises over the water. Service is seamless, gracious. If you prefer a quiet party for two in your pavilion, you can call on room service any hour.

You'll find a wide range of water sports activities on the beach, including sailing, sailboarding, Hobie-Cats, and snorkeling. Amanpuri has an excellent marina and maintains more than twenty yachts, available for charter. Pack a picnic, your snorkeling gear, and flippers, and explore some of the neighboring islands and bays close to the resort. Or climb aboard a restored classic Chinese junk for a sunset cruise.

Want to see some of the wonderful life beneath the sea? Check out the H2O Sportz operation, a full-service PADI facility geared to scuba divers of all abilities. The resort course will give you a basic introduction to diving; for the more advanced and certified divers, there are trips to a number of world-class dive sites for exploring underwater caves and crevices as well as coral reefs and walls.

The resort has a library with a collection of more than 1,000 books and a gift shop where you can purchase a variety of Asian artifacts, including jewelry, textiles, pottery, and small sculptures.

It's a long way to this part of the world, so consider seeing both Thailand and Indonesia. Stay at Amanpuri in Thailand, Amandari in Indonesia, and/or Amanwana, a luxury "tented" island resort on the tiny island of Moyo, near Bali. All are members of the Amanresorts group.

Address/Phone: Pansea Beach, Phuket Island, Thailand; 011–66–076–324–333; fax 011–66–076–324–100 or 324–200

E-mail: amanpuri@loxinfo.co.th

Web Site: www.amanresorts.com

U.S. Reservations: (800) 447–7462 or (800) 421–1490; (212) 223–2848 in New York or (818) 587–9650 in Los Angeles

Owner/Manager: Amanresorts Ltd., owner; Anthony Lark, general manager

Arrival/Departure: Complimentary transfers provided from Phuket Airport; frequent air service from Bangkok daily (1-hour flight)

Distance from Phuket Airport: 12 miles (20 minutes)

Distance from Phuket Town: 10 miles

Accommodations: 40 pavilions, each with its own outdoor *sala* (sitting area); also 30 guest villa homes, with two-, three-, or five-bedroom homes, each with a black-tiled pool and separate dining room, living room, and bedroom. A live-in maid and cook attend to all guest needs.

Best Room/Suite: Numbers 103 and 105, with ocean views

Amenities: Hair dryer, toiletries, air-conditioning, ceiling fans, mosquito netting, twin vanities, minibar/refrigerator, sundeck, in-room safe, stereo cassette system; 24-hour room service

Electricity: 220 volts

Sports and Facilities: 2 floodlit tennis courts, pool, gym, beach club, sailing, sailboarding, snorkeling, waterskiing, deep-sea fishing, scuba diving; golf nearby; island cruises

Dress Code: Smart casual

Weddings: Can be arranged

Rates/Packages: Pavilions, $390–$1,120 per couple, per night; villa homes, $1,080–$6,000 per couple per night, including transfers

Payment/Credit Cards: Most major

Deposit: Guarantee with credit card deposit within 7 days of acknowledgment from the Bali Central Reservations Office; should a reservation be canceled within 7 days of arrival date or in the event of a no-show, the first night's charge along with transfer costs will be charged to the credit card or deducted from the prepayment

Taxes: 21 percent tax and service

Entry Requirements for U.S. Citizens: Passport that is valid for duration of stay and ongoing or round-trip airline tickets. *Please note:* It is recommended that you start taking antimalaria medication (e.g., doxycycline) before you arrive.

AFRICA

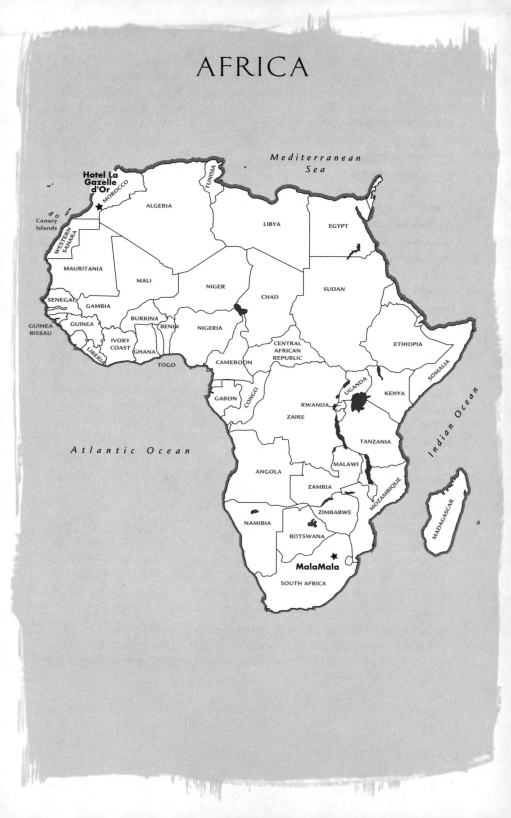

Mediterranean Sea

Hotel La Gazelle d'Or ★

Canary Islands

TUNISIA

MOROCCO

ALGERIA

LIBYA

EGYPT

WESTERN SAHARA

MAURITANIA

MALI

NIGER

CHAD

SUDAN

SENEGAL

GAMBIA

GUINEA BISSAU

GUINEA

BURKINA

BENIN

NIGERIA

IVORY COAST

GHANA

TOGO

LIBERIA

CAMEROON

CENTRAL AFRICAN REPUBLIC

ETHIOPIA

SOMALIA

GABON

CONGO

RWANDA

ZAIRE

UGANDA

KENYA

Atlantic Ocean

TANZANIA

Indian Ocean

ANGOLA

MALAWI

ZAMBIA

MOZAMBIQUE

MADAGASCAR

ZIMBABWE

NAMIBIA

BOTSWANA

MalaMala ★

SOUTH AFRICA

MOROCCO

≋

Hotel La Gazelle d'Or

Location: Ten minutes from Taroudant, a medieval walled city.
Romantic Features: Little stone villas in what was once the private hunting lodge of a French baron; lovely grounds fragrant with rose gardens and citrus orchards.

Having risen late, a couple called room service to ask until what time breakfast was served. The captain grandly responded, "Whenever you like. All we ask is that you finish breakfast before you have lunch."

That's the personal attention you can expect at La Gazelle d'Or, a hideaway just outside the medieval walled city of Taroudant. It's the kind of place where the maître d' reserves your unfinished bottle of wine from the night before, and the attendant calls to ask if you'd care to swim before he covers the pool for the night.

Built in 1948, the enclave was the private hunting reserve of French Baron Jean Pellenc; it became a hotel in 1961. Formerly the baron's residence, the main building is opulently decorated with camel saddles, antique rifles with mother-of-pearl stocks, and magnificent mosaics, most notably the gilt-trimmed floor of the Zodiac Room.

The resort encompasses twenty-five acres of tropical gardens, which cast the intoxicating fragrances of rose and citrus onto the breezes. There are just thirty stone cottages, draped with bowers of bougainvillea and overlooking orange groves, gardens, and the Atlas Mountains.

Cottages face a broad, emerald lawn shaded by palms, cedars, and olive trees and bordered by beds of roses. You'll find the same profusion of roses gathered into bouquets in your room—vivid arrangements of alabaster, pink, coral, and crimson. Cottages are large, each with an entrance foyer leading to a separate bedroom and bathroom. Furnishings capture the romance of the Arabian Nights, with blue-and-white terrazzo floors, mosaic tables, and filigreed plasterwork over the bed. A corner fireplace adds to the romantic ambience. The bathrobes for your use are thick and heavy—it seems as if they weigh nearly ten pounds.

La Gazelle d'Or is a place for utter relaxation and sensual pleasure—the hardest thing you might have to do is brush bougainvillea blossoms off your chairs on the terrace.

Your day might begin with a jog through the citrus groves and alleys of roses. Then order breakfast, which will be brought to your private terrace by a white-robed attendant. The ample continental repast includes a large glass of fresh-squeezed orange juice (from the hotel's own trees) and a platter of ripe nectarines, grapes, and melon. In the basket of breads, you'll find croissants, rolls, and *pain au chocolat,* the filling still warm from the oven. You'll probably make friends with some of the resident cats, who drop by not just to mooch extra milk but also to appeal to your sense of largesse—they are especially fond of the crisp corners of the croissants.

Read and sun by the magnificent large pool, lined with blue tiles and shaded by ancient olive trees. Then play tennis or go horseback riding on one of the fine Arabians, trotting through the Souss valley, where doves skim along the breezes.

If you can tear yourself away from this peaceful oasis, tour nearby Taroudant, a walled city with ramparts dating back to the twelfth century. A city of 35,000 inhabitants, it is nonetheless an exotic desert outpost, the street thronging with horse-drawn buggies and Berber women draped in black. Visit the market, where vendors sell amber, musk, kohl, and huge piles of fragrant spices looking like they were poured from a child's sand pail. The hotel can arrange excursions to the waterfalls at Amagour or the beaches near Imouzer.

Dinner is served in a circular, tented dining room that recalls the tales of Scheherazade. In this delicious, five-course repast, portions are sized just right, providing a parade of exquisite tastes without leaving you overly stuffed. You might start with a shrimp bisque enlivened by ripe tomatoes, or fish soufflé, brought to the table at the peak of its crescendo. Entree choices can include a chicken fricassee or *tagine* of lamb with okra—the meat is so tender, it flakes off the bone. Desserts are heavenly, like the lemon tart, heady with citrus flavor.

After dinner head to the adjoining salon, where mint tea is served with a flourish by gentlemen who pour from a metal pot held several feet above the tiny glass cups. Enhancing the magic, manager Adam Stevenson plays tunes ranging from Gershwin to Rachmaninoff on the piano.

"We have found our Paradise," one honeymoon couple inscribed in the hotel guest book. All who sojourn at La Gazelle d'Or are sure to agree.

Address/Phone: BP 260, Taroudant, Morocco; 011–212–8–85–2039, fax 011–212–8–85–2737

E-mail: gazelle@marochet.net.na

U.S. Reservations: Contact the hotel directly or Casablanca Tours, (212) 697–7511

Owner/Manager: Rita Bennis, owner; Adam Stevenson, general manager

Arrival/Departure: Transfers can be arranged, about $60 each way

Distance from Agadir Airport: 50 miles (45 minutes)

Distance from Taroudant: 1 mile (5 minutes)

Accommodations: 30 rooms in stone cottages

Best Room/Suite: Suites

Amenities: Ceiling fans (some), hair dryer, minibar, toiletries, bathrobes; private terrace

Electricity: 220 volts

Sports and Facilities: Large heated swimming pool, 2 clay tennis courts, riding stables, croquet, *hammam* (traditional steam bath), massage and beauty center

Dress Code: Casual elegance; jacket and tie for dinner

Weddings: The resort does not arrange weddings for U.S. citizens. However, there is a Christian church in the town of Taroudant where you can be married. La Gazelle d'Or will provide assistance.

Rates/Packages: $395 ($885 in large suite) per couple per night, including dinner and continental breakfast

Payment/Credit Cards: Most major

Deposit: Normally, a deposit of 1 night is expected except during peak periods, such as Christmas, when full prepayment is requested. Cancel 14 days prior to arrival date for full refund.

Government Taxes: Included

Service Charges: Included in rate; gratuities at discretion of guests

Entry Requirements for U.S. Citizens: Valid passport

SOUTH AFRICA
≋

MalaMala

Location: MalaMala is one of three safari camps located on the MalaMala Game Reserve, a private, 45,000-acre game preserve adjacent to the Kruger National Park, in the northeastern part of the country.

Romantic Features: Moonlight safaris; thatched *rondavels* overlooking Sand River.

At MalaMala your wake-up call comes about 5:30 A.M., just in time to watch the moon set into the shelter of the distant hills over the Sand River. After a cup of tea or coffee in the lodge, you climb into an open Land Rover and, with a ranger-driver and armed tracker aboard, head into the bush for a magic morning of game viewing. You may see a mother cheetah sitting under a tree with her four cubs lazing about in a heap around her, or you may pick up the trail of a lioness loping along, her tail swaying back and forth.

You'll get close to giraffes and elephants, warthogs, kudu, and waterbucks. Later, back at the lodge, you'll chow down on a lavish breakfast.

Coming to MalaMala and not participating in the early morning and late evening game-viewing safaris would be like visiting the Tuileries and passing over the flowers. Everywhere you go in this amazing camp, you are reminded that you are in the heart of the largest tract of privately owned big-game territory in South Africa. Walk around the grounds in the evening and you hear the cries and calls of the animals stirring, the sounds of their nighttime activities of roaming, eating, and mating.

Rooms at MalaMala are in spacious, ochre-colored *rondavels* (bungalows), which sit on a knoll overlooking the Sand River, where animals come daily to drink. The rooms are remarkably luxurious for the bush. They come with "his and her" bathrooms; comfortable, oversize Posturepedic twin beds; and high thatched ceilings. Norma Rattray, who oversees the designs of the interiors, says, "Just because you come to camp doesn't mean you have to be uncomfortable." Large window walls give you wonderful views of the river, and rooms are furnished with rattan furniture and nature prints.

Afternoons at camp are spent as the animals spend them: leisurely. You can take a nap, swim in the pool, or sip a cool drink under the shade of a tree.

Night drives begin in late afternoon while the sun is still hot, but beware: Once the sun goes down, it cools off rapidly, especially in the winter. Then you'll need some warm clothing—think "layered look." As it gets dark, the rangers slowly drive the Land Rovers into the bush. The tracker holds a spotlight, which would seem to intrude on the animals' privacy and to frighten them. It doesn't. Over the years the animals have become accustomed to the light and the sounds of the vehicles' engines and accept these things as just part of their world.

The light finds a lion and her two cubs finishing their meal of impala. Later the Land Rover slowly rolls off the path into the center of a large buffalo herd. A large, mud-caked bull shakes his thick horns as he grazes—just 3 feet away from the Rover's passengers. The motor is turned off, and you can hear the animals rustle through the low bush and the night sounds all around. Behind the buffalo, acacia trees are silhouetted by a full, white moon hanging in the African sky.

Back at the lodge meals are served in an air-conditioned dining room. Dinner can really be fun on the nights you eat in a reed enclosed *boma*, a traditional South African round open-air area. You sit in a large circle with everyone facing a log fire blazing in the center of the area. Your meal includes beautifully prepared fresh local fruits and vegetables and game meats such as venison and impala. After dinner, dancing and entertainment is provided by the staff under the starry South African skies.

There is a cozy bar where people gather in the evenings after the game dri-ves to compare their sightings. It's always a challenge to see if you qualify for the prestigious "Big Five Club": More than three-quarters of MalaMala's guests achieve membership in the club after spotting lion, leopard, rhino, elephant, and buffalo. Rangers join in exchanging tales of animals they have known, such as Mafunyane, an old elephant with tusks so long they reached the ground. MalaMala's rangers are highly trained and qualified; all have university degrees in areas like ecology or zoology, and all have an intimate understanding of ani-mals and their relationship to their environment.

The Buffalo Lounge is just what you'd imagine it would be: casual, walls decorated with animal heads and skins; native artwork; and a high, vaulted, wood and thatch ceiling. The lounge opens onto an expansive veranda, a good place to watch the rhinos and other animals coming for a drink in the river below. It's also a great place to relax at the end of the day with a glass of fine South African wine. MalaMala has an excellent and extensive collection of tasty regional wines.

The romance of MalaMala is a heady concoction of exotic safari experi-ences, warm knowledgeable people, exceptional accommodations, and brilliant African skies.

Address/Phone: MalaMala Game Reserve, Box 2575, Randburg 2125, South Africa; 011–27–789–2677; fax 011–27–886–4382; fax to camp: 011–2713–735–5686

U.S. Reservations: Tim Farrell & Associates, P.O. Box 3029, Westport, CT 06880; (203) 845–0304; fax (203) 845–0448; e-mail:safaritim@aol.com

Owner/Manager: Michael Rattray, C.E.O./managing director; Nils Kure, camp manager

Arrival/Departure: By air. MalaMala offers daily direct flights from Johan-nesburg into the MalaMala airstrip in chartered, pressurized King Air Aircraft. You can also fly from Johannesburg to Skukuza Airport, where you will be met by rangers from the MalaMala camp.

Distance from Skukuza Airport: 14 miles (½ hour); 1-hour-and-10-minute flight from Johannesburg International Airport to Skukuza

Distance from Skukuza: 13 miles

Accommodations: 25 twin *rondavels*

Best Room/Suite: Suites

Amenities: Air-conditioning, electric shaver plug, PABX telephone/intercom, extra-large twin beds, ice service, heated towel racks, *New York Times* fax daily

Electricity: 220 volts

Sports and Facilities: Wild game viewing, swimming, guided bush walks, walking safaris

Dress Code: Bushveld casual, but a sweater may be required at any time; during winter (May to September) very warm clothes, including a windbreaker, are essential

Weddings: Can be arranged

Rates/Packages: From $580 per person per night; includes twin *rondavel* accommodations, all meals, snacks, teas, game drives, walking safaris, laundry, and transfers from Skukuza Airport.

Payment/Credit Cards: Most major

Deposit: 50 percent deposit required to secure accommodations; balance due 30 days prior to arrival. Cancellation fees apply as follows: 5 percent, 90 days prior to arrival; 25 percent, 21 days prior; 50 percent, 7 days prior; 100 percent, 24 hours or less prior. Special policies for high-season periods.

Government Taxes: Room tax, R5.70 per person per night

Service Charges: Included

Entry Requirements for U.S. Citizens: Passport and return or onward ticket required. Check whether visa is necessary.

Indexes

Alphabetical Index to Romantic Resorts

A

Ahwahnee, The, 17
Akti Myrina Hotel, 263
Amandari, 305
Amanpuri, 313
Amanwana, 307
Anse Chastanet, 192
Auberge du Soleil, 20

B

Balance Rock Inn, 76
Banff Springs Hotel, 109
Barcelo Playa Tambor, 213
Bedarra Island, 287
Bitter End Yacht Club, The, 145
Boca Raton Resort & Club, The, 43
Bora Bora Lagoon Resort, 299
Boulders, The (AZ), 12
Boulders, The (CT), 41

C

Cambridge Beaches, 139
Caneel Bay, 208
Cap Juluca, 122
Casa de Campo, 160
Château du Domaine Saint-Martin, 254
Château du Sureau, 23
Château Eza, 256
Château Lake Louise, 112
Cobblers Cove, 137
Curtain Bluff, 125

D

Disney's Grand Floridian Resort & Spa, 46

E

Equinox, The, 97
Excelsior Palace Hotel, 266

F

Feathers Hotel, The, 239
Four Seasons Biltmore, 26
Four Seasons Resort Maui at Wailea, 57
Four Seasons Resort Nevis, 180

G

Gleneagles, 282
Golden Lemon Inn & Villas, 190
Grand Hotel Punta Molino Terme, 268
Grand Lido Sans Souci, 165
Greenbrier, The, 105

H

Hacienda Katanchel, 216
Halekulani, 60
Half Moon Golf, Tennis, and Beach
    Club, 168
Hartwell House, 242
Hayman, 289
Horned Dorset Primavera Hotel, 185
Hotel Bora Bora, 301
Hotel Danieli, 270
Hotel Goldener Hirsch, 237
Hotel Hana Maui, 64
Hotel La Gazelle d'Or, 317
Hotel Villa del Sol, 219
Hyatt Regency Aruba Resort &
    Casino, 128
Hyatt Regency Dorado Beach, 188

Hyatt Regency Grand Cayman, 157

I

Inn at Spanish Bay, 28
Inn of the Anasazi, 91

J

Jasper Park Lodge, 114

K

Kamandalu Resort & Spa, 310
Kona Village Resort, 68

L

La Casa Que Canta, 222
La Pinsonnière, 117
La Samanna, 205
Las Hadas, 225
Le Manoir aux Quat' Saisons, 245
Le Sport, 197
Little Dix Bay, 150
Little Palm Island, 49
Lygon Arms, The, 249

M

MalaMala, 319
Manele Bay Hotel, The, 71
Maroma, 228
Mauna Lani Bay Hotel and
    Bungalows, 73
Meadowood, Napa Valley, 30
Melhana Plantation, 55

N

Negresco, 259
Nisbet Plantation, 182

O

Ocean Club, 131
Old Fort Inn, 79

P

Peter Island Resort and Yacht
    Harbour, 153
Post Ranch Inn, 33
Pousadas of Portugal, 276

R

Radisson Edwardian Hampshire
    Hotel, 252
Reefs, The, 142
Reid's Palace, 279
Ritz-Carlton, Cancun, The, 233
Ritz-Carlton, Naples, The, 53

S

Sandals Resorts, 172
Sandals Royal Bahamian Resort &
    Spa, 135
Sandals St. Lucia Golf Resort & Spa, 200
Schlosshotel Lerbach, 261
Sherman House, The, 36
Silky Oaks Lodge, 292
Sonnenalp Resort, 38
Spice Island Beach Resort, 162
Swept Away Negril, 177

T

Turtle Island, 295

V

Villa d'Este, 272

W

Wauwinet, The, 84
Wawbeek, The, 93
Westin Brisas Ixtapa, 231
Whalewalk Inn, The, 88
White Barn Inn, 81
Windjammer Landing, 203
Woodstock Inn & Resort, 101

Seaside Resorts

Akti Myrina Hotel, 263

Amanpuri, 313

Amanwana, 307

Anse Chastanet, 192

Balance Rock Inn, 76

Barcelo Playa Tambor, 213

Bedarra Island, 287

Bitter End Yacht Club, The, 145

Boca Raton Resort & Club, The, 43

Bora Bora Lagoon Resort, 299

Cambridge Beaches, 139

Cancel Bay, 208

Cap Juluca, 122

Casa de Campo, 160

Château du Domaine Saint-Martin, 254

Château Eza, 256

Cobblers Cove, 137

Curtain Bluff, 125

Excelsior Palace Hotel, 266

Four Seasons Biltmore, 26

Four Seasons Resort Maui at Wailea, 57

Four Seasons Resort Nevis, 180

Golden Lemon Inn & Villas, 190

Grand Hotel Punta Molino Terme, 268

Grand Lido Sans Souci, 165

Halekulani, 60

Half Moon Golf, Tennis, and Beach
    Club, 168

Hayman, 289

Horned Dorset Primavera Hotel, 185

Hotel Bora Bora, 301

Hotel Hana Maui, 64

Hotel Villa del Sol, 219

Hyatt Regency Aruba Resort &
    Casino, 128

Hyatt Regency Dorado Beach, 188

Hyatt Regency Grand Cayman, 157

Inn at Spanish Bay, 28

Kona Village Resort, 68

La Casa Que Canta, 222

La Samanna, 205

Las Hadas, 225

Le Sport, 197

Little Dix Bay, 150

Little Palm Island, 49

Manele Bay Hotel, The, 71

Mauna Lani Bay Hotel and
    Bungalows, 73

Negresco, 259

Nisbet Plantation, 182

Ocean Club, 131

Peter Island Resort and Yacht
    Harbour, 153

Reefs, The, 142

Reid's Palace, 279

Ritz-Carlton, Cancun, The, 233

Ritz-Carlton, Naples, The, 53

Sandals Resorts, 172

Sandals Royal Bahamian Resort &
    Spa, 135

Sandals St. Lucia Golf Resort & Spa, 200

Spice Island Beach Resort, 162

Swept Away Negril, 177

Turtle Island, 295

Villa d'Este (Lake Como), 272

Wauwinet, The, 84

Westin Brisas Ixtapa, 231

Windjammer Landing, 203

Resorts with Tennis

Akti Myrina Hotel, 263

Amandari, 305

Amanpuri, 313

Anse Chastanet, 192

Auberge du Soleil, 20

Barcelo Playa Tambor, 213

Bedarra Island, 287

Boca Raton Resort & Club, The, 43

Bora Bora Lagoon Resort, 299

Boulders, The (AZ), 12

Boulders, The (CT), 41

Cambridge Beaches, 139

Caneel Bay, 208

Cap Juluca, 122

Casa de Campo, 160

Cobblers Cove, 137

Curtain Bluff, 125

Disney's Grand Floridian Resort & Spa, 46

Equinox, The, 97

Four Seasons Biltmore, 26

Four Seasons Resort Maui at Wailea, 57

Four Seasons Resort Nevis, 180

Gleneagles, 282

Golden Lemon Inn & Villas, 190

Grand Lido Sans Souci, 165

Greenbrier, The, 105

Half Moon Golf, Tennis, and Beach Club, 168

Hayman, 289

Hotel Bora Bora, 301

Hotel Hana Maui, 64

Hotel La Gazelle d'Or, 317

Hotel Villa del Sol, 219

Hyatt Regency Aruba Resort & Casino, 128

Hyatt Regency Dorado Beach, 188

Hyatt Regency Grand Cayman, 157

Inn at Spanish Bay, 28

Kamandalu Resort & Spa, 310

Kona Village Resort, 68

La Samanna, 205

Las Hadas, 225

Le Manoir aux Quat' Saisons, 245

Le Sport, 197

Little Dix Bay, 150

Lygon Arms, The, 249

Manele Bay Hotel, The, 71

Mauna Lani Bay Hotel and Bungalows, 73

Meadowood, Napa Valley, 30

Melhana Plantation, 55

Nisbet Plantation, 182

Ocean Club, 131

Old Fort Inn, 79

Peter Island Resort and Yacht Harbour, 153

Reefs, The, 142

Reid's Palace, 279

Ritz-Carlton, Cancun, The, 233

Ritz-Carlton, Naples, The, 53

Sandals Resorts, 172

Sandals Royal Bahamian Resort & Spa, 135

Sandals St. Lucia Golf Resort & Spa, 200

Schlosshotel Lerbach, 261

Silky Oaks Lodge, 292

Spice Island Beach Resort, 162

Swept Away Negril, 177

Villa d'Este, 272

Wauwinet, The, 84

Wawbeek, The, 93

Westin Brisas Ixtapa, 231

Windjammer Landing, 203

Woodstock Inn & Resort, 101

Resorts with Golf on Premises

(*Note:* Many other resorts offer golf nearby.)

Boca Raton Resort & Club, The, 43

Boulders, The (AZ), 12

Casa de Campo, 160

Disney's Grand Floridian Resort & Spa, 46

Equinox, The, 97

Four Seasons Resort Nevis, 180

Gleneagles, 282

Greenbrier, The, 105

Half Moon Golf, Tennis, and Beach
Club, 168

Hyatt Regency Aruba Resort &
Casino, 128

Hyatt Regency Dorado Beach, 188

Hyatt Regency Grand Cayman, 157

Inn at Spanish Bay, 28

Kona Village Resort, 68

Manele Bay Hotel, The, 71

Mauna Lani Bay Hotel and
Bungalows, 73

Meadowood, Napa Valley, 30

Sandals Resorts, 172

Sandals St. Lucia Golf Resort & Spa, 200

Woodstock Inn & Resort, 101

Resorts with Horseback Riding

Ahwahnee, The, 17

Barcelo Playa Tambor, 213

Boulders, The (AZ), 12

Greenbrier, The, 105

Hotel Hana Maui, 64

Inn at Spanish Bay, 28

La Casa Que Canta, 222

Maroma, 228

Nisbet Plantation, 182

Schlosshotel Lerbach, 261

Turtle Island, 295

In-City/Town Hotels

Balance Rock Inn, 76

Equinox, The, 97

Feathers Hotel, The, 239

Hotel Danieli, 270

Hotel Goldener Hirsch, 237

Inn of the Anasazi, 91

Lygon Arms, The, 249

Negresco, 259

Old Fort Inn, 79

Pousadas of Portugal, 276

Radisson Edwardian Hampshire
Hotel, 252

Sherman House, The, 36

White Barn Inn, 81

Woodstock Inn & Resort, 101

Resorts with Area Skiing

Ahwahnee, The, 17
Boulders, The (CT), 41
Château du Sureau, 23
Equinox, The, 97
Hotel Goldener Hirsch, 237

Inn of the Anasazi, 91
Sonnenalp Resort, 38
Wawbeek, The, 93
Woodstock Inn & Resort, 101

Adventure/Safari Lodges and Resorts

Ahwahnee, The, 17
Barcelo Playa Tambor, 213
MalaMala, 319

Silky Oaks Lodge, 292
Wawbeek, The, 93

Resorts with Private Pools

Ahwahnee, The, 17
Amandari, 305
Cap Juluca, 122
Cobblers Cove Hotel, 137
Golden Lemon Inn & Villas, The, 190
Hacienda Katanchel, 216
Half Moon Golf, Tennis, and Beach
    Club, 168
Hotel Bora Bora, 301
Hotel Villa del Sol, 219

Kamandalu Resort & Spa, 310
La Casa Que Canta, 222
La Samanna, 205
Las Hadas, 225
Sandals Resorts, 172
Sandals Royal Bahamian Resort &
    Spa, 135
Sandals St. Lucia Golf Resort & Spa, 200
Spice Island Beach Resort, 162
Windjammer Landing, 203

Resorts with In-Room Fireplaces

Ahwahnee, The, 17

Auberge du Soleil, 20

Balance Rock Inn, 76

Boulders, The (AZ), 12

Boulders, The (CT), 41

Château du Sureau, 23

Equinox, The, 97

Feathers Hotel, The, 239

Four Seasons Biltmore, 26

Hartwell House, 242

Hotel La Gazelle d'Or, 317

Inn at Spanish Bay, 28

Inn of the Anasazi, 91

La Pinsonnière, 117

Le Manoir aux Quat' Saisons, 245

Lygon Arms, The, 249

Meadowood, Napa Valley, 30

Melhana Plantation, 55

Old Fort Inn, 79

Post Ranch Inn, 33

Sonnenalp Resort, 38

Wawbeek, The, 98

Whalewalk Inn, The, 88

White Barn Inn, 81

Woodstock Inn & Resort, 101

About the Author

KATHARINE D. DYSON is a freelance writer who specializes in travel. For this book her work has taken her around the world researching and writing about the best romantic spots. Her articles have appeared in many newspapers and magazines, including *Modern Bride, Romantic Escapes, Country Victorian, Bridal Guide, Golfweek, Specialty Travel Index, Golf Digest,* American Express's *Golf, Golf and Travel,* and *Jax Fax Travel Marketing.* She writes a bi-weekly travel and food column for several Fairfield County, Connecticut, newspapers. She is a member of the Society of American Travel Writers, a recipient of the Quill and Trowel Award from the Garden Writers Association of America, and a consultant for A&E network for their "Top 10 Most Romantic Resorts" series.

For further information log on to www.honeymoonsaway.com.